TOBIAS SMOLLETT
Critic and Journalist

TOBIAS SMOLLETT
Critic and Journalist

James G. Basker

DELAWARE
NEWARK: UNIVERSITY OF DELAWARE PRESS
LONDON AND TORONTO: ASSOCIATED UNIVERSITY PRESSES

Associated University Presses
440 Forsgate Drive
Cranbury, NJ 08512

Associated University Presses
25 Sicilian Avenue
London WC1A 2QH, England

Associated University Presses
2133 Royal Windsor Drive
Unit 1
Mississauga, Ontario
Canada L5J 1K5

The paper used in this publication meets the requirements of the American National
Standard for Permanence of Paper for Printed Library Materials Z39.48-1984.

Library of Congress Cataloging-in-Publication Data

Basker, James G.
    Tobias Smollett, critic and journalist.

    Bibliography: p.
    Includes index.
    1. Smollett, Tobias George, 1721–1771—Knowledge—
Literature.   2. Criticism—Great Britain—History—
18th century.   3. Journalism—Great Britain—History—
18th century.   4. Book reviewing—Great Britain—
History—18th century.   5. English periodicals—
History—18th century.   I. Title.
PR3698.L5B37   1988   820'.9   86-40430
ISBN 0-87413-311-4 (alk. paper)

Printed in the United States of America

To
JAMES W. BASKER
and
ANNE GLYNN BASKER

Contents

Preface

To study Smollett's brilliant career as a journalist is first of all to reconceive the whole shape of his canon, adding perhaps as many as 270 new items (most of them book reviews) to the list of his writings. Of even more interest is the intellectual range of these writings, comparable to the range of Samuel Johnson's writings during the years that he contributed so heavily to the *Gentleman's Magazine* and single-handedly conducted the *Literary Magazine*. Quite naturally our interest in Smollett over the years has been focused on the novels. What this book attempts to do is to explore another, and very substantial, part of his writing through which we perceive a more widely knowledgeable and ambitious intellect than we have usually thought of him as being.

For more than seven years at the height of his career in the 1750s and 1760s, Smollett was London's leading book reviewer and arguably its most influential editor. It was a period in which literary journalism—especially in magazines and review journals—came into its own. Not only Johnson and Smollett, but Fielding, Goldsmith, Boswell, and many others were finding journalism an increasingly important critical and creative medium. During these decades many features of the modern literary world were emerging for the first time, such as the shift to review journals as the dominant critical forum and the serialization of novels in magazines, and Smollett was at the forefront of each of these developments.

Using the more comprehensive lists established in this study of Smollett's articles in the *Critical Review* and the *British Magazine*, one can follow his critical discussions of major authors—Shakespeare, Pope, Voltaire, Johnson, Hume, Sterne, among others—and of general topics in language and literature, historiography, scientific method, contemporary art, and more. We also see Smollett's innovations: not only the serialization of a full-length novel fully seventy years in advance of Dickens and his contemporaries, but the introduction of systematic foreign correspondence despite England's being at war with France and the coverage of contemporary art even before the first public art exhibition had been held.

There is also genius in Smollett's achievement as a literary editor, as he became the first genuine man of letters to edit a review journal of the recognizably modern kind—under pressure to be literate, comprehensive, prompt, and profitable all at once. Smollett succeeded in enlisting some of the great writers of his time—Goldsmith, Johnson, Hume—and in extending his influence through literary circles that included Richardson, Burke, the Wartons, the Burneys, Kames, Walpole, and Gray—virtually all the British and many of the European literati of the day.

But as much as it touched the literary elite, Smollett's work may be more significant for its part in developments on the broader fronts of the Enlightenment. Journals like the *Critical Review* enabled a rising and eager middle-class audience to share in the intellectual and cultural explorations of the times. This new spread of literary and cultural interest proved to be essential to the Europe, and the English-speaking world, of the nineteenth century, when great sociological changes were to take place. In the middle of the eighteenth century many of the most gifted writers were concerned with trying to convey to the general public the intellectual developments going on in every field of learning, from the *philosophes* in France to Franklin and Jefferson in America. In Britain the Scottish writers, feeling themselves on the periphery of an older, native-English culture, tried to combine the spread of learning with a new cosmopolitanism. And among these anxious Anglo-Scots, Smollett was the most prominent and the most energetic at the midcentury.

In mapping Smollett's career as journalist and editor, I hope to provide a new perspective on the literary history of what has come to be called the "Age of Johnson" but of which one critic has also said that Smollett was "a kind of literary protector in the interregnum between Pope and Johnson." Smollett and others, by involving a wider readership in the intellectual and cultural life of the day, fostered what might be called "the democratization of culture." At the same time, his pioneering work in criticism and journalism contributed to the emergence of a new kind of literary establishment, the structures and norms of which are still evident in the literary world as we know it today.

Among the many to whom thanks are due for help in the conception and preparation of this study, I wish to mention particularly Susan A. Barton, Jerry Beasley, Diane Bowen, O M Brack, Jr., Robert Adams Day, James Engell, Antonia Forster, David Foxon, Scott Gordon, Alan Heimert, Blair Hoxby, Marten Liander, April London, John Manners, Derek Roper, Donna Salli, Major Patrick Telfer-Smollett, Kevin Van Anglen, Sir Edgar Williams, and Karina Williamson. I am also grateful for their assistance to the staffs of the Bodleian Library, British Library, National Library of Scotland, Houghton and Widener Libraries at Harvard, Beinecke Library, Huntington Library, the Library Company of Philadelphia, National Library of Congress, University of Oregon Library, and the Public Records Office in London. For financial support, I am indebted to the Rhodes Trust in Oxford and the Clark Fund at Harvard University. Finally, for their advice and support at so many stages, I am most grateful to W. J. Bate, Paul-Gabriel Boucé, Gail Finney, and Roger Lonsdale.

Guide to Dates and Volume Numbers
of the *Critical Review* Frequently Cited in This Study

Year	Vol.	Pages	Month
1756			
	Vol. 1	1– 96	Ja/Fe
		97–192	Mr
		193–292	Ap
		293–388	My
		389–484	Jn
		485–572	Jl
	Vol. 2	1– 96	Au
		97–192	Se
		193–288	Oc
		289–384	No
		385–482	De
1757			
	Vol. 3	1– 96	Ja
		97–192	Fe
		193–288	Mr
		289–384	Ap
		385–480	My
		481–558	Jn
	Vol. 4	1– 96	Jl
		97–184	Au
		185–280	Se
		281–376	Oc
		377–472	No
		473–552	De
1758			
	Vol. 5	1– 88	Ja
		89–176	Fe
		177–272	Mr
		273–360	Ap
		361–448	My
		449–528	Jn
	Vol. 6	1– 88	Jl
		89–176	Au
		177–264	Se
		265–352	Oc
		353–438	No
		439–526	De
1759			
	Vol. 7	1– 88	Ja
		89–184	Fe
		185–288	Mr
		289–382	Ap
		383–470	My
		471–558	Jn
	Vol. 8	1– 88	Jl
		89–176	Au
		177–260	Se
		261–340	Oc
		341–420	No
		421–500	De
1760			
	Vol. 9	1– 80	Ja
		81–160	Fe
		161–244	Mr
		245–324	Ap
		325–420	My
		421–494	Jn
	Vol. 10	1– 80	Jl
		81–160	Au
		161–248	Se
		249–328	Oc
		329–408	No
		409–488	De

1761			*1762*		
Vol. 11	5– 80	Ja	Vol. 13	1– 80	Ja
	81–168	Fe		81–168	Fe
	169–256	Mr		169–284	Mr
	257–340	Ap		285–364	Ap
	341–420	My		365–444	My
	421–500	Jn		445–524	Jn
Vol. 12	1– 80	Jl	Vol. 14	1– 80	Jl
	81–160	Au		81–160	Au
	161–236	Se		161–240	Se
	237–320	Oc		241–320	Oc
	321–404	No		321–400	No
	405–484	De		401–[380]	De
				(for 480)	

TOBIAS SMOLLETT
Critic and Journalist

[1]

Grand Designs: Smollett's Plan for an English Academy and the Birth of the *Critical Review*

Nothing in the first fifteen years of Smollett's literary career gave any hint of the grand design for an English academy of the belles lettres he was to propose in the last months of 1755. It was audacious. Smollett had come to London in 1739 trained as a surgeon but, much like Thomson and Johnson before him, with his hopes really riding on a verse tragedy, *The Regicide*. Frustrated in his attempts to get his play accepted (as he would be for another ten years), Smollett served a stint as a surgeon's mate in the Royal Navy, followed by a period in the early 1740s of practicing medicine in London while trying to get started as a writer. Gradually the publications came: his ballad, "The Tears of Scotland," two verse satires in the style of Pope, *Advice* (1746) and *Reproof* (1747), and then the breakthrough as a novelist, with *Roderick Random* (1748), *Peregrine Pickle* (1751), and *Ferdinand Count Fathom* (1753). Two major translations, *Gil Blas* (1748) and *Don Quixote* (1755), also gained attention and generated income, but there was little sign of a budding academician in any of this.

Still, Smollett had a breadth of intellect and talent beyond what these early writings could show, all of them (one must remember) written by the time he was thirty-one years old. In his midthirties, new dimensions in Smollett began to unfold. His career changed course. Always an energetic exponent of what we now call the Enlightenment, Smollett shared with his contemporaries—especially his fellow Scots—not only a belief in the value of reason and methodical inquiry, but a desire for an overarching cosmopolitanism in learning and the arts. He was also deeply ambitious. Thus, it is completely in character that Smollett originally envisaged the *Critical Review* as the journal of this English academy of letters that he began to propose in late 1755. He explained his plan to his friend John Moore, the Scottish novelist and man of letters, in a letter of August 1756, describing the *Critical Review* as merely "a small Branch of an extensive Plan which I last year projected for a sort of Academy of the belles Lettres, a Scheme which will one day, I hope, be put in Execution to its utmost Extent."[1] It is an indication of the strength of his hopes for this "extensive plan" that even as he wrote, six issues of the *Critical Review* had already appeared and his proposals had been in circulation for several months, with no sign that they would ever be realized. Yet he persisted, and although his envisaged academy never came to exist, his ideas for it gave form and purpose to the *Critical*.

Smollett's idea, as he was well aware, was not new. Since the time of the Restoration, prominent literary figures had been calling for some sort of English academy. Sprat, Dryden, and Roscommon in the 1660s, Prior and Defoe at the turn of the century, Addison and Swift in the 1710s, and even Voltaire in the 1730s had all remarked on the need for such a body in England.[2] Thomas Sprat's proposal, as described in his *History of the Royal Society* (1667), was among the earliest and most detailed. It represented a synthesis of the ideas of his fellow members of the Royal Society in the 1660s and was often taken as a prototype by subsequent supporters of the idea. That Smollett had read Sprat's *Royal Society* is evident: he measured Birch's *History of the Royal Society* against it in a review in 1756 (Ja/Fe '56, 41). In this light, the main points of Sprat's proposed academy take on added interest: it was to imitate and rival the French Academy; it was to be government-sponsored and composed of "sober and judicious" gentlemen of letters; it would have authority to improve and regulate the English language; it would establish a board of critics "according to whose Censure, all Books or Authors, should either stand or fall"; it would finance and organize major projects of scholarship, particularly works of history.[3] The similarity of these ideas to much of what can be gathered about Smollett's proposal in 1755–56, suggests that, consciously or unconsciously, Smollett adopted many of his ideas from Sprat. He was placing himself in a tradition, asserting neoclassical notions of authority, rules, and standards, to meet current conditions in the republic of letters.

Like Sprat, Smollett respected the institutions that promoted the progress of the arts and sciences on the Continent and hoped to see England emulate them. From the beginning, as Walter Graham's comprehensive study shows, the development of English literary periodicals was influenced by Continental journals.[4] Smollett, too, was familiar with the learned journals of Europe. Although he described it as "a paultry Bookseller's Jobb [*sic*]," he had translated a collection of essays from the *Journal oeconomique* in 1754.[5] In the "Foreign Articles" section of the *Critical*'s second issue, he translated two articles from the newly established *Journal encyclopédique* (Mr '56, 181–84)[6]—a journal the *philosophes* were using to promote their *Encyclopédie*.[7] Directly and indirectly, in small details and larger principles, the *Critical* was to show signs of the influence of Continental, and especially French, journalism. The *Critical*'s title page, for example, bore the legend "By a Society of

Gentlemen," similar to a device frequently used by French journals ("Par une société de gens de lettres"), including the *Journal encyclopédique*, one of Smollett's acknowledged sources.[8] When Smollett announced in his proposals for the *Critical* that the authors "have established a Correspondence with France, Holland, Germany, Italy and Spain; which will enable them to entertain their Readers with the Literary News of those different Countries,"[9] he was allying himself in spirit and manner with the truly international journals of Europe. Their shared premise was, as one scholar describes it, "that the republic of letters should never recognise the limitations of national frontiers."[10]

In seeking to present the British public with comprehensive information about the arts and sciences throughout Europe, Smollett—who could be stridently nationalistic in other contexts—was following the cosmopolitan pattern of earlier periodicals published in London: de la Crose's *Universal Historical Bibliothèque* (1687) and his *History of Learning* (1691–92); Dunton's *Compleat Library* (1692–94); *The History of the Works of the Learned* (1699–1712); de la Roche's *Memoirs of Literature* (1710–17), *New Memoirs of Literature* (1725–27), and *Literary Journal* (1730–31); Reid's *Present State of the Republic of Letters* (1728–36); and the *History of the Works of the Learned* (1737–43).[11] He may also have been impressed by the example of Matthieu Maty's elegant and erudite *Journal britannique* (1750–57), which had been the basis for Maty's election to the Royal Society in 1751.[12] Although it was designed primarily to present readers abroad with reviews of English publications, it was set up partly as an attempt to improve on the *Monthly Review* and it was compiled (although not published) in London.[13] Maty, its author and editor, was prominent in learned circles in London—he and Smollett had such friends in common as Dr. William Hunter—and his journal had a considerable readership in England.[14] But because it was written in French for an elite international audience, Maty's journal could not, finally, reach the general British public in the ways Smollett intended for the *Critical*.

In his designs for the *Critical* and for an academy, Smollett was responding to a widely perceived need in England in the mideighteenth century. There were many suggestions in the 1750s for some sort of regulatory authority to set standards for the theater and for the republic of letters generally. The author of *The True Briton* called in 1752 for some authority to recommend "proper books" in all fields to the public and to combat the corrupt transmission of classical texts by supervising their publication.[15] Also in 1752, as Read has pointed out, Dr. George Harris proposed that Parliament establish an academy to standardize and regulate by force of law all English spelling.[16] In 1753, William Whitehead (soon to become poet laureate) suggested to the authors of *The World* that they assume the role of censors and adjudicate on the merits of contemporary fiction.[17] There were especially frequent demands for regulation of the theaters coming from playwrights, players, and the public alike, to the extent that several writers called for the government to take over the management of the theaters and supervise the selection of plays to be staged.[18] A character in Smollett's own *Peregrine Pickle* argues "that plays ought to be exhibited at the expence of the state" and, accordingly, "that proper judges should be appointed for receiving or rejecting all such performances as are offered to the public" (chap. 55). Other distinguished authors shared these concerns. Although it came to naught, the poet William Collins projected a new review journal about 1750, to be conducted under the auspices of Oxford University and compiled by himself, John Gilbert Cooper, and Thomas Warton.[19] One of Fielding's purposes in founding *The Covent-Garden Journal* in 1752, he announced in the first number, was to retrench the field of criticism along classical lines: "The Constitution of Aristotle, Horace, Longinus, and Bossu, under which the State of Criticism so long flourished, have been entirely neglected, and the Government usurped by a Set of Fellows, entirely ignorant of all those Laws."[20] The founding of *The Edinburgh Review* in 1755 by Adam Smith, William Robertson, and Hugh Blair, and of *The Literary Magazine* in 1756 by Johnson, manifested something of the same concern.

During the 1750s there was also a surge of interest in public bodies designed to promote the arts and sciences. The London Society for the Encouragement of Arts, Manufactures, and Commerce, founded in 1753, was a body Smollett would praise effusively in his *Continuation* in 1760: "In a word, the society is so numerous, the contributions so considerable, the plan so judiciously laid, and executed with such discretion and spirit, as to promise much more effectual and extensive advantage to the public, than ever accrued from all the boasted academies of Christendom."[21] Its Edinburgh counterpart was founded in 1755–56 and among its founders were several friends of Smollett's, including George Drummond and Lord Elibank.[22] In 1755 there appeared "An Essay in two Parts, on the Necessity and Form of a Royal Academy for Painting, Sculpture, and Architecture," written by John Nesbitt, first cousin to Smollett's then-close friend John Wilkes; perhaps in this connection, as Lewis M. Knapp has suggested, Smollett had a special interest in the proposal.[23] Proposals for various kinds of academies and societies continued to appear throughout the latter half of the eighteenth century, as has been documented by Allen Walker Read.[24] Under Smollett's editorship, the *Critical* was to support such proposals repeatedly (Ja/Fe '56, 1–2).[25]

It was more than a public-spirited interest in resurrecting standards and patronizing merit, however, that made Smollett want to establish a new authority over English letters. He drew on a deep fund of bitter personal experience. "I have been frustrated in all my attempts to succeed on the Stage," he complained in 1750, "not by the Publick which I have always found favorable and propitious, but by the Power of two or three Persons who (I cannot help saying) have accepted and patronized the works of others, with whom, in point of Merit, I think myself, at least, upon a par."[26] Smollett also felt abused by the booksellers and resented their unofficial but extensive control of the publishing world. He exulted in his "Advertisement" to the second edition of *Peregrine Pickle* (1758), "At length Peregrine Pickle makes his appearance in a new edition, in spite of all the art and industry that were used to stifle him in the birth, by certain booksellers and others, who were at uncommon pains to misrepresent the work and calumniate the author."[27] Smollett never lost an opportunity to satirize the corruption and chaos, as he saw it, of the literary world: in Melopoyn's tale in *Roderick Random*, the college of authors in *Peregrine Pickle*, and several scenes in *Ferdinand Count Fathom*.[28] In all these scenes there are hints of Smollett's underlying fantasy, to be invested with the power to regulate the literary world. As the narrator says of Peregrine Pickle when he begins to resent all the false patrons, sham critics, and bad poets he sees around him: "Had the executive power of the legislature been vested in him, he would have doubtless devised strange species of punishment for all offenders" (chap. 93). Never satisfied with the treatment his own works received or with the general trend of things, by 1754 Smollett seemed to feel about the whole literary scene (as he said of the theater) that "Goody Criticism has been delirious a long time, but now she is quite lethargic."[29]

It is still difficult to determine the exact nature of Smollett's academy scheme. If he circulated printed proposals (as he had for printing *The Regicide* by subscription and for his translation of *Don Quixote*), no copy has survived. Some valuable indirect evidence assembled in studies by Claude E. Jones and Knapp in the 1940s has shown, however, that some of Smollett's contemporaries noticed and remembered his academy project.[30] From their various descriptions and allusions, some idea of its form can be gathered. Smollett's enemy Joseph Reed, the rope-maker and would-be playwright, recalled it as late as 1759 in his pamphlet attack, *A Sop in the Pan for a Physical Critick*, where he travestied the scheme:

> In the close of the Year 1755, a certain Caledonian Quack, by the Curtesy of *England*, call'd a *Doctor of Physick*, whose real, or assum'd Name was FERDINANDO MAC FATHOMLESS, form'd a Project for initiating and perfecting on the Male-Inhabitants of this Island, in the Use and Management of the *Linguinary Weapon*, by the Erection of a *Scolding Amphitheatre*. For this Purpose, he selected, and engag'd, on weekly Salary, about a Dozen of the most eminent Professors of *Vociferation* in this Academy: but, after he had been at a considerable Expence, the unfortunate *Emperic* could not get his Project licenc'd.
>
> The Doctor was greatly mortified at his unexpected Disappointment, but being resolved that *his own*, and the *Sisterhood's* Talents should not be lost to the World, *he* set about publishing a periodical Work, called the *Hyper-Critical Review*.[31]

Beneath the parody, Reed's account suggests a basic outline. Smollett seems to have been acting principally on his own, the chief if not sole proponent of his academy scheme in 1755, and of its offshoot, the *Critical Review*. He had been "at a considerable Expence" in promoting it—perhaps in advertising or printing proposals—and it had gained the attention, if not the approval, of individuals beyond his immediate circle of friends and colleagues. Despite the blatant sexual innuendo, the idea of perfecting men in the use of the "linguinary weapon" seems to indicate a primary purpose of improving and standardizing the English language. Perhaps the selection of "a dozen of the most eminent professors of vociferation" corresponds to the scale of membership actually proposed. Reed's allusion to the failure of Smollett's efforts to "get his Project licenc'd" suggests that Smollett had unsuccessfully sought government support or, perhaps, private patronage. Understandably, Smollett felt "greatly mortified" at his failure.

This disappointment probably contributed to Smollett's morose mood in December 1755 when, in answer to his friend Moore's request for Smollett's influence on his behalf, Smollett wrote:

It is with great Mortification I now assure you that I have no sort of Connexion with the Great Man [unidentified] who is to decide between you and your Competitor. Far from being used to the Great, as you seem to imagine, I have neither interest nor acquaintance with any Person whose Countenance or Favour could be of advantage to myself or my friends. I live in the shade of obscurity, neglecting and neglected.[32]

Smollett lacked influential connections, his proposal was languishing, and he felt depressed, but still he persisted.

He discussed his project with his friends and succeeded in involving several of them in it. John Armstrong and John Wilkes had both been consulted, as can be seen in a letter Armstrong wrote to Wilkes on 6 January 1756: "Smollett imagines he and I may both make Fortunes by this project of his; I'm afraid he is too sanguine, but if it should turn out according to his hopes farewell Physick and all its Cares for me and welcome dear Tranquility and Retirement."[33] Just how Smollett's scheme might make their fortunes remains unexplained, but Armstrong did contribute to the *Critical's* first issue and regularly thereafter for at least a year.[34] Wilkes was clearly familiar with the project and may have participated, although there is no firm proof that he did. Another member of their circle of friends definitely did join in: the Scotsman Patrick Murdoch, who contributed two major reviews, including the lead article, to the first issue of the *Critical Review*.[35] Another friend Smollett consulted about his plan was Dr. George Macaulay, husband of the historian Catherine Macaulay. In April 1756, Smollett wrote to ask his help in the form of a loan to cover a financial embarrassment, saying: "This disgrace hovers over my imagination so as that I shall be rendered incapable of prosecuting my scheme."[36] Smollett's letters also indicate that he revealed his plan to John Moore and others of his friends in Scotland.[37]

Information and rumors about Smollett's academy project had reached a much wider audience, however, than has previously been shown. To the information collected by Jones and Knapp there can now be added new evidence about others who knew of the scheme, what some of its details were, and how the idea was received.

Long before Reed's pamphlet attack in 1759, for example, another irate author had invoked the academy project to goad Smollett about the pretensions of his *Critical Review*. Resentful at an unfavorable review in the *Critical* (Ja/Fe '56, 85–88), the *Universal Visiter* printed in its issue for March 1756 a sham letter "From *Edmund Curl*, to the principal Author of a Thing *Called* the *Critical Review*."[38] Offering mock congratulations to Smollett for succeeding as "a critic without taste, genius, judgement, learning, candour, or common sense," this "ghost" of Curl (Pope's well-known adversary) announces that the pack of quarrelsome hack writers he had once kept in his pay "would undoubtedly have deemed it an honour to have been acquainted with a hug-bug-rub-drug, pug-scrub, *Acad. &c. Soc.*" The abbreviated but derisory reference in the last phrase to the academy scheme shows that at least one writer on the staff of the *Visiter* had somehow heard, by March 1756, of Smollett's proposal. The *Visiter* had an impressive list of contributors, including Christopher Smart (who, with Richard Rolt, was chief compiler), Samuel Johnson, David Garrick, and Dr. Thomas Percy;[39] whichever of them wrote this mocking piece, they were all figures who would have been very useful, *had* they been involved in Smollett's project. But none was. Indeed, with all their talent, prestige, and connections, they represent a circle without which it would have been nearly impossible to establish a meaningful sort of English academy in the mideighteenth century.

However, Smollett's envisaged academy did receive support from other quarters. In the *Old Maid* for 6 December 1755 there is evidence that the editor, Frances Brooke, and Smollett may have been subtly promoting each other's interests—hers in her new periodical, his in founding an academy. In that issue a letter signed "T. S."—quite possibly by Smollett—urges the *Old Maid* to devote occasional essays to criticism of the theater in an effort "to put things on a right footing."[40] "Mary Singleton" (Brooke) answers the letter by recommending instead the more comprehensive authority of an academy:

I agree with my correspondent as to the utility of the stage, and believe whatever may have been wrong in the management, is to be in great measure charged upon the Town, which often condemns and approves without knowing why. As I think a good critic a friend both to authors and actors, I could wish a society of real judges were incorporated, by way of an

academy, to take the theatres under their inspection: till that happens I
have some thoughts of establishing a little court of female criticism.

Brooke's support for the idea of an academy at just the time when Smollett's
proposal was circulating may have been mere coincidence, but further evidence suggests otherwise. In a later issue devoted to criticizing the rise of
Methodism, she lavished praise on the *Critical Review*, "the ingenious and
judicious authors of which masterly performance, have with true wit and
humour exposed, the folly of this prevailing and pernicious spirit of
enthusiasm."[41] On his part, Smollett showed special favor toward Brooke's
tragedy, *Virginia*. Reviewing it immediately after its publication in April
1756, he sympathized with her over its rejection by the theater managers (like
his own *Regicide*, it was never staged), applauded her decision to bypass them
by publishing it anyway, and praised it—despite some flaws—as "truly moral and poetical" (Ap '56, 276–79). Significantly, it was treated more favorably
by Smollett, who did most of the drama reviews for the *Critical* himself, than
any other play he reviewed in 1756.[42] Whether or not they were acquainted,
as the warmth of their mutual praise and other signs would suggest, and
whether or not she even knew Smollett was behind the academy scheme, it
seems very likely that her expression of support for an academy in late 1755
resulted from hearing about his proposal, and her emphasis on its usefulness
in supervising the theaters probably derives from one of its main points.
    Early in January 1756, only days after reading the *Old Maid*'s endorsement
of the academy idea, the public heard another literary figure announce his
support, this time in more detail. The actor Theophilus Cibber, feeling himself unfairly blackballed from his profession, hired a theater and began
delivering to paying audiences his "Two Dissertations on Theatrical
Subjects."[43] In the first of them, after complaining of the mismanagement of
the two principal theaters (Rich's Covent Garden and Garrick's Drury Lane),
he described a very interesting remedy:

> I have heard of an Academy,—intended to consist of a select Number of
> Gentleman, iminent for their Taste of the *Belles Lettres*; and some, whose
> Works have the deserv'd Estimation of the Public:—On which Plan it will
> be propos'd, to support Authors of Merit;—to give Praise to the Deserv-
> ing, and due Censure to the Dull and Presuming;—to shew the many, why
> they are pleas'd,—and with what they ought to be delighted:—May that
> laudable Scheme succeed, and prevent the Depravity we are falling into,
> by rescuing sound Sense, and Morality, from the barbarous Attacks of
> Ignorance and Gothism! I have also heard a Weekly Paper, under their
> Inspection, will be publish'd, entitled, *The Theatre*; wherein no mean Arts
> will be us'd, to prejudice the Public in favour of an unworthy Author, or
> Actor; nor will any Writer, or Performer, of any Degree of Merit, be de-
> preciated thro' the Wantonness of Mirth, or to gratify the Vanity, or

Spleen, of another. . . . Thus may the encroaching Power of Managers be properly check'd, and rational Entertainments alone become the polite Amusement of the town. . . . 'Till this Plan is put in Execution,—and I hope the Interim will be but short,—permit me humbly to propose an Expedient, for the immediate Correction of Theatrical Misconduct.[44]

Cibber's description becomes especially significant for two reasons. First, since March 1754 Cibber had been reviewing drama and other works for the *Monthly* on a regular basis (obviously he didn't regard it as the answer to the woes of the literary world).[45] Second, Smollett and Cibber had been friends for several years, perhaps since the 1740s (if allusions to Cibber in *Roderick Random*[46] are any indication) and certainly since the early 1750s when both were working for Ralph Griffiths, Smollett reviewing for the *Monthly* and Cibber writing such works as *A Lick at a Liar* (1752), *Lives of the Actors* (1753), and *Lives of the Poets* (1753), all Griffiths publications. We have further evidence of their continuing friendship and literary consultations in 1758 in a story told by Joseph Reed:

My Manager Mr. THEOPHILUS CIBBER, of wrong-headed Memory, about three Weeks before the Exhibition of my Tragedy [*Madrigal and Trulletta*, staged 6 July 1758], told me he had made Mention of that Piece to Dr. SM+LL+T, whom he represented as a great Admirer of Performances of the *burlesque* kind, and desired to know if it were agreeable to me that the Play should be read to the Doctor. I told Mr. CIBBER I had no Objection. On which he pulled out the Copy, and desired me to strike out, at least to mark, all the Passages I had borrow'd from the REGICIDE, that he might drop them in the Reading: for, added he, tho' the Doctor should ever so highly admire the humorous Ridicule, which you have levelled at his poetical Brotherhood, he would not fail of being greatly enraged at the Freedom you have taken with his REGICIDE. It will, continues my *upright* Manager, be your Interest to make a Friend of the Doctor. As he presides over the poetical Province in the CRITICAL REVIEW, your Piece will, in all Likelyhood, have a favourable Character, if you strike out Passages, which immediately affect him.[47]

For his own reasons, the volatile Reed was at pains to verify this incident, citing the "many Persons of Credit" who heard the story before Cibber died and the material proof of the marked copy he had prepared for Smollett's inspection, which was still in John Rich's possession.

Reed's efforts via Cibber to secure a favorable review in the *Critical* failed: he fell out with Cibber over production details, printed the play complete with the *Regicide* passages, and received a predictable damning in the *Critical* (Au '58, 168). Cibber, however, always received very generous treatment from the *Critical*, still another aspect of his continuing friendship with Smollett. His interest with Smollett would explain how his egotistical *Dissertations*, with their extended criticism of Garrick, could receive a balanced, largely favorable review (by Smollett) in the *Critical* for August 1756, at a time when Smollett was acutely sensitive about his relations with Garrick (Au '56, 48).[48] Two years later, Smollett took the opportunity in a review of Aaron Hill's *Insolvent, or Filial Piety* to interject a personal plea on Cibber's behalf. Although conceding that the play suffered in performance due to the "rawness of Mr. Cibber's actors," Smollett urges charity: "We think the town ought to have overlooked these defects in favour of a veteran comedian, from whose theatrical talents they have formerly derived so much mirth and entertainment; and encouraged him in the day of distress, not only in remuneration of his own services, but also in regard to the memory of his father" (J1 '58, 17). Not only does this special pleading differ from much of the dramatic criticism in Smollett's *Critical*, it runs counter to the current anti-Cibber mood in the theater that was driving Cibber to take work abroad with Sheridan's company in Dublin.[49]

If it can be assumed, then, that in 1755–56 Cibber had heard about Smollett's academy project from Smollett himself, his description of it takes on special interest. The academy was to be composed of a number of gentlemen selected for their taste and accomplishments in literature, and its basic aim would be to praise the worthy, censure the dull, and refine the public's critical taste and understanding. These features correspond both to Smollett's own description of the project in his letter to Moore and to points in the manifesto he published in advertisements for the *Critical*.[50] But two points in Cibber's version do not resemble anything that appears in Smollett's proposals for or conduct of the *Critical*, points that seem to represent ideas in the original academy scheme that never came to fruition.

The first is the provision for the Academy members to take the theaters "under their inspection" and to exert their influence, via a theatrical review journal, to raise the theaters' standards. It was this function the *Old Maid* had also singled out for particular approval. The idea that an English academy should control the theaters had antecedents as far back as Defoe in 1697,[51] but neither in his day nor in Smollett's was any such authority created. Smollett's own enthusiasm for the idea may have dwindled as he became friendly with Garrick during 1756 and his *Reprisal* was accepted for production in 1757.[52] From this time on, the *Critical* consistently applauded Garrick both as performer and as theater manager.

The other distinctive feature in Cibber's account was the suggestion that this academy would "support authors of Merit"—that is, financially reward or perhaps even subsidize worthy authors and projects. This was very much the system on the Continent. Academies and societies offered prizes for works of literature and science, and promising authors could gain encouragement and financial relief, as Jean-Jacques Rousseau had in 1750 when his

Discours won the Dijon literary prize. Many of the learned journals, such as the *Journal des Savants* and the *Mercure de France* (1672–1791), enjoyed government subsidy and protection.[53] The *Mercure de France* even rechanneled its profits into grants-in-aid for writers.[54] Perhaps Smollett had envisioned a similar system in England when he assured Armstrong that they would all make fortunes through his scheme. Smollett's bitterness over the decline of patronage and the neglect of merit lasted all his life. In the encomium on the Society for the Encouragement of the Arts he delivered in his *Continuation*, he compared the achievements of that body of private citizens to those of the academies of Europe, and he lamented the failure of the English government and monarchy to provide any such institutions or patronage:

> No Maecenas appeared among the ministers, and not the least ray of patronage glimmered from the throne. The protection, countenance, and gratification, secured in other countries by the institution of academies, and the liberality of princes, the ingenious in England derived from the generosity of a public, endued with taste and sensibility, eager for improvement, and proud of patronizing extraordinary merit.[55]

A year later, summarizing literary achievement during the reign of George II, he wrote: "Never was the pursuit after knowledge so universal, or literary merit more regarded, than at this juncture by the body of the British nation; but it was honoured by no attention from the throne, and little indulgence did it reap from the liberality of particular patrons."[56] Having listed the greatest authors of the age, he then remarked on the very few who had received patronage and concluded: "None of the rest, whom we have named, enjoyed any share of the royal bounty, except W. Whitehead, who succeeded to the place of laureat at the death of Cibber; and some of them, whose merit was the most universally acknowledged, remained exposed to all the storms of indigence, and all the stings of mortification."[57] Undoubtedly Smollett included himself among the latter. His language here repeats the phrases and metaphors used in his many private complaints about the hardships of his career.[58] Behind this indictment one senses Smollett's bitterness not only at the neglect he had suffered personally, culminating later in life in his inability to secure a pension or a consular sinecure,[59] but also at the failure of government and private powers to support his academy proposal or to provide an alternative.

Through Cibber, the academy proposal gained considerable, if less than ideal, publicity. Besides the audiences who actually heard Cibber deliver his "Dissertations," others in the public read excerpts from them—featuring the endorsement of the academy proposal—in the newspapers.[60] When published, the *Dissertations* went through two editions in three years, the first appearing in the summer of 1756 and the second (brought out to capitalize on the news of Cibber's recent death) early in 1759. But despite this publicity, the approval of the *Old Maid*, and whatever other support Smollett could enlist, his academy proposal faded into oblivion, remembered chiefly by his literary enemies only to nettle him.

In arguing the need for an academy, Smollett had identified an issue that would persist in English letters from the Restoration well into the twentieth century. Throughout the later eighteenth century, Thomas Sheridan, Arthur Murphy, Isaac Disraeli, and a host of others continued to recommend the establishment of such an authority in England. Among those who examined the issue in the nineteenth century was Matthew Arnold, who, in his essay "The Literary Influence of Academies," tried to assess the consequences for English literary history of not having had an academy. Similarly in this century, Harry Levin raised the issue by way of inquiring into the historic differences between the English and French languages in his essay, "The War of Words in English Poetry." And more recently, John Barrell has presented an excellent discussion of the sociopolitical implications of the academy debate in "The Language Properly So-Called: The Authority of Common Usage."[61] But Smollett of course could know none of this, only the mounting frustration he felt as his grand designs gave way to what could easily have become just another Grub Street project.

The Young Pretender: Smollett's Challenge to Johnson and Others

There was one other figure who remembered Smollett's academy proposal and later turned it to mockery, a man whose support more than that of any other single person, ironically, might have enabled it to succeed: Samuel Johnson. To aspire to literary eminence in the 1750s was almost inevitably to come into contact with Johnson, as Smollett was to discover. Certainly a proposal as ambitious and nationally significant as an academy would attract his attention. But Johnson was strenuously opposed to the idea of an English academy and remained so throughout his career. As early as 1748 he had written against the idea in his "Life of Roscommon" in the *Gentleman's Magazine* (18:216), and he was to repeat and elaborate his opposition in the Preface to his *Dictionary* (1755), an *Idler* essay (no. 61, 16 June 1759), and his lives of "Swift" and "Roscommon" in the *Lives of the Poets*.[1]

There may have been other reasons, of course, why Johnson was not taken with Smollett's proposal. Early on, the two of them seemed to have caught sight of each other out of the corners of their eyes. Johnson had been moved to write his famous *Rambler* no. 4 on fiction by the recent successes of *Roderick Random* and *Tom Jones*, and in that essay he made it clear that he didn't approve of the new realism as practiced by Smollett, Fielding, and others. On his part, Smollett poked fun at a "college of authors" in *Peregrine Pickle* (chap. 101) that included an unmistakably Johnson-like figure who "projected a variety of plans for new dictionaries, which were executed under his eye by day-labourers." Then, too, it didn't help that Smollett was a Scot. And to Johnson it must have seemed particularly inappropriate, perhaps even presumptuous, that Smollett should propose founding an academy of letters in 1755, just months after Johnson had published his *Dictionary*—a work that many, including Johnson himself (one may infer from his *Dictionary* preface), thought had obviated the need for such a body by fulfilling its primary objective of standardizing the English language.

But however it originally came to Johnson's attention—whether by hearsay or in a proposal he actually read—we can now see that Johnson incorporated recognizable details of Smollett's failed academy scheme into his *Idler* sketch of Dick Minim the critic:

> Minim professes great admiration of the wisdom and munificence, by which the Academies are formed on the Continent, and often wishes for some standard of taste, for some tribunal, to which merit might appeal from caprice, prejudice, and malignity. He has formed a plan for an Academy of Criticism, where every work of Imagination may be read before it is printed, and which shall authoritatively direct the theatres what pieces to receive or reject, to exclude or review.
>
> Such an institution would, in Dick's opinion, spread the fame of English Literature over Europe, and make London the metropolis of elegance and politeness . . . where nothing would any longer be applauded or endured that was not conformed to the nicest rules, and finished with the highest elegance.
>
> Till some happy conjunction of the planets shall dispose our Princes or Ministers to make themselves immortal by such an Academy, Minim contents himself to preside four nights in a week in a Critical society selected by himself, where he is heard without contradiction, and whence his judgment is disseminated through the great vulgar and the small.[2]

This passage contains many echoes from the various accounts of the academy proposal: the patronizing of neglected merit, the regulation of the theaters, the reformation of public taste, and the elevation of English letters to European standards. Moreover, Minim's experience is remarkably similar to Smollett's. Unable to secure powerful patronage for the proposed academy, he is forced to settle for a lesser undertaking, a critical society selected by himself whence his opinions are disseminated. The only detail missing to make the parallel complete is a journal like the *Critical Review*. But perhaps this was deliberate, because Johnson avoided directing the satire overtly at Smollett. The relevant passage contains only a small part of Minim's antics and Minim is, after all, a composite caricature drawn from various coffeehouse-critic "types." Besides, Johnson rarely indulged in personal satire and it would have been especially inopportune in mid-1759 when Johnson was still seeking Smollett's help in obtaining the release of his servant, Francis Barber, from the Navy.[3] Finally, it is worth noting that here, as in his other expressions of opposition to the establishment of an English academy of letters, Johnson dismissed it not because of its aims and ideals, but because of the impracticability of founding and operating such an institution.[4] For Smollett, as for Minim, the obstacles apparently proved insurmountable and no miraculous "conjunction of the planets" ever occurred to make his dream come true.

In the end, the only concrete result of Smollett's academy proposal was the *Critical Review*. In this "small branch" of his original scheme he obviously invested innovative ideas and high aspirations. His contentious "Proposals" for it began appearing in the newspapers in December 1755. Because these "Proposals" bear the marks of his academy ideas, intermingled with transparently commercial tactics, they are here reprinted in full:

PROPOSALS
FOR PUBLISHING MONTHLY,
THE PROGRESS OR ANNALS
OF
LITERATURE AND THE LIBERAL ARTS

In a succinct and faithful Detail of the Performances on the Subjects of Theology, Metaphysics, Physics, Medicine, Mathematics, History and the Belles Lettres; which shall occasionally appear at Home or Abroad; together with an accurate Description of every remarkable Essay in the Practical Part of Painting, Sculpture, and Architecture, that may do Honour to modern artists of this or any other Kingdom.

This Work will not be patched up by obscure Hackney Writers, accidentally enlisted in the Service of an undistinguishing Bookseller, but executed by a Set of Gentlemen whose Characters and Capacities have been universally approved and acknowledged by the Public: Gentlemen, who have long observed with Indignation the Productions of Genius and Dullness; Wit and Impertinence; Learning and Ignorance, confounded in the Chaos of Publication; applauded without Taste, and condemned without Distinction; and who have seen the noble Art of Criticism reduced to a contemptible Manufacture subservient to the most sordid Views of Avarice and Interest, and carried on by wretched Hirelings, without Talent, Candour, Spirit, or Circumspection.

Urged by these considerations, they have resolved to task their Abilities, in reviving the true Spirit of Criticism, and exert their utmost Care in vindicating the Cause of Literature from such venal and corrupted Jurisdiction.

They have no Connexion to warp their Integrity; they have no Prejudices to influence their Judgment; they will not presume to decide upon the Merits of a Work in an arbitrary Sentence unsupported by Evidence; they will not condemn or extol, without having first carefully perused the Performance; they will not affect to draw odious Comparisons, where there is no Resemblance or Relation; they will not invidiously seek to wrest the Sense, misinterpret the Meaning, or misquote the Words of any Author, who may fall under their Inspection; they will not exhibit a partial and unfair Assemblage of Beauties or Blemishes of any Production; they will not venture to criticize a Translation, without understanding the Original, or fill up the page with long insipid Transcripts: In a Word, they will not commend with Reluctance, or censure with Hesitation; they scorn to act as

Ministers of Interest, Faction, Envy, or Malevolence; they profess themselves indeed the Enemies of Dullness; but their favourite Aim is to befriend Merit, dignify the Liberal Arts, and contribute towards the Formation of a public Taste, which is the best Patron of Genius and Science.

They pretend to delineate the Plan of every Work with Accuracy and
Candour; to point out the Excellencies; hint at the Defects; and whenever
they signify their Disapprobation; they promise to illustrate their Censure
with proper Quotations, from which the Reader may appeal to his own
Understanding.

In these Sentiments they have established a Correspondence with
France, Holland, Germany, Italy and Spain; which will enable them to
entertain their Readers with the Literary News of those different Countries, and to translate such Productions, as shall seem to bid fairest for
succeeding in an English Dress.

The Work will be comprehended in a Pamphlet of six Sheets, to be
published in the First Day of every Month, and the first Number to make
its Appearance on the first Day of February 1756.[5]

Here much derives from the academy scheme: the elite, highly qualified
board of gentlemen critics; the systematic coverage of all the arts and sciences, including the visual arts; and the extensive attention to foreign literary
news through a network of correspondents. And at the heart of this manifesto, conveyed in characteristic phrases, is Smollett's abiding purpose: his
"favourite Aim . . . to befriend Merit, dignify the Liberal Arts, and contribute towards the formation of a public Taste, which is the best Patron of
Genius and Science." This is the language of noble purpose. Assuming for
the *Critical*'s "society of gentlemen" the authority and role of an academy,
the manifesto proclaims a critical reformation, intended to restore traditional
order and values to the realm of English letters.

But for all these professions of lofty ideals, this manifesto also evinces baser
motives. Smollett aimed, as Armstrong stated, to get rich from his scheme.
The *Critical Review* was a commercial publishing venture and Smollett meant
to make money by it. Normally the publisher whose name appeared on the
title page of such publications was the man who financed them, reaped the
profits, and in some measure controlled their editorial conduct. But, despite
the appearance of the publisher's imprint of "R. Baldwin" on the title page of
the first four volumes (January 1756 through December 1757), there can be
little doubt the real proprietors were Smollett and his friend Archibald
Hamilton. Baldwin's name was a cover—perhaps a limited share soon bought
out—for this irregular arrangement. No contractual documents have survived, but an editorial note written by Smollett in the second issue (in answer
to an attack by the *Monitor*) indicates an unusual author-publisher relationship in the *Critical*: "He [the *Monitor*'s author] will do well in the mean-

time, to correct a mistake under which he seems to lie, in affecting to suppose, that the Critick of the *third Letter* [Smollett], is Mr. *Baldwin*'s author; whereas, in fact, Mr. *Baldwin* is no more than the said critick's publisher" (Mr '56, 192). Baldwin served Smollett, not the other way around. Again in 1758, a writer in the *Critical* referred to Smollett's originally having "set up the Critical Review" himself (Se '58, 226–27). This is entirely consistent with Smollett's history of resistance to the usual practice whereby an author sold his entire copyright to the bookseller-publisher with the manuscript. Smollett had published *The Regicide* by subscription in 1749, and he had retained shares in the copyright of many of his other works, including his opera *Alceste* (never published), *Peregrine Pickle* (1751), and his edition of Smellie's *Treatise on Midwifery* (1752).[6] His knack for commercially successful publications later showed itself in his *History*, its *Continuation*, the *Present State of All Nations*, and his edition of the *Works of Voltaire*, all of which he arranged to have published serially as well as in volumes. Perhaps in 1755–56, tired of the spasmodic lump-sum income most authors had to live on, he sought to regularize his income on a monthly basis. If so, it was a delayed success at best, for he revealed in 1762 that he had only recently begun to make money from the *Critical*: "As I am Proprietor of that work [the *Critical*], I should be a fool to give it up at a Time when it begins to indemnify me for all the Vexation and Loss I have sustained by it."[7] Clearly financial interests sometimes overshadowed literary ideals.

Smollett's straitened finances in 1756 could never have supported such a venture alone, so he turned to the printer Hamilton who had recently left William Strahan's shop to set up on his own. It was probably through Strahan that Hamilton met Smollett and, significantly, observed the profits to be made by a printer's branching out into publishing. Although printers rarely did so, Strahan held shares in many publishing ventures, including Smollett's own *Peregrine Pickle, Ferdinand Count Fathom*, and the *Compendium*; he discreetly concealed this unorthodox practice by keeping his name off the title page.[8] Hamilton's name only began appearing on the title page as publisher of the *Critical* in 1758 but, as his obituary and numerous contemporary accounts confirm, he was a proprietor from the outset.[9] Most likely, Hamilton's was a proprietory partnership with Smollett wherein the latter contributed copy and editorial labors while Hamilton provided for printing, copyediting, and other expenses such as advertising.

When their aggressively worded advertisements began to appear in December 1755, an unexpected competitor responded immediately. Within days, on 25 December, there suddenly appeared an advertisement for a forthcoming rival, highly indignant at the *Critical*'s pretensions:

On Monday Feb. 2 will be published,
THE LITERARY MAGAZINE.

Giving an Account of all the Books and Pamphlets published in Great-Britain, with Remarks upon, and Characters of them. This work will be carried on by Gentlemen who write for their Amusement, and whose Circumstances and Situation in Life are such, as to render them entirely independent of Booksellers, from whom they have nothing to hope or fear. Having had various Transactions with this Body of Men, they have had Occasion to be well acquainted with their Arts of *Puffing*; and it is Part of the Plan to lay these Arts before the Public from Time to Time; which, it is to be hoped, will be both useful and entertaining.

The Grand Aim of this Undertaking is to encourage all Works of Genius when they have a Tendency to Promote the Interests of Truth and Virtue, of solid and useful Learning, to instruct, entertain, and polish Mankind, and to discourage every Thing that is calculated to serve the Cause of Vice and Infidelity. The Gentlemen concerned in the Undertaking don't pretend to have *no Connections to warp their Integrity, no Prejudices to influence their Judgment*, honestly acknowledging themselves vastly inferior, in this Respect, to those exalted Intelligences (see Public Advertiser for Friday last) the Monthly Annalists [i.e., the *Critical*]; nor do they take upon them to censure the Productions of those who are concerned in Undertakings of the same Kind. The Public must judge of their respective Merits; and to the Decisions of this Tribunal they entirely refer themselves.

The Work will be comprehended in a Pamphlet of four Sheets, to be published on the first Day of every Month, at the Price of 6d. each Number; and all proper Care will be taken to distribute it throughout the Island, without any Connection with or Dependence upon the Trade.[10]

Behind this modest announcement and its sarcastic allusions to the *Critical* lies an extraordinary coincidence: unknown to either, at the same time that Smollett was organizing the *Critical Review*, Johnson was planning a literary journal of his own, the *Literary Magazine*.[11] Both of their journals were to be literary reviews; both aimed to redeem critical journalism from the control of booksellers; and both were scheduled to begin publishing on virtually the same date, the first of February, 1756. Even the titles they had originally devised were similar. Smollett's projected title, "The Progress or Annals of Literature and the Liberal Arts," was later modified to "The Critical Review or Annals of Literature," but it closely resembled a prospective title that Johnson had first considered, according to Boswell:

In one of his little memorandum-books I find the following hints for his intended Review or Literary Journal:

"*The Annals of Literature, foreign as well as domestick.* Imitate LeClerk—Bayle—Barbeyrac. Infelicity of Journals in England. Works of the learned. We cannot take in all. Sometimes copy from foreign Journalists. Always tell."[12]

Regardless of his antipathy to the idea of an English academy, Johnson had independently reached similar conclusions about the state of English literary journalism. Like Smollett, Johnson emphasized the importance of covering foreign literary news, elevating the general tone of criticism, and employing independent "Gentlemen" in the undertaking. As every detail—even the titles[13]—suggests, Smollett and Johnson were looking to the learned journals of Europe as models for reform.

Although open hostilities between Smollett and Johnson never broke out, and certainly there was no all-out warfare of the sort that Grub Street was used to, the simultaneous commencement of the *Critical Review* and the *Literary Magazine* in 1756 marked the beginning of a period of tension between them. In the first issue of his *Literary Magazine*, Johnson used a footnote to defend his friend Arthur Murphy's *Apprentice* from negative reviews in both the *Critical* and the *Monthly*, and the same year, in an article in the *Universal Visiter*, he remarked disparagingly on the recent proliferation of new magazines and review journals.[14] A year later, Johnson observed that the lack of a good literary journal had been "for a long Time, among the Deficiencies of English Literature, but," he added sardonically, "as the Caprice of Man is always starting from too little to too much, we have now, amongst other Disturbers of human Quiet, a numerous Body of *Reviewers* and *Remarkers*."[15] For his part, Smollett occasionally took issue with Johnson's views, both as critic and lexicographer, in the pages of the *Critical*. In reviewing Warton's *Essay on Pope* in 1756, for example, Smollett disputed several of Warton's and Johnson's criticisms of Pope (Ap '56, 231–32). In 1759, in reviewing a pamphlet attack by James Grainger, Smollett pointed out some errors in Johnson's *Dictionary* simply to score a point of argument in his wrangle with Grainger (Fe '59, 155). Johnson was so annoyed that he sent off an angry note to the printer Hamilton, a note that Smollett saw and dismissed as "a very petulant Card . . . concerning an Article in the last Review."[16] All this occurred in the same month that Smollett privately, and not without a hint of irreverence, dubbed Johnson "that great Cham of Literature" and went on in the same letter to explain that he and Johnson "were never cater-cousins."[17] Johnson's sketch of Minim the critic appeared in the *Idler* about two months later, in June 1759.

Yet through it all Smollett and Johnson remained civil and even did favors for each other. Smollett tried to help Johnson get his servant Frank Barber freed from the Navy and in return Johnson gave Smollett permission to reprint *Idler* essays in his *British Magazine* and donated at least one original article to help launch its first issue.[18] By the 1760s, all signs of their brief and muted rivalry had disappeared. Smollett praised Johnson lavishly in his *Continuation* and a decade later Johnson insisted on writing a Latin inscription for a memorial to Smollett.[19]

Perhaps one reason their potential rivalry passed so quickly was that for all the prepublication verbal sparring, in the event Johnson's *Literary Magazine* had proved to be something other than a true literary review. Its size (fifty-six pages), price (six pence), and format were those of a magazine, as were its miscellaneous contents. Despite the fact that Johnson compiled the first few issues almost single-handedly and included many book reviews and other literary articles, the *Literary Magazine* became steadily less literary and more political in content. Johnson soon left the magazine and it thereafter lost all claim to being a literary journal.[20] It ceased altogether in 1758. That Smollett's journal established itself and flourished for another half century, while Johnson's faltered and failed, is one measure of Smollett's achievement in a period that would come to be called "the Age of Johnson." But the efforts of both reflect a shared sense of literature and criticism at a crisis in the 1750s. Both sensed, as Johnson had noted, the "Infelicity of Journals in England." But it was more. The rapidly growing reading public, the changing standards of taste, the proliferation of publications, the shifting terms of success and survival for the professional author, and above all the increasing power of booksellers were developments that concerned them both. Thus, when founding their journals, they shared a fundamental concern to distinguish them from the mainstream of the commercial publishing world—i.e., from booksellers and their mediocre, self-interested periodicals.

For Smollett, this meant Ralph Griffiths and his *Monthly Review*. He rightly saw it as the only real predecessor to the *Critical* and its natural rival. Founded in 1749, the *Monthly* had by 1755 come to represent a new category of literary periodical—the review—primarily by virtue of one distinctive feature: its comprehensiveness. Unlike the magazines and miscellanies on the one hand, which included reviews of a few recent publications as only a small part of their offering, and the learned journals on the other, which attended only to selected works of letters and scholarship, it attempted to review every work of every kind published in England. In this approach, the *Critical* joined the *Monthly*, and together they made the second half of the eighteenth century unique in English literary history: neither before nor since could the reader find nearly every published work, from low pamphlet to learned tome, reviewed in a single periodical and collected in its annual volumes.[21]

Thus the aggressive advertisements for the *Critical* were aimed unmistakably at Griffiths and the *Monthly Review*, the "undistinguishing Bookseller" and his staff of "obscure Hackney writers," their journal damned as "a contemptible Manufacture . . . carried on by wretched Hirelings, without Talent, Candour, Spirit, or Circumspection." These prepublication insults were harsh even by contemporary standards, and the *Literary Magazine*'s proprietors expressed disapproval of the *Critical* for censuring "the Productions of those who are concerned in Undertakings of the same Kind" (thereby committing, of course, a milder form of the same offense). But something more than commercial rivalry must have moved Smollett to this level of animosity.

He may have disdained Griffiths's rather poor reputation as a publisher, tarnished by a history of prosecutions for seditious and obscene publications in the late 1740s.[22] There is evidence, for example, that Griffiths was still publishing the unexpurgated version of *Fanny Hill* clandestinely and illegally throughout the 1750s and 1760s.[23] Perhaps Smollett bore a grudge against Griffiths for publishing such troublesome works as *Lady Frail* (1751)—John Hill's attempt to preempt the readership of *Peregrine Pickle*—and *A Vindication of the Name and Random Peregrinations of the Family of Smallwits* (1751)—a personal attack on Smollett.[24]

But it seems also that Smollett genuinely disapproved of Griffiths's intrinsically compromised position as both bookseller and contributing editor of a review journal and the ways in which he capitalized on that position. In assessing Griffiths's *Monthly*, no modern scholar has so far found anything terribly corrupt or unusually self-serving about his editorial practices, and a detailed treatment is beyond the scope of the present work.[25] Although, as Edward Bloom has shown, self-serving practices were common in journals conducted by booksellers,[26] there were nevertheless enough "infelicitous" practices on the *Monthly* (practices that Smollett had observed firsthand while working for it in 1751–52) to explain at least why Smollett's idealism might be offended and how he could make some of the accusations he did. For example, the practice on the *Monthly* of a writer's reviewing one of his own works, which Benjamin Nangle thought not to exist but which was discovered recently by Roger Lonsdale, was actually indulged in repeatedly.[27] In addition to the single instance Lonsdale found of Cleland reviewing his own work, *The Case of the Unfortunate Penlez*, in 1749, a study of Griffiths's own marked copy of the *Monthly* in the Bodleian Library reveals several other instances between 1749 and 1756. John Hill reviewed his own novel, *Adventures of Mr. Loveill* (1750) and, two months later, his book *The Actor, A Treatise on the Art of Playing*.[28] John Berkenhout reviewed his own translation of *Letters from an Old Man to a Young Prince* in 1756.[29] Smollett himself had been allowed in 1751 to review a book he had edited and in which he owned part of the copyright, Smellie's *Midwifery*.[30] In 1755, Griffiths appended to the March issue an eight-page essay written by the "Reverend Mr. Brown" to puff his own book, *A New Form of Prayer*—itself a Griffiths publication.[31] Nor was the practice halted in 1759. The same source reveals William Kenrick reviewing his own works in 1759, 1761, and 1762–63.[32] Griffiths also often printed straightforward advertisements for his own publications in the *Monthly*, not an uncommon practice in journalism but one hardly redolent of impartiality in a review.[33] In one case he even advertised a forthcoming publication and in another he issued with the *Monthly* a catalog of seventy-one publications available from his shop. These seventy-one were among the scores of Griffiths publications that the *Monthly*, in the natural course of its work, found itself reviewing. The *Monthly* also reviewed many other books that, although published by other booksellers, were retailed from Griffiths's shop; their sales, therefore, were also of interest—if less directly—to him. Some, including many contemporary publishers and editors, would probably have regarded this as just good business, but the stigma of being a "house-organ" was inevitable and it was alluded to in many of the printed attacks on the *Monthly* in its early years.[34] Although, as Smollett was to discover, such attacks were part of the reviewing business and not a very objective measure of a journal's worth, their numbers show that in the 1750s many shared his view of the *Monthly*'s shortcomings.

Thus Smollett's exalted tone in announcing the aims of the *Critical* grew from several causes: the twin desires to found an English academy and to rescue criticism from mercenary hands; the need to succeed commercially; a strong sense of rivalry with the *Monthly* and at least initially with Johnson's *Literary Magazine*. Each was to affect the early course of the *Critical*'s life, together fostering a pattern of apparent ambivalence in the *Critical*'s editorial conduct. Smollett was to find it impossibly difficult to maintain the manner and tone of an elite, learned journal, while still trying to hold his own in the knockabout world of Grub Street.

It was indicative that, from the very outset, Smollett began to experience the headaches and setbacks of an editor: for all its prepublication hauteur, the *Critical* was delayed in making its debut. A notice in the *Public Advertiser* of 2 Feburary 1756 explained the postponement of the first issue (which was to have appeared that day) "till March, in expectation of some foreign articles." On 1 March a combined January-February issue did appear, offering ninety-six pages of copy containing reviews of seventeen different books, all for one shilling. In content and format both, it signaled a challenge to the *Monthly Review*, its older sibling and still the only journal of its kind. More importantly, the appearance of the *Critical*'s first issue marked the beginning of a new era in the history of criticism and journalism. And the quality of that first issue, like the success of the *Critical* throughout its early years, was due almost entirely to Smollett's own enormous exertions.

[3]

The Man of Letters as Review Editor:
Problems and Policies

Although Smollett's direct involvement with the *Critical Review* covered more than seven years, 1756–63, this chapter focuses primarily on his editorial role during 1756. It was in 1756 that the *Critical Review* established the basic format and practices it was to follow throughout Smollett's tenure and for many years thereafter. And it is for 1756 that by far the most extensive and reliable information about its authorship is available, thanks to the discovery by Derek Roper in 1957 of annotated copies of the volumes for 1756 that establish the authorship of almost all the articles for that year.[1] Because of the detailed information these annotations provide, the character of Smollett's own writings and of his editorial control can be seen with greater clarity for 1756 than at any time thereafter.

So much rests on the authority of this annotated copy of the *Critical* (vols. 1 and 2) that it is necessary first to clarify its origins. Roper's account, although accurate and informative, does not determine the identity or authority of the person who made the annotations and, accordingly, leading Smollett scholars such as Knapp and Paul-Gabriel Boucé have been understandably cautious about accepting them.[2] However, after an examination of the annotated volumes, a comparison of handwritings, and further analysis of the circumstantial evidence, it is clear that the volumes were originally part of the printer Hamilton's own set and it was he who recorded the authorship of each of the articles.[3]

The evidence is briefly summarized. As Roper reported, the annotations were jotted down hastily, with a lead pencil, in an eighteenth-century hand, at an early date before the leaves were trimmed for binding. Like the corresponding annotations in Griffiths's marked set of the *Monthly Review*, the entries vary in form—for example, "Derrick," "D—k", "Der–k", "Der", "D"—suggesting that they were recorded at different times.[4] All this is consistent with the way a printer would mark up his file copy of a periodical as a kind of payroll record, to keep track of who wrote what and therefore how much each should be paid. Moreover, like Griffiths, Hamilton is known to have kept such a marked copy, although it was thought to have disappeared,[5] and the handwriting of these annotations is similar to the few available specimens of his own.[6] One of Hamilton's chief assistants, Thomas Wright, was also known to have kept a marked file of the *Critical*,[7] but as he did not even come to work for Hamilton until almost three years later (December 1758),[8] these detailed ascriptions for 1756 certainly are not his.

Only someone with comprehensive inside information could have made such thorough ascriptions, but all the other possible sources—namely the reviewers themselves—must also be eliminated. By analyzing the instances where the ascriber had made corrections by penciling in a second name over the initial ascription, Roper showed that Smollett, Francklin, and Derrick must be ruled out. The names of each of the three appeared in these corrections and presumably each would have known from the start whether he had written a given article. It is even more improbable that either Patrick Murdoch, who contributed only two reviews to the first issue and then spent most of 1756 in Germany,[9] or John Armstrong, who contributed relatively few articles and none at all in some issues, compiled these notes. Indeed, the procedure by which copy for each issue was sent in from the various authors enabled only the printer to know who wrote each piece, as can be gathered from an editorial note in 1757:

> The gentlemen chiefly concerned with the Critical Review, live at a considerable distance from the press; and sometimes the printer has been so hurried towards the latter end of the month, by their sending in the copy so late, that he could not possibly furnish them with proof sheets for their correction. (No '57, 472)

In short, the ascriptions must be Hamilton's and as such constitute the most reliable guide to authorship one could ask for.

Hamilton's annotations immediately reveal a great deal about the organization and editorial conduct of the *Critical*. Besides disclosing the Herculean scale of Smollett's work as a reviewer (more than seventy reviews, comprising about a third of the total text[10]), they confirm that in 1756 at least, the *Critical* was very much Smollett's project, written by men he had enlisted, under his editorial supervision. As with any new publishing project, there were innumerable decisions to be taken and tasks to be performed, ranging from what editorial policies to adopt down to what typeface to use. In his valuable unpublished study, "English Book-Reviewing 1749–1800," W. Denham Sutcliffe summarizes the difficulties a review editor faced:

> The lot of a Review's editor was not an easy one. Upon his head descended

all the violent abusive wrath of offended authors and publishers; on his shoulders lay the responsibility of making the Review a profitable concern. As the only unifying force in a straggling group, he had to watch over the paper's policy. He had to find reviewers; critique, curtail, or expand their articles; determine rates of payment, and keep his staff satisfied with them; he had to whip up the dilatory, and get the paper into the post-chaises on time every month or face irate subscribers. No wonder he was often harrassed and irritable.[11]

The job seems even more complicated and hectic when one considers the procedure for compiling each issue. It involved several steps. Early in the month, it had to be decided what books would be reviewed and by whom and whether each merited a main article or a brief notice. Copies of the necessary works had to be procured and distributed to the appropriate reviewers. The reviewers sent their copy to the printer or editor, who was often the same man (as with Edward Cave and the *Gentleman's Magazine*) but not always, as in the case of Hamilton and Smollett's division of labor. Proofs were run off and sent back for correction, although there wasn't always time for this before deadline (Mr '57, 288, "Errata"). It had to be decided in what order the articles would appear and where they had to be cut or abridged to improve the text or to fit the layout. Gradually the issue took shape, each sheet printed as soon as complete, leaving, if possible, only the last sheet for the busy days just before publication. To the last sheet, the editor added replies to correspondents and critics, announcements and other editorial notes, and an errata list.

Smollett and Hamilton shared these responsibilities. If Smollett could be said to be "editor-in-chief," then Hamilton served as a kind of managing editor, combining the duties of copy editor and business manager in one. But in these early days of journalism, the role of editor was still evolving; there were no clear-cut lines of demarcation among the duties of chief editors, subeditors, and printers. As writer, editor, and coproprietor, Smollett had a special interest in every aspect of publication, down to the smallest detail. It is not surprising, then, that Smollett worked closely with Hamilton, occasionally performing some of the more mundane and mechanical tasks that one might expect to fall to the printer or subeditor. There is evidence, for instance, that Smollett sometimes took charge of distributing review copies of books to the reviewers and that their written copy was sometimes sent to him, rather than to Hamilton directly.[12] Smollett also wrote most of the short notices and replies to correspondence at the back of each issue.[13] He and Hamilton cooperated closely on the editing of copy. By 1761, the regular treks to Chelsea by printer's devils from Hamilton's shop, carrying copy for Smollett to edit, were so frequent and so well known that the *Court Magazine* parodied the routine: it printed a mock complaint ostensibly from one of

Hamilton's devils who had missed George III's Coronation Day festivities because Hamilton had sent him that day "with a proof half sheet of the *Review*, three times to Dr. S[mollett] at Chelsea."[14] The traffic was not one-way. Smollett's editorial duties brought him into town on a regular basis. Once a week he visited Forrest's Coffee House in Charing Cross, according to his friend Alexander Carlyle, who observed with amusement there one of his conferences with his various literary assistants.[15] Smollett must also have paid regular visits to Hamilton's shop, especially in the first year of the project he prized so highly. In later years it was remembered as a comfortable meeting place for authors, described by John Nichols as "the literary conversational lounge at Archibald Hamilton's."[16]

Precisely how Smollett and Hamilton divided and coordinated their efforts may never be fully known, but one lingering myth can be dispelled: that Hamilton, either in desperation for copy or to indulge his own literary inclinations, wrote reviews for the *Critical*. The records show he wrote nothing, not even editorial notices. Smollett himself was adamant on this point. In refuting Charles Churchill's accusation, in 1761, that Hamilton wrote reviews, Smollett declared that Hamilton "never in the whole course of his life wrote one single article in the Critical Review" (My '61, 411). Indeed, it is unlikely that Hamilton ever participated as a reviewer himself, even years later when Smollett had left and he had become sole proprietor. In 1770, a writer in the *Critical* described the staff's reviewing procedure in a way that indicated Hamilton still refrained altogether from reviewing or even voicing an opinion on books under review (De '70, 464–66). Instead, he hired literary editors to supervise the work for him, including, at various times, William Guthrie, Percival Stockdale, and George Steevens.[17]

Hamilton's nonparticipation as writer or contributing editor underscores the unusual degree of editorial control that Smollett retained to himself. This policy distinguished the *Critical* from the *Monthly*, where the bookseller Griffiths reserved editorial authority to himself and thus gave substance to one of Smollett's favorite claims for the *Critical*: that unlike the *Monthly*, it was not patched together by an "undistinguishing bookseller" whose taste and impartiality were equally suspect. This distinction, which was from Smollett's point of view terribly important, is difficult to discern at two hundred years' distance. But it is true that, as Griffiths's own records show and Smollett undoubtedly knew, Griffiths regularly reviewed works for the *Monthly*.[18] His critical efforts produced some curious results. Once, for example, he acclaimed an obscure novel, *The Adventures of Joe Thompson*, as superior even to *Don Quixote*, although he openly admitted he had not read it through.[19] On another occasion, he devoted the longest review of a work of fiction ever to appear in the *Monthly* (thirty-five thousand words) to a now long-forgotten novel, *The Life of John Buncle*, and praised its author, the eccentric Thomas Amory, as "master of a vast compass of literary knowledge."[20]

The key issue was conflict of interests. Unlike Griffiths, Hamilton had no proprietary interest in any current publications and was never, therefore, in Griffiths's position as editor-proprietor of a journal that reviewed his own publications. In 1755 and 1756, to cite pertinent years, the *Monthly* reviewed twenty-nine Griffiths publications, all favorably,[21] and at least three of these reviews were written by Griffiths himself.[22] Although Griffiths's list of new titles shrank over the years, in 1761 the *Monthly* still reviewed twelve Griffiths publications—again, no surprise, all favorably.[23] By contrast, not even the *Critical*'s nominal connection with the publisher Baldwin seems to have influenced its staff: several Baldwin publications were damned outright in 1756, and most were relegated to the "Monthly Catalogue" where they received only cursory notice (Ap '56, 246–48).[24] No one reviewer was responsible for this treatment of Baldwin's publications either. The negative reviews are distributed among Smollett, Francklin, and Derrick. Perhaps this display of impartiality explains the early disappearance of Baldwin's name from the *Critical*'s title page. It is important to remember, however, that it was Smollett's idealism, and not Griffiths's pragmatism, that was at odds with the everyday practices and ethics of the publishing world. Indeed, one cannot imagine a time in the last 250 years that it would not have seemed hopelessly idealistic to curtail the symbiotic relationship between publishers and review journals.

The identities of the authors revealed to be contributors to the *Critical* in 1756 confirm that Smollett, rather than Hamilton (as many sources allege),[25] was the organizer who brought them together. Each of the three who joined with Smollett to produce the first issue—Patrick Murdoch, John Armstrong, and Samuel Derrick—had close connections with him. Armstrong was Smollett's close friend and, like Murdoch, a central figure in the coterie of London Scots centered on James Thomson with which Smollett had been familiar since the 1740s.[26] Derrick, meanwhile, had served as Smollett's amanuensis on earlier projects and was soon, if not already, living at Smollett's house in Chelsea.[27]

At least as far as Murdoch and Armstrong were concerned, the stature of these contributors fulfilled Smollett's claim for the *Critical* reviewers, that they were "a Set of Gentlemen whose Characters and Capacities have been universally approved and acknowledged by the Public."[28] Murdoch's accomplishments were various. Although an ordained clergyman he had distinguished himself at the University of Edinburgh in mathematics. By 1745, he had been elected a Fellow of the Royal Society.[29] He wrote many treatises on scientific and mathematical topics, including eight papers published in the Society's *Philosophical Transactions*. A close friend of James Thomson's, he contributed a stanza to his *Castle of Indolence* (1748) and eventually was to write a "Life of Thomson" (1762), the first important biography of the poet and a principal source for Johnson's "Life of Thomson."

Armstrong, too, conformed with Smollett's desired image of his reviewers as gentlemen of letters. Educated at Edinburgh, he was a practicing physician who had attained some fame for his poetry and medical essays. The publication of his mildly erotic poem, *The Economy of Love*, had aroused some objections in 1736, but his reputation was more than redeemed by his widely acclaimed *Art of Preserving Health* in 1744. He also contributed four stanzas to Thomson's *Castle of Indolence*. In the medical field, he produced *A Synopsis of the History and Cure of the Venereal Disease* in the 1730s and gained appointments first as a physician to the Hospital for Lamed, Maimed, and Sick Soldiers in 1746, and later as physician to the army in Germany in 1760.[30] His critical views, particularly as encapsulated in his poem *Taste, An Epistle to a Young Critic*, jibed with Smollett's. In fact, when *Taste* was published anonymously in 1753, Smollett was among the first to applaud it and to attribute it to Armstrong.[31]

When Thomas Francklin joined the *Critical* a month later (his first review appeared in the March issue), he brought with him comparable credentials. Educated at Westminster and Trinity College, Cambridge, he took holy orders and became a Fellow of Trinity. In 1750, he was appointed professor of Greek at Cambridge.[32] He published many sermons and, in 1753, a poem called *Translation* which also contained his proposals for publishing by subscription a translation of the works of Sophocles (eventually published in 1759), a project on which he was still working when he joined the *Critical*. Aside from classical translations and sermons, his literary productions included an essay-periodical, *The Centinel* (January–December 1757), several volumes of a joint translation with Smollett of Voltaire's *Works* (1761–65), and four plays, among them the tragedies *The Earl of Warwick* (1766) and *Matilda* (1775). He went on to become part of Johnson's circle in the 1770s and he succeeded Goldsmith as honorary professor of ancient history to the Royal Academy in 1774.[33] When he died in 1784, he was eulogized as having been "long a favorite in the literary world."[34]

The only exception to the *Critical*'s generally high standard of writers in 1756, and a source of occasional embarrassment to Smollett, was the lowly and laughable Samuel Derrick. Having started life as apprentice to a linen-draper in Dublin, Derrick had come to London in 1751 where, after an abortive attempt at an acting career, he made shift to survive as a hack writer. His early writings consisted of undistinguished translations, minor verse, and bits of journalism, including a brief run of his *Dramatic Censor* in 1752. They gained him little reputation and less pay. Johnson used to tell a story about Derrick's having to sleep in the streets in his early London days.[35] Perhaps out of charity, Smollett patronized Derrick, hiring him as his amanuensis sometime in the mid-1750s, subscribing to his *Poems* in 1755, and taking him into his own home for all or part of the period 1755–58.[36] But Derrick's personal reputation was worse than his writings, and Smollett obviously kept his distance. He admitted to John Moore in 1757 that he had employed Derrick "as a Trash reader for the Critical Review, but," he added, "you are not to number him among my Companions, nor indeed does his Character deserve any further Discussion."[37] Not that the job was inescapably ignominous: Coleridge was to work for a time as the *Critical*'s trash reader—a self-described "hireling" who reviewed "sundry Fungi of the Press"—in the 1790s.[38] Derrick was no Coleridge, but he must have had some useful qualities for editors—whether diligence, versatility, or the compliant eagerness of the needy—because Johnson also considered hiring him for a journal he was projecting in the 1750s.[39] But even after Derrick's elevation to the post of Master of Ceremonies at Bath in 1763, he was still regarded by many—including Johnson, Boswell, Strahan, and John Home—with a mixture of sympathy and contempt.[40] Smollett was to ridicule him later, in *Humphry Clinker* (1771).[41] Smollett can hardly have prided himself, then, on having hired Derrick as a contributor to the first issues of the *Critical*, a lapse he glossed over in affirming to Moore in August 1756 that "the Critical Review is conducted by four Gentlemen of approved abilities."[42]

On balance, however, Smollett's early collection of contributors to the *Critical* confirms his seriousness about reclaiming review criticism from Grub Street. A Cambridge professor of Greek, a Fellow of the Royal Society, a prominent physician and poet: these were the kinds of credentials and institutional connections that would lend his journal authority and prestige. It was an attempt to create a new kind of literary establishment that whatever its immediate success, foreshadowed the direction of criticism in the nineteenth century and beyond. In the context of the contemporary literary scene, the prestige of the *Critical*'s writers was confirmed, unwittingly, in an anonymous magazine article of 1761, in which fifty-six contemporary authors are ranked "by degree of merit." It listed John Armstrong tenth, Thomas Francklin seventeenth, and Smollett himself twenty-fourth. The same chart had Edward Young first, Samuel Johnson second, and Oliver Goldsmith—who joined the *Critical* in 1757–sixteenth.[43] The point is that four of the *Critical*'s main writers during its first eighteen months were, at least by one account, among the best twenty-five writers alive in Britain.

While they were organizing a staff of reviewers, Smollett and Hamilton also had to make decisions about format and other technical matters, decisions that were to prove important not only in the success of the *Critical Review* but in the emergence of the review journal as a new genre of literary periodical. It was natural that they took the *Monthly Review* as their model because both had a working familiarity with it. Smollett had written for the *Monthly* in 1751–52 and Hamilton, who until 1755 had worked as a manager of William Strahan's shop where the *Monthly* was printed, had supervised its printing.[44] The specific features they imitated from the *Monthly*, however, have never been clearly identified. In his pioneering study, "Smollett and the *Critical Review*," Jones contended that "the *Critical* [borrowed] from the

Monthly a policy of anonymity, the practice of publishing each month's issue at the beginning of the following month, the inclusion of a 'Monthly Catalogue' for brief mentions, and the use of extensive quotation in long reviews."[45] But in fact, except for the "Monthly Catalogue," all these practices were conventional in eighteenth-century periodicals. Led by the *Gentleman's Magazine* (founded in 1731), most monthly journals practiced anonymity, published on the first of the month, and, if they had a small review section, used extensive quotation in long reviews, with brief notices or, more often, simple lists of new titles.

But the review *was* a new and distinctive genre of periodical, as C. L. Carlson, the historian of the *Gentleman's Magazine*, was among the first to conclude: "Virtually all magazines established in England during the eighteenth century imitated the *Gentleman's* in vital respects. The most notable exceptions were the reviews."[46] What really distinguished the *Monthly* and *Critical* was a combination of factors: the exclusive attention to new publications in their contents, their attempt at comprehensive coverage of both learned and popular works, and their use of a regular format consisting of a few major reviews followed by a section of minor notices (the "Monthly Catalogue").[47] By contrast, the magazines offered a wide variety of subject matter of which book lists or review sections were only a minor part—when they weren't omitted altogether—and they reviewed or printed excerpts from at most a handful of books. Price and size also differed. The reviews contained five or six sheets (eighty to ninety-six pages) of text each month and sold for a shilling, while the magazines usually filled three and one-half sheets (fifty-six pages) and sold for six pence. These details, although small in themselves, represent an enormous difference for the reading public. In the course of a year the sheer volume of literary and cultural information (as opposed to news and light entertainment) a review provided would amount to many times that contained in a magazine.

That the *Critical* had imitated the format and contents of the *Monthly* would have been evident to every reader as soon as its first issue appeared on 2 March 1756. That it also posed a serious challenge was equally clear. It offered more text, for example: the *Monthly* had been offering eighty pages for its one-shilling cover price up through 1755, so the *Critical* offered ninety-six pages of contents in every issue of 1756. The *Monthly*'s response was a portent for the future of their relations. Griffiths immediately increased the *Monthly*'s size to ninety-six pages in the February issue and a fierce, but productive rivalry was underway.

The *Critical*'s first issue was published in conventional blue wrappers, undoubtedly with its title and table of contents on the front cover, just as they are on the only recorded copy of the *Critical* to survive in its original covers "as issued," that for May 1758, now in the Public Records Office.[48] The first issue (and probably the next few) had Smollett's "Proposal" for the *Critical* printed on the back cover, as one of the first writers to attack the *Critical* referred to having read it there.[49]

The covers themselves raise issues. How Smollett and Hamilton chose to use them and whether they accepted paid advertisements became significant questions in light of Smollett's defiance of commercial influences on literature. Many years later, in 1772, printing advertisements on the covers had become a regular practice for the *Critical*. An editorial note in the issue of December 1772 explained the policy in replying to an angry correspondent: "Can it be necessary to inform M W. that the advertisements on our Blue Cover make no part of the Review?—He, or any one else may advertise there, on paying the usual prices" (De '72, 480). But in the 1750s, although advertisements were common practice and a useful source of revenue, some felt they carried a stigma of compromised integrity. The editor of the *True Briton*, after proudly stating that he had "avoided receiving any advertisements" throughout his first year, regretfully announced in January 1752 that he was now forced to do so for financial reasons.[50] Such scruples were rare. The *Gentleman's Magazine* had been printing advertisements both in the body of the magazine and on its covers since its beginning in 1731 and continued to do so throughout the eighteenth century.[51] So, too, did Woodville's *Grand Magazine of Magazines* (1750–51?) and Martin's *General Magazine of Arts and Sciences* (1755–65). Martin, like Cave, usually advertised works in which he himself had a financial interest, including "optical apparatus" (telescopes, microscopes, and spectacles) for sale in his shop.[52] But the *Grand Magazine of Magazines* was more catholic: one surviving copy (May 1751) contains paid advertisements for new books from eight different publishers.[53]

Thus Griffiths did no more than conform with normal business practices when he printed advertisements for his own publications in the *Monthly*. His acceptance of paid advertisements from other publishers, however, raises subtler issues. One of the few available copies of the *Monthly* in its original covers (for October 1764) bears advertisements on its front and back covers for books published by Becket and De Hondt. The first book listed in the advertisements, a translation of Voltaire's *Treatise on Religious Toleration*, is also—by remarkable coincidence—the subject of the lead article in that issue, a long and favorable review of Voltaire's *Treatise*.[54] Of course to correlate advertising space with the treatment of a particular publishing house might be revealing in any review journal, whether mideighteenth or late twentieth century. And copies in original covers of the *Monthly*, as with any eighteenth-century periodical, are too scarce to shed much light. But the available evidence suggests that already in the infancy of review journalism, paid advertisements could have a direct connection with the allocation of critical favor by review journals.

Against this background, Smollett's apparent policy not to accept advertisements in the *Critical* stands out all the more. No advertisements ever appeared in the pages of the *Critical* during his editorship or any time after.[55] His overriding concern to dissociate the *Critical* from booksellers and their commercial interests must have impelled him to extend that policy to its covers as well. Certainly on the one available copy of the *Critical* in covers (May 1758) there are no advertisements, nor do any contemporary sources refer to anything on the *Critical*'s covers except editorial announcements.[56] This idealistic policy may help explain why Smollett made so little money from the *Critical* in its first few years.

Advertising for the *Critical* itself was another task. Normally the publisher or printer would see to it, but as Smollett was coproprietor, he must have taken a close interest. In 1760 he was to show great interest in marketing tactics for the *Universal History*, a project in which he was merely an editor and writer; he drew up an analysis of the *Universal History*'s faltering sales, with a proposal of how they might be increased, and submitted it to Richardson's approval before passing it on to the other proprietors.[57] Besides writing the copy for the *Critical*'s "Proposals," Smollett probably helped plan the advertising strategy to insure that it was well-announced throughout the provincial, Scottish, and London press. It is impossible to ascertain the full scope of that advertising, but it is indicative that besides running advertisements in such London papers as the *Public Advertiser* (19, 24, and 30 December 1755 and 1 February 1756), they advertised intensively in such provincial newspapers as *Jackson's Oxford Journal*, in which ads ran for three weeks to announce the *Critical*'s first issue (14, 21, and 28 February 1756). On this scale, advertising could be expensive. The standard rate was 2s.6d., plus one penny per line over twenty lines, per insertion;[58] the preliminary advertisements for the *Critical* often ran to seventy lines and more. The initial cost to Hamilton must have been considerable, not much less than the figure of sixty pounds cited by John Murray about 1780 as the minimum cost to advertise just the first issue of a new review.[59] After the initial promotion subsided, the advertising budget would settle somewhere between five and ten pounds per month.[60]

Other costs had to be met for printing and distribution. Hamilton's printing expenses can be estimated from what is known of Griffiths's expense in printing the *Monthly*. Between 1749 and 1767, Strahan charged Griffiths just over one penny per copy to print the *Monthly*.[61] But if Strahan took his profit on the same scale as Richardson, as R. A. Austen Leigh has suggested,[62] then the actual cost to him would have been only about $\frac{7}{10}$d. or $\frac{8}{10}$d. per copy. Assuming that Hamilton had adopted the same business practices as his mentor Strahan, then, based on these figures, one can estimate that the cost to Hamilton of printing one issue in a run of twenty-five hundred copies (comparable to the *Monthly*) would have been just under ten pounds. A one-time extra cost would have been incurred, of course, if Smollett and Hamilton decided to distribute the first issue free, as new journals commonly did to stimulate circulation.[63] Also, discounts were often granted to wholesalers and distributors; if the *Critical* followed the practice of the *Grub Street Journal* (1730–37) or *London Magazine* (1732–85), the discount could have been as high as twenty-five percent.[64]

Authors had to be paid for copy. Here again evidence is scarce, but contemporary accounts suggest that the standard rate for reviewing was two guineas per sheet.[65] This included quoted material, a very important consideration when reviews often consisted of eighty to ninety percent excerpts transcribed from the work under review. Thus, theoretically, the payroll for each issue of the *Critical*, containing six sheets, would have come to about £12 6s. But was this much actually paid out? In later years, the *Critical* had a reputation for low rates of pay; according to Stockdale it paid its reviewers two guineas per sheet in 1770, at a time when the *Monthly* was paying four.[66] Lowly Derrick, as Smollett's amanuensis, may not have been paid as much as the more prestigious writers.[67] Griffiths had a policy like this, setting different rates of pay for reviewers according to their talents.[68] Pay may have been one reason Armstrong left the *Critical* in late 1756 or early 1757. Contributions by Armstrong—who had told Wilkes of Smollett's original sanguine hopes of riches for them all—dwindled noticeably towards the end of 1756, to a total of three in the last four issues combined,[69] and sometime in the next few months he withdrew from the *Critical*.[70]

Smollett himself may have foregone his pay as a reviewer to make up his share of the proprietary capital (or simply to minimize losses); it is apparent that the *Critical* yielded him little or no income in 1756, one of the worst periods of financial stress in his life. His private correspondence shows him repeatedly appealing to Rivington, Macaulay, and others for loans to fend off the creditors who so beseiged his house in Chelsea that he yearned to flee "to some corner where I may work without being distracted and distressed, for here I can do nothing."[71] Yet, in itemizing the sources from which he could expect any financial relief—advances against his *History*, proceeds from his play, revenue from his wife's assets in Jamaica—Smollett never once mentioned the *Critical*. It wasn't until 1762 that Smollett spoke of the *Critical*'s providing him any income, and then in a way that suggests it had only just become profitable.[72] In 1756, finances were a sore point. When one pamphleteer sneered that if the *Critical* reviewers were to curb "their passionate way of writing . . . their finances might be affected," Smollett replied testily that he should "have had more urbanity than to reflect upon the finances of those whom he does not know" (Se '56, 191). Under such financial pressures, it must have been as difficult to continue publishing as to preserve one's dignity.

How did Smollett and his reviewers acquire copies of the more than 245 works they reviewed in 1756? This question, most recently raised by Donald Eddy in his study of Samuel Johnson as book reviewer,[73] deserves attention not only to illuminate a point of publishing history, but to clarify the pattern of relationships among review journals and publishing houses and their connection with editorial policy. Undoubtedly the books reviewed in the first issue of the *Critical* had to be bought or borrowed, as Hamilton published none of his own and no publisher or author was likely to donate a review copy to a journal which did not yet exist. But as the *Critical* got started, new books got into reviewers' hands several different ways.

Some books were borrowed from friends who already had them or would have purchased them anyway, as Smollett revealed for example in a letter to Philip Miller in 1759, written to accompany the books he was returning.[74] This was not unusual. The staff of the *Gentleman's Magazine* also borrowed books to review, according to Carlson.[75] Other times the need to acquire a review copy and the need to pay a reviewer were obviated when a correspondent sent in an acceptable review based on a copy he owned.

In this category also are a few books that Smollett had acquired by subscription, but passed along to members of his staff, apparently, rather than review them himself. Smollett is known to have subscribed for the following books between 1756 and 1765, all of which were reviewed in the *Critical*, although in no case does the review bear signs of Smollett's authorship:

> Samuel Boyce, *Poems on Several Occasions*, Dodsley, 1757 (Se '57, 193–95).
> [Miss Smythies of Colchester], *The Brothers*, Dodsley, 1758 (Ja '59, 79).
> [William Woty], *The Shrubs of Parnassus*, Newbery, 1760 (Mr '60, 217–21).
> Francis Fawkes, *Original Poems and Translations*, Dodsley, 1761 (Jn '61, 485–87).
> Christopher Smart, *A Translation of the Psalms of David*, Bathurst, 1765 (Se '65, 208–16).[76]

In fact none of these reviews is particularly enthusiastic and at least two, those of Smythies and Smart, are decidedly negative. Whatever Smollett's reasons for subscribing to each, they did not translate into favored treatment in the *Critical*. It has been suggested that the names of famous authors sometimes got onto subscription lists without the subscription fee's being paid, as a promotional favor to publishers with whom they had regular business dealings.[77] Although Smollett had business relations with Newbery and Dodsley, it is very unlikely that he engaged in this practice. Otherwise it is difficult to explain why his name appeared in so few subscription lists at a time when his influence on the *Critical* would have been so useful to publishers of unknown authors. Smollett genuinely believed in publication by subscription as a way to circumvent the booksellers' control—not to further their interests—and, perhaps remembering his own difficulties in securing subscribers for *The Regicide*,[78] he had subscribed for works by struggling authors long before his connection with the *Critical* began.[79] Allowing his name to be used this way would have been the kind of practice Smollett abhorred. In 1763, for example, he responded indignantly to such rumors circulating in America: "I am much mortified to find it is believed in America that I have lent my name to Booksellers; that is a species of Prostitution of which I am altogether incapable."[80]

Before the end of the *Critical*'s first year, of course, some review copies of new books began to arrive as "gifts" from authors, publishers, and their friends. The *Monthly* had experienced this too and Griffiths took no pains to conceal donations, tacitly acknowledging them by occasionally omitting the price of a book from its publication details or printing instead "Price unknown to us."[81] So too with the *Critical*. William Huggins, for example, sent Smollett a copy of his *Orlando Furioso* in late 1756 and Smollett reviewed it favorably in the May 1757 issue (My '57, 385–98).[82] Either Charles Jenty or his friends sent a copy of his *Structurae Humanae Demonstratio* to the *Critical*, but Smollett so resented the accompanying letters of recommendation that the tactic backfired and he criticized it severely (No '56, 373–74). Undoubtedly a review copy was readily available when one of the reviewers himself published a book, such as Smollett's *Compendium of Voyages*, which Francklin reviewed in May 1756 (309–12), but of course these instances were very infrequent. Occasionally reviews appeared without any mention of price, probably signifying other gift copies (Mr '56, 172).[83] In later years, reviewers would often report that the copy under review was donated (Ja '57, 74).[84] Derrick's correspondence during the years 1756 to 1763 shows him receiving books from various friends in Ireland, including the bookseller George Faulkner, who obviously hoped for favorable reviews.[85] One correspondent, Thomas Wilson, alluding to an unspecified book in which he had an interest, wrote Derrick, "When Pub[lication] is done, I will send a Rv^{rs} [Reviewers] copy to Dr. Smollet."[86]

What is most interesting, however, is that these contributions seem to have failed to effect the desired result. Only one of those mentioned in Derrick's correspondence was reviewed in the *Critical*—William Dunkin's *Funeral Obsequies on Lawson's Death*, published in Dublin by Faulkner—and it received largely negative treatment in a review based on a copy not of Faulkner's, but of a London publisher's edition (Mr '60, 232). That this avenue failed for Faulkner and others may be no more than a reflection of Derrick's meager influence with Smollett and the *Critical*, although it also contributed to Faulkner's sense of prejudice against Irish and Scottish publications in the English review journals.[87] Writers such as Fielding and Shebbeare made jokes about themselves and other critics who favored books that were donated to them,[88] but for Smollett and the *Critical* it became a serious issue. By 1763, the practice of receiving complimentary copies was common enough to be used by the *Critical*'s enemies as grounds to impugn its reputation. In an editorial response, Smollett admitted that "a few books, at their first publication, have been sent as presents, to one or other of the supposed writers of the work" but he vigorously denied that this constituted receiving "any present or bribe, or other unfair consideration, for any article that it ever contained" and offered a reward of fifty guineas to anyone who could prove a single instance of real corruption in the history of the *Critical* (Ja '63, 21). On balance, the evidence suggests that the practice of sending review copies to the *Critical* was a growing but still relatively infrequent phenomenon and most unpredictable in its result.

The vast majority of publications reviewed in the *Critical* simply had to be purchased. Other review journals had had to do this. The authors of the *True Briton*, which printed some reviews, complained in 1751 of the expense involved: "The bare Purchase of the Publick Papers and Pamphlets, and the collecting of News, will (exclusive of Books to be bought) amount to a very considerable yearly Sum."[89] Aside from his own publications, Griffiths presumably had to buy books to review also, which might explain his anger in 1757 at one of his reviewers (Oliver Goldsmith) who had failed to return the volumes he had been lent to review.[90] For the *Critical*, too, there was no escaping the onerous necessity each month of buying large numbers of publications, many of them mediocre or worse. One reviewer in 1759 confirmed that this was the procedure as he wryly explained why authors should not abuse reviewers:

> If the truth were known, we are the very best and most constant friends they have in the world; since, let them be never so dull, we are obliged to buy their performances. The rest of the world may forsake them; but they are still sure of one purchaser: and, if upon paying a shilling for a book scarce worth an headless pin, it would be very hard to refuse us the consolation of grumbling a little at our bad bargain. (No '59, 412)[91]

Into the mid-1760s at least, reviewers continued to refer occasionally to the practice of buying publications to review as if it were quite common.[92]

The expense would have been considerable, and some scholars have doubted that the journals could have afforded to buy review copies and still remain in business.[93] But clearly they did buy the books they reviewed and they did remain very much in business. In fact, the total cost of purchasing at full price every publication reviewed in the *Critical* in 1756 (omitting Smollett's *Compendium*) would have amounted to £35 2s. 10d.—high, but affordable. The cost per month would have averaged £3 3s. 1d., ranging from a low of £1 3s. in September to a high of £5 7s. 4d. in June. When compared with the hypothetical monthly costs discussed above for printing (£10), payroll (£12 6s.), and advertising (£5–10), it was far from the highest overhead cost.

This is an area of expense where Griffiths, with a shop full of new books, was at a competitive advantage. A Griffiths advertisement in 1752–53 listed more than seventy titles in which he had a proprietary interest;[94] another in 1760 listed more than eighty "books and pamphlets printed for, and sold by R. Griffiths" at that time.[95] None of these, presumably, had to be purchased to review. Here was another financial handicap, like the policy against taking in paid advertising and the refusal to publish semiannual supplementary issues as the *Monthly* did, under which the proprietors of the *Critical* labored. One can safely assume that these financial matters were mainly left to Hamilton's competence, which must have been considerable, judging by his later reputation as not only a fine printer,[96] but a financially successful one too.[7] Smollett showed his trust in Hamilton's abilities by granting him a power of attorney when he left England in 1763[98] and by making him an executor of his will before he died.[99]

Editorial problems were more Smollett's province. Smollett must have taken upon himself—especially in the early stages—the responsibility for decisions about what works were to be reviewed and by whom. For the first issue, these decisions were probably made rather informally. In his eagerness to enlist the support of Murdoch and Armstrong, Smollett must have been quite accommodating, encouraging them to review a recent work or two of their choice. That Murdoch contributed only two reviews and Armstrong only one suggests that they cooperated less than enthusiastically. Murdoch chose Sheridan's *British Education* (a review Smollett distinguished by making it the lead article) and James MacKnight's *Harmony of the Four Gospels* and reviewed both favourably (Ja/Fe '56, 1–10, 23–41). Armstrong reviewed Thomas Blackwell's *Memoirs of the Court of Augustus*, welcoming it, despite many faults, as a "learned work" (Ja/Fe '56, 66–74). The rest fell to Smollett and Derrick, who between them reviewed at least twelve works.[100] Derrick's reviews were assigned him by Smollett and already in the first issue he complains in the voice of a conscripted "trash reader": "Nothing could have obliged us to the perusal of a performance so wearisome as the *Fortune-teller*, but the absolute necessity under which we are laid by our plan, of giving some account of every thing that appears in print" (Ja/Fe '56, 53). Not surprisingly, Derrick found scarcely a redeeming feature in any of the five minor works he reviewed. Smollett chose for himself, however, seven publications (from a variety of publishers) in which he had a real interest:

James Grieve, trans., *Of Medicine*, by A. Cornelius Celsus, 6s., Wilson.
Thomas Birch, *History of the Royal Society*, £1 5s., Millar.
William Borlase, *Observations on the Islands of Scilly*, 6s., Sandby.

Samuel Pegge, *Dissertations on Anglo-Saxon Remains*, 2s. 6d., Whiston.
Arthur Murphy, *The Apprentice*, 1s., Vaillant.
Samuel Foote, *The Englishman Return'd from Paris*, 1s., Vaillant.
[John Shebbeare], *A Third Letter to the People of England*, 1s., Scott.[101]

He also reviewed, in Article 17, a painting by Hamilton, three drawings by Strange, and a statue by Rysbrack. Although a fastidious critic, Smollett in general found much more to approve in his reviews than did his assistant, as will be seen.

Even with the first issue, Smollett experienced the editor's perennial difficulty in getting enough copy together by the publishing deadline. Perhaps Murdoch or Armstrong needed coaxing, perhaps Smollett and Derrick were overextended: either way, an advertisement appeared on the originally scheduled date of publication—2 February 1756—to announce that the inaugural issue was "postponed till March in expectation of some foreign articles."[102] This excuse appears slightly disingenuous, for the three "foreign articles" in the first issue were not dispatches from foreign correspondents, but instead reviews by Derrick of three foreign publications available in London bookshops (Ja/e '56, 90–93).

Still, it is possible that Smollett, after waiting in vain for the expected foreign correspondence, had made the difficult decision to go to press without it. This touches another area of his editorial problems. He had stated in his proposals that the *Critical* reviewers "have established a Correspondence with France, Holland, Germany, Italy and Spain; which will enable them to entertain their Readers with the Literary News of those different Countries, and to translate such Productions, as shall seem to bid fairest for succeeding in an English Dress." How he set about this ambitious scheme is not certain. He probably used the contacts he had established (especially among Scottish expatriates) on his tour of Holland, Flanders, and France in 1749 and his visit to Paris in 1750;[103] he may also have used whatever foreign connections his literary friends in London could offer. Inevitably, problems arose. Years later it was revealed, for example, that extensive coverage of Italian publications had "originally formed a part of [the *Critical*'s] plan; but the difficulty of procuring early a judicious assortment of Italian books, interrupted the design" (Ja '61, 63). He made a limited start with the section in the March issue, printing two articles from the *Journal encyclopédique* (Liege) that he translated himself and some reviews collected by Derrick on drama, art, and books from Paris, Vienna, and Zürich (Mr '56, 185–90).[104] Gradually the foreign correspondence grew more regular and comprehensive. After six issues, Smollett acknowledged his early setbacks but expressed satisfaction with recent progress and promised further improvement:

Hitherto, the public has seen but the infancy of their correspondence, which they found great difficulty in establishing; and this hath lately suffered some interruption from our hostilities with *France*, in consequence of which, they have been obliged to alter one canal of communication: but now a certain intercourse is settled with *Paris, Rome, Lucca, Florence, Berlin* and the *Hague*, which they flatter themselves will produce an ample fund of amusement, the more acceptable as *Europe* is likely to become the scene of events uncommonly interesting, and the war will stop many other usual sources of literary intelligence. (Ja/Fe '56, [ii])

Only one of these foreign correspondents can be identified: Patrick Murdoch, whose occasional correspondence from Berlin began appearing with the July issue (Jl '56, 564).[105] Whatever his other "canals of communication," especially with France in the midst of the war, Smollett showed vision and resourcefulness in his innovative scheme for foreign correspondence. Although the *Gentleman's Magazine* had included occasional notices about foreign literature since 1736, and more regularly after 1741,[106] it did not compare in range or in style with Smollett's plan. As for the *Monthly*, it had not yet offered any such feature, and when it did (from 1757) its foreign section proved an irregular and inferior imitation.[107]

Still another editorial headache Smollett suffered in 1756 was a shortage of reviewers. Because of Armstrong's limited involvement and Murdoch's sudden departure for Germany, after the first issue Smollett faced the prospect of compiling the *Critical* virtually on his own, with only the assistance of Derrick. In his apologetic address "To the Public" at the end of the first issue, Smollett appealed for contributors:

Far from thinking ourselves infallible in the art of criticism, we shall thankfully acknowledge any hints or assistance we may receive from the learned and ingenious of every denomination. We request the favour of *their* remarks; and, in a particular manner, address ourselves to the GENTLEMEN OF THE TWO UNIVERSITIES, for whom we profess the most profound veneration, and with whom we shall be proud to cultivate an occasional correspondence. (Ja/Fe '56, 96)

Coming from Smollett, who was of course a complete outsider to the Oxbridge world, this appeal is quite telling. By seeking to enlist university academics, as he had tried to arrange a network of correspondents in European centers of learning and culture, Smollett was pushing a program that would have transformed the practice of criticism in his time. It was too ambitious to succeed (and the takeover of criticism by academics remained for the twentieth century to implement), but it reveals much about Smollett's perception of what conferred cultural authority and where it was centered. In his attraction to powerful institutions, Smollett was uncannily prescient of the state of modern letters.

Whether it was indolence (of the kind Gibbon described) or indifference to vernacular literature (as opposed to classical learning), there was little response to Smollett's appeal. Fortunately, it did produce one well-qualified volunteer—Thomas Francklin—who joined the *Critical* at this point and whose assistance probably enabled it to survive. Son of the printer R. Francklin and now professor of Greek at Cambridge, Francklin knew both worlds, academe and Grub Street. He was ideal. There is no evidence that Francklin and Smollett were acquainted before the former joined the *Critical*; nowhere in Smollett's correspondence is he mentioned, nor does Smollett's name appear in the list of subscribers to his translation of the *Works of Sophocles* for which subscriptions had been solicited since 1753. Francklin started modestly, contributing only two reviews to the March issue, neither of which, in their comparatively tentative tone, displays the authoritative manner which would come to characterize his reviews later on (Mr '56, 148–62, 175–81). Smollett was obviously relieved to have Francklin's assistance. A note of thanks appeared at the end of the March issue: "Dr. F——— is desired to accept the thanks of the Society for the present of his ingenious performance" (Mr '56, 192).[108] Francklin was not yet Smollett's "right-hand man," as Roper describes him later on,[109] but some formal agreement must have been reached soon after this, for there were five reviews by Francklin (including the lead article) in the April issue and in June Francklin assumed primary responsibility for the "Monthly Catalogue," writing the introduction and supplying most of the copy in June, July, and August (Jn '56, 480).[110] His participation steadily increased and, by the end of 1756, Francklin had reviewed sixty-one separate works in only ten issues of the *Critical*.

After the first issue, distinct departments began to emerge. Francklin filled the gap left by Murdoch's departure, covering all the works on theology, an area in which Smollett had very little interest.[111] Some literature, consisting of classical translations and minor poetry, plays, and novels, also fell to him. Armstrong's eighteen reviews were chiefly of medical and scientific works, with a sprinkling of novels and works on painting. Smollett shared with Armstrong the fields of medicine and science, but he reserved to himself (almost exclusively) the important works in his areas of interest: history, drama, politics, and literary criticism. To Derrick was left the "trash," the majority of the less important works in almost every field from farriery to poetry. He labored diligently, if not always happily, commenting on seventy-four publications in 1756, more than anyone else.

Perhaps after these areas of specialization emerged, certain works were automatically sent off to the respective specialists on the staff. But there still remained for Smollett the enormous task of central organization, not only with his own staff but with the occasional correspondents he continued to solicit. In the September issue he announced:

> The authors of the CRITICAL REVIEW having been informed by letters and otherwise, that some gentlemen of taste and learning are disposed to communicate their observations occasionally, on new performances, could they be certain that the same articles are not already discussed by the Proprietors and Undertakers of the REVIEW; all those who may be inclined to correspond with the Society in this manner, are desired to signify, by letter to the publishers, the particular books they intend to consider. (Se '56, 192)

Privately, he solicited specific articles from various friends who were not regular contributors. In December 1756, for example, he wrote to George Macaulay: "I wish you could get an Article for the next number of the Review, on painting, Statuary or Engraving."[112] Although Smollett's tone suggests this was not the first time he had asked Macaulay to contribute and that he had reason to expect his compliance, no such article appeared in the next few issues of the *Critical*, another illustration of Smollett's vexations as an editor.

One of the most important questions about Smollett's editorial conduct is to what extent and how he controlled the opinions expressed by his reviewers. It is evident that Smollett did not read and approve every article before it went into print. For example, one of his reviewers managed to insert a slur on Admiral Byng into his mocking review of a pamphlet on the Pennsylvania Quakers; he ridiculed the Quakers' pacifism as folly and cowardice, and speculated that a "certain Admiral" (Byng) had imbibed their spirit by stopping "at *Pennsylvania* in his way to *Port-Mahon*" (Au '56, 96). Smollett could not have approved this review. Not only was the remark extraneous to the subject under review, it was exactly the kind of inflammatory jeer that Smollett (who reviewed all of the pamphlets on the Byng controversy himself) continually inveighed against. Striving to maintain the *Critical*'s impartiality, Smollett condemned the "cruelty of spiriting up popular prejudice against an accused person before he is convicted" (Oc '56, 252). One can only imagine his reaction when he saw in print this lapse from decorum.

His reviewers surprised him more than once. In reviewing a minor novel for the April 1756 issue, Derrick interjected a completely gratuitous insult to Samuel Richardson about his prolixity (Ap '56, 261). Clearly, Smollett had not seen the article. He forced Derrick to make amends by generously complimenting Richardson in the next issue (My '56, 315). He also apologized to Richardson through Andrew Millar and later in a letter to Richardson himself.[113] Smollett's correspondence reveals similar incidents occurring repeatedly, although sometimes in periods when he had temporarily relaxed his supervision of the *Critical*. He expressed regret at the rough treatment Home's *Douglas* received in the *Critical*, but protested to John Moore that "the Remarks upon Home's Tragedy I never saw untill they were in print."[114]

In 1761, in a similar apology to Garrick, he admitted that he had not "examined the article upon the Rosciad before it was sent to the press."[115]

Smollett seemed to grant his reviewers considerable independence as a matter of policy. In theory, at least, he had enlisted able men whose views he respected and trusted. It was on general principles—religious orthodoxy, political moderation, high standards of criticism and taste—that he sought conformity, not on particular judgments. That his reviewers might occasionally disagree and contradict one another was an inevitability that Smollett confronted in 1759, in a revealing statement of policy. Responding to Grainger's accusation that two reviews in the *Critical* had expressed contradictory opinions, Smollett asked rhetorically:

> Is it impossible that two persons, who wrote in the same Review, should be of different opinions touching the same performance?
> The Critical Review is not written by a parcel of obscure hirelings, under the restraint of a bookseller and his wife, who presume to revise, alter, and amend the articles occasionally. The principal writers in the Critical Review are unconnected with booksellers, unawed by old women, and independent of each other. (Fe '59, 151)

Eschewing what he considers Griffiths's self-interested and dictatorial practices, Smollett implies that the *Critical*'s policy is to publish without editorial interference the critical opinions of qualified judges. Behind the arrogant tone, there is again a residuum of Smollett's unrealized academy scheme wherein the journal would publish the findings and views of its members, in this case a society or syndicate of independent scholars and critics, without being subject to the censorship of a central editorial authority.

Smollett's policy was not, however, completely laissez-faire. He retained and occasionally exercised editorial powers over his writers. He did, after all, force Derrick to make amends to Richardson. He saw to it that the *Critical* printed a correction to the regrettably negative review of *The Epigoniad*, in the form of a long epistle of praise from David Hume, and Smollett introduced it with an editorial apology:

> By perusing the following article, the reader will perceive, that how subject soever we, the Reviewers, may be to oversights and errors, we are not so hardened in critical pride and insolence, but that, upon conviction, we can retract our censures, and provided we be candidly rebuked, kiss the rod of correction with great humility. (Ap '59, 323)

He assured Garrick, in 1761, that had he seen the article on *The Rosciad* before it went to press, "I should have put my negative on some expressions in it."[116]

But the fact that Smollett refrained from interfering as much as he did and publicly announced the absolute independence of his authors distinguished his policy from Griffiths's on the *Monthly*. Griffiths supervised his writers more closely and maintained much stricter control. When Goldsmith left the *Monthly* in 1757, he cited Griffiths's continual interference with his copy as a principal reason. It is probably information from Goldsmith that Smollett drew on to make mockery of Griffiths's editorial practices.[117] But there was a grain of truth in the taunts. Griffiths's correspondence (preserved in the Bodleian) shows him as late as the 1790s instructing his reviewers how to treat certain works assigned them. In 1791, he advised William Taylor to review favorably a book by fellow *Monthly* writer Arthur Murphy and on another occasion he sent Taylor a covering letter with a review copy, directing him to judge kindly a work by Thomas Wallace, also on the staff.[118] Another time Griffiths returned to John Walcot his review of Erasmus Darwin's *Botanic Garden* and insisted that he rewrite it more favorably; Walcot reluctantly complied, out of "friendship" for Griffiths, he said, but repeated that it was still contrary to his true opinion.[119]

Again it must be stressed that Griffiths's editorial procedures, not Smollett's, were the standard practices of the time, the same practiced by the editors of the *Gentleman's Magazine* and others throughout the century.[120] By the 1780s and 1790s, long after Smollett's departure, the *Critical* had a fully centralized editorial authority exactly like the *Monthly*, as Coleridge, William Taylor, and others found out.[121] Then, too, if Smollett did not send out letters of instruction with review copies, he probably communicated his views on certain works to his reviewers informally when they had working dinners together in town or dined at his house on Sundays.[122] When he told Strahan in 1757 that "I shall not fail to insist upon Mr. Derrick's doing you Justice" he may have been alluding to a review Derrick was doing of a book in which Strahan was proprietor.[123] Whether by explicit instruction or not, the same kind of reciprocal-courtesy reviewing prevailed among the staff of the *Critical* as that which Griffiths arranged at the *Monthly*. Nonetheless, Smollett's editorial policies were new and noteworthy. The typical editor exercised a methodical, centralized control: every piece of copy would pass under his scrutiny, subject to rejection or revision by his hand—practices from which Smollett's policies were a limited but conscious departure.

Other distinctions between the *Critical* and *Monthly* were less subtle and had become evident even by the end of the first year of their rivalry. From the competition between them one not only gains a sense of the ways they were rapidly molding each other into the shape that reviews would take for the next fifty years or more, but one also finds measures of Smollett's success as an editor in his first year.

Smollett had set his review a formidable goal when he announced in his proposals that the *Critical* would review all "the Performances on the Subjects of Theology, Metaphysics, Physics, Medicine, Mathematics, History

and the Belles Lettre; which shall occasionally appear at Home or Abroad."
Obviously the first issue fell short of this aim, reviewing only sixteen publications, although a note on the last page promised that "the Articles omitted in
this Number will be taken notice of in the next." By comparison, the *Monthly*
managed to review forty-eight works in its January 1756 issue and another
eleven in February, meanwhile also publishing (in late January) the supplement to volume 13 (July–December 1755) containing another twenty
articles.[124] But for both, the sheer number of publications made truly comprehensive coverage impossible: in those same months of January and February 1756, according to the book lists in the *Gentleman's Magazine*, there were
137 new titles published—scores more than either review had covered.[125]
For the editors it was a problem just to keep track of all the new publications.
Among other practices, Smollett and his staff (according to an editorial
note in 1757) resorted to scanning the back pages of "the Public and Daily
Advertisers" where new books were advertised (Se '57, 256–57). Smollett
also solicited and acted on information from correspondents; one finds him
apologizing repeatedly in the correspondence columns for having overlooked
particular works (Mr '56, 192).[126] Sometimes even after a new title was
brought to his attention, the book proved difficult to obtain: a note in 1759
acknowledged receipt of "a letter from Brecon, desiring they would take
notice of a certain performance; but they cannot find it, either at the places
described, or anywhere else in London" (Ja '59, 88).[127]

There simply had to be some limits on coverage. The *Critical* restricted
itself to new publications, for instance, and refused to review later editions of
previously published works. There were some notable exceptions to this policy, but they were carefully justified on the grounds that the new editions
contained significant revisions to the original or had new relevance because of
recent controversies (Se '56, 155).[128] More importantly, like the *Monthly*, the
Critical silently exercised some selectivity, a policy from which—despite
occasional complaints about omissions—reviewers and readers alike benefited. No one could have minded, for example, that the *Critical* actually
reviewed only one or two of the fifty sermons published between January and
April 1756 (Ap '56, 291–92).

In terms of total numbers of books reviewed, the *Critical* was decidedly
inferior to the *Monthly* in 1756. The *Monthly* reviewed a total of 455 publications in 1756 in fourteen issues (twelve monthly numbers plus two supplementary issues), the *Critical* only about 245 in eleven issues (January–
February combined in one issue). But in view of the *Critical*'s disadvantages,
starting a new journal, drawing on fewer writers, overcoming organizational
problems, and meeting high initial costs, its performance was not discredit-
able. Smollett put a brave face on it. In the preface to the first volume, Smollett noted proudly that the reviewers "claim some merit from having presented the essence of near 120 British performances in the small compas of six

numbers [and] of about 30 foreign articles." In the last five months of the year, the *Critical* reviewed about 115 publications in only five issues (August–December), despite covering only thirteen in September. The September downturn reveals an unexpected aspect of a literary review's dependence on the cycle of the publishing seasons: in the winter, the peak months for the publishing business, the large numbers of publications would crowd their capacity, but in the lean late-summer months, especially September, the reviewers could suffer a shortage of works to review. Thus, in September 1757, an editorial note explained an unusual preponderance of foreign material:

> Never was such a strange famine in the land of literature as seems at present to begin amongst us—in vain does the eye run over the last page of the Public and Daily Advertisers: nothing is there to be seen but new editions of Brown, Hervey, &c. without one new performance to attract the attention, laughter, or indignation of the public. . . . After all, the present dearth of wit, like that of our corn, is probably rather artificial than natural; and owing, perhaps, to the same covetous disposition in the engrossers, who keep up both in hopes of a better market the ensuing winter. (Se '57, 257)[129]

But in fact the alleged manipulation by the booksellers was really a simple market reaction to the depressed demand for books during the annual lull in town life.

The *Critical* did succeed, however, in maintaining a more consistent number of articles per issue than the *Monthly*, with generally twenty to thirty works reviewed per issue. The regularity of its contents had its effect. Never again would the *Monthly* offer only five book reviews in an issue, as it had in April 1755, or serialize other Griffiths publications as filler in its text, as it had in several issues in 1750.[130]

In another of its aims, the *Critical* easily excelled the *Monthly*: promptness in reviewing new works. In taking stock of their achievement after six issues, Smollett pointed out with pride that the *Critical* reviewers

> value themselves upon having reviewed every material performance, immediately after its first appearance, without reserving productions for a dearth of articles, and then raising them, like stale carcasses from oblivion, after they have been blown upon by every minor critic, and the curiosity of the public is gorged even to satiety. (Ja/Fe '56, [ii])

This was no empty boast. Throughout 1756, the *Critical* consistently reviewed new publications more promptly than did the *Monthly*. Of the 183 works reviewed in 1756 by the *Critical* that were also reviewed in the *Monthly*, forty-six (twenty-five percent) were reviewed by both in the same month's issue, forty-one (twenty-two percent) were reviewed first in the *Monthly*, but the majority—ninety-six (fifty-two percent) of them—were reviewed first in the *Critical*. This superiority in promptness held true in every month's issue except two, August and September. In one instance, the *Critical* even succeeded in reviewing one of Griffiths's own publications before the *Monthly* got around to it: a translation of the Marquis d'Argens's *Philosophical Visions* was reviewed by Francklin in the *Critical* in November 1756 (331–40) and reviewed by Griffiths himself in the *Monthly*, but not until January 1757 (16:25–32). The *Critical* also avoided the technique of serializing a review through two or more issues, which had been common in the *Monthly*, but which must have frustrated readers who wanted to know all about a new work at once. One issue of the *Monthly* (October 1756), for example, contained seven main articles, of which three were continuations from previous issues and, of these three, one was only the second installment of a three-part serialization and another was the continuation of a review begun in the July issue three months earlier. Smollett's unpleasant image of "raising stale carcasses" was not so excessive as it first seemed. But again, the point is that practices changed very rapidly, as competition brought improvements to each.

In the eyes of public, the *Critical*'s superior promptness in reviewing new titles must have offset its initial inferiority to the *Monthly* in gross numbers of works reviewed. The eighteenth-century publisher Charles Dilly is reported to have preferred the *Critical* to the *Monthly* precisely because "it was more prompt to review his publications."[131] The *Critical*'s promptness also showed the kind of temerity the stock-type coffeehouse critic lacked: a willingness to venture an opinion before the public consensus was established. Leading rather than following public opinion was a necessary precondition for Smollett's campaign to reform public taste; or, to use one of Smollett's favorite images, exerting the keen faculties of a good bloodhound to lead the critical pack rather than serving as a mere babbler to fill up the chase (Ap '56, 227).[132] On a more practical level, there was an immediate consequence that also had an effect on the future of literary journalism. Promptness became imperative. Griffiths again responded to the *Critical*'s lead and after 1756 the disparity between them on this, as on so many competitive points, rapidly disappeared. For future review journals, getting out the earliest reviews of new books was to remain an essential goal even if, as in the case of the *General Magazine and Impartial Review* in the 1780s, it was the only boast an otherwise mediocre journal could make.[133]

That Smollett was directly connected with this achievement is indicated by two facts. First the issue in which the *Critical* was the most dilatory—August—was the one issue in 1756 with which he was least involved. (Perhaps he had taken a holiday during the annual slow period.) Of the works reviewed in that issue, eleven had already been discussed in the *Monthly* at least one issue previously, while only five were being reviewed in advance of the *Monthly*. Smollett's one new review in the August issue, of Shebbeare's *Fourth Letter* (2:35–44), was also one of the few speedy ones: the *Monthly* reviewed the book a month later, in September (15:292–93). Second, Smollett's promptitude compared exactly with the *Critical*'s overall. Of the fifty-five works reviewed by Smollett in 1756 that were also reviewed in the *Monthly*, thirteen (twenty-four percent) appeared in the same month's issue, twelve (twenty-two percent) were reviewed earlier in the *Monthly*, but thirty (fifty-five percent) appeared in the *Critical* first. Smollett may have reserved certain books for his own attention, but he was not dilatory in reviewing them. One must suppose that he encouraged in his staff the same assiduousness he practiced himself.

Beyond all the hard work and careful management, one of Smollett's greatest editorial achievements in 1756 was the introduction of innovative new features in addition to the standard fare of book reviews. In each case it was Smollett who actually wrote the new feature. He contributed the first two pieces to the "Foreign Articles" section in March 1756, a feature that was to appear regularly in the *Critical* until Smollett's departure in 1763. He wrote the first articles for the art review section (Ja/Fe '56, 94–96), another important innovation that, like the foreign correspondence, the *Monthly* had not offered and about which more will be said later on. A third innovation, a section called "Arts and Sciences," was short-lived, lasting one issue only (No '56, 373–74). But like the other two, it was the product of an ambitious imagination, a mind full of the intellectual currents of the time, from the encyclopedic urge to systematize knowledge to the cosmopolitan aim of disseminating foreign culture and learning to the English middle classes.

There came a point, however, at which Smollett's personal and editorial resources were exhausted. With the completion of the *Critical*'s first year, Smollett announced his decision not to issue a supplementary issue, which had been standard practice with the *Monthly*, as well as the *Gentleman's Magazine, London Magazine*, and so many others. Smollett explained that

> the difference of five or six sheets will hardly appear in the binding; *a great book* (according to the *greek* proverb) *may be a great evil*, an adage, which some brother critics would do well to consider; and the proprietors are resolved to avoid supplements, as an unnecessary incumbrance on their readers. They will take care to leave no matter for such a clumsy appendage, which the work drags heavily along, like a huge mortified excrescence. (Au '56, [i])

The *Monthly* had been issuing two forty-page supplementary issues per year since 1753. Griffiths used them to clear out the backlog of material that had overflowed from the crowded monthly catalogs. But they also served, of course, to extract one more shilling from each subscriber and Griffiths did not hesitate to promote them as absolute necessities, "without which no sets of the Review are compleat."[134] Here again Griffiths's financial acumen shines through, and he undoubtedly succeeded in making the *Monthly* a far more profitable publication than the *Critical*. As Smollett announced his apparently principled decision not to publish these lucrative "excrescences," he was not being entirely candid. We can see now that he simply lacked the manpower and the time to produce an additional issue every six months, an impossible burden if added to his already enormous workload. But his editorial chores were only part of that workload. The other part—no less taxing but perhaps more agreeable to a man of letters—was the actual reviewing.

[4]

A New Critical Vehicle: Smollett's Technique
as Book Reviewer

When Smollett plunged into review journalism at the beginning of 1756, both the review journal as a specialized kind of periodical and the art of book reviewing itself were still very much in their formative stages. Yet within a few years Smollett would have emerged as the leading book reviewer of the period (at least by virtue of experience) and many of the features of what twentieth-century readers would recognize as review journalism would have become standard. From the start Smollett had to face many issues about reviewing technique: whether to stress standards and accuracy over generosity and kindness, how to apportion quotation and abstract versus critical analysis, how to balance information and entertainment. Obviously these issues are not fully resolved even today and never can be, but Smollett's attempts at resolving them are nonetheless edifying. So, too, are the broader issues that recur in Smollett's review criticism: his concern for the correctness of language; his ambivalence about Scottish writings; his (undeserved) reputation for severe and negative criticism; his perception of the *Critical*'s readership and the ways he adjusted his critical manner to suit that readership.

One sees these elements most clearly in Smollett's book reviewing during 1756, a period for which we have a full and representative body of his reviews and in which he was reviewing most intensively, at a rate of about five or six books a month. Specifically, in the eleven issues of the *Critical* published in 1756, Smollett reviewed (according to Hamilton's notations) sixty-one separate works, thirty-five of them in full-length reviews (averaging ten pages) and the other twenty-six in short notices (under two pages). To these one must add several reviews that, although left unascribed by Hamilton, can be attributed confidently to Smollett.[1] Two of his reviews were so long they had to be published in three monthly installments.[2] One of these serialized reviews—that of the Royal Society's *Philosophical Transactions* for 1755—

really amounted to several reviews in one, as it required giving some account of each of the more than forty essays the volume contained. In recognition of the huge burden this would place on a single reviewer, Ralph Griffiths often assigned two or more *Monthly* reviewers to each volume; he assigned five to the volume for 1755.[3] Smollett, however, did it alone.

Nor were book reviews all. Smollett contributed translations of three French essays and he wrote three articles about recent works of art in which he commented on paintings and sculpture by six different artists.[4] In addition to all this, he wrote five substantial editorial addresses and nine installments of brief answers to correspondence.[5] This remarkable journalistic productivity in one year by someone who until then had written scarcely a handful of reviews in all his life seems even more impressive in view of the other projects he was working on at the same time: his seven-volume compilation, *A Compendium of Authentic and Entertaining Voyages* (1756), his farce *The Reprisal* (1757), and his four-volume *Complete History of England* (1757–58).

At first sight, nothing about Smollett's reviewing technique seems particularly innovative. As he had modeled the *Critical*'s format after that already established by the *Monthly*, so he also followed conventional practices in writing the reviews themselves. Quotation and summary were the mainstays; they constituted the bulk of almost every review. If Murdoch's statement in the lead article of the *Critical*'s first issue that "we are no great friends to quotation" (Ja/Fe '56, 7) raised expectations of a radical departure from the conventional form, they were quickly dispelled. Like the rest of his staff, Smollett built his reviews around large blocks of quotation. The basic pattern included an introductory section of general comment, followed by long extracts interspersed with critical observations, and then a paragraph or two of closing remarks. In this, he resembled most mideighteenth-century reviewers, even the most brilliant of them, as the reviews of Johnson in the *Literary Magazine*, Goldsmith in the *Monthly*, and Burke in *The Annual Register* readily show.[6] Smollett and Johnson reviewed several of the same books for their respective journals in 1756 and a comparison of selected examples illustrates their similarity in method, especially their heavy reliance on quoted material. In reviewing Birch's *History of the Royal Society*, Smollett allotted ninety percent of his eleven-page review to quotation, Johnson eighty percent of his three-page review; similarly, with Browne's *History of Jamaica*, Smollett's twenty-page review contained eighty-five percent quotation, Johnson's ten-page review, ninety-five percent.[7] Although both recognized the seminal importance of a book like Warton's *Essay on Pope* and treated it specially— Smollett's fourteen-page review was more than seventy percent critical analysis, Johnson's four-page article ninety percent[8]—the norm was nearer twenty to thirty percent commentary, the rest quotation.

By 1756, this was generally true of reviews in the *Monthly* as well, although the *Monthly* was still vacillating between its original commitment to providing abstracts without criticism and the natural tendency of its reviewers to add critical commentary. As Sutcliffe has pointed out, Griffiths had originally eschewed criticism (in the *Monthly*'s first issue in 1749) for what he called the "much more agreeable and useful method" of printing extracts.[9] Griffiths restated his aversion to criticism in 1750: "Our business is to enter no farther into the province of criticism, than just so far as may be indispensably necessary to give some idea of such books as come under our consideration."[10] By 1757, Griffiths was being urged by one writer to extend the plan of the *Monthly* "so as to admit, besides a mere extract of books, something in a more critical way, especially upon subjects of controversy."[11] In discussing these developments, Sutcliffe suggests that this episode in 1757 marked an abrupt change in the *Monthly*'s critical approach. Few changes, however, occurred so decisively. Although, as Sutcliffe concludes, competition from the newly established *Critical* provided additional incentive, the *Monthly* had been offering varying amounts of criticism in at least some of its articles since 1750. But the *Monthly* reviewers, like Johnson, Smollett, and their whole generation of journalists, had inherited from the abstract journals a set of reviewing conventions based on epitome and quotation and, although the *Monthly* and the *Critical* were to be leaders in the transition from epitomizing to criticizing in eighteenth-century book reviewing, in 1756 the trend was just emerging.[12]

Smollett's extensive use of quoted material can be seen in part, therefore, as an acknowledgement of this tradition and its value: to present the reader with impartial summaries and to let him sample the book's style and contents for himself. "With respect to the elegance and perspicuity of his stile," Smollett wrote of Grieve's *Celsus*, "the reader may judge for himself from the following quotations" (Ja/Fe '56, 13). In discussing characterization in Murphy's *Apprentice*, Smollett introduces a specimen of dialogue, he explains, so "that the reader may judge for himself" (Ja/Fe '56, 81). There is sometimes a sense of Smollett consciously doing the author justice by letting him speak for himself. Thus he introduces a long quotation from Birch's *History of the Royal Society* by saying, "let us hear the account the learned doctor gives of his own work" (Ja/Fe '56, 42). Even in reviewing a work of which he did not entirely approve, such as *The Monitor*, Smollett could be fair enough to quote at length the author's own plan (No '56, 334).

Many observers have tended to see in this (at best) a kind of critical neutrality and (at worst) an evasion of the critic's responsibility to criticize. Some of Smollett's less generous contemporaries accused him of using extensive quotation as the easiest way to provide copy or, as the phrase went, "to eke out the volume." In view of the pressures under which Smollett worked, it must have been an attractive and sometimes irresistible practice. Modern scholars, however, have generally under-estimated the significance of how reviewers like Smollett used quoted material, going only so far as to remark

on the high proportion of it in reviews and from that to conclude that voluminous quotation was divorced from critical assessment. Although, as Roper
rightly observes, the relative proportion of critical comment and quotation
"varied from Review to Review and from article to article,"[13] most scholars
accept Sutcliffe's generalization that, "as a rule, a review of four pages contains as much remark as a review of twenty; the difference lies in the amount
of quotation."[14] This emphasizes the wrong perspective, looking backward
with the knowledge of what the review journal was yet to become, rather than
contrasting it with that from which it was evolving. It was to this evolution,
resulting in the establishment of the review as a distinct periodical genre, that
Smollett was so energetically contributing.

To dwell on the residual features of the abstract journal or on the occasional expressions of critical neutrality in deference to the public's judgment, is to
slight Smollett's avowedly didactic purpose and its influence on his reviewing
technique. He aimed to revive "the true Spirit of Criticism," subdue the
"Chaos of Publication," and "contribute towards the Formation of a Public
Taste."[15] He preferred to identify himself not with journalists but with
writers of formal criticism, such as Joseph Warton:

> The man of taste must expend his labours in reforming the judgement
> and enlightening the understanding of these pretenders, and other novices
> of sensibility, before they are qualified to maintain the character they
> assume. This charitable task of improvement, the learned, who enjoy their
> ease, ought to undertake for the benefit of mankind. This is the professed
> aim of us, who publish our monthly lucubrations in the *Critical Review*;
> and we cannot help looking upon the author of the *Essay* now before us, as
> one of our coadjutors in the laudable scheme we have projected. (Ap '56,
> 227)

Despite the pomposity, one can see that Smollett considered the techniques
and tenor of abstract journals insufficient for his purposes: they were too
neutral and critically reticent. He saw the potential of book reviewing as a
truly critical and edifying science.

In this context, he treated the use of quotation as integral to true criticism.
He had promised, in his "Proposals," that the *Critical* reviewers would not

> invidiously seek to wrest the Sense, misinterpret the Meaning, or misquote
> the Words of any Author, who may fall under their Inspection; they will
> not exhibit a partial or unfair Assemblage of the Beauties or Blemishes of
> any Production . . . [and] whenever they signify their Disapprobation;
> they promise to illustrate their Censure with proper Quotations, from
> which the Reader may appeal to his own Understanding.[16]

Smollett knew that the reviewer's mere choice of passages to quote and his presentation of them affected the reader's perception, sometimes in subtle ways. Authors realized this too. One offended writer complained that, in his review, Smollett had chosen to quote the single worst passage in his whole book and he accused Smollett of having "*private Reasons* for [making] such a disingenuous Extract."[17]

Almost invariably, even when reprinting very long quotations, Smollett evaluated them critically. He used them to illustrate his points and influence the reader's opinion, as a sampling of the critical remarks with which he introduced long quotations reveals:

> As a specimen of the work itself, and of the scrupulous caution and judgment with which the first founders of the society proceeded in their enquiries, observing every where the rules and examples left them by the immortal *Bacon*, take the two following articles. (Birch, *History of the Royal Society*; Ja/Fe '56, 44)

> As the author's conjecture concerning the depopulation and division of those islands, is curious and well supported, we shall insert a few pages in his own words. (Borlase, *Islands of Scilly*; Ja/Fe '56, 58)

> Maxims, we apprehend, ought to be equally concise and perspicuous, so as to flash conviction at sight; but some of those before us, seem rather as riddles to exercise the imagination, than apothegms to convince the mind, and take possession of the memory. For example . . . . (*Maxims, Characters, and Reflections*; Ap '56, 222)

> We defy the most phlegmatic of our readers to pass over the following paragraph without a smile. (*A Serious Defence of Some Late Measures*; Se '56, 122)

> Having thus finished the disagreeable part of criticism, we shall entertain the reader with some quotations which will give a much more advantageous idea of this author's abilities. The state of *England*, immediately after the death of *Charles I* he has thus explained in a concise, distinct, masterly manner. (Hume, *History of Great Britain*; De '56, 395)

No reader could miss the critical comment in such remarks or fail to apply it to the accompanying quotations. When presented this way, long quotations served not as filler but as extra weight reinforcing critical opinion. Certainly this was far from the fully developed critical analysis offered by reviews at the beginning of the nineteenth century such as the *Edinburgh* and the *Quarterly*, but Smollett's reviewing technique had begun to resemble more closely that analysis than the epitomizing methods of journals at the eighteenth century's beginning. Under Smollett's leadership, the *Critical*—along with the *Monthly*—was setting what Bloom has described as the "trend toward more fully developed critical evaluation."[18]

This trend was not universally welcomed. Rather than faulting the reviews for containing too much quoted material, many of Smollett's contemporaries felt they offered too little. One author complained in 1764 that both reviews contained too many "short malevolent criticisms, without quotations."[19] The eccentric etymologist Rowland Jones objected to the *Monthly*'s criticism of his last work because "they have exhibited [i.e., quoted] nothing more in support of their assertion than a marginal note in the preface."[20] Another writer accused the *Monthly* of trying to "stifle the Reputation of [his] Book" by giving so few quotations from it.[21] Journals were founded with the purpose of returning to reviewing that was *less* analytical. In 1764, the *St. James's Magazine* proposed to give accounts of books but without presuming to "expatiate or dictate *ex cathedra*, on the particular merits or demerits of any piece whatever."[22] In 1769, William Kenrick, the quarrelsome former *Monthly* reviewer, founded his own review, *The Critical Memoirs of the Times*, and in its preface attacked both the *Monthly* and the *Critical* for presuming to criticize rather than merely epitomize books. He accused them of arrogance toward the public, "whom they seem to think," he wrote, "more solicitous about *their* opinion of a book, than about what the author has advanced on his subject. From this motive they give in to a practice of censure and cavil, totally deviating from the purpose of their institution."[23] Neither journal succeeded for long: both found it impossible to refrain, in fact, from commenting critically on books reviewed. Like other such signs of reaction, they signaled, ironically, the inexorable progress of the very change they sought to arrest. But the reading public's continuing demand for substantial extracts and its occasional resistance to critical evaluation were conditions to which Smollett had to accommodate his method of reviewing.[24]

There was one other issue connected with the practice of extensive quotation: whether or not it hurt the sale of books by preempting their readership. Many authors feared that it did. The author of *Tyburn to the Marine Society* (1758) asked the reviewers not to quote anything from his book, contending that

> when a new book appears, you never fail to transplant from it into yours the choicest and most beautiful flowers.... These being now most judiciously culled, and ready-made up into six or twelve-penny nosegays, the reader, for whose sake, only, you take all this periodical trouble, will neither be inclined to purchase, nor even to look into the rifled nursery where they originally grew.[25]

James Ralph used the same argument, in his better-known work, *The Case of Authors by Profession*, to urge the establishment of a copyright law.[26] Clara Reeve was to echo the sentiment in the 1780s, describing it as "injurious to authors" that magazines and anthologies reprinted excerpts of their work and thus preempted readers (like Lamb, who told Coleridge he read Southey's poetry in review journal extracts, to avoid buying his expensive books), although Reeve specifically exempted reviewers, who, she said, "ought to have an exclusive right to give extracts of every publication that deserves their recommendation."[27] Samuel Johnson once explained his very brief quotations in a review of the *Philosophical Transactions* by saying, "we desire to promote, not to hinder the sale of these valuable collections."[28] Smollett, too, sometimes curtailed quoted material, explaining as he did in the case of one pamphlet that "we have omitted many other excellent strokes in this little piece, that we might not totally anticipate our reader's pleasure in the perusal of it" (Se '56, 126).

Most authors and readers seemed to agree, however, that extensive quotation in reviews ultimately helped more than hindered sales. Kenrick defended the practice and William Enfield, an experienced reviewer for the *Monthly*, declared that "extracts make the original work better known, and generally promote its sale."[29] In response to Ralph's plea for copyright protection from such quotation, a correspondent wrote from York to say that he and other readers—especially those in the provinces—depended on the journals to know "what books are published" and that the "little extracts from them . . . for the most part raise a curiosity not to be gratified but by buying the books themselves."[30] That Smollett believed this too is amply demonstrated in the way he had his own works reviewed in the *Critical*. The reviewer of Smollett's *Continuation*, for example, included generous extracts that he prefaced by saying "that we may not waste the reader's time with our own reflections, we shall proceed to lay before him specimens from our author, which we doubt not will sufficiently justify our encomiums" (Oc '61, 284–85). In reviewing volumes of *The Universal History*, a project in which he had an authorial and editorial if not proprietary interest, Smollett regularly gave abstracts of whole volumes and extracts extending to many pages.[31]

How to balance the proportions of quotation and critical commentary was only one of many problems Smollett faced in deciding how to write reviews. While pursuing his idealistic aims of promoting learning and reforming taste, he also had to please a broad and diversified reading public. Above all, therefore, he had to be entertaining. This he acknowledged in the preface to volume 1 where he outlined the four basic aims of the *Critical* reviewers:

> to exhibit a succinct plan of every performance; to point out the most striking beauties and glaring defects; to illustrate their remarks with proper quotations; and to convey these remarks in such a manner, as might best conduce to the entertainment of the public. (Ja/Fe '56, [i–ii])

Here was that difficult middle ground: how to be a serious journal of learning and letters, such as the learned journals had been, and yet to be interesting and entertaining for the general reader whom those journals had never reached. It was this point that Smollett immediately elaborated:

> As variety is the soul of such entertainment, and the confined nature of the plan would not admit of minute investigation; they have endeavored to discover and disclose that criterion by which the character of a work may at once be distinguished, without dragging the reader through a tedious, cold, inanimated disquisition, which may be termed a languid paraphrase rather than a spirited criticism. (Ja/Fe '56, [ii])

As always, the elegant formula *utile et dulce* described the ideal, but as Smollett knew all too well their actual success would be anchored in the hard truth of publishing: entertaining works sell, tedious ones do not.

Smollett's talents as a satirical novelist suited him, perhaps better than any of his contemporaries, to write entertaining book reviews. In his eagerness to do this, as well as to present "spirited criticism" rather than "languid paraphrase," he relied heavily on the tools of satire. His technique varied. Often he would pick a theme or phrase from the work under review and play on it to expose the work's absurdity, as in his review of a pamphlet on the cause of earthquakes:

> The professed aim of this curious piece, is to prove, that earthquakes are occasioned by electricity; and to explain the *great thump that was generally heard in the upper part of houses.*—We are afraid the learned gentleman's own upper story has received a rude *thump*, which we shall not pretend to explain. (Jn '56, 457)

This kind of parody, so characteristic of Smollett, was employed much more whimsically elsewhere, as in his review of a pamphlet in which the author had proposed that

> one or two gentlemen of genius should be employed in composing songs to celebrate the atchievements of the *British* Navy; that the sailors, by getting them by heart, and singing them occasionally, might be warmed into a nobler spirit of courage and emulation. We approve of the expedient, and hope that the Lords of the Admiralty will, without loss of time, appoint a poet, and his crew, for the use of the navy. The marine laureat may wear a tiara of seagreen bays; and his mates be distinguished by cockle-shells, as the boatswains drivers are known by their whistles. He may have a cabin on the poop as the part analogous to a cock-loft, and his women and people may be differently employed in picking sentiments, splicing syllables, reeving rhymes, and caulking stanzas. (De '56, 481)

Here, as in so many of his reviews, the creative impulses of the comic novelist enliven his observations as literary reviewer. Especially with such obscure pamphlets, satire was an entertaining alternative to tedious fault finding or plain condemnation. It must also have been a means of diverting himself in the midst of his drudgery.

Not always parodic, Smollett's satire could be dry and ironic. In presenting a specimen of Rolt's *History of South America*, for example, Smollett remained ostensibly objective:

> We shall now entertain the reader with a few quotations, by which he will become still better acquainted with the talents of this historian; and first let us see how he is qualified to yield entertainment:
> "The principal rivers of *Peru*, which rise on the West-side of the *Andes*, and fall into the *Pacific* ocean, are, 1st. The *Coloncha*, which empties itself into the sea, in 2 deg. of South latitude. *2d, 3d, 4th, 5th* and *6th*. The *Daule*, or river of *Guiquil*, and the *Narangal*, in 3 degrees: the *Bolas*, *Tenques*, and *Jubones . . . 20th*. The *Pica*, in 21 deg. *21st*. The *Salado*, in 25 deg. (Mr '56, 101)

Only as the tedious passage drags on and on does the ironic trap close on the reader. Smollett could be especially wry in debunking pseudolearning:

> In the twelfth article, we are given to understand, by *John Canton*, A.M. and *Henry Miles*, D.D. that on the eighth and ninth days of *February, 1755*, the weather was cold in *Spitalsquare, London*, and at *Tooting* in *Surry*. This might have remained a secret to the end of time, had not those literati kept a register of their thermometers. (Jl '56, 530)

At other times, he could be mannered and discursive in the style of the great moral-essayists. In reviewing Warton's *Essay on Pope*, for example, he digressed on a favorite topic:

> Of those who affect to read the *Belles Lettres*, one half do not presume to judge for themselves, and at a moderate computation, two thirds of the other half, judge amiss; and yet they shall be all professed critics. He of the first species, conscious of his own defect, peruses a new performance with the same secrecy and circumspection that a pickpocket uses in making a conveyance of your handkerchief; and if questioned concerning the work, will deny his having seen it with all the prevarication of a veteran delinquent at the bar of the *Old Bailey*. This reserve he maintains until he has extracted the opinion or decision of some oracle, in whose infallibility he confides. Then no man assumes a more dogmatical air, in distributing applause or denouncing censure.—Those of the other class are a kind of ferocious hussars, who skirmish on the skirts of dulness, and her phalanx. They are sudden, rash, impetuous, and desperate, and slash away at random without order, skill, piety, or remorse. They have a great deal of presumption, and some spirit, which, properly restrained and regulated by

discipline, might qualify them to fight in the ranks of true criticism. The first are like your babblers in the chace, which without any sagacity of their own, can only serve to fill up the cry; the second sort resemble a breed for forward mongrils, not altogether devoid of noses, but totally destitute of breeding. (Ap '56, 226–27)

Smollett invests this passage with as much imagination and humor as he would a scene in one of his novels; in fact, the image of "babblers in the chace" is a reworking of a comic passage in *Peregrine Pickle*.[32]

His satire was often ribald. A ludicrous pamphlet about a childish squabble between two self-important citizens of York, entitled *An Account of what passed between Mr. George Thompson of York, and Dr. John Burton of that City, Physician and Man-midwife at Mr. Sherriff Jobb's Entertainment, and the Consequences thereon, By Mr. George Thompson*, provided Smollett ample material for satiric humor:

This notable transaction was (it seems) a fray occasioned by Mr. *Thompson*'s proposing what he calls a test toast at a sheriff's entertainment. Dr. Burton, physician and man-midwife, refusing to conform, a dispute ensued; and, after some altercation, the said Dr. *Burton* broke the head of one of his fellow guests. This exploit, however, he did not atchieve with impunity; in as much as he was collared, philliped, and scratched, saw his shirt torn and his cudgel broke, and was dismissed from the company with some ignominious remembrances *a posteriori*, which he did not patiently retain. Instead of wreaking his resentment upon the proper object, he had recourse upon Mr. *George Thompson*, who declared, that far from assaulting the doctor, he secured him from severe chastisement. He complains, therefore, that he was not only sued unjustly, but also maltreated by the council of his adversary, and cast upon false evidence. Mr. *Thompson* seems to think he [Burton] fell a sacrifice to the virulence of a faction, in whose cause the doctor has suffered heretofore.

Had it not actually happened, this episode might have been lifted straight from a Smollett novel, and he obviously enjoyed inventing his own facetious conclusion to the tale:

If that be the case, he [Burton] has been twice happily *delivered*; but one time or another his head may be jammed in such an untoward pelvis, that even his own *tire tête* [footnote here: "A curious instrument so called, contrived by Dr. *Burton*, to extract the head of a foetus from a narrow pelvis"] will not extricate him; so that the operator must have recourse to the noose, which is but a rough and disagreeable expedient. (Oc '56, 281)

This rough, sometimes scurrilous ridicule appeared most frequently in the "Monthly Catalogue," where the proportion of minor and bad books was very high. But it could also surface in longer reviews, often as a moment of comic relief in an otherwise serious and favorable review.

The point is that throughout his reviews, Smollett was striving for entertaining effects. He was highly conscious of his readership, comprising mostly nonspecialists of diverse backgrounds, interests, and levels of education. He could expect their interest in a learned work such as Dr. Rutherforth's *Institutes of Natural Law* to be limited, so he carefully interjected, wherever possible, an element of human interest. In discussing one of Rutherforth's legal problems, Smollett observes that

> if a man stipulates to marry a woman, with the proviso that she is a virgin, and afterwards discovers that she is not a virgin, the Doctor seems to think the contract would hold, because he must give her possession of his person, by taking possession of hers, before he can make this discovery; and by so doing he gives up his conditions, and binds himself absolutely.—But, no offence to the learned doctor, we apprehend a man may make this discovery, without giving her possession of his body. (Se '56, 177)

The passage selected, the common sense applied to it, and even the hint of titillation elicited from it all suggest the kind of audience Smollett was addressing. In the same review, Smollett added a touch of homely humor to Rutherforth's views on a husband's authority over his wife:

> He takes notice, that . . . the subjection of a wife was appointed by positive institution, as a punishment for that crime, into which the first husband was seduced by the first wife; that it might be a standing lesson of humility to all future wives, reminding them, that through the weakness of their sex, a curse has been entailed upon the whole species.—Hear this, O ye wives, and be meek, humble and obedient! (Se '56, 177)

This closing injunction, obviously facetious, gently mocks the severity of Biblical law, as well, perhaps, as the balance of power in Smollett's own household. More significantly, it is a light and human touch introduced into the evaluation of a learned and specialized tome, typical of Smollett's efforts to enlighten without alienating the general reader.

These efforts to write entertainingly, however, do not overshadow the essential seriousness of Smollett's approach to reviewing. Although written in a more entertaining style and for a broader audience than earlier review journals, the *Critical* was not—as the magazines were—primarily a popular entertainment. Very serious concerns about language, learning, and social issues pervade Smollett's reviews and dominate his method. Most of these concerns are reminiscent of his aspirations for an English academy of the belles lettres and finally they, more than his comic talents, shape his reviewing technique.

Smollett was very sensitive about the use, and abuse, of language. As a kind of linguistic archconservative, Smollett fought the decline (as he saw it) of the English language in all its manifestations: barbarisms, neologisms, and solecisms of every kind. The earlier proponents of an English academy and their supporters—Sprat, Defoe, Prior, Swift, Addison, and others—had all seen one central purpose of such an academy as being to standardize and regulate the language.[33] It is evident that Smollett had also envisaged some such function for his academy. Reed, in his travesty of Smollett's academy proposal, had mocked it as a "Project for initiating and perfecting the Male-Inhabitants of this island, in the Use and Management of the *Linguinary Weapon*, by the Erection of a *Scolding Amphitheatre*."[34] Despite the sexual innuendo, the "Linguinary" concerns were obviously central. Then, too, in the *Critical*'s first issue Smollett saw to it that the lead article featured Murdoch's review of Sheridan's *British Education*, with a firm endorsement of Sheridan's "design to revive the long lost art of oratory, and to correct, ascertain, and fix the *English* language" (Ja/Fe '56, 1–2). Throughout Smollett's own reviews, his unflagging attentiveness to language, verging on obsession, reveals that behind his penchant for linguistic humor based on dialects and malapropisms in his novels and plays, Smollett had a deep respect for the form and rules of language.

In all his reviews, Smollett assiduously pointed out grammatical errors, sometimes gently, as with Mrs. Brooke's *Virginia*:

That there are a few inaccuracies in the diction, we cannot deny; such as, "to this alone *is* owing our defects,"—"a soul *susceptive*"—"and applicate the *goddess*' aid,"—&c. But, these are trivial defects. (Ap '56, 277)

and sometimes harshly, as with the anonymous military treatise, *The Target*:

It were to be wished, however, that the treatise had been translated into *English*. In its present appearance, we know not to what dialect it belongs. (Jn '56, 438)

At times, Smollett seemed to scan for errors with the cranky severity of a pedant, transcribing his notations directly into the review. In one article, for example, even while admitting that "it is an invidious task to hunt after blemishes," he nevertheless lists error after error, merely labelling them according to where they occur: "In page 3, he tells us. . . . In the very next page we find. . . . Page 7. . . . Page 10. . . [etc.]" (Ja/Fe '56, 10–12). Nor did he confine this close scrutiny to the kinds of works in which correctness of language might seem most important, such as translations and learned treatises. He cited grammatical mistakes in such various works as Shebbeare's *Fourth Letter to the People of England*, Norden's *Voyage to Aegypt and*

Nubia, Pegge's *Anglo-Saxon Remains*, and *The Monitor* (Au '56, 35–36).[35]

He was equally strict on orthography. He rarely passed over in silence accidental errors and sometimes listed them in detail: "*lossed* for lost, *fiveteenth* for fifteenth, *titule* for title, [etc.]" (Mr '56, 170). The implicit equation was always between flawed language and flawed intellect. Smollett rejected deliberate archaisms and any other systematic deviations in orthography, no matter how well supported theoretically. He criticized Hume for using "the *Roman* orthography in spelling words derived from the *Latin*, such as *favor, labor, honor, ardor*, &c." (De '56, 393). For Smollett, in such cases usage dictated. He did not, however, ignore the perpetual problem of the lexicographer: how to reconcile the urge to fix and preserve the language with the realization that the language is always and inexorably changing. Smollett addressed this question in his review of Lucas's *Essay on Waters*. Lucas had invented his own system of orthography and tried to justify it by invoking history: "Why did not *Spencer* follow *Chaucer*; *Milton* or *Cowley*, *Spencer*; or *Dryden, Pope* or *Swift* literally follow the steps of these?" Smollett answered him simply:

> We find no other reason that should have induced the more modern of those authors to differ from the more ancient, but that the ancient method was become obsolete, which I believe the doctor will not say is the case with those modes, from which he hath swerved. (My '56, 324)

Smollett recognized, in other words, that the evolution of language was inevitable and that writers must use the language as it descends to them, but they must not anticipate or accelerate its change. That way lies babel, as Smollett illustrated in his parodic extension of Lucas's orthographical principles:

> *Aguard* to be sure is happily substituted in the room of *aware*; but as it is not to be found in common dictionaries, might not the word be altogether changed into *a la garde*, which every smatterer in *French* well understands? We meet with *conceled* for *concealed*; but why not *celed*, without the aggregating particle *con*, which is improperly applied to a single object? . . . . Besides these singularities, we find *none air* for no air, *whea* for why—why not *whew*?—*immerged* for immersed, *scholes* for schools, . . . and, we suppose, the doctor would write *geberous* for gibberish, which is derived from *Geber* the *Arabian* alchymist, of whom our author might, from his writings, be supposed a worthy disciple. (My '56, 323)

Beneath the mockery, there is a firm belief that without standards and rules, language rapidly degenerates into gibberish.

Smollett also resisted neologisms. He ridiculed Shebbeare's *Fourth Letter* for its new-coined words:

the compound epithet *seen-service*, is a valuable acquisition to the *English* language. The hint may be extended, in it's application to a great many different classes of men, for example, *seen-simple apothecaries, seen-pillory politicians*, and *seen-fee physicians*, in contradistinction to *sans-fee*. *Seen-service*, however, yields in dignity of derivation to the word *posspolite*, which we wish he had explained for the benefit of his *English* readers. But, we meet with a parallel instance of this author's genius, in improving and enriching his mother tongue, with the noun substantive *parallellarity*. (Au '56, 36)

But Shebbeare could be discounted as an errant hack. When he criticized a more serious work, such as Pegge's *Dissertations*, Smollett explained his views more thoroughly; Pegge's language, he wrote,

we are afraid is not *Sterling English* throughout; not to mention some words, such as the adverb *groundedly*, and the verb *dissertate*, which seem to be of Mr. *Pegge*'s own *coining*. But the *English* language will probably grow neither the richer nor the baser for them. For harsh ill-sounding awkward words do not easily become current in our language, even tho' the learned and great *opiniatre* their establishment. (Ja/Fe '56, 75)

This was not, as might be inferred, a sweeping rejection of the authority of the "learned and great" in linguistic matters. Rather, it was a rejection of specious learning as a basis for artificial alterations in the language. The views of the truly learned would take into account the natural order and harmony of the language, as well as the power of common usage to resist arbitrary interference. As if even in the year after Johnson's *Dictionary* had appeared there was still a lack of a proper authority, Smollett and his staff were apparently assuming that role themselves, as protectors of the language and arbiters of usage—a kind of English academy *de facto*, as Robert Spector has suggested.[36]

Pegge's other offense, according to Smollett, was the use of barbarisms. In noting the several words of foreign origin in Pegge's language, Smollett concludes that "perhaps he is only endeavouring to stiffen it with *Latin*, or inervate it with *French* words and phrases" (Ja/Fe '56, 75). The two were distinct. In the case of Latin, Smollett of course venerated it as a classical tongue and accepted that English derived in large part from it. What he objected to was the artificial and awkward introduction of Latinisms for the sake of affectation, or "stiffening," especially when they clashed with normal usage and as much obscured as conveyed the sense. Thus, he attributed the lack of clarity in one book to the fact that "the language is stiffened with some uncouth phrases, borrowed from the classics" (Ap '56, 223). Smollett also found fault with Hume for this "affected mode of expression" and, after quoting a sentence of awkward Latinate construction, stated simply: "Our language does not require such Latin idioms." Having rebuked Hume for his borrowings and other Latinate affectations, Smollett relented enough to allow some exceptions, explaining himself with characteristic verve:

> If we adopt foreign words, it is but reasonable that we should alter them according to the genius and fashion our own language. Had we occasion to inlist a number of *Persian* recruits, we should not allow them to wear their long cloaths and turbans. Besides, we did not derive those words immediately from the *Latin*; but borrowed them at second-hand from the *French.*—In such cases, we think, custom ought to determine: and therefore we do not approve of *emergence* and *inconsistence,* which Mr. *Hume* uses for *emergency* and *inconsistency. Verba valent usa.* (De '56, 393–94)

Here, Smollett may have unwittingly detected a general quality of his fellow Scot's style that supports James Sutherland's thesis about the distinctive prose style of most Scots in the eighteenth century. Sutherland argues that, because of "the peculiar linguistic situation in which the Scot was placed"— speaking in one idiom, but writing in another—the Scots commonly used a "much less idiomatic mode of writing based on the language of scholars and divines."[37] This contributed to the transition in prose style from the "Addisonian" to the "Johnsonian"; that is, from an idiomatic and conversational to a more scholarly and rhetorical style of writing. Hume's Latinisms fit the pattern. Ironically, however, although Hume is not mentioned by Sutherland as an example of this stiff and formal Scottish style, Smollett is—although with what justice is hard to see. William Wordsworth, who was no mean judge of language, once complained that in the eighteenth century all the "Scotch historians [had done] infinite mischief to style, with the exception," he noted, "of Smollett, who wrote good pure English."[38]

Smollett had less patience with gallicisms. He repeatedly described the effect of introducing French words into English as "inervating," implying the same kind of enfeeblement and moral corruption in borrowing from the French language as there was in imitating French manners.[39] In his review of *Maxims, Characters and Reflections,* Smollett strongly objected to

> the use of *French* words and phrases, which, notwithstanding the apology made in the preface, we are sorry to see introduced into any *English* performance of merit; because we are fully persuaded, that there is no idea which an *Englishman* may not express in his own tongue. Such promiscuous use of foreign words and idioms, relaxes the nerves and destroys the uniformity of our language. An *English* performance, bespangled in this manner, looks like a piece of broad cloth intersected with threads of tinsel. (Ap '56, 221)

Tinsel and promiscuity: the images suggest the connection in Smollett's mind between the corruption of language and the many other symptoms of cultural decline. It was another violation of the moral and aesthetic order, based on Augustan ideals, which Smollett tried to uphold. It was another manifestation of what John Sekora (in his excellent study, *Luxury: The Concept in Western Thought, Eden to Smollett*) defines as "luxury," the pervasive decay—as classical conservatives like Smollett saw it—of culture and society.[40]

To understand Smollett's fastidiousness about language, it must be seen in this context. He was exacting. He relentlessly criticized not only errors in grammar, vocabulary, and orthography, but instances of verbosity, mixed metaphor, and other stylistic misdemeanors. His scrutiny was not limited to English for, at various times in his reviews, he corrected errors in Latin, French, Greek, and Spanish.[41] But he acted more out of principle than pettiness. He had a special view of the role of language in transmitting knowledge and preserving civilization, a view he articulated in an editorial response to a newspaper attack on the *Critical* by the naturalist, Dr. J. Parsons. Feigning disbelief that the hostile article was actually written by Parsons, Smollett cites the

> strange doctrine which this disguised enemy of Dr. Parsons advances: that a man, who writes of matters and importance, ought not to trouble his head about diction: that is to say, if your intention is to communicate knowledge, no matter whether you be, or be not, understood: for, we apprehend, that diction is the vehicle in which an author's meaning is conveyed; and if no regard is to be paid to this vehicle, it may be conveyed in *Arabic* as well as in *English*. This assertion is like that of an honest gentleman, who affirmed he had seen an *Irish* manuscript that contained a thousand curious particulars, a good number of which he recounted, adding that it was written in characters which no man alive understood. As this cannot be the case, with the writings of Dr. *Parsons*, so neither can we believe he would make such a wild declaration, as, that diction is not to be minded by a philosopher. (Se '65, 189)

For Smollett, poor language not only impaired the transmission of knowledge, it reflected a muddled intellect—an idea he was to pursue in his portrayal of the fraudulent, patois-speaking Dr. Fizes in the *Travels* and of such malapropistic characters as Tabitha Bramble and Winifred Jenkins in *Humphry Clinker*.

Thus Smollett valued the traditional role of Latin. In reviewing a recent medical treatise written in Latin, Smollett stated:

> We cannot but applaud the foresight and philanthropy of those authors who, conscious of the importance of their own works, as well as the perishable nature of every living language, transmit their labours in a tongue that will never alter or decay while learning shall remain, and thus perpetuate their productions for the benefit of posterity. (Ap '56, 246)

At such moments Smollett exhibited little confidence in the power of his own or anyone else's efforts to check, ultimately, the decline of English. In an equally philosophical manner, a little tinged with sadness, Smollett was to discuss in his *Travels* the origins of the patois of Nice: "the language that rose upon the ruins of the Latin tongue, after the irruptions of the Goths, Vandals, Huns, and Burgundians, by whom the Roman empire was destroyed." He conjectured that the language had been thoroughly corrupted "in the course of so many ages, especially as no pains have been taken to preserve its original purity, either in orthography or pronunciation."[42]

Smollett did not, however, indiscriminately prescribe that all learned works be preserved in Latin. One medical author's Latin was so error-ridden, Smollett observed, that "it is a pity he should have taken so much pains to write bad *Latin*, while those for whose benefit he has professedly submitted to this toil and labour, could just as easily have understood his aphorisms in plain *English*, as if he had *swaddled them up* in *Ciceronian* or *Caesarean Latin*" (Ap '56, 244). Aside from the author's inability to communicate in Latin, two other reasons for its unsuitability are urged. First, the audience aimed at—primarily midwives—is unlikely to be well-versed in Latin. Second, as Smollett says, "we do not recollect above one sentence throughout the whole performance, which could justly give offence to the most virtuous and delicate lady in *Britain*" (Ap '56, 244). In denying its necessity here, Smollett was reaffirming another function of Latin in eighteenth-century society: to preserve decorum by distancing and purifying otherwise unmentionable topics such as gynecology and obstetrics. The suitability of language to its purpose, like correctness and purity, was another aspect of Smollett's comprehensive view of the interdependence of language and culture. To establish and preserve a great culture, Britain no less than Rome had to attend to its language. In his rejection of barbarisms and his insistence on the sufficiency of English, there is also an element of nationalistic pride, not unconnected with the kinds of views he expounded on British art and letters generally.

Smollett also justified his minute corrections on practical grounds. In his detailed corrections of Grieve's *Celsus*, Smollett foresaw that the author, as "a man of learning," would "no doubt rectify those little oversights, should the translation come to second edition" (Ja/Fe '56, 12). The *Critical* was performing a valuable service, not only by its idealistic insistence on the correct transmission of knowledge, but in the more mundane sense of textual editing and correction. Smollett's policy of corrections in the *Critical* itself was consistent with this view. He frequently included errata lists for past issues in the current ones, and he welcomed corrections from correspondents of even the smallest details:

The typographical errors pointed out to us by our obliging correspondent *A.M.* shall be taken notice of in our errata: the advice which he has given will be followed, and the uniformity which he recommends, observ'd. (No '56, 384)[43]

This was not done merely to oblige correspondents. Smollett saw the *Critical* as a kind of archive or repository, a cumulative record of the progress of the arts and sciences in his time, and, as such, meant it to be as correct as human effort could make it.

The real bugbear of Smollett's campaign to purify and preserve the English language—and that with the broadest ironic implications—was the use of Scotticisms. Smollett's sensitivity to Scotticisms and, seemingly, to all things Scottish, shaded his approach to many of the works he reviewed. He detected Scotticisms in Grieve's *Celsus*, for example, discreetly referring to them as "some incorrectness in the language, which very few writers, who are not born in *England*, can avoid" (Ja/Fe '56, 10). In the case of another Scot's book (Home's *Experiments on Bleaching*), he was more explicit:

> The language in some places is a little uncouth.—We meet with some *Scottish* words and measures, which an *English* reader will be at a loss to understand. Such as *tramp* for treading under foot, *lint* for flax, *dreeper* for a dripping-stand, *bittling* for beetling, *mutchkin* for pint, *chopin* for quart, *Scots pint* for two quarts, *Scots gallon* for sixteen quarts, &c. (Mr '56, 114)

Scotticisms were also a problem in Hume's prose, according to Smollett, although he admitted that only "some few, and but a few *Scotticisms* have escaped our author." He listed them as "*had been* (instead of *would have been*). . .; the words *rescind* and *succumb*; the phrases *of deliberating what use* [and] *prevent like confusions WITH those*" (De '56, 394). The irony here is that Hume shared Smollett's concern that Scotticisms not encroach on correct English and to that end he had published in 1752 a list of Scotticisms and their English meanings in an appendix to his *Political Discourses*.[44] One of the Scotticisms Hume included on his list—*adduce*—was among those cited by Smollett in reviewing another work by an anonymous author whom he felt sure was a Scotsman:

> We shall first mention a few inaccuracies in the language by which we should judge the author to be a North-Briton; for he uses the word *adduce*, a word peculiar to the *Scotch* dialect, and several uncouth phrases, which do not seem to be of *English* growth; such as *attention irresistibly awoke—development, untuneableness, musicalness, seeming originality*, English language whose original,—*arrived at a poem*, &c. (Ap '56, 228)

Unfortunately, the anonymous work under review was *An Essay on the Writings and Genius of Pope* and its author, Joseph Warton, was decidedly not Scottish. If all this suggests the degree of Smollett's sensitivity to Scotticisms, it indicates at least as much about the uncertain state of the English language in the mideighteenth century.

But in addition to decrying Scotticisms, Smollett had a penchant for making other anti-Scottish remarks in his reviews. Most were jocular. In discussing Home's *Experiments on Bleaching*, Smollett quipped that "linen manufacture. . . is the staple commodity of his country, unless the breed of Authors produced in *Scotland*, comes in competition with this branch of industry" (Mr '56, 106). In another review, he mocked an author for "owning himself proud of being an apothecary: a declaration," said Smollett, "like that of a certain member of the house of commons, who in a speech to the chair, took occasion to thank God, that he was born a *Scotchman* and bred a presbyterian: upon which another gentleman rose up and observed, that the other he believed was a good christian, for he thanked heaven for small mercies" (My '56, 326). These mild jests would be insignificant in themselves except that elsewhere Smollett's anti-Scottish remarks cut nearer the bone. In criticizing Murphy's *Apprentice*, Smollett observed that Murphy's caricature of a Scot, "the Caledonian spouter," was less than accurate in "foible and dialect" but agreed that he "is dismissed with great propriety to translate *Tacitus* or *Grotius*; for," he continued, "it is a melancholy truth, that every idle *Scotchman* who cannot, or will not earn his bread by the employment in which he was brought up, commences author, and undertakes to translate books into a language of which he is entirely ignorant" (Ja/Fe '56, 80–81). Read in one way, this is a sweeping condemnation of Scottish authors and indeed, eleven years later, the editors of the *Critical*, faced with continuing accusations of a pro-Scots bias, quoted it to demonstrate a long-standing policy of strict impartiality, even antipathy towards Scottish authors (Ja '67, [ii]). But there is something a bit troubling about Smollett, safely concealed behind the veil of anonymity, writing in these ways about Scottish authors in the 1750s. It is not hypocrisy but something nearer to self-protective humor, scarcely concealing the underlying anxiety and conflict.

Of course Smollett was not alone in his concern to eradicate Scotticisms and to purify the English used by Scots. Hume, for instance, not only published his list of Scotticisms, but privately corrected Scotticisms in the works of friends such as William Robertson.[45] Scotticisms were also one of the categories of words proscribed by Johnson in his *Dictionary* and Boswell, who was constantly sensitive to Scots accent and usages, even went so far as to avoid the company of Scotsmen because of their bad influence on his speech.[46] And there were many other men of letters seeking linguistic purity on a grand scale by organizing societies and lecturing on oratory and the belles lettres; among them were Thomas Sheridan, Lord Kames, Lord Auchinleck, Hugh Blair, William Robertson, Adam Ferguson, and Adam Smith.[47] As Sutherland has suggested, their efforts may have had a significant influence on the development of literary language during the century, although not, according to Wordsworth, an entirely felicitous influence.

But Smollett was more conscious than most of the clash between the two cultures, Scottish and English. Throughout his career, he experienced the difficulty of being an ambitious Scot in the London literary world. His ballad "The Tears of Scotland" and the story of its composition attest to the trauma he suffered over the Scots Rebellion in 1745.[48] Indeed, the night news of Culloden reached London in 1745, an event occurred that must have been permanently scarring for Smollett. He and his friend Alexander Carlyle, another Scot, were trying to walk home across London but (in Carlyle's words) "the mob were so riotous, and the squibs so numerous and incessant" that the two men took off their wigs and drew their swords for self-protection; Carlyle then remembers Smollett "cautioning me against speaking a word, lest the mob should discover my country and become insolent."[49] Smollett considered himself a loyal English subject but he could never completely escape his Scottish heritage. This dilemma was to lead to a crisis in his life with the *Briton-North Briton* paper war of 1762–63, when dialects and accents took on serious political overtones and the debate became fierce, with painful consequences for Smollett.[50] But even by 1755 Smollett had become sensitive enough about Scotticisms (as well as gallicisms and other stylistic "flaws") to edit them out of the fourth edition of *Roderick Random*.[51]

Thus in the early days of the *Critical*, he must have been continually worried about how it might look if it were known that three of its writers (Murdoch, Armstrong, and himself) were Scottish. His enemies plagued him on this score. In 1757 Smollett took the trouble to publish an editorial statement in the *Critical* insisting that only one of five writers on the staff was a Scot (Oc '57, 333). Accusations of pro-Scots bias persisted, despite denials and evidence to the contrary. In 1758 Smollett apologized to John Moore for the harsh treatment two books by Scottish authors (John Home and William Wilkie) had received in the *Critical* and then complained that

> notwithstanding the Censures that have been so freely bestowed upon these and other Productions of our Country, the Authors of the Critical Review have been insulted and abused as a *Scotch Tribunal*. The Truth is there is no Author so wretched but he will meet with Countenance in England if he attacks our Nation in any shape.[52]

It is with these inner tensions and in this "climate of opinion," then, that Smollett saw himself launching and conducting a review that was to be one branch of a scheme for an *English* academy of letters. Not surprisingly, his self-consciousness in this position seems to have impelled him to establish from the outset the thoroughly *English* attitudes and policies of the *Critical*: almost to out-English the English.

There was one other principle, not unconnected with his call for an English academy, that governed Smollett's treatment of every kind of publication: his idealized image of the author's role in society. To Smollett, Warton was a paradigm of "the learned, who enjoy their ease," yet undertake the "charitable task" of "enlightening the understanding" of the less favored (Ap '56, 227). Similarly, in reviewing the publications of a "Society in *Edinburgh*," Smollett praised the society as

a community composed of persons endowed with learning and probity, [which] will contribute to the improvement of philosophy, not only by their own hints and discoveries; but also by exciting and diffusing a spirit of inquiry and emulation among people who without their example, would never have dreamed of exercising their faculties in these pursuits, or of publishing the remarks they might have made in the course of their observations. (Jn '56, 409)

In Smollett's view, the learned had a responsibility to society, not only in the arts and theoretical sciences, but in practical matters too. Accordingly, he lauded one author's proposed method of making buildings fireproof (Ap '56, 263) and another's proposal for tax reforms, including voluntary sacrifices by the wealthy, to relieve "the present exigencies of the state" (Ap '56, 265). But society, in turn, had a responsibility to encourage not only such civic-minded publications but any literary work that would be a credit to the nation.

Smollett was deeply distressed, therefore, at the increasing commercialism of the publishing industry; he deplored the pernicious consequences of the decline of patronage and the growing power of booksellers. This led him to comment frequently even on the physical qualities of books: their format, printing, illustrations, and bindings (Ja/Fe '56, 57).[53] But he was especially concerned about the neglect of worthy authors and projects, and he editorialized on this theme in several reviews. He took the opportunity in one review, for example, to laud the author's latest publication as an exemplary service to the nation:

Mr. *Postlethwayt* gently complains of the little encouragement he has found for devoting his studies to the service of his country; and indeed nothing will reflect more disgrace upon the memory of our late ministers, than their neglect of genius and ability. But times we hope are changed. Every body knows that Mr. *Postlethwayt* is author of the Dictionary of Trade, a work which has been candidly received by the public, as a national advantage. (De '56, 433)

Smollett found Postlethwayt's accomplishment doubly impressive when compared with that of Savary, his counterpart in France, who compiled a similar dictionary but with the advantages of patronage, paid amanuenses, and a lucrative pension. By contrast, Smollett explained, Postlethwayt "had no coadjutors, and no other recompence but virtue, which, to be sure, is its own reward, though so unsubstantial that a man cannot live upon it." The parallels with Johnson's experience in compiling his *Dictionary* are obvious. For Smollett, such examples were noble but alarming. He used his reviews not only to applaud individual authors, but to urge those in power to revitalize the patronage system, private and public, for the betterment of the nation and the benefit of needy authors.

He used the same rationale to explain the growing numbers of trivial and slipshod publications. In his review of one such work, Rolt's *History of South America*, Smollett painted a dismal picture of the author's plight under the depraved patronage of the booksellers:

> The *British* learning of this age is grown into contempt among other nations, by whom it was formerly revered; and nothing has contributed to this disgrace, so much as the inundation of mean performances, undertaken for the emolument of booksellers, who cannot distinguish authors of merit, or if they could, have not sense and spirit to reward them according to their genius and capacity. Without considering the infinite pains and perseverance it must cost a writer to form and digest a proper plan of history; compile materials; compare different accounts; collate authorities; compose and polish the stile, and complete the execution of the work; he furnishes them with a few books, bargains with him for two or three guineas a sheet; binds him with articles to finish so many volumes in so many months, in a crouded page and evanescent letter, that he may have stuff enough for his money; insists upon having copy within the first week after he begins to peruse his materials; orders the press to be set a going, and expects to cast off a certain number of sheets weekly, warm from the mint, without correction, revisal, or even deliberation. Nay, the miserable author must perform his daily task, in spite of cramp, colick, vapours, or vertigo; in spite of head-ach, heart-ache, and *Minerva*'s frowns; otherwise he will lose his character and his livelihood, like a taylor who disappoints his customer in a birth-day suit.—What can be expected from a wretched author under such terrors and restraints, but a raw, crude, hasty, superficial production, without substance, order, symmetry or connection, like the imperfect rudiments of nature in abortion; or those unfinished creatures engendered from the mud of the *Nile*, which the old philosophy fabled as the effect of equivocal generation. (Mr '56, 97–98)

Smollett drew on personal experience for this depiction of life in Grub Street, a subject he had treated often before in his novels and other works.[54] But he did not allow sympathy to cloud his judgment: he thoroughly damned Rolt's *History* as "a very trivial, insipid, injudicious and defective performance, without plan, method, learning, accuracy or elegance" (Mr '56, 98). To understand conditions was not to accept them.

There is a final outstanding characteristic of Smollett's reviewing technique that, because of his exacting standards and his reputation—fueled by angry pamphleteers—as a "hypercritic,"[55] is also the most surprising. Smollett was overall much more positive than negative as a critic. He found much to praise in the works he reviewed and most of the time he chose to extol the virtues of good works rather than dwell on the failings of poor ones, as the following chart suggests:[56]

A BREAKDOWN OF REVIEW ARTICLES IN 1756

	favorable	mixed	unfavorable
Smollett	18	9	9
Francklin	14	7	11
Armstrong	6	5	2
Murdoch	2	0	0
Derrick	3	7	8
Total	43	28	30

Of the thirty-six books to which Smollett devoted a full review article (usually eight to twelve pages), three-quarters met with either overwhelming approval or approval mixed with criticism; only one in four of the books he took the trouble to review in full did he find irredeemably bad. The pattern in the "Monthly Catalogue" notices was a little different: a higher proportion were condemned, although of course being relegated to this section amounted to tacit discounting in the first place. But even here Smollett alone of the *Critical* staff gave favorable or mixed notices to more than half:

MONTHLY CATALOGUE NOTICES IN 1756

	favorable	mixed	unfavorable
Smollett	7	12	17
Francklin	5	6	17
Armstrong	0	1	4
Murdoch	0	0	0
Derrick	6	9	26
Total	18	28	64

Once the veil of anonymity is pulled aside, Smollett becomes a critic of a very different temperament indeed! It is also significant that in 1756 the *Critical* gave favorable or mixed reviews to more than three-quarters of all the books reviewed in the main articles and only once in eleven issues did the lead article present an unfavorable review. This evidence of a relatively generous approach to reviewing, in spite of his rigorous standards, helps to explain Smollett's subsequent frustration and resentment at the public's widely varying response to the *Critical* in its early years. Indeed, the number of complaints and quarrels continued to rise so that by 1759 Smollett felt as if he were being (in his words) "baited like a bear by all the hounds of Grub-Street."[57]

The Republic of Letters: Smollett's Writings on Literature and History in 1756

i. CRITICAL RANGE

Pope, who was in so many ways Smollett's idol and model, advised the would-be critic to "Be sure *your self* to know, / How far your *Genius, Taste,* and *Learning* go"; and urged him to stick to his areas of real expertise because "One *Science* only will one *Genius* fit; / So *vast* is Art, so *narrow* Human Wit" (*Essay on Criticism,* 48–49 and 60–61). The extraordinary range of subjects and genres that Smollett took under his critical purview remind us of his exceptional combination of abilities—novelist, historian, poet, translator, physician, and scientific writer—not unlike such other distinctively eighteenth-century polymaths as Voltaire and Johnson.

Even if we focus on Smollett's critical output during just his first year of book reviewing, we find a variety of kinds of books and fields that scarcely seems possible. The works he reviewed in that year range from single poems to multivolume histories, from farces to scientific treatises, from political pamphlets to paintings and sculpture. In each month's issue, one must remember, Smollett's freedom to choose his own topic and expound his own ideas was circumscribed by the variety and quality of recent publications. It should be remembered also that, Johnson's writings in the *Gentleman's* and *Literary* magazines notwithstanding, Smollett was the first major writer to subject himself to precisely these conditions and produce a significant body of writing. Smollett had to respond to the whole flood of contemporary publications each month—and to no others—whether in his own critical articles or by editorial assignment. Smollett's freedom was further restricted within each review article by the limits of space and, as has been seen, by the inherited conventions of abstract-style reviewing and the demands of the public for summary and quotation. It is senseless to seek, therefore, a sustained and systematic critical theory being expounded in the course of these assorted reviews; one cannot finally compare the sum of Smollett's opinions in the *Critical Review*, however voluminous in toto, with the cogent theses developed in such works as Warton's *Essay on Pope* or Hurd's *Letters on Chivalry and Romance*.

Nonetheless these scattered writings open new vantages on both Smollett's critical thinking and that of his age. One need not share the enthusiasm to appreciate the perception of John Wilson, the nineteenth-century critic who, in asserting the value of journalistic writings in his own time, wrote appreciatively of the many

> crack contributors to the Reviews, Magazines, and Gazettes, who have said more tender, and true, and fine, and deep things in the way of criticism, than ever was said before since the reign of Cadmus, ten thousand times over,—not in long, dull, heavy, formal, prosy theories,—but flung off hand, out of the glowing mint—a coinage of the purest ore—and stamped with the ineffaceable impress of genius. Who so elevated in intellectual rank as to be entitled to despise such a periodical literature?[1]

This is no less true of Smollett than of Goldsmith, Johnson, and other talented periodical writers of the eighteenth century. Whether expressed in substantive critiques or isolated remarks, Smollett's critical opinions help to illuminate aspects of his own thinking and to trace important threads in the complex fabric of ideas in the mid-eighteenth century.

The works Smollett reviewed fall into five basic areas, the first two of which comprise the products of Smollett's cherished (if notional) "republic of letters" and will be considered in this chapter: *literary works* (including poetry, drama, fiction, translation, and criticism) and *history*. The remaining three areas, which include *contemporary works of art*, *science and medicine*, and *politics*, will be discussed in chapter 6, where each of these miscellaneous and in some cases unexpected fields can be given separate attention.

ii. LITERATURE

Smollett's view of the state of literature in his own day seemed to vary according to his mood and the particular work at hand. At one point, he pronounced rather gloomily that Warton's *Essay on Pope* "is one of the few productions of this Gothic age, which we can with pleasure recommend to the public notice" (Ap '56, 227). But elsewhere in the same issue, in a very different mood, he proclaimed that "nothing is more unjust, than the common observation that genius no longer blooms in this degenerate age; that science expired with *Newton*, and poetry perished with *Pope*" (Ap '56, 276). Where the paucity of good publications had dismayed him in the Warton review, here he maintains the opposite: "We could enumerate many living authors,

whose works, we apprehend, are not inferior to those of *Pope* himself. . . .
We can boast a *Young*, an *Armstrong*, an *Akenside*, a *Gray*, a *Mason*, a *Warton*,
and a *Whitehead*, with many others who possess the true spirit of poetry"
(276). But these stellar poets did not publish every day, or even every year,
and from the reviewer's point of view, they could be lost in the growing
crowds of mediocre and bad authors. As he made explicit in his prefatory
manifestoes, Smollett saw his primary task as that of befriending merit
amidst "the chaos of publication." Understandably, therefore, he concentrated on reading and reviewing good books rather than denouncing the bad.

This partly explains why in 1756 Smollett reviewed almost nothing in two
fields in which he could have been expected to take a keen interest: fiction
and poetry. Of the two, it is perhaps most surprising to find that Smollett,
already one of the most successful novelists of the century, did not review a
single novel that year. This was not due to any decline in respect on his part
for the novel as a genre. He had conducted his most elaborate and spirited
defense of the novel as a literary form in *Ferdinand Count Fathom* (1753), his
last novel before he founded the *Critical*.[2] It is also clear that he was still
reading contemporary fiction in the early 1750s. In various contexts, he demonstrated familiarity with many recent novels, including: *An Apology for the
Life of Bampfylde-Moore Carew* (1749),[3] John Hill's *History of a Woman of
Quality* (1750) and *The Adventures of Mr. George Edwards* (1751), *The Adventures of Mr. Loveill* (1750), *The Adventures of Joe Thompson* (1750), Eliza
Haywood's *History of Miss Betsy Thoughtless* (1751), Cleland's *Memoirs of a
Coxcomb* (1751),[4] Christian Gellert's *History of the Swedish Countess of G——
——* (1752),[5] Shebbeare's *Lydia: or filial piety* (1755),[6] and Edward Kimber's
Juvenile Adventures of David Ranger (1756).[7] And of course he knew well the
novels of Richardson, his friend and later business associate, and Fielding, of
whose fiction he was acutely aware because of their rivalry and the prickly
exchanges that ran from the publication of *Tom Jones* in 1749 through *Peregrine Pickle* (1751) and *Amelia* (1752), at least.[8]

Thus the real reason for Smollett's apparent disregard for fiction in 1756
stems, paradoxically, from the very seriousness of his belief in the novel as a
distinct and important genre. Its very survival was imperiled, he felt, by the
proliferation of trashy fiction. He had addressed this problem as early as 1751
in his review of Cleland's *Coxcomb*: "In this work we meet with nothing so
surprising, as that an author of merit should attempt to entertain the public
with a species of writing which is of late so justly grown into disrepute, on
account of the many wretched productions it hath brought forth." When
talented writers publish a novel, he went on, they "run the risque of being
seen and confounded with those who are condemned by the lump, to the
gulph of oblivion."[9] Various details in the *Critical* in 1756 evince his continuing sense of the novel's stature and tradition, as when he detects a plagiarism from *Joseph Andrews* (Au '56, 38) or invokes the memory of Defoe's

achievement to condemn Shebbeare (Oc '56, 279). In later years, he was to review various novels, including *Candide* and *Tristram Shandy*, for the *Critical*. But in 1756 he remained aloof, avoiding any involvement with the paltry fiction on offer, as if refusing to dignify it with his attention. His attitude is best represented in the way he responded to Kimber's *David Ranger*: although it can be shown that he had read it, he left it to Francklin to review in the "Monthly Catalogue" (De '56, 379).

His treatment of poetry was similar. Again, although he was a poet himself,[10] he reviewed almost no poetry in 1756, delegating it to Derrick and Francklin who in turn granted most of it only a brief notice in the "Monthly Catalogue." (The chief exception was William Mason's *Odes*, to which fellow Cantabrigian Francklin devoted a major review in April 1756, 208–14.) Smollett reviewed only four works of poetry that year, all in short notices. One—the anonymous *Essays Pastoral and Elegiac*—he dismissed out of hand as "extremely tedious" and unreadable (Jn '56, 482–83). A second was a collection of Latin verse fables, *Fabulorum Aesopiarum libri quinque*; Smollett's general praise for them may have been in part an effort to promote his friend Foulis's scholarly publications and in part an experiment to test his readership's receptivity to quotations in foreign languages.[11] About John Duncombe's collected *Poems*, Smollett was unenthusiastic, although he found them "not wholly void of merit" (Ap '56, 262). Collections aside, the only separately published poem Smollett reviewed was the anonymous ode to *The Genius of Britain. . . . Pitt*, in the course of which he offers a glimpse into his method of practical criticism. He observes of one line "that *grammar* (as is frequent in our best poets) is sacrificed to *poetry*, the preposition *to* being omitted, which at the same time renders the verse obscure" (De '56, 470). But this point about the artificiality of poetic diction—so promising in itself—is dropped without elaboration and the poem, because of its diminutive size and significance, receives overall only a short notice (De '56, 470–71).

By contrast, Smollett devoted almost as much space as any of these notices to discussing one small point of literary opinion raised by Hume in the course of his *History of Great Britain*. It concerns Milton:

We think Mr. *Hume* is too severe on the character and abilities of *Milton*. He says, (p. 125) "he prostituted his pen in factious disputes, and in justifying the most violent measures of his party."—We have a better opinion of *Milton*.—He was an enthusiast; but, surely no prostitute. Neither do we find his prose writings disagreeable; nor any of his poetical performances flat and insipid. We cannot think that near one third of his *Paradise Lost* is devoid of harmony, elegance, and vigor of imagination. (De '56, 388)

Smollett went on to refute Hume's contention that Milton was inferior to

Homer, Lucretius, and Tasso. This was perfectly in keeping with Smollett's lifelong esteem for Milton. From his earliest major poem, *Advice* (1746), through his great last novel, *Humphry Clinker* (1771), Smollett's creative works contained echoes and lines from Milton's verse, particularly *L'Allegro* and *Paradise Lost*, and in his *History of England* he referred to Milton as "one of the great geniuses for epic poetry that ever the world produced."[12] The point is that it seemed to Smollett more important to pause and defend Milton from a passing attack than to discuss any of the minor poetry of the day.

Not surprisingly, Smollett's longest and most elaborate review of a literary work in 1756 is that on Warton's *Essay on Pope* (Ap '56, 226–40). His interest was inevitable. He greatly admired Pope, whom he once called "the prince of lyric poetry," and his works bear innumerable signs of Pope's influence.[13] But he also had the critical acumen to recognize—as did Johnson later the same month[14]—the crucial importance and potentially revolutionary implications of Warton's reassessment of the eighteenth century's most celebrated poet. Smollett's review of Warton offers a paradigm of his critical ambivalence and uncertainty about such issues as neoclassical rules and the value of imagination, responses typical not only of his own critical outlook, but of his age. For these reasons, the review deserves to be considered in some detail.

In order best to understand the significance of the Warton review, however, one must first differentiate between Smollett's own critical opinions and those generally attributed to the *Critical* as a whole. Distinctions have been obscured. Scholars who have studied the critical standards of the *Critical Review* have tended to subsume Smollett's own critical ideas in the general patterns they perceive. Joseph Heidler, in his study of eighteenth-century criticism of prose fiction, argues that under Smollett's guidance the *Critical* practiced more sophisticated and progressive criticism of the novel than did the *Monthly*.[15] Yet his discussion is based on only five selected reviews, of which two are now known to be by Derrick and the authorship of the other three is still uncertain.[16] Similarly, in a brief survey entitled "Change in the Criticism of the Novel after 1760," William Park brushes over direct contradictions among the opinions of different reviewers on the *Critical*.[17] Studies by Edward Hooker and Jones have offered equally broad generalizations about the *Critical*'s attitude toward what they call the "new criticism" and its view on poetry and drama.[18] The differences in their findings are striking: "The dominant trend of the reviews," writes Hooker, "was liberal, or 'romantic.'"[19] "Despite these romantic leanings," answers Jones, "the general tone of the *Critical Review* is conservative and reactionary."[20] Clearly generalizations about the critical ideas and practices of the *Critical* reviewers are dangerous, if not self-defeating.

In the first place, uniformity of outlook on the staff of a single journal cannot be assumed.[21] It was decidedly not true of the *Critical*, as a handful of examples will illustrate. It has already been shown, for example, that Smollett disagreed with Derrick about the quality of Richardson's fiction and forced him to atone in print for his "silly, mean Insinuation against Mr. Richardson's Writings."[22] Smollett differed with Francklin on the practice of altering or "correcting" Shakespeare's plays; he was far less opposed to the practice than was Francklin, if their reviews of two such alterations in the March 1756 issue are an indication.[23] In reviewing Armstrong's *Sketches*, Smollett disagreed with Armstrong about such things as the nature and value of "genius" in poetry, arguing that Armstrong undervalued it (My '58, 381).[24] Smollett disowned and appeared to regret many of the opinions expressed in the *Critical*'s review of Home's *Douglas* (Mr '57, 258–68).[25] Ironically, this particular review has been singled out by at least one scholar as the best example of the *Critical*'s dramatic criticism.[26]

To collect Smollett's own literary opinions and examine them separately accomplishes two things that the studies cited above, notwithstanding their other merits, do not. First, it shows that Smollett's critical thinking, marked by ambivalence about the neoclassical rules and what are often called "preromantic" trends—either of which *could* be seen as ascendant in, for example, his treatment of Warton—accurately reflects the uncertain and transitional state of literary criticism in the period generally. Most modern criticism characterizes the period this way, in terms of complexity and conflicting critical values. Northrop Frye, among others, has pointed out the inadequacy of traditional notions of "Augustanism" and "preromanticism."[27] René Wellek speaks of the tensions inherent in the neoclassical creed "breaking out" in the mideighteenth century, but he warns that "it would be an error to think, however, that these diverse reinterpretations and innovations followed a logical or chronological order. Rather all these positions were taken up almost simultaneously and became sorted out only very slowly."[28] Bertrand Bronson has ably summed up the whole problem of attempting to generalize about the tenets and tendencies of eighteenth-century literature in his essay "When Was Neoclassicism?" The eighteenth century is a region, he writes,

> of the most baffling complexity and self-contradiction, in which can be found almost anything we choose to seek. Wherever we pause, we are bewildered by the diversity that surrounds us: not alone in the conflict of opinion but shot through the very texture of every considerable author's or artist's work. Of even the chief spokesmen this is probably true. Pope is no exception. The difficulty of making a consistent pattern of Johnson's thinking is notorious. Yet when we look at the authoritative surveys of critical historians, such is not the impression we receive.[29]

Here Bronson touches on the second point to be made about Smollett's critical opinions: they place him in the critical tradition of Pope and Johnson who, although inclining toward rules and standards, practice the distinctively English style of neoclassicism with its case-by-case flexibility and its grounding in audience impact, illustrious precedent, and common sense. Smollett's regard for rules and standards is tempered with the wisdom of Pope's dictum: "Great Wits sometimes may *gloriously offend*, / And *rise* to *Faults* true Criticks *dare not mend*";[30] in practice, his criticism shares the spirit of Johnson's sensible allowance that when an effective work of literature cannot be reconciled with traditional rules, "there is always an appeal open from criticism to nature."[31]

Nowhere is this truer than in Smollett's review of Warton's *Essay*. It is therefore useful to examine closely Smollett's discussion of Warton's *Essay* as a paradigm of Smollett's critical outlook precisely because in that review (to borrow Bronson's phrase) "can be found almost anything we choose to seek." In it contradictions abound. A mixture of close practical criticism and broad theoretical observation, of quibbles based alternately on points of fact and on subjective interpretation, Smollett's review is a quarry from which could be mined material to support critical views ranging from strict neoclassical conservatism to lively "preromantic" sympathies.

The signs of an Augustan outlook are many. Smollett begins the review with a discussion of the function of the critic reminiscent of Pope's *Essay on Criticism*, emphasizing the powers and concomitant responsibilities of the critic: "The man of taste must expend his labours in reforming the judgment and enlightening the understanding of these [critical] pretenders, and other novices of sensibility. . . . This charitable task of improvement, the learned, who enjoy their ease, ought to undertake for the benefit of mankind" (Ap '56, 227). There follows a critique of Warton's language that (as has been noted) in its insistence on purity and correctness links Smollett to a century-long tradition of linguistic conservatism. In discussing imagery, Smollett often applies notions of propriety and correctness, defending (for example) the propriety in one of Pope's pastorals of a swain complaining of immoderate heat because such heat actually occurs in English summer days (Ap '56, 228). But on similar grounds, Smollett faults the imagery of Akenside's "Ode to the Earl of Huntingdon"—which Warton exalts above any lyric of Pope's—for being undignified, unnatural, and incorrect (Ap '56, 231). Warton also, according to Smollett, "seems to undervalue the merit of versification" (Ap '56, 228), a grave lapse in judgment by neoclassical standards. Thus Smollett disagrees with Warton's praise for Dyer's "Grongar Hill" in part because of its "hobbling measure" (Ap '56, 230). Among other criteria applied by Smollett are the traditional ideas of decorum and aesthetic propriety, of suiting the sound to the sense in poetry. On this basis, he disputes the judgment of Warton (and indirectly of Johnson, whom Warton cites in support) on various verses of Pope's (Ap ' 56, 231–32).

On a different plane, Smollett disagrees with Warton's assertion "that the sciences cannot exist but in a republic," responding to it with characteristic conservatism: "This assertion savours too much of a wild spirit of *Democratic* enthusiasm, which some people have imbibed from the writings of the *Greeks*" (Ap '56, 233). Finally, Smollett finds Warton overenthusiastic (his attitude verging on "superstitious adoration") about Homer and Shakespeare and, by way of rebuttal, lists examples of their frequent "incorrectness." Notably, in the case of Shakespeare Smollett cites examples of what he calls "glaring improprieties" drawn from *Hamlet, Othello,* and *Macbeth*, all having to do with improbability, the unsuitability of speeches to particular characters, and the mixing of vice and virtue (Ap '56, 234–35). These are the same kinds of faults that Johnson was to cite a decade later, even as he was exculpating Shakespeare of others, in his famous reappraisal of Shakespeare in the preface to his edition of 1765. Such concerns, in other words, were central to the critical reexamination of Shakespeare in the mideighteenth century.

But for all the standard terms and attitudes of neoclassical criticism in Smollett's discussion, the diligent seeker of signs of "preromantic" attitudes would be equally rewarded. There is, first, Smollett's acquiescence in Warton's central thesis: that a careful reappraisal of Pope's poetry justifies reassigning him to a lower level of poetic achievement. Then there is Smollett on the topic of versification, describing it as more than mere decoration or "colouring"; it is the drawing of a figure, Smollett contends, that gives it "energy and warmth" (Ap '56, 228). In a revealing comparison, he upholds poetry's effect on the imagination over its artificial correctness: "Let two writers, for example, produce the same image upon paper, in verse; the one shall be awkward, lifeless, and insipid, tho' exhibited in proper language and studied cadence; while the other shall strike the imagination with all the force of expression and all the fire of enthusiasm" (Ap '56, 228). In the same vein, where Warton criticizes Pope's pastorals for introducing pagan mythological figures into Christian poems, Smollett again upholds imaginative power over propriety: "This practice, tho' perhaps a sort of impropriety, forms a kind of wild *prosopopeia*, which pleases the fancy, and conjures up an agreeable scene of ancient allegory" (Ap '56, 229).

In his rather surprising defense of poetic license, Smollett more than once charges Warton with being too strict. He defends a wildly fanciful image used by Petronius from Warton's charge that it "confounds" animal with vegetable generation, excusing scientific inaccuracy in the interests of sublime effect: "There is something great, stupendous, and venerable in the idea of the earth as the general parent producing all the animals to which it affords subsistence; and the image of a creature's cleaving the solid soil and starting into existence, is extremely picturesque" (Ap '56, 232). Although perhaps in part moved to defend Pope from Warton's strictures, Smollett's language— "strike the imagination," "the fire of enthusiasm," "pleases the fancy"— suggests criteria that anticipate the poetic values of the romantic era. It is certainly not the language one would expect from a devotee of Augustan correctness, such as Smollett has often seemed.

Near the end of his review, Smollett singles out for quotation a passage from the *Essay* that more than any other supports a view of Warton as a precursor of romanticism. That its full force and the significance of Smollett's endorsement of it may be conveyed, it is here repeated:

> In no polished nation, after criticism has been much studied, and the rules of writing established, has any very extraordinary work ever appeared. This has visibly been the case, in *Greece*, in *Rome*, and in *France*, after *Aristotle*, *Horace*, and *Boileau*, had written their *Arts of Poetry*. In our own country, the rules of the drama, for instance, were never more completely understood than at present: yet what *uninteresting*, though *faultless*, tragedies, have we lately seen? So much better is our judgement than our execution. How to account for the fact here mentioned, adequately and justly, would be attended with all those difficulties that await discussions relative to the productions of the human mind, and to the delicate and secret causes that influence them. Whether or no, the natural powers be not confined and debilitated by that timidity and caution which is occasioned by a regard to the dictates of art: or whether, that philosophical, that geometrical, and systematical spirit so much in vogue, which has spread itself from the sciences even into polite literature, by consulting only reason, has not diminished and destroyed sentiment; and made our poets write from and to the head rather than the heart: or whether, lastly, when just models, from which the rules have necessarily been drawn, have once appeared, succeeding writers, by ambitiously endeavouring to surpass those just models, and to be original and new, do not become distorted and unnatural, in their thoughts and diction. (Ap '56, 238–39)[32]

The significance of this statement did not escape Johnson, who introduced his quotation from it in the *Literary Magazine* by describing it as "a remark which deserves great attention."[33] But Johnson quoted only the first sentence. It was Smollett who considered the passage important enough to quote it in full, with its pervasive antipathy to critical rules and its implication that true poetic genius invariably transcends them.

It is not the case that Smollett was advocating a revolutionary poetic ideal. Quite the contrary. But if it can be said (as one critic puts it) that Warton's *Essay* is an "attempt to identify the distinctive features of poetry as affective rather than formal,"[34] it is evident that Smollett embraced Warton's idea in practice, if not in theory. It is in terms of effect that Smollett disputes with Warton the value of various lines and images, repeatedly excusing violations of the rules and breaches of poetic decorum if the transgressing figure excites or moves the reader's imagination. It is noteworthy that when Smollett disagrees with Warton, it is not to uphold points of orthodox taste, but the other way round; it was usually to defend Pope from the orthodox standards Warton himself was applying or to argue that the specific image achieved impact on the reader that Warton denied it. At such moments, Smollett, like Johnson in much of his criticism, showed himself to be much more reader-centered than formalistic in his critical approach. In surveying the responses of contemporary reviewers to Warton's *Essay*, Joan Pittock comments that "none of the [reviewers'] reactions sees the questioning of Pope's appeal to the reader as having a substantial importance."[35] Unfortunately, she had overlooked Smollett's review in the *Critical*.[36] Although difficult, complex, and not always consistent, it·is perhaps the most seminal and provocative literary review that Smollett ever wrote. Equally significant is the context of the criticism. When such a critical discussion took place in a review journal like the *Critical*, with a circulation of twenty-five hundred or three thousand and a readership perhaps several times that, it reached a more numerous and varied audience than a specialized critical essay with limited readership such as Warton's. It was through articles like Smollett's that the new critical ideas of thinkers like Warton became first the common terms of discussion and then the new orthodoxy among the educated reading public.

Drama, however, was Smollett's true passion. From the moment of his arrival in London in 1739, Smollett's fondest dream was to become a successful playwright. It was never realized. The story of his dogged but unsuccessful efforts to get his *Regicide* staged (and the shadow tales of frustrated playwrights in his novels) has been told by Knapp.[37] During his career Smollett wrote at least five dramatic works, only one of which—*The Reprisal*, still in preparation in 1756—was staged in his lifetime.[38] Moreover, evidence of his having written still other unsuccessful plays continues to surface.[39]

With his own farce in progress, Smollett took a lively if somewhat vested interest in the drama of 1756. He reviewed at least seven plays:

Arthur Murphy, *The Apprentice* (Ja/Fe '56, 78–82).
Samuel Foote, *The Englishman Return'd from Paris* (Ja/Fe '56, 83–85).
Charles Marsh, *The Winter's Tale. . . alter'd from Shakespeare* (Mr '56, 144–45).
[Henry Dell], *The Spouter; or the Double Revenge* (Mr '56, 146).
Frances Brooke, *Virginia* (Ap '56, 276–79)
[Anon.], *The Sham Fight; or Political Humbug* (Oc '56, 280).
David Garrick, *Lilliput* (De '56, 474).

He also reviewed one other work about theater, Theophilus Cibber's *Two Dissertations on the Theatres* (Au '56, 48–51).[40] In two sentences, he dismissed Dell's *Spouter* as ridiculous, perhaps because he had no desire to become involved in the paper feud between the two theaters (Rich's *Covent Garden* and Garrick's *Drury Lane*) that had engendered it. But to the others, he devoted considerably more attention.

A careful distinction was drawn between performances and the published texts of plays and, as a literary reviewer rather than a theater critic, Smollett reviewed only the latter.[41] As a result, Smollett sometimes found himself at odds with the theater managers and their audiences, using literary criteria in one case to extol the virtues of a tragedy that was never acted (Brooke's *Virginia*) and, in another, to denigrate the qualities of a comedy (Murphy's *Apprentice*) that was very popular in performance. Regarding the latter, Samuel Johnson at one point defended his friend Murphy's play by pointing out exactly this discrepancy between audience approval and negative reviews of the printed play, all by way of rebuking the review journals.[42]

As in his review of Warton, Smollett applied the vocabulary of rules and genre criticism to the drama, with varying degrees of clarity and consistency. With regard to the "unities and manners of the drama," he found *The Sham Fight* beneath consideration (Oc '56, 280). He methodically faulted Murphy's *Apprentice* for its lack of a clear "moral," lapses in "probability," flaws in "character," and inaccuracies in "dialect" (Ja/Fe '56, 79–81). Further, Smollett disapproved of Murphy's prologue and epilogue because they followed the (admittedly common) modern practice rather than the strict model of ancient drama (Ja/Fe '56, 82). Garrick's *Lilliput*, on the other hand, was praised for its "moral end" and its style of burlesque, patterned after classical comedy (De '56, 474). While he admired Foote's *Englishman Return'd from Paris*, Smollett considered the central character imperfectly "designed" and the denouement too "abrupt" (Ja/Fe '56, 83). The checklist of features with which he closed this review may suggest his rather formulaic method: "The reflections are, in general, just and pertinent, the dialogue spirited, and the incidents entertaining; tho' there is no intrigue, recognition, nor change of fortune in the conduct of the drama" (Ja/Fe '56, 83).

In his only review of a tragedy—Brooke's *Virginia*—Smollett displayed both a sense of the divergence of modern tragedy from classical models and an unusually tactful critical manner. He delivered his criticisms of the play indirectly, by speculating on what reasons a theater manager might have had for refusing it:

> Perhaps the manager to whom this piece was offered, found it too thin of incidents for a modern audience: perhaps he disapproved of the catastrophe, in which *Virginia*'s fate is narrated, and not acted on the stage: tho' these objections would have had no weight with a circle of *Greeks* or *Romans*; perhaps he did not think there was enough of fire, fury, bitter altercation, cursing and blasting in the dialogue: perhaps, he thought the fable was not *simplex duntaxat et unum*, that the unity of action was not preserved, that the scene flagged after the death of *Virginia*. That there are a few inaccuracies in the diction, we cannot deny. . . . But, these are trivial defects (Ap '56, 277)

Smollett's comments are noncommittal, but perhaps with reason. In writing and revising his own tragedy, he had sought assiduously (as he explained in the preface to *The Regicide*) to "mould it into a regular tragedy, confined within the unities of the drama."[43] But perhaps disappointment and the passage of time had softened his views. Perhaps also, as has been suggested, Smollett was friends with Frances Brooke and this tempered his tone. In either case, Smollett remained thoroughly ambivalent about the classical rules of tragedy, as applied to this play. "Probability is not preserved in the catastrophe," he observes; "the imagination cannot conceive, that during the representation of two very short scenes *Virginia* could walk to the Forum, be judged by *Appius*, killed by her own father, and the tidings be brought back to the house of *Virginius*" (Ap '56, 279). Yet in the very next sentence, Smollett defies classical authority: "With all due deference to *Aristotle*, *Horace*, and the *French* critics, we should have been pleased to see that august, affecting, horrid scene, in which the father sacrifices his darling daughter" (Ap '56, 279). (As powerful as this scene seemed to him now, his daughter and only child just turned eight, how unbearable it would have been to him seven years later when her sudden death devastated him.) Here, as elsewhere, it seems that classical rules and categories were a convenient way to talk about poetry and drama, but with no well-defined or consistent critical creed attached to them. In each case, common sense, audience impact, and personal taste counted at least as much as formal criteria.

The definitive test for critics was Shakespeare. For Smollett, as for Johnson, Shakespeare's plays were undeniably products of genius, but also fraught with "irregularity" and "incorrectness," which made them terribly problematic. Confronted with Marsh's adaptation of *The Winter's Tale*, Smollett took a middle course. He first praised Shakespeare's transcendent powers and warned against presuming to correct him:

> The practice of altering *Shakespear*, is like that of mending an old *Roman* causeway by the hands of a modern paviour; tho' far less excusable, because not undertaken for use or convenience. A man of true taste will have more pleasure in seeing the ruins of a *Grecian* temple, than in examining all the commodities of the neatest box in *Hackney*, or in *Hammersmith*: even the irregularity of some *Gothic* edifices, exhibits a rude, stupendous grandeur, which, notwithstanding all its incorrectness, strikes the beholder with admiration and awe.
>
> Mr. *Marsh* has been frugal in decorating the ground of *Shakespear* with his own embroidery; and so far he is commendable. (Mr '56, 144)

But no sooner is this said, than Smollett does an about-face. He not only proceeds to applaud Marsh for correcting some of Shakespeare's inaccuracies and improbabilities, but then suggests still more irregularities that he missed, including anachronisms and the mixture of comedy and tragedy. "For," says Smollett, "since the garment of our *British Homer* was to be new cut, it might have been reduced entirely to the fashion" (Mr '56, 145). This apparent lack of resolution about how to cope with Shakespeare need not, however, invalidate Smollett's critical judgments. In fact it makes them paradigmatic. In them is mirrored the continuing struggle of the eighteenth century to evolve critical ideas that would be rigorous and exact, yet capacious enough to accommodate irregular genius and to explain aesthetic pleasure.

Smollett's dramatic criticism in 1756 was not always as impartial and objective as it might have been. Self-interest and prejudice crept in. He criticized *The Sham Fight* for its poorly written French dialect (Oc '56, 280) and faulted Foote for his excessive antigallicism, asking, "Is not the author too national in his sarcasms upon the *French*? Are not such reflections so many sacrifices made to the galleries, at the expence of politeness and common justice?" (Ja/Fe '56, 83). But Smollett's own farce, *The Reprisal; or the Tars of Old England*, which he was even then preparing for the stage, depends heavily on just this kind of dialect and foible to mock the French ruthlessly. In it, Smollett, as much as Foote or any of his contemporaries, was playing to the galleries, capitalizing on the rising tide of anti-Gallic sentiment excited by the war with France.

For obviously personal reasons, Smollett reserved his severest criticism for Murphy's *Apprentice*. While *The Apprentice* was not markedly better or worse than the common run of such farces, its humor is built on the mockery of several recent tragedies, among them Smollett's own *Regicide*. One of Murphy's characters is a histrionic Scot who in the course of his ridiculous utterances mentions the time "when I enacted in the *Reegeceede*" (Ja/Fe '56, 80–81). This stab at *The Regicide*, complete with Scottish accent, touched Smollett on his sorest spot. Perhaps too sensible to attempt to defend *The Regicide* directly (he even quotes the offending line in his review), Smollett nevertheless lashed the play and included a gratuitous slur on Murphy's character for good measure (Ja/Fe '56, 79). Although Murphy's little jest had touched things off, Smollett's vitriolic response insured that bad blood would continue between them, as it did for years.[44]

In contrast with Murphy, Garrick benefited from Smollett's self-interest. At least in part owing to his desire to get *The Reprisal* staged, Smollett had by the end of 1756 completely reversed his former animosity toward Garrick. The attacks and mockery implanted in both *Roderick Random* and *Peregrine Pickle* gave way to praise for him as actor, manager, and playwright.[45] In his scathing review of *The Apprentice*, Smollett managed to insert a panegyric on Garrick and his company for having transformed what he deemed a miserable play into a successful entertainment (Ja/Fe '56, 78–79). Perhaps at Smollett's urging, Francklin made a similar point in his review of *Athelstan*, lauding Garrick's power "of turning all that he touches into gold"—in this case, a poor tragedy into a theatrical success (Mr '56, 149). Where Francklin and Derrick were sometimes critical of Garrick's abilities as a playwright, condemning (respectively) his *Catharine and Petruchio* (Mr '56, 145–46) and

The Tempest. . . Taken from Shakespeare (Mr '56, 147–48), Smollett was kinder. Smollett's brief but favorable notice of Garrick's farce *Lilliput* in the December issue (De '56, 474), accorded perfectly with the gratitude and indebtedness he expressed in letters to Garrick about a month later. Sometime before 24 November 1756, Garrick had agreed to produce *The Reprisal* at Drury Lane; in thanking him, Smollett avowed that "I shall not rest satisfied until I have an opportunity to convince Mr. Garrick that my gratitude is at least as warm as any other of my passions."[46] A few days later, Smollett again wrote Garrick: "Should it ever lie in my way to serve Mr. Garrick, I hope he will command me without Reserve."[47] During this time, Smollett also sent Garrick a copy of his *History* as a gift.[48]

There were obvious ways that Smollett, as editor and reviewer on the *Critical*, might "serve" Garrick's interests. Garrick published more than thirty separate works (mostly plays and adaptations) during his career, three in 1756 alone. There were rumors (circulated by Shebbeare, among others) that some such interest had prompted Garrick to accept Smollett's play, in response to which Smollett wrote Garrick: "I, in justice to myself, take the liberty to assure you that if any person accuses me of having spoken disrespectfully of Mr. Garrick, of having hinted that he solicited for my farce, or had interested views in bringing it up on the stage, he does me wrong, upon the word of a gentleman."[49] But the interests were mutual and the reconciliation welcome. The friendship that ensued was cordial, if not intimate, and lasted many years without problems.[50] Smollett subsequently reviewed with approval other works by Garrick, replaced his mockery with praise for Garrick when he revised *Peregrine Pickle* for a second edition (1758), inserted a compliment for him in *Sir Launcelot Greaves*, and eulogized him at length in his *Continuation*.[51] On his part, Garrick granted Smollett special terms in calculating his royalties from *The Reprisal*, visted him during his imprisonment in the King's Bench, sent him complimentary copies of his plays, and, as late as 1768 when Smollett was convalescing in Bath, asked him to help write a pamphlet against his antagonist Baretti.[52]

What is most noteworthy about Smollett's relations with Garrick from 1756 on is that they are an early and positive example of the kind of power, as a literary arbiter, that began to accrue to Smollett from his involvement with the *Critical*. That Garrick, a prominent and influential man in his own sphere, should seek good working relations with someone who had earlier vilified him is dramatic testimony to that fact. Not that there were specific "deals" made between them; their mutual support was subtler than that. Garrick's most recent (and definitive) biographers, George Winchester Stone and George M. Kahrl, note Garrick's eagerness to cultivate good press relations but rightly find it "unthinkable" that Garrick had "any censoring hand" in newspapers "or," they add, "in Smollett's *Critical Review*, or in Johnson's *Idler* or *Rambler*, or Murphy's *Gray's Inn Journal*."[53] (It may have been a slightly different story, however, with Garrick's ties to Smollett's *British Magazine* in the 1760s, as will be discussed in chap. 9 below.) But that Smollett had been admitted to such circles, his influence acknowledged and his goodwill cultivated—all through the agency of his new review journal—marked a fundamental change in his relationship to the literary establishment of his day.

Smollett's position also exposed him to difficulties, as when Garrick was attacked in Cibber's *Two Dissertations on the Theatres*, for Cibber was also a friend of Smollett's. In his review of Cibber's book, Smollett handles this delicate situation tactfully and impartially. Due credit is given to Cibber for the "taste and judgment in many of his observations" (Au '56, 48). It is noted that Cibber "has candour enough to do ample justice to the merit of a gentleman [i.e., Garrick] who seems to be the particular object of his resentment" (Au '56, 49). The thrust of Cibber's attack—denouncing Garrick's innovative and highly animated acting technique (which Smollett had also mocked in *Peregrine Pickle*)[54]—is softened and diffused by the observation that Cibber "singles him out as an instance of faults which are perhaps too common on the stage" (Au '56, 49). Tacitly granting the truth of some of Cibber's complaints, Smollett also gently chastizes him for committing a "trespass" against Garrick of the same kind of which he accuses him (Au '56, 50). Apparently the balanced and diplomatic treatment worked. Cibber, like Garrick, continued to respect Smollett's judgment and authority, submitting manuscripts to him for his approval and in 1758 urging an aspiring playwright "to make of Friend of the Doctor [Smollett]," reasoning that "as he presides over the poetical Province in the CRITICAL REVIEW, your Piece will, in all Likelyhood, have a favourable character."[55] This pattern of authorial deference and solicitation repeated itself with increasing frequency over time and, although less obvious than the public protests of offended authors, formed an equally significant counterpoint to their complaints and threats.

One of the more unusual works Smollett reviewed in 1756 was the anonymous *Maxims, Characters, and Reflections* (Ap '56, 220–26).[56] Treating it first as a work of literature, Smollett again demonstrates his propensity for rules and genre criticism, insisting that even maxims have certain forms and standards. "Maxims," he writes, "ought to be equally concise and perspicuous, so as to flash conviction at sight"; they "ought not only to be clear, but also conveyed in all the beauty and energy of expression" (Oc '56, 222). But the review is most important because Smollett uses it as a pretext to make some serious observations about English society. He notes that the most distinctive quality of the English is their unparalleled diversity:

> *England* certainly produces a greater variety of character, than any other country in the known world; and the peculiarities of each individual are more strongly marked in this than in any other climate. We are indeed a

nation of originals; and our oddities are so remarkable, that the natives of other countries never behold an *Englishman*, without expressing curiosity or surprize. (Mr '56, 220)

This statement illuminates one aspect of the comic vision behind Smollett's novels. It suggests that in his role as satirical novelist and caricaturist supreme, Smollett is actually celebrating, reveling in the eccentricities and foibles of the English people.[57]

In explaining how this healthy diversity of character came to be, Smollett emphasizes political and social influences over natural or climactic causes:

> But, our characters are perhaps more strongly influenced by that spirit of liberty and independence, which enables every man to pursue his own natural byas and turn of thinking, without fear of punishment and censure. Our singularities grow up as nature implanted them. Our education is as various as the whims and caprices of our parents: our enquiries are unlimited and unrestrained. We are not overawed in our politics, or restricted in our notions of religion; but at liberty to drink at every fountain of science, and give a loose to every flight of imagination. (Mr '56, 220)

Despite its nationalistic overtones and passing glance at French authoritarianism, this round affirmation of the liberty and enlightenment the English enjoy suggests Smollett's view of the advantages of England's (relatively) free marketplace of ideas. In giving a hearing to both sides of controversies, sometimes even inviting exchanges in the pages of the *Critical* itself, and attempting to mediate impartially, Smollett tried to uphold the ideals and methods of what he perceived as the ongoing Enlightenment in England.

The remaining literary articles Smollett contributed in 1756 are all translations of articles from the French *Journal encyclopédique*. The first is an exchange of letters between Voltaire and the French Academy concerning piracies of his publications. They are drawn from articles in the January 1756 issue of the *Journal* (interestingly enough without his citing the source),[58] and printed in the *Critical* as:

> "A Letter from Monsieur *de Voltaire* to the *French* Academy, concerning two performances, which have been lately published in his name" (Mr '56, 181–82).
> "The Answer, by Mr. *Duclos*, secretary, in the name of the *French* Academy" (Mr '56, 182).
> "A second Letter from M. *de Voltaire* to the same Academy" (Mr '56, 182–84).

The second is a translation of "A Letter from an *Englishman* to the authors of the *Journal Encyclopédique*, at *Paris*" (Mr '56, 184–85), concerning the riotous reception at Drury Lane of a French ballet production in November 1755.[59] These articles reveal one important source of foreign news other than correspondents and raise the question of how far Smollett was dependent on and influenced by foreign journals. More significantly, they are typical of Smollett's efforts to keep the British public in touch with the network of learned journals and societies on the Continent. That he translates these articles into English suggests both the kind of audience he imagined he was reaching—literate, but not learned—and his desire to accommodate it.

The subjects of the articles he chose to reprint are noteworthy. Voltaire's letters complain of unscrupulous and inaccurate piracies and the use of his name to sell fraudulent works, both practices Smollett knew and loathed from his own experience of the publishing world. That Voltaire could appeal to an authoritative body such as the French Academy and publish his corrective statements through their agencies, probably drew Smollett's admiration and fueled his sense of the need for such resources in England. Perhaps, too, be anticipated the *Critical*'s partially filling that role. The articles also show early signs of Smollett's interest in Voltaire, an interest that would flower in the 1760s when he became, together with Francklin, the first author to present the English public with a translation of Voltaire's complete works.[60]

The "Letter from an Englishman" describes a disgraceful episode at Garrick's Drury Lane Theatre in the fall of 1755. Garrick had invited the French ballet master Noverre to stage his celebrated *Chinese Festival*; the result, according to the correspondent, was that despite a "magnificent" production, a Francophobe mob forced it to close unceremoniously. The praise for Garrick's initiative and his production management, the disdain for the "ridiculous national prejudices" of the mob, and the idea that art transcends national boundaries all conform with Smollett's own views. Despite this and the fact that the article had interest as an account of an occurrence in England, it is still remarkable that Smollett chose to present the English reading public with such an unflattering image of itself, as reflected through the unsympathetic medium of a French journal. Cosmopolitan they would need to be to accept such an embarrassing episode.

iii. HISTORY

History was another field in which Smollett took a very personal interest. He had been writing since mid-1755 his *Complete History of England*, three volumes of which were to appear in April 1757 and the fourth in January 1758.[61] Although its critical reception was mixed, it was a tremendous commercial success; further editions were immediately called for and by 1765, according to the advertisements, "nearly 20,000 copies" had been sold.[62] It was followed by the equally successful *Continuation of the Complete History of*

England, which Smollett began publishing serially in May 1760.[63] In addition, Smollett had been involved in compiling and editing the multivolume *Modern Part of the Universal History* at least since 1754 and perhaps as early as 1751.[64] Then, too, as Wordsworth's high opinion of Smollett's prose suggests, his historical writing was stylish and readable. It is understandable, therefore, that he considered himself an authority on history-writing.

He reviewed three works of history in 1756:

> Richard Rolt, *A New and Accurate History of South America* (Mr '56, 97–106).
> [Anon.], *Letters on Mr. Hume's History of Great Britain* (Ap '56, 248–53).
> David Hume, *The History of Great Britain*, vol. 2. (De '56, 385–404).[65]

The importance of Hume's *History* was self-evident, but the reasons for devoting a full review (the lead article of the March issue) to Rolt's *History* are less obvious. Smollett categorically denounced it as "a very trivial, insipid, injudicious and defective performance, without plan, method, learning, accuracy or elegance; an unmeaning composition of shreds, rags, and remnants" (Mr '56, 98). Why then review it at length? The explanation lies in Smollett's sense of the dignity and importance of history-writing and his perception that Rolt's *History* amounted to a gross imposture on the public that had to be exposed. In methodically analyzing its flaws, Smollett outlined his own ideas about historiography.

He begins with sources and authorities. The good historian, in Smollett's view, is careful to draw on comprehensive and authoritative sources; he will "compare different accounts" and "collate authorities" (Mr '56, 98). Smollett castigates the artlessness of Rolt's pilferage from some authorities, the inaccuracy and deceit of his references to others, and the ignorance he shows in failing to consult still others of the highest authority (Mr '56, 98–100). Organization and narrative flow are also essential, but here too Rolt fails: "Instead of proceeding with the history of *America*, he, like the crab, seeming *downwards to climb, and backwards to advance*, retires in the second chapter as far back as *Minos* king of *Crete*, from whom he makes a sudden transition to the *Pisans, Florentines, Genoese, Venetians, Vasco de Gama*, and *Christopher Columbus*" (Mr '56, 99). Errors of fact are especially intolerable to Smollett and he ridicules such examples as Rolt's observation that in the tropics subterranean gold deposits are generated by the heat of the sun (Mr '56, 100). Above all, history must be entertaining. Rolt's failure on this count is so egregious that Smollett contents himself with facetiously quoting long and impenetrably dull specimens of Rolt's prose (Mr '56, 101–6).

But Smollett's most serious lamentation about Rolt's *History* is that it is a kind of national disgrace: "We own ourselves warmed with a sort of national indignation, against those who by their presumptuous ignorance depreciate and degrade the character of their country" (Mr '56, 98). Historical writings, it seems, are a particularly important measure of a nation's intellectual achievement. Largely because such works are produced under the corrupt patronage of the booksellers, Smollett complains, "the British learning of this age is grown into contempt among other nations" (Mr '56, 97).

In these remarks, Smollett was not merely setting the stage for the appearance of his own *History*: this is amply proved by his favorable treatment of Hume's *History* the same year (De '56, 385–404). Although Smollett endorsed some criticisms of Hume's *History* in his review of the *Letters on Mr. Hume's History of Great Britain* (Ap '56, 248–53) and raised others in his own review of it, Smollett pronounced it overall "one of the best histories which modern times have produced" (De '56, 404). This would seem finally to dispel suspicions (lingering well into the twentieth century) that Smollett's own *History* was written primarily to displace Hume's and usurp its commercial success.[66]

In his review of *Letters on Hume's History*, however, Smollett fully supported the author's main argument: that Hume had unduly characterized the Protestant Reformation as prone to "enthusiasm" and "fanatacism" (Ap '56, 250). On this, Smollett could readily agree, secure in his own religious orthodoxy and, presumably, that of his readership. But what principally attracted Smollett to this particular critique of Hume, out of the many then being published, was its restrained and reasonable manner. "We could wish to see," he wrote, "the rest of Mr. *Hume's* performances as impartially canvassed and as fairly refuted as those parts which have fallen under the inspection of the author of these letters" (Ap '56, 253). No subscriber to Hume's rational skepticism or reputed atheism, Smollett nevertheless respected his genius. Differences of opinion notwithstanding, therefore, what mattered most to Smollett in such disputes were the merits of argument and the level of discourse.

Smollett's review of Hume's *History* brought into contact the two most prominent British historians of the mideighteenth century, with revealing results. The article opens with glowing praise for "one of the few performances of modern authors, which we can read with satisfaction and commend with pleasure" (De '56, 385) and closes twenty pages later with a summary tribute to "one of the best histories which modern times have produced" (De '56, 404). But between these panegyrical brackets, Smollett devotes much of his attention, in carefully modulated phrases, to the book's "little blemishes"—the flaws that, in Smollett's opinion, mar Hume's historical judgment and method.

Like Hume, Smollett was to be criticized as historian for his supposed Jacobite sympathies and bias.[67] His name and Hume's were often linked together: the two were reviled as biased "Scotch historiographers,"[68] an association not discouraged in later years when publishers commonly spliced Smollett's *Continuation* onto Hume's *History* and published them as one.[69] Yet in his review, Smollett takes issue with Hume on just this point, accusing him of showing "a warm (not to call it a weak) side towards those princes of the *Stuart* family who have sat upon the throne of *England*" (De '56, 385). In particular, Smollett criticizes Hume for treating Charles II and James II with "overstrained tenderness" and proceeds to redress Hume's depiction of them by repainting them, in long descriptive passages, as unredeemed villains and cowards (De '56, 389–92). Ironically, one of Smollett's first detractors was to accuse him, when his *History* appeared a year later, of being too soft on the villainy of another Stuart: James I.[70] This distinction between Smollett and Hume, really one of degree between two totally un-Jacobitical historians, was lost on the blindly anti-Scottish public of the 1750s and 1760s; but it was one that Smollett, ever self-conscious about his position in English letters and affairs, was careful to draw, even through the anonymous channel of his review.

Also noteworthy are Smollett's Whiggish objections to Hume's views on monarchical power and the constitution. Smollett quotes Hume's statement that "the power of the sword had, in all ages, been allowed to be vested in the crown; and though no law conferred this prerogative, every parliament, till the last of the preceding reign, had willingly submitted to an authority more antient, and therefore more sacred than that of any positive statute" and then responds to it:

> That it is was more ancient than any positive statute may be doubted. Those who imagine all the liberty of the subject is the gift of the sovereign, may be of that opinion. We can conceive original monarchies formed by a contract between king and people, and in that case the sovereign could have no authority but what he derived from that compact. . . . Neither do we think the antiquity of any custom renders it the more sacred. Were customs to be sanctified in that manner, we should have retained to this day, many barbarous practices which are now happily laid aside and forgotten. (De '56, 387–88).

In asserting the notion of the British constitution as a mutual and vital "contract," Smollett shows a more liberal and progressive view of social and political change than his arch-Tory reputation might suggest. Smollett's differences with Hume—on the regicidical "prostitute" Milton, on royal prerogative, on the sanctity of tradition—support Donald Greene's conclusion that Smollett's reputation as a strict Tory is unfounded. As Greene found, Smollett's political views are "difficult to fit into any neat predetermined pattern" and rather than "Tory" or "Whig" they are best described as "independent."[71]

Smollett's crucial difference with Hume, however, centered on historical method. Smollett used the review to present his objections to what might be called the "new history"—history based on interpretation and analysis or, in Smollett's term, "philosophizing." Treating Hume with tact and circumspection, Smollett writes:

> Were we disposed to find fault, we should disapprove of the numerous reflections which occur in every page, and instead of elucidating the subject not only perplex the reader, but also serve to fix upon the historian the charge of vanity, singularity, and affectation. This rage of reflecting, and even of dogmatizing, seems to have possessed all the late compilers, in this as well as in other countries of *Europe*. Histories are metamorphosed into dissertations; the chain of events is broken, the reader's attention diffused; and his judgement anticipated: peculiar incidents that distinguish the complexion of times, and form the features of the most remarkable individuals, are overlooked and omitted, and all character distorted into grotesque figures made up of conceit and antithesis.———This, however, is not the case with Mr. *Hume*. His reflections are, for the most part, just, tho' sometimes superfluous. (De '56, 386)

For Smollett, the straight narration of events with a minimum of commentary was both the essence and the highest grace of history. In his sensible reappraisal of Smollett the historian, Greene has argued that, although subsequent developments in historiography proved Hume's the more forward-looking and Smollett's the outmoded method, this fact does not make Smollett's historiography less valid or less valuable than either Hume's or much of the history that followed in the nineteenth century. Especially in the second half of the twentieth century, of course, the ideological assumptions and methods of interpretive history are again highly suspect.

These ideas led Smollett to emphasize the importance of narrative style. On this count he found Hume too often "inflated or affected" and "perhaps . . . in the main, deficient in weight and simplicity" (De '56, 392). Both the passages that Smollett quotes from Hume in his review and those that Greene compares in his study with parallel passages from Smollett's *History* demonstrate the justice of his criticism. In fact, Smollett may have been generous: Joseph Priestley, in his school textbook *The Rudiments of English Grammar*, quoted Hume more than twice as often as any other author to give examples of bad grammar and other errors.[73] For Smollett, historical prose should be vivid and interesting, and Hume wrote too "tamely," especially in describing battles. "Nothing is more agreeable to an *English* reader," Smollett says, "than a battle well told" (De '56, 394). Coming from a successful novelist, as Greene observes, these views "are not too surprising."[74] The differences evident here concerning purpose, style, and perhaps, by extension, even readership, are borne out in their different ideas about methods of publication.

The success of Smollett's *History* was fostered by its publication in serial numbers, a method of which Smollett greatly approved, as indicated by his boasting to Moore in 1758 that "the weekly Sale of the *History* has increased to above Ten thousand."[75] By contrast, as his letters to his publisher Millar reveal, Hume despised such commercial tactics. "I like much better your publishing in Volumes than in Numbers," he wrote to Millar in 1762. "Tho' this last Method has been often practic'd, it has somewhat of a quackish Air, which you have always avoided as well as myself."[76] Indeed, in the same letter, he instructs Millar not even to include an engraved frontispiece in his *History*—as Smollett had done—saying: "I do not imagine, because these Ornaments have help'd off the Sale of Smollett's History, that mine would be the better for them."

Yet despite all these differences, Smollett and Hume genuinely respected each other as historians. Hume was of course aware of their unavoidable rivalry. In 1758, without a trace of rancor, he wrote to console Millar: "I am afraid, this extraordinary Run upon Dr. Smollett has a little hurt your Sales: But these things are only temporary."[77] Hume's esteem for Smollett as a historian emerges in his light hearted remark to another prominent historian, William Robertson: "A plague take you! Here I sat near the historical summit of Parnassus, immediately under Dr. Smollett; and you have the impudence to squeeze yourself by me, and place yourself directly under his feet."[78]

To his credit, Smollett had set the tone for their relations in his review in 1756. He passed up the opportunity to undermine a major rival—perhaps the clearest such opportunity of his career—in order to pay due respect to Hume's accomplishments and to promote his *History*, even as his own was forthcoming. They remained friends and mutual supporters thereafter. Hume was to pay high praise to the *Critical* and its writers in 1759, even as he wrote to rebut an earlier article with which he totally disagreed (Ap '59, 323–34). A decade later, they were exchanging warm compliments as Smollett prepared to go abroad for the last time. Rather emotionally, Smollett closed in saying: "I shall always remember with Pleasure, and recapitulate with Pride, the friendly Intercourse I have maintained with one of the best men, and, undoubtedly, the best writer of the age."[79] That "friendly Intercourse" with one of the greatest thinkers of the century, initiated and partly conducted in the pages of the *Critical*, approaches very near to Smollett's original ideal of the *Critical*'s function in the republic of letters.

"His Several Provinces": Smollett on Art, Science, and Politics

Pope's cautionary advice to critics not to overextend themselves that "Each might his sev'ral Province well command" (*Essay on Criticism*, 66) was lost on Smollett. His ambitions for his journal and its readership were too great. Of the three major areas beyond history and literature that he covered—art, science, and politics—there was little in his background to indicate particular competence to discuss any of them, except perhaps, because of his medical training, science. Yet he took them on, reviewed energetically and intelligently, and displayed a facility for communicating these subjects to the general public in clear, accessible terms. Although wildly different, each of these areas of his reviewing adds in its way to our understanding of Smollett's thought and writing, the aims and achievement of the *Critical*, and the state of culture and society in the mideighteenth century.

i. ART

Perhaps nothing is more surprising about Smollett's contributions to the *Critical* in 1756 than the discovery that he was the chief art critic. This has gone almost completely unnoticed. Roper duly reported the 1756 attributions by article number but, as his focus was on books reviewed, understandably gave no titles of works of art reviewed.[1] In fact there has been little or no mention of these art reviews anywhere in eighteenth-century scholarship, with the sole exception of a short passage in Ronald Paulson's superb biography, *Hogarth: His Life, Art, and Times*. And even Paulson focuses briefly on only one of the art reviews, that of Hogarth's triptych altar painting for St. Mary Redcliffe in Bristol, and was apparently unaware that Smollett had actually written the article himself.[2] Yet in tracing through Hamilton's annotations as reported by Roper, one finds that Smollett introduced and largely conducted a regular feature on painting, sculpture, and engraving throughout the first six months of the *Critical*. Although the articles are short, in the course of them Smollett appraises the following recent works by contemporary artists:

> Gavin Hamilton, *An Allegorical picture . . . for his Grace the Duke of Bedford* (Ja/Fe '56, 94).
>
> Sir Robert Strange, "Drawings for three different prints [taken from paintings by Pietro de Cortona and Salvator Rosa]" (Ja/Fe '56, 94–95).
>
> John Michael Rysbrack, *Hercules* [sculpture] (Ja/Fe '56, 95–96).
>
> Giovanni Battista Plura, *Diana and Endymion* [sculpture] (Ja/Fe '56, 96; Mr '56, 192).
>
> Joseph Wilton, [several pieces of sculpture, including:] *Belvidere Apollo, Venus de Medicis, Alexander the Great,* and *The Dancing Fawn* (My '56, 387).
>
> William Hogarth, [triptych painting] *The Sealing of the Sepulchre, The Ascension,* and *The Three Marys* (Jn '56, 479–80).[3]

The significance of these articles is at least threefold. First, they are a historical breakthrough: they constitute the first attempt by an English periodical to present a regular review of current works of art and they include what appears to be the first review in a periodical of an exhibition by a contemporary artist. Second, they put Smollett and the *Critical* in the forefront of the widespread efforts in mideighteenth-century England to develop and publicize a national art. Third, they radically alter Smollett's traditional image—fostered both by his detractors and by some of the fictional personae he created—as a boorish, cantankerous Philistine, undiscriminating and largely uninterested in art.

There were magazines and newspapers that had offered, before the *Critical*, occasional notices about works of art. But these were infrequent and irregular, and they tended to be either obituaries and biographical notes about famous artists or brief announcements of new monuments and statues that focused on the celebrity of the subject and sponsor, rather than the talents of the artist and the qualities of the work itself.[4] Thus in general, sepulchral monuments and statues of famous men got some attention, while other works were ignored. In the absence of public galleries and exhibitions, the artist's best hope for publicity was to publish prints of his works.[5] As late as 1760, according to William T. Whitley, "and for many years afterwards, the press paid little attention to picture galleries or questions relating to the fine arts, and it was not until after 1770 that the newspapers began to review exhibitions systematically."[6] Both Whitley and Andrew Shirley point to the *Imperial Magazine*'s review of the first exhibition by the newly formed Society of Artists in 1760 as a landmark in the history of art criticism: the first review in a periodical of an art exhibition.[7] Gradually thereafter, writes

Shirley, "newspapers began to take art seriously and to report the exhibi-tions, until by Johnson's death such reviews were stock-in-trade."

But now it can be shown that Smollett's *Critical Review* was the real pioneer in art criticism for the general public. Several years before the first public exhibitions were held under the auspices of the Society of Artists (1760) and the Free Society of Artists (1761), Smollett presented his readers with a review of a private exhibition by the sculptor Joseph Wilton:

> A man who visits Mr. Wilton's performances, can hardly help imagining himself in the [*ergasterion*: a studio or workshop] of a *Grecian* artist. There we see the elegance of the *Belvidere Apollo* starting from the block that seems to have inclosed him. There we view the *Venus de Medicis* emerging from the marble, with all the graces of feminine beauty. There we behold an admirable colossal bust of *Alexander the Great*. There we admire the dancing fawn, copied from the original statue of *Florence*, and executed with such a tender chisel, with such delicacy, taste, and precision, that we cannot conceive it inferior to the figure from which it was delineated. (My '56, 387)

Having followed the typical pattern of British artists of the period, Wilton in 1756 had just returned from a preparatory period in Italy and was now living in his father's house in London, which probably served also as studio and gallery.[8] Obviously, Smollett had visited him in his studio, for he comments on a work still in progress: "Besides these . . . Mr. *Wilton* has almost finished a fine expressive bust of the learned *Cocci*, member of the Academy of *Flor-ence*" (My '56, 387). Here, as in other articles, it is significant that Smollett seems to encourage his readers to visit the artist's gallery and view the works for themselves. In the corrective notice of Plura's (not Rysbrack's) *Diana and Endymion*, it is mentioned that this "ingenious artist" had died since the first notice was published (Ja/Fe '56, 96), but it is added that "he lived in *Oxford Road*; and there are to be seen, in the possession of his widow, some speci-mens of his skill, well worth the attention of the curious" (Mr '56, 192). Whether this encouragement had the desired effect cannot be determined, but certainly the artists must have appreciated the publicity.

While Smollett's contributions to this art section concentrated solely on domestic productions, installments in other issues (ascribed to Derrick, but evidently translated from foreign correspondence or journals) were devoted to foreign works of art. A statue by Perrin, tapestries by the Marquis de Marigny, maps engraved by Le Rouge, prints by Chenu and Poussin, and mezzotints by Marcadel are all briefly noted (Mr '56, 190–192 and Ap '56, 286). Under Smollett's direction, the *Critical* was fulfilling the pledge made in its "Proposals": to provide, in addition to book reviews, "an accurate Description of every remarkable Essay in the Practical Part of Painting, Sculpture, and Architecture, that may do Honour to modern artists of this or any other Kingdom."[9] Smollett was fully aware of the distinctiveness of his innovation. In summing up the achievements of the *Critical* after its first six months, he stated that the *Critical* reviewers took pride not only in the range of book reviews offered, but in "those [articles] upon painting and statuary, in which they stand unrivalled by any periodical writer of this kingdom" (preface, Ja/Fe '56, [ii]).

There were obviously problems in providing this feature each month and it appeared at irregular intervals. After the June issue, for example, no more articles appeared in 1756; there were only two in 1757 (Fe '57, 173–74 and My '57, 479) and one in 1758 (Mr '58, 265–66). But Smollett never abandoned the idea. One finds him in December 1756 appealing to Macaulay for an article on art, even proposing a possible subject: "I wish you could get an Article for the next number of the Review, on painting, Statuary or Engraving. What do you think of the Bacchus?"[10] But apparently Macaulay did not comply and the pressure of other duties prevented Smollett from doing it himself, all of which underscores the degree to which the art reviews were Smollett's own idea and responsibility. Except for Derrick, who worked under Smollett's supervision, and perhaps Macaulay, none of the other staff writers is known to have written even one art review. The arts feature may have been ahead of its time or at least ahead of the opportunities for the general public to view and comment on contemporary art. Certainly it stirred little response: in Smollett's exchanges with the public in the correspondence section printed at the end of each issue, the topic of art never arose. Nevertheless, as a pioneering effort, Smollett's arts feature helped prepare the way for the increasing attention paid to the arts by the periodical press and by the general public from the 1760s on.

One purpose runs throughout Smollett's art reviews: to announce and promote the emergence of a distinctly British school of artists, equal to any on the Continent. In one article he concludes: "We cannot help congratulating our country, on having produced such an artist as Mr. *Strange*, with whom very few engravers in *Europe* can come in competition" (Ja/Fe '56, 95). Of Hogarth's altar painting, he observes that "if this noble ornament should make its way into our churches, it will be the likeliest means to raise a *British* school of painters" (Jn '56, 479). The grandest proclamation comes in his review of Wilton:

> Our neighbors on the continent, will no longer reproach us with want of talent for the arts of Painting, Engraving, and Sculpture. We can boast a *Hogarth* and a *Hayman* for design; a *Strange* and a *Grignion* for drawing and engraving; and in statuary, a *Wilton* who has imported from *Italy*, the strength and accuracy of a *Bona Rota*, with all the taste and delicacy of a *Bernini*. (My '56, 387)

In addition to native-born (but usually European-trained) artists, Smollett extended his notice to such foreign-born artists as Plura and Rysbrack presumably because they had long worked in England and represented London's emerging reputation as an international center for artists.

However sanguine his opinions, Smollett shared the spirit of the many artists and friends of art who had been trying for years to organize some kind of an English academy of art. Several of those who schemed and negotiated for such an academy throughout the 1740s and 1750s were friends of Smollett's, including Hogarth, Hayman, and Wilkes.[11] Hayman, who had known Smollett since 1750 when he interceded unsuccessfully on Smollett's behalf with Garrick,[12] headed the committee of artists that negotiated with the Dilettanti Society about forming an academy in 1755; Wilkes, one of Smollett's closest friends until 1762 and one of those privy to Smollett's own academy plan in 1755, emerged as president of a group of artists who supported Hayman's plan for an exhibition in 1759.[13] Whatever Smollett's connection with any of their plans, it is clear that he directed the *Critical*'s art coverage in pursuit of similar goals.

But most of all, Smollett's art reviews signalize the unfairness and inaccuracy of his long-standing reputation for being tasteless, ignorant, and irreverently skeptical about art. That reputation largely stems from his *Travels* or, more precisely, from the distorted image projected through Sterne's caricature of Smollett as "Smelfungus" in *A Sentimental Journey through France and Italy*:

> I met Smelfungus in the grand portico of the Pantheon—he was just coming out of it—'*Tis nothing but a huge cock-pit*, said he—I wish you had said nothing worse of the Venus of Medicis, replied I—for in passing through Florence, I had heard he had fallen foul upon the goddess, and used her worse than a common strumpet, without the least provocation in nature.[14]

In his scholarly introduction to the *Travels*, Frank Felsenstein documents the sudden reversal of Smollett's reputation as a result of Sterne's and others' satirical attacks in the late 1760s.[15] Despite a revival of interest in the *Travels*, the "Smelfungus" myth has not died out. One modern scholar has said of Smollett: "His connection with Hogarth is the more striking when one considers that Smollett knew literally nothing about any other painter. Except when he speaks of Hogarth, his judgments on pictorial art are absurd."[16]

Smollett made no claims for himself as a connoisseur. In fact, his many self-effacing remarks seem to have contributed to his reputation. "After all," he writes in the *Travels*,

> I do not set up for a judge in these matters, and very likely I may incur the ridicule of the virtuosi for the remarks I have made: but I am used to speak my mind freely on all subjects that fall under the cognizance of my

senses; though I must freely own, there is something more than common sense required to discover and distinguish the more delicate beauties of painting.[17]

In both *Peregrine Pickle* (chaps. 46, 67, 68, and 113) and *Ferdinand Count Fathom* (chap. 32), Smollett had mocked the ignorance and pretentiousness of self-avowed art fanciers who hold forth authoritatively, but invariably prove to be parvenus, fools, or con men. In *Humphry Clinker*, Matthew Bramble is made to say at one point: "I must own I am no judge of painting, though very fond of pictures. I don't imagine that my senses would play me so false, as to betray me into admiration of anything that was very bad; but, it is true, I have often over-looked capital beauties, in pieces of extraordinary merit."[18] Even if one overlooks the problem of the "autobiographical temptation" to treat such remarks as Smollett's own opinions (as Boucé cautions us),[19] the bulk of opinions expressed in his books simply will not support a construction of them as signs of Smollett's inability to appreciate art. Bramble's remark, in fact, merely prefaces his accolades for the paintings of a "young gentleman of Bath."[20] And, while Smollett did cautiously and self-disparagingly express reservations about the *Venus de Medicis*, most of his comments about works of art in the *Travels* are appreciative, perceptive, and often enthusiastic.[21] Smollett's art reviews confirm this. The attitude of a man who could rhapsodize about Titian's *Venus* that it "has a sweetness of expression and tenderness of colouring, not to be described"[22] accords better with the tone of Smollett's art reviews than the grumblings of Sterne's Smelfungus.

No one would argue that Smollett's critiques are either theoretically sophisticated or deeply insightful. But for all the standard and somewhat superficial terms of description, there is also an appealing air of excitement and imaginative response. He describes Strange's engraving of "the finding of Romulus and Remus" thus:

> A shepherd presents one of the infants to his wife, who receives it with all the eagerness of benevolence, at the door of a cottage; while a little boy holds up his hands in a transport of childish curiosity, as if wishing to handle the prize: the daughter, within the cottage, eyes the scene with a look of meekness and satisfaction: a pigeon fondly flutters on a corner of the roof; and the back-ground exhibits a charming pastoral landscape, on which we see at a distance the wolf suckling the other twin. (Ja/Fe '56, 94–95)

Under Smollett's touch, the scene is not only described but animated; he invests figures with character and emotion, and, by way of closing, communicates a personal response: "Every figure in this performance is beautiful, benign, and expressive, and contributes to dispose the mind to peace, benevolence, and satisfaction" (Ja/Fe '56, 95). In describing Wilton's statues, Smollett's tone conveys imaginative engagement: the reader is made to feel the tension between the solid stone and the sculpted form, as he describes "the *Belvidere Apollo* starting from the block that seems to have inclosed him" (My '56, 387). At times his enthusiasm leads to hyperbole: "The accurate elegance, and delicacy of the drawing, are almost inconceivable" (Ja/Fe '56, 95). But some of his observations are quite perceptive. In describing Hogarth's *Ascension*, he points out a special effect: "The back ground is shut up with rocks, and the bottom of the cloudy mass, except on one side, where, under the skirts of the low-hung clouds, part of a magnificent city (supposed to be *Jerusalem*) appears to great advantage at a distance, illuminated by a flash of lightening under a darkened sky, which casts a vivid gloom over it" (Ja/Fe '56, 479). It is this same detail that art historian David Bindman singles out as one of the "extraordinary felicities" of the painting; Bindman's efforts to rehabilitate the painting's reputation in our time at least partly vindicate Smollett's unstintingly favorable appraisal in 1756.[23]

Rather remarkably, unlike any other category of Smollett's reviews, none of his art reviews contains a single word of negative comment. It was not his intention to make balanced appraisals. In the interest of promoting a British school of art, he offered nothing but encouragement to the artists. Still, in closing his review of Hogarth's painting, he expressed a mild reservation about Hogarth's abandoning caricature altogether for history painting: "It would be a just subject of public regret, if Mr. *Hogarth* should abandon a branch of painting in which he stands unrivalled and inimitable, to pursue another in which so many have already excelled" (Jn '56, 480). Perhaps in Smollett's words there is just a hint of friendly caution. But taken in sum, his encomiastic article on the *Ascension* triptych gave encouragement to Hogarth in pursuit of his private dream: to be a serious history painter.[24] By choosing to discuss Hogarth's work in this genre in the *Critical*, Smollett obviously meant to shape public perceptions of Hogarth as a serious artist, again perhaps with personal knowledge of Hogarth's aspirations. Such articles led some people to suspect that Hogarth had self-serving connections with the review journals. In 1763 Charles Churchill, for example, was to attack the satiric manner of Hogarth's works, together with the "Reviews [that] conspired thy wrath to swell" (*Epistle to William Hogarth*, 1. 228). The Smollett-Hogarth connection was certainly one of Churchill's targets here, and the *Critical Review* shared Hogarth's dubious distinction of having an entire Churchill satire devoted to it: *The Apology Addressed to the Critical Reviewers* (1761).

Smollett was to extend support to Hogarth often over the years. In 1759 he exposed the imposition of an opportunistic poet who claimed to have Hogarth's authorization for his *Poetical Description of Mr. Hogarth's Election Prints* (Ap '59, 274–75). In Smollett's *Continuation*, Hogarth comes in for special praise for having "excelled over all the world in exhibiting the scenes of ordinary life" (4: 131). Smollett's novels repeat the standard compliments so often paid to Hogarth by comic novelists of the time, typically an invocation beginning "it would require the pencil of Hogarth himself to. . ." (*Roderick Random*, chap. 47). More importantly, Smollett's close attention to Hogarth's works shaped his own creative imagination, as Robert Moore, Paulson, and others have shown. The inverted connection between the prostitute Miss Williams' reformation in *Roderick Random* (chap. 23) and the first plate of the *Harlot's Progress* and the debt to Hogarth's *Gate of Calais* for the details of an Anglo-Gallic confrontation in *Ferdinand Count Fathom* (chap. 28) are striking examples, although the most extensive imagistic evidence of Smollett's affinity for Hogarth is in *Sir Launcelot Greaves*, as will be seen below in chapter 9.

Smollett extended his encouragement to lesser-known artists as well. The thirty-three-year-old Gavin Hamilton whose "allegorical picture" Smollett generously praised (Ja/Fe '56, 94) did not really gain prominence until he began exhibiting through the Society of Artists (1762–71) and Royal Academy (1770–88) and even then he was "perhaps better known abroad than in Britain."[25] If Smollett knew Hamilton personally—both Scots, they had overlapped at Glasgow University in 1738 and maintained many ties with the same circles in Glaswegian society—then he may be "that poor man Mr. Hamilton" whom Smollett was trying to help through the charity of Macaulay in 1756.[26] Smollett paid Wilton a nice public compliment when, in *Sir Launcelot Greaves*, the narrator asserts that it would take the combined talents of "Praxiteles, and Roubillac, and Wilton" to design a beauty comparable to Aurelia (chap. 3). In a similar vein, Smollett has Matthew Bramble digress effusively on the merits of the young landscape painter, John Taylor of Bath; Bramble concludes that "this artist, I apprehend, will make a capital figure, as soon as his works are known."[27] The point of this episode has sometimes been misconstrued as a measure of Smollett's poor judgment, rather than what he meant it to be, a boost for a promising young artist.[28]

Throughout his career, Smollett also provided more material support for artists. In the course of publishing his works, Smollett and his publishers hired the services of many engravers, including notables such as Hayman, Strange, Grignion, and Ravenet, as well as lesser figures like Aliamet, Miller, Benoist, Clowes, Bannerman, Halett, and Walker.[29] In Hayman's case, Smollett commissioned his friend to design twenty-eight engravings for the translation of *Don Quixote* that he published by subscription in 1755. The illustrations were a major selling point for the book. Advertisements emphasized them and invited subscribers to come see the engravings on display in the shop.[30] Hayman also designed the engravings for the fourth edition of *Roderick Random* (1755). In 1760, Aliamet was hired to engrave a portrait of Smollett for the frontispiece of the first volume of the *Continuation*. There is

little evidence about what paintings or sculpture Smollett bought in his lifetime, except that he is known to have commissioned five portraits of himself;
they include paintings by Willem Verelst, Nathaniel Dance, Thomas Gainsborough, Joshua Reynolds, and an unknown Italian painter of the 1760s.
There may have been still another portrait, painted "a short time before his
death, at the particular request of Voltaire," if a rumor circulating in November 1771 had any truth to it.[31]

Although never an aficionado, Smollett was in the true sense an amateur of
the art world. Socializing and scheming with many artist friends, commis-
sioning various works for his publications and for his personal pleasure, and,
most significantly, introducing into the history of journalism and of art criticism a feature devoted to reviewing contemporary art, Smollett was perhaps as
active in support of the arts in England as any professional writer of his era.

ii. SCIENCE AND MEDICINE

In terms of quantity, Smollett devoted more attention to scientific and medical publications than any other kind of literature in 1756. This was unavoidable. The number of scientific works then being published, combined with
the *Critical*'s commitment to review every new publication, led to the allocation of more than thirty percent of the *Critical*'s contents to these subjects.[32]
In 1756 Smollett reviewed some twenty himself, including the voluminous
compilations of scientific papers published as *The Philosophical Transactions
of the Royal Society*. This emphasis was also a reflection of his priorities for
the *Critical*. Of course, as an experienced physician, his interest in medical
treatises is understandable. Moreover, Smollett had written *An Essay on the
External Use of Water* (1752), edited William Smellie's books on obstetrics (to
one of which he contributed a case history), and had reviewed two medical
works for the *Monthly* in 1751–52.[33] However, although his formal education
in science was limited to his medical training in Glasgow (not inconsiderable
in itself),[34] Smollett's reviews evince his interest and reading in many
branches of science. In the course of them, he analyzed—often minutely and
authoritatively—essays in chemistry, physics, geology, archeology, anatomy,
astronomy, natural history, and medicine.

No attempt will be made here to appraise the scientific merits either of the
works under review or of Smollett's ideas. It suffices to say that the consensus
among the scholars who have considered Smollett's scientific opinions is that
they are neither greatly advanced nor retarded for his time.[35] Yet from other
perspectives, even a cursory examination of his reviews illuminates many of
his general attitudes about science and society, about academic versus
amateur scientists, about the role of learned societies, and about that collec-
tive enterprise of the Enlightenment, the compilation, systemization, and

dissemination of knowledge.

In one of his first reviews, on Birch's *History of the Royal Society*, Smollett proclaimed his faith in the supreme value of scientific inquiry. Conceding that wrong-headed or trivial essays occasionally appear in the Royal Society's *Transactions*, he finds them ultimately harmless:

> In this detail, 'tis true, we meet with some things that may appear trifling, and some that are fictitious and unphilosophical. Mention is made of *sympathetic* powders, a lunar sphere, the art of flying, &c. but these can give no offence, if it is considered, that as no fact or opinion is admitted in experimental philosophy but upon the faith of experiments, neither ought any thing to be exploded, till it has undergone the same test. Besides, such things are accidentally useful in another way; they are the *straws* and *feathers* with which crazy fellows tickle themselves, till they expose their own futility and ill-nature. (Ja/Fe '56, 42)

He then continues with a remarkable statement about science as the highest field of intellectual endeavor:

> Let such [the frivolous and skeptical] laugh; let even a poet, enraptured with the dreams of a sublimer but less intelligible philosophy, call the *society* an assembly of *dunces*; experimental philosophy, conscious of her own dignity, smiles at the vain insult; and shall continue to diffuse useful and ornamental improvements thro' human life, when all our rhimes, perhaps the art of rhiming itself, shall be buried in eternal oblivion. (Ja/Fe '56, 42)

Such a statement, its terms distantly foreshadowing those of C. P. Snow's *The Two Cultures* two centuries later, comes as something of a surprise from a poet, playwright, and novelist, a self-professed gentleman of letters steeped in the tradition of Pope and Swift. In the contest between Ancients and Moderns, although Smollett is usually seen as the staunch advocate of classical learning, here he declares himself at least as steadfast an ally of modern science.

Smollett's defense of the Royal Society in this review helps to counterbalance his criticisms of it elsewhere and his reputation for disapproving of the Royal Society as elitist, ineffectual, and excessively speculative. As G. S. Rousseau has pointed out, Smollett's support for the Society of Arts in part grew out of his disillusionment with the Royal Society.[36] And in the *Continuation*, Smollett remarks at one point that the Society "seems to have degenerated in its researches."[37] But Smollett's criticisms must not be exaggerated. He was not blindly prejudiced against the Royal Society. He did in fact mention the Royal Society with approval at other points in his *Continuation*, as for example when he gave a complimentary account of the Royal Society's parties of astronomers sent to Africa and the East Indies in 1760 to observe a solar eclipse.[38]

Smollett's review of Birch's *History* provides further evidence of his esteem both for the Society itself and for individuals connected with it, such as Boyle. It is an article on Boyle's experiments with gases that Smollett chooses to quote as a specimen "of the scrupulous caution and judgment with which the first founders of the society proceeded in their enquiries, observing every where the rules and examples left them by the immortal *Bacon*" (Ja/Fe '56, 44). He refers to the Royal Society as "that illustrious body" (Ja/Fe '56, 41) and expresses approval of its basic purpose and practices. In other reviews, even when he complains of lapses in the quality of papers in the *Transactions*, it is primarily out of regard for "the reputation of the Society" (Jl '56, 528).

Smollett had a basically "democratic" or, more precisely, "meritocratic" attitude toward science, as Rousseau has argued,[39] and his reviews confirm and clarify this attitude. In reviewing Dr. Robert Taylor's presidential address to the College of Physicians (*Oratio Anniversaria in Theatro Collegii Regalis Medicorum Londinensium*), Smollett sharply criticizes Taylor's elitism. To Smollett's annoyance, Taylor seems to be an educational bigot who believes that only Oxford and Cambridge offer genuine learning and that "there is no learning without their own pale" (Mr '56, 173). Bitterly resenting (for obvious reasons) Taylor's attempt to preserve "the great monopoly of medicine," Smollett points out that fine medical education can be acquired at other institutions, as well as from simply reading the proper authorities (Mr '56, 173). Here again there is an undercurrent of the provincial outsider resenting the exclusivity, real or imagined, of elite English institutions.

The same democratic attitude appears in other reviews. In discussing the *Essays and Observations* published by "a Society in Edinburgh," Smollett perceives a double benefit resulting from their efforts:

> Such a community composed of persons endowed with learning and probity, will contribute to the improvement of philosophy, not only by their own hints and discoveries; but also by exciting and diffusing a spirit of inquiry and emulation among people who without their example, would never have dreamed of exercising their faculties in these pursuits, or of publishing the remarks they might have made in the course of their observations. (Jn '56, 409)

Approval of one society did not, however, entail the rejection of others. Smollett championed the whole concept of such organizations and therefore approved of any, whether learned or amateurish, elite or humble, that contributed to the progress of the arts and sciences and to the dissemination of knowledge through all levels of society. Thus in addition to this society in Edinburgh, he could support both the Society of Artists *and* the Royal Society, as well as the Society for the Encouragement of Arts, Manufactures, and

Commerce, and the many academies and societies on the Continent whose publications were regularly reported in the foreign section of the *Critical*.

Smollett's science reviews show him, as one would expect, emphasizing experimental proofs in the best Baconian tradition and upholding the value of scientific discoveries with practical applications over the more theoretical and purely speculative branches of science. But there are also some surprises. In two of his reviews in 1756, for example, Smollett speaks out vehemently against experimentation that inflicts extreme suffering on laboratory animals. In one review, Smollett examines the report of a scientist who tested the function of opium on the nervous system of animals. Smollett is outraged. "This article," he writes, "is filled with the account of such barbarities, as must fill every humane reader with horror. Such as opening animals alive, plucking out their hearts, pinching and burning their spinal marrow, poisoning them with glysters, injections, *&c.* in order to ascertain the *modus operandi* of opium" (Jn '56, 414). After describing a gruesome list of procedures, Smollett closes with an objection:

> From these and other experiments Dr. *Whytt* infers, that the effects of opium are not owing as some have thought, to its producing sleep; on the contrary, the sleep which it occasions, seems to be only a consequence of its impairing the sensibility of the whole nervous system. Is this really a discovery? Or, supposing it to be a discovery, is it of consequence enough to justify such a series of cruel executions, as one would be apt to imagine, must destroy that humanity and tenderness of heart by which every physician ought to be distinguished? (Jn '56, 415)

In a second review, Smollett protests the same kinds of experimental techniques even more vehemently because their findings had already been demonstrated by an earlier experimenter (Au '56, 32–33). This is hardly the voice of the novelist with whom (perhaps more than with any other) one associates cracked pates, broken limbs, bloodied noses—physical pain, pranks, and deformity of so many kinds. In his stance as an early and outspoken critic of vivisection and unnecessary cruelty to experimental animals, Smollett anticipates attitudes that were not to become commonplace for many years and certainly did not find such fervent expression in many quarters in the eighteenth century. Here again one is forced to temper or modify the traditional image of Smollett as a rough satirist, a hardened veteran of wartime naval surgery, and a rather crusty character all around.

Despite these instances of humane objections to certain experiments, however, it is true that Smollett emphasized the importance of experimental proofs and practical application in scientific research. For this reason, he was particularly hard on the "antiquarians"—the fledgling archaeologists who were beginning to examine and interpret the remains of antiquity. Smollett mocked the triviality of Pegge's findings in his *Dissertations on Some Anglo-Saxon Remains* (Ja/Fe '56, 74–75) and those of Ward and others in the *Philosophical Transactions* (Au '56, 29–30 and Se '56, 129). Yet it was not a blanket prejudice: he quoted approvingly and generously from reports on the important discoveries at Herculaneum (Au '56, 15–19) and endorsed Borlase's researches into the antiquity of the Scilly Islands (Ja/Fe '56, 56–65). On the kindred sciences of geology and paleontology he could also be severe, as in his facetious remarks on Parson's observations on rocks and fossils (Au '56, 25); yet he treated with respect another paleontologist's account of a fossilized fish (Se '56, 129–30).

Books on natural history and geography, especially of distant lands, held a special interest for Smollett. He was attentive to the field perhaps in part because he relied on such books for material to fill out the sections on non-European countries in the *Universal History*.[40] Years later, he was to consider writing a natural history of Nice himself.[41] Thus he took interest in Frederic Norden's *Voyage to Egypt and Nubia*, calling it "the best description now extant of the course of the *Nile*, and the monuments of antiquity in upper *Ægypt*" (Se '56, 188). He was less satisfied with Borlase's *Observations on the Islands of Scilly* (Ja/Fe '56, 56–65), Browne's *Civil and Natural History of Jamaica* (Jn '56, 389–409), and *A Letter from New Jersey* (Oc '56, 280–81), but he attributed this more to the "barrenness" of the subjects described than to the talents of the authors. In each case, he tried to salvage a few points of interest for the general reader, whether about sugar cane (Jn '56, 393–400), the manufacture of kelp (J/Fe '56, 64–65), or American rattlesnakes (Oc '56, 280–81). At his best, Smollett seemed to understand how much more useful it was for his reader to get an interesting fact from a book than simply to learn that it was bad; in fact, his journal might serve to rescue and transmit to the wider public one of the few valuable bits in a book that would itself sink from sight.

Practical utility was for Smollett the highest end of science. Thus he singled out Home's *Experiments on Bleaching* as "a very valuable attempt to extend the use of chymistry to purposes subservient to a national advantage" (Mr '56, 106). A short tract on *The Manner of Securing Buildings from Fire* he welcomed as a "laudable instance of true patriotism and national improvement" (Ap '56, 263). Essays by Dr. Stephen Hales received glowing approval as the products of one "who has always dedicated his excellent talents to the immediate service of his fellow-creatures" (Se '56, 132). On the same grounds, he approved of investigations into methods of estimating population (Se '56, 126–29) and new techniques in cataract surgery (Jn '56, 415–19).

By the same standards, Smollett was highly intolerant of the foolish and specious. The theory that earthquakes are caused by electricity, posited in *A Plain Account of the Cause of Earthquakes*, is greeted with ridicule (Jn '56, 457–58). So also are a simplistic report of cold weather in Surrey (Jl '56, 530) and selected oddities from various works, including Lucas's *Essay on Waters* (My '56, 321–45), Linden's *Treatise on the Waters at Llandrindod* (Se '56, 97–109), and Mooney's *Dissertation on Venereal Disease* (Jn '56, 459–62). Smollett's insistence on common sense above all is perhaps best exemplified by his response to one author's theory that "water-spouts" (a kind of cyclone or tornado moving over water) are merely heavy downpours of rain from thick clouds. To refute this theory, Smollett argues that these waterspouts actually draw water up from the body beneath, and he characteristically rests his case on a concrete proof: the fish that are invariably reported to fall from them (Au '56, 22–23).

Also in the Baconian tradition, Smollett attends closely to questions of experimental method. Thus, he rejects the conclusions in one pamphlet on inoculation primarily because they are based on "hear-say" evidence (Oc '56, 278). Conversely, he approves of Simpson's refinements on the experimental methods of astronomers, endorsing Simpson's demonstration that taking the mean of many observations gives more reliable results than "one single observation, taken with due care" (Au '56, 13–14).

This is not to say, however, that Smollett completely rejects the more theoretical branches of science. His and the other *Critical* writers' emphasis on applied science has led at least one scholar to conclude that, of all the contemporary periodicals, "the *Critical* was probably the most conservative periodical in the scientific attitude it presented."[42] But if one looks no further than Samuel Johnson's reviews of many of the same books, one finds them at least as conservative in attitude as Smollett's. Like Smollett, Johnson gives special praise to such practical treatises as Home's *Experiments on Bleaching* and his quoted selections tend to be about practical matters, such as articles on china varnishes, the manufacture of kelp, and methods for softening water.[43] Johnson also emphasizes the importance of proper experimental methods.[44] In fact Johnson raises an objection to the Royal Society's *Transactions* of a kind that appears nowhere in Smollett's reviews: in one of his reviews in the *Literary Magazine*, Johnson bids the Society attend "more to the sacrosanctity of religion, which seems treated with too little reverence when it is represented as hypothetical and controvertible, that all mankind proceeded from one original."[45] One can readily imagine where Johnson's views would have placed him in the Darwinian debates of the next century; but, more to the point, such a statement places Smollett's scientific attitudes by comparison rather nearer the center of the intellectual spectrum.

Moreover, although his personal preference was for practical discoveries, Smollett expressed appreciation for the theoretical sciences and the pure spirit of intellectual inquiry behind them:

When we consider any production of nature or of art, we are not satisfied with viewing it in its more advanced state, or in its maturity, and perhaps enumerating the various uses to which it may be applied: our curiosity leads us farther, to enquire into its origin, its early culture, and the successive slow steps by which it arrives at perfection; for without these we can have but an imperfect knowledge of the subject we are examining. (Ja/Fe '56, 41)

Smollett readily approved of discoveries in fields where no immediate practical application was evident, such as mathematics (Jl '56, 528), astronomy (Se '56, 134), and electricity (Se '56, 130–32). He actually defended theoretical speculation: "As no fact or opinion is admitted in experimental philosophy but upon the faith of experiments, neither ought any thing to be exploded, till it has undergone the same test" (Ja/Fe '56, 42). That Smollett regarded the pursuit of knowledge for knowledge's sake as a noble undertaking is indicated in his treatment of the amateur scientist George Richmann's death. Richmann was killed by lightning while trying to reenact Benjamin Franklin's experiments on electricity, a circumstance that might have elicited mockery. Instead, Smollett introduces a long account of Richmann's death with the sober statement, "This gentleman fell a sacrifice to his thirst after knowledge and improvement" (Jl '56, 533).

What finally emerges from Smollett's scientific reviews is that he saw the *Critical*, which he had originally intended to be the journal of an academy itself, functioning in parallel with the learned societies on two levels. On the first, it served to circulate ideas among the learned and to subject those ideas to critical scrutiny and experimental probation. This explains the close and often contentious analysis of so many of these works, the call for the Royal Society to "weed" its publications more carefully, and the approval for publishing in Latin those learned tracts that were aimed at specialists, thus enabling them to circulate internationally.

But perhaps the *Critical* was less pretentious and more useful on the second level: as a conduit of information, carefully summarized and interpreted, for the general reader. This explains, for instance, Smollett's thorough treatment of the *Philosophical Transactions*. Where Johnson in the *Literary Magazine* minimized the excerpts he presented so as "not to hinder the sale of these valuable collections,"[46] Smollett methodically summarized and evaluated virtually every article for his readers. He undoubtedly recognized that the majority of common readers were not the sort who would otherwise buy or read the huge volumes of the *Transactions*. In the same spirit, Smollett encouraged translations from the learned languages that made valuable works accessible to the less educated among the lower professions (midwives, apothecaries, etc.) and the general public (Ja/Fe '56, 10–23 and Ap '56, 244). A work such as Ferguson's *Astronomy* earned his special approval because it explained an abstruse subject in ways suited "to the apprehension of the meanest capacities"; it is equally noteworthy that he also approved of Ferguson's book for making the subject intelligible to female readers (Jl '56, 516 and 511). The result was that along with other journals of the time, the *Critical* was contributing to the circulation of scientific information and ideas among the general public to an extent never before realized.

iii. POLITICS

The tangled condition of British politics and foreign relations in 1756 and especially the outbreak of hostilities with France in what was to become the Seven Years War produced a flood of political pamphlets and related publications. Smollett retained coverage of this material almost exclusively to himself, reviewing about thirty separate publications.[47] Included under this heading are a few more substantial books that did not depend on current affairs for their interest and would doubtless have attracted his attention anyway: books on economics and political philosophy such as Postlethwayt's *Great Britain's True System* (De '56, 432–48) and Rutherforth's *Institutes of Natural Law* (Se '56, 160–81; Oc '56, 227–43; and No '56, 299–315), and treatises on the military arts such as Molyneux's *The Target* (Jn '56, 438–43) and the anonymous *Cadet* (Oc '56, 244–51). These received serious treatment in major articles. But the large majority are ephemeral pamphlets that merited only brief notices in the "Monthly Catalogue."

It is a bleak irony that Smollett, like Johnson with his *Literary Magazine*, had chosen the year 1756 in which to found his journal, for the historical accident of the outbreak of war that year cast a pall over both their projects. Johnson was forced to abandon the *Literary Magazine* late in 1756, according to Greene, in large part because his political views did not suit either his readers or his publishers.[48] Smollett was his own man on the *Critical*, but he too felt the pressure of political developments. As the year wore on, he was forced to divert more and more of his attention from books on the arts and sciences to the increasing numbers of political pamphlets. This became especially obvious toward the end of the year. Of some thirty works that Smollett reviewed in the last three issues of 1756, only six were not related to current affairs and he found time to treat only two of these in full-length articles. This trend proved ominous. Even as he was describing the *Critical* in August of 1756 as one branch of a projected "Academy of Belles Lettres" and asserting in the same letter that "I never dabble in Politics,"[49] Smollett was entering a period of growing political involvement that would lead to the Admiral Knowles libel case in the late 1750s, the pro-Bute writing and furious political wrangling of the *Briton* years 1762–63, and ultimately the acrimonious retrospect on politics in *The History and Adventures of an Atom* in 1769.

Smollett's political views have been analyzed repeatedly in recent studies and will not be examined again here.[50] Nor will Smollett's writings for the

Briton be taken up for, as political journalism, their discussion properly belongs in other contexts. In terms of the *Critical*, it is important to remember at the outset that, all the accusations by contemporaries notwithstanding, the *Critical* was in no way established or conducted as a Tory party organ. That myth has long since been dispelled,[51] and there is not a single detail in the story of how the *Critical* was founded (recounted above in chap. 1) to suggest otherwise. Moreover, during the last few decades, Smollett's reputation as a dyed-in-the-wool Tory has been steadily qualified and corrected.[52] What will be considered here is how Smollett responded to political publications as a kind of literature and how he tried to maintain his position as an impartial observer and conductor of a *literary* journal, even as he was being drawn inexorably into the political controversies themselves.

It is evident that Smollett perceived the importance, as well as the volatility, of the emerging controversies. This explains his care to review most of the material himself. It is equally clear, however, that he was reluctant to allow these matters to fill up the pages of the *Critical*, even if they did occupy increasing amounts of his time. Thus most were treated summarily, dismissively, mockingly. In his *Appeal to the Commons and Citizens of London*, Charles Lucas becomes so "overheated," says Smollett, that he "bewilders himself" in his own arguments (Mr '56, 170). Another pamphleteer's arguments are so convoluted they become as much a "secret of state" as those he pretends to disclose (De '56, 481). One pamphlet is peremptorily dismissed: "In a word, it is a very contemptible performance" (Oc '56, 279). Others are treated with mock seriousness, in a tone of resignation in the face of their unintelligibility: "This is one of those motly performances which a reader does not well know whether to interpret into jest or earnest" (No '56, 375).

The prolific and strident Shebbeare, by virtue of his many writings, earned more abuse than anyone else. Smollett was both relentless and resourceful. At various times he likened Shebbeare to a lunatic, a fishwife, a bedlamite, and a pestiferous insect; he termed one of Shebbeare's metaphors "such a childish conceit as a boy would have been whipped for in school" (Au '56, 38). When Shebbeare resorted to publishing a pamphlet in answer to himself (*A Full and Particular Answer to . . . a Pamphlet, Called a Fourth Letter to the People of England*), Smollett responded with mock pity: "We wish the G[overnmen]t would take some notice of him, otherwise the poor creature will break his heart" (Oc '56, 280). To Smollett, Shebbeare represented the worst kind of political writer: "a desperate incendiary" (Au '56, 44). In exposing and ridiculing such pamphleteers as Shebbeare, Smollett's overriding purpose was to keep political discussion calm, reasonable, and restrained. "Let us not," he urges, "at such a crisis, be hurried into rash and dangerous resentments, they may produce convulsions in the state, by the insidious suggestions of an obscure scribler" (Au '56, 44).

To this end, Smollett insisted on good prose, sound argument, and reasonable manner, regardless of political stance. He could easily admire the "cool, candid, dispassionate manner" of one writer with whose views he agreed (Ap '56, 263); but in the case of another political writer with whom he also agreed, he would not tolerate poor form: "The reflections, however, are just in the main; but they are at the same time trite and hackneyed, so as to have lost all effect upon the public, and the stile is for the most part insipid and *verbose*: inflated with gigantic metaphors jumbled together in the utmost confusion and impropriety" (No '56, 345). Smollett might observe that Lucas's prose style, which produced at one point a sentence of eighty lines that ended in a question mark, reflected his addled state of mind (Mr '56, 170), but he could also admit that another pamphlet with which he disagreed was "well written" and "shrewd" (No '56, 377). Similarly, he welcomed political opinions buttressed with the intelligent application of historical precedents—as in *An Address to the Electors of England* (De '56, 471–72)—but would not tolerate errors of historical fact such as *The Monitor* contained, despite agreeing with its opinions on current issues (No '56, 345–46).

The biggest controversy of late 1756—and the one to generate the most pamphlets—was the Admiral Byng affair. Having failed to defend Minorca from the French in a muddled sea battle, Byng was being tried for negligence; he was persecuted in the press (partly by government writers) in an effort to shift the blame for this setback from the government onto him. He was eventually convicted and executed in March 1757. Like Voltaire, who tried to intervene in his behalf,[53] and Johnson, who defended him in the *Literary Magazine*,[54] Smollett was upset at the government's machinations and the public's clamor against Byng. In the first of more than ten reviews of publications concerning the Byng controversy, Smollett emerged as an early and consistent defender of the persecuted admiral. In the October issue, he devoted seven pages to supporting a pamphlet that disclosed how the government, in its publications, was abridging and misquoting Byng's own statements to stir public feeling against him: "We cannot help thinking that pains have been taken to charge upon him the loss of *Minorca*, which it was not in his power to save" (Oc '56, 257). Later in the same issue, Smollett denounces another pamphlet as "the production of a venal pen hired to keep up the clamor of the populace, against the scape-goat of the m[inistr]y" (Oc '56, 286). It should be noted that while Voltaire's and Johnson's efforts on behalf of Byng have been well-remembered as laudable examples of their humane activism,[55] Smollett's have not fared so well. Even in the years since Roper's discovery that Smollett reviewed the Byng pamphlets himself, there has been almost no notice taken of these reviews, apart from Spector's discussion of them in the context of the political history of the period.[56] But as his reviews reveal, like Voltaire and Johnson, Smollett's humanity and sense of fair play were aroused by Byng's persecution. It is another instance, as with his feelings about vivisection and cruelty to animals, of our tendency to see the

Smollett we are used to seeing and unconsciously failing to factor into our inherited idea of him such contradictory or complicating information.

If one looks again, in fact, Smollett made more of a sustained cause of the Byng affair even than Voltaire, whose darkly satiric "rationale" for Byng's execution ("pour encourager les autres") is always remembered. In addition to his many comments in the *Critical*, Smollett devoted long passages of his *Continuation* to the case. There he described Byng "as the scapegoat of the ministry," his failure "thrown out like a barrel to the whale, in order to engage the attention of the people, that it might not be attracted by the real cause of the national misfortune," which was, in Smollett's view, the "supine negligence, ignorance, and misconduct" of the ministry.[57] After recounting in great detail Byng's trial and execution, Smollett offered a summary judgment: "Thus fell, to the astonishment of all Europe, admiral John Byng, who, whatever his errors and indiscretions might have been, seems to have been rashly condemned, meanly given up, and cruelly sacrificed to vile considerations."[58] Smollett took up Byng's cause again years later, in the *History and Adventures of an Atom*, wherein Byng ("Bihn-goh") is offered up as "a human sacrifice" to the mob by a vile, self-serving government. Smollett even invents a dark detail by way of a damning postscript: after Bihn-goh's death, the ministry defiles his memory by circulating a rumor that Bihn-goh "had bribed a person to represent him at his execution, and be sacrificed in his stead."[59] Ludicrous and impossible, of course, but it is another measure of the intensity of Smollett's feelings about the case.

As a critic whose interests in 1756 were not political, Smollett quickly grew exasperated with the many unnecessary and inflammatory pamphlets. He openly discouraged pamphleteering on both sides of controversies. He lamented, for example, the appearance of one poorly written but pro-Byng pamphlet "which we are afraid, will do no service to the prisoner" (Oc '56, 285). Another he questioned on its own terms: "If the gentlemen by whom the admiral will be tried, are above all prejudice and prepossession, to what purpose was this pamphlet published?" (Oc '56, 281). The heights of absurdity were reached when a pamphlet appeared that condemned the writing of pamphlets: *A Modest Remonstrance to the Public, Occasioned by the Number of Papers and Pamphlets Published about Admiral Byng*. Predictably, Smollett lampooned this ridiculous tract, likening its author in Swiftian terms to "the fat publican in the throng, who cursed the people for mobbing in such a manner, not considering that he himself was one of the most insignificant individuals that constituted the very mob against which he exclaimed" (De '56, 473).

Smollett's distaste for most political writings and his resentment at having to review so many emerge most clearly in his treatment of that rarity, a genuinely witty and entertaining political satire. Entitled *A Serious Defense of Some Late Measures of the Administration*, it was anything but serious in

content. Significantly, Smollett allotted as much space to this thoroughly facetious piece—six pages—as to any of the serious political pamphlets
he covered elsewhere. After liberally quoting some of its wittier passages,
Smollett writes that he

> cannot conclude this article without recommending that concealed author's
> method to our present race of political writers, who seem utterly to have
> forgotten that there are such things in the world as *wit* and *humour*, which
> might be occasionally made use of to recommend their works to the age
> they live in, and (if they extend their hopes so far) perhaps secure them a
> favourable reception with posterity. (Se '56, 126)

Burdened with increasing numbers of dreary political publications, Smollett
the comic novelist felt that their only possible redeeming virtue was a good
laugh. His words ironically foreshadow the failure of his own most regret-
table (because most earnest and impassioned) work, *The Briton*.

With war in the air, treatises on the military arts became timely. Smollett
reviewed two: Molyneux's *The Target* (Jn '56, 438–43) and the anonymous
Cadet (Oc '56, 244–51). But in both cases, he refrained from any reference to
current events, confining his remarks to the merits of the author's ideas about
military tactics and strategy in the abstract. He singled out the most sensible
innovations suggested in each and, typically, corrected errors in grammar
and style and translated the military jargon into plain English. Above all,
Smollett emphasized the educational value of these works in preparation for a
military career, recommending them "to the attention of all the youths that
embrace a military life; in full confidence that they will find [them] replete
with useful maxims" (Oc '56, 251). These military treatises, like so many of
the publications he reviewed, provided Smollett with raw material that later
got transmuted into the comic art of his novels; the "science" of military
formations gathered from these books resurfaces, for example, as parody in
Adventures of an Atom.[60]

In the midst of the political uproar, two other books of substance captured
Smollett's attention. The first was Thomas Rutherforth's *Institutes of Natural
Law*, a learned philosophical treatise on law, the rights of man, and the nature of society. Treating it much as he had the *Philosophical Transactions*,
Smollett carefully summarizes the work chapter by chapter, explaining and
commenting on the main points in a manner suited to the general reader's
understanding. The review is one of his longest, running to more than fifty-
five pages serialized over three issues (Se '56, 160–81; Oc '56, 227–43; No
'56, 299–315). Again here, as with the *Philosophical Transactions*, rather than
directing the reader to a book that is formidable in size and price and probably difficult of access in every sense, Smollett aims to convey the substance
of the work to his readers himself, as if assuming they are unlikely to read
such a learned tome themselves. In such instances, Smollett's aims approach

more nearly those of the *philosophes*, with their *Encyclopédie*, than those of a mere book reviewer.

The second book was Malachy Postlethwayt's *Great Britain's True System*, a study of England's economic system and its relation to foreign policy. More topical than Rutherforth's book, it nevertheless commanded Smollett's respect as a comprehensive and intelligent analysis of Britain's current condition and policies, by a respected authority. This last point he made by reminding his readers that Postlethwayt was the author of the *Dictionary of Trade*, a work widely acclaimed as "a national advantage" (De '56, 433). While Smollett obviously agreed with the political implications of its analysis—"We hope it will find its way into the hands of the ministry" (De '56, 448)—its scope and manner were elevated far above any mere political tract. For example, Smollett quotes with approval Postlethwayt's advice that the English could learn much from the economic policies of the French government (De '56, 441–43)—hardly a common opinion in late 1756.

Although Smollett must have welcomed such important and substantial books in the midst of the political pamphleteering, they were by contrast with the others an added reminder of the topics that were coming to dominate English thought and letters—the whole "climate of opinion"—of the late 1750s.[61] Smollett's dismay was perhaps compounded by the realization that as he diverted more of his attention to these topics, prized features of the *Critical* such as the art review and the foreign articles section were being interrupted or displaced. Perhaps he also sensed that, with them, some of his original ideals for the *Critical* were slipping away.

[7]

"Tied Down to the Stake": Smollett as Editor and Reviewer from 1757 to 1763

i. REVIEWER

There are no exact records, no article-by-article ascriptions, of Smollett's contributions (or anyone else's) to the *Critical* after 1756. Nevertheless it is clear both that he remained in editorial control and that he continued to contribute reviews on a major scale from 1757 until mid-1763. Given the impossibility of the most exhaustive or definitive kinds of investigations, it seems wise to examine Smollett's journalism during these years with three aims in mind: to determine as far as possible the extent of Smollett's involvement as reviewer and editor; to survey the body of reviews identifiable as Smollett's, noting especially the most important of them; and to evaluate the editorial policies and performance of the *Critical* under Smollett's guidance.

At the end of 1756, having contributed more than seventy articles, amounting to over 350 pages in total, Smollett was compiling the *Critical* almost by himself, with the assistance of only Francklin, Derrick, and occasionally Armstrong, and with no relief in sight. Smollett began soliciting help both publicly in the pages of the *Critical* itself (Mr '56, 192) and privately in letters to his friends;[1] already in the January 1757 issue one sees signs of a response, with two reviews identified as contributions from correspondents. Sometime in early 1757, Smollett temporarily reduced his involvement. By his own report, he contributed nothing at all to the March issue[2] and in January 1758 he told John Moore: "I have for some time done very little in the Critical Review."[3] Smollett's sense of "very little," however, must be seen on the scale of his normal workload: "very little" as opposed to "nearly everything," one might say. When he reiterated in September 1758, "I have not had Leisure to do much in that work [the *Critical*] for some time past," he went on to make it clear that he meant a reduced but still substantial involvement: "Therefore I hope that you will not ascribe the articles indiscriminate-

ment: "Therefore I hope that you will not ascribe the articles indiscriminately to me for I am equally averse to the Praise and Censure that belong to other men."[4] Indeed, even in this period of "very little" work for the *Critical* from early 1757 to mid-1758, there are more than forty articles that bear enough distinctive marks of his authorship to be identified with confidence as his.[5] Moreover, Smollett openly acknowledged the centrality of his role when, in the August 1757 issue, he responded seriously to a printed attack that named him as "the author of the Critical Review"; with the writer's identification of him as head of the *Critical* Smollett had no quarrel, only with the pamphleteer's nasty remarks about the *Critical* (152).[6]

By late 1758, having finished his *Complete History of England*, revisions for the second edition of *Peregrine Pickle* (1758), and various booksellers' jobs,[7] Smollett was apparently able—despite his continuing commitment to the *Universal History*—to devote more time to the *Critical*. His correspondence affords glimpses of him, at the beginning of 1759, handling editorial chores: borrowing books to review, engaging writers like Philip Miller to contribute articles, and conferring with Hamilton about a complaint received from Samuel Johnson regarding a recent article.[8] His duties grew burdensome. In April 1759, for instance, he declined a social invitation from his close friend Wilkes because he was too busy "reading dull books and writing dull Commentaries *invitâ Minerva*."[9] New projects such as the *Continuation* of his *History* and the *British Magazine* so added to his labors, that by early 1761 Smollett said that he felt "tied down to the stake by periodical Publications."[10]

Throughout this period, Smollett's involvement with the *Critical* seems to have been continuous, despite his writing to Garrick in April 1761, "I have been so hurried since my enlargement [from the King's Bench in late February 1761] that I had not time to write one article in the Critical Review except that upon Bower's History, and perhaps I shall not write another these six months."[11] This statement was misleading and probably deliberately so. Smollett had been using Garrick as an intermediary to settle a quarrel with Colman over a review in the *Critical*, a review Smollett had not written. Long since tired of such quarrels, which always seemed to land at Smollett's door, he was leading Garrick to think that he had detached himself from the *Critical* and was not responsible, undoubtedly in the hope that Garrick would spread the rumor. In August 1762, when he really had cut back on his labors for the *Critical*, Smollett confided to Moore that "I still write some articles in the Critical Review," adding: "As I am Proprietor of that work, I should be a Fool to give it up at a Time when it begins to indemnify me for all the Vexation and Loss I have sustained by it; but the Laborious Part of Authorship I have long resigned."[12] Again here, Smollett's account suggests that what he considered "the Laborious Part of Authorship" must have amounted to a substantial portion of the *Critical* over the years, undoubtedly hundreds of reviews and thousands of pages of copy.

Smollett confirmed as much in 1763 when, in summarizing his literary output, he listed among his works "Great Part of the Critical Review."[13] Smollett's use of the phrase "Great Part" must be seen in perspective. In that same list he took credit for "A very small part of a Compendium of Voyages," which as Louis Martz has demonstrated amounted to compiling some sixteen hundred pages (of a total of twenty-two hundred),[14] and "A Small Part of the modern Universal History," which, again according to Martz, amounted to responsibility "for nearly 3000 folio pages (almost a third of the work) . . . a total of about three million words."[15] Smollett's understatement suggests a scale by which even the more than 250 articles attributed to Smollett in appendix A of this study undoubtedly fall short of his actual contribution.

But it is a start. The list of attributions in appendix A has been compiled as carefully as possible, based on evidence that is summarized briefly for each attribution in the appendix. The identification of Smollett's articles in 1756[16] significantly increased the possibilities of identifying later reviews on the basis of internal evidence. The slowly growing fund of biographical information and the scholarship of Martz, Knapp, and others, together with Smollett's many other writings, all afford various kinds of evidence. Bearing in mind the tentativeness of much of the canon thus established and the possibility that future additions may significantly alter its composition, one can nevertheless form an approximate idea of the kind of reviewing that Smollett was doing between 1757 and 1763 and its relation to his literary interests and friendships, to the editorial policies of the *Critical*, and to the *Critical*'s fluctuating fortunes.

Two general characteristics are immediately evident in this list of reviews. First, a considerable number of his reviews deal with works by or somehow connected with friends of Smollett's. This bias is as much the result of the available biographical evidence, which naturally clusters around such relationships, as it is a reflection of Smollett's policies. It is equally significant that Smollett's friends valued his support in the *Critical* and that other writers cultivated his acquaintance for the same reasons, about all of which more will be said below. Second, during this period Smollett's reviews cover the same wide range of topics they had in 1756, including literature, history, works of art, science, medicine, and politics. It is useful, therefore, to survey these reviews according to the same topical categories.

ii. LITERATURE AND HISTORY

In literature, although Smollett continued to review some plays after 1756, his attention to drama declined. This resulted in part from Smollett's personal situation, living in Chelsea at a distance from the theaters, frequently housebound with illness and work, and his interest in other plays subsiding as the excitement of staging his own *Reprisal* faded in memory. Then, too, of all branches of literature, published plays were uniquely troublesome and unrewarding to review. By the time the reviewer dealt with a play, public opinion was firmly established: managers had decided to produce or reject the play, audiences had applauded or booed it in production. Thus the reviewer faced the choice of passively echoing public opinion or risking the consequences of defying it.

As a result, Smollett's drama reviews, like those of the *Critical* in general, became cautious and diffident. Smollett's guarded and ambivalent treatment of Colman's *The Jealous Wife* is typical:

> From the thundering peals of applause with which this performance hath been received on the theatre, we flattered ourselves with the hope of enjoying it with rapture in the closet . . . but we cannot help owning ourselves disappointed. The town has of late been troubled with violent convulsive fits of liking, which seem to prognosticate a total privation of sense. In these paroxisms it falls, seemingly by accident, into the arms of some authors, whose good fortune is at least equal to their merit. . . . Far be it from us, however, to rank Mr. Colman among those lucky writers, who have been born with cawls on their heads. We always respected him as a man of genius, and have such reverence for the manager's [Garrick's] taste in dramatic writings, that we impute our disappointment in the article of this play, to our own want of discernment, or rather to our having preconceived too sanguine expectations of the piece. (Fe '61, 131–32)

Thus tacitly accepting the theater public—despite its capricious tastes—as first and final judge, Smollett refrains from applying rigorous critical standards. In another case, he could safely applaud Garrick's method of correcting Shakespeare in his adaptation of *The Winter's Tale*, *Florizel and Perdita*, both as a gesture to a friend and as an acknowledgement of the play's popularity in performance. Where Garrick had let stand one of Shakespeare's "irregularities," Smollett explained it away as a defect that Garrick "(probably) thought would admit of no remedy, without making too free with his revered author" (Fe '62, 157). Smollett was similarly ambiguous about critical standards in reviewing Whitehead's *The School for Lovers*: "Our author has preserved the unities of time and place with the most scrupulous exactness; though we have lived to hear this censured as a defect" (Fe '62, 137). Clearly Smollett's critical views about drama were, to say the least, tentative and mutable by the late 1750s, perhaps a sign of the transitional state of critical ideas generally.

If Smollett became less severe and more deferential in his dramatic reviews after 1756, he was still willing to speak up on behalf of neglected merit— especially if it belonged to a friend. In reviewing two unsuccessful plays— Cibber's edition of Aaron Hill's *The Insolvent* (Jl '58, 17–25) and Cleland's

Tombo-Chiqui (Mr '58, 199–206)—Smollett took the opportunity to plead quietly on behalf of friends. In the case of Cibber, Smollett explained the play's unpopularity in performance in terms of Hill's faults as a playwright and the poor acting of the supporting cast, while appealing to the public to recognize Cibber's accomplishments as an actor (Jl '58, 17). With Cleland's rejected comedy, Smollett gently urged that its qualities "would have ensured its success on the stage under the conduct of a Garrick," while also suggesting revisions that would make it more stageable (Mr '58, 206). Behind the compliment to Garrick one senses a subtle attempt by Smollett to mediate between Cleland and Garrick, both friends of his, although of course it was true that Garrick's fame and talent almost guaranteed box office success, whatever a play's literary merits. As will be seen, however, drama was not the only field in which Smollett's impartiality was sometimes open to question.

With poetry, the evidence suggests that Smollett reviewed considerably more in later years than he had in 1756 and often in major articles: at least sixteen works of translated and original verse.[17] It seems to be true, as Cibber is reported to have said, that Smollett presided "over the poetical Province in the *Critical Review*."[18] Some of the poetry he reviewed was by friends— Armstrong's *A Day: An Epistle to John Wilkes* (Ja '61, 73–75), Cleland's *The Times* (My '60, 417–18), and Huggins's *Orlando Furioso* (My '57, 385–98 and De '58, 506–8)—and of course was reviewed favorably. The majority was by poets who, although celebrated in their own day, have since declined in importance, including Arthur Murphy, William Kenrick, John Gilbert Cooper, and Charles Churchill. It is more interesting to observe that, with one exception,[19] Smollett applauded or found something good to say about every one of them, even those such as Murphy and Churchill who were openly hostile towards Smollett and the *Critical*.

One of Smollett's poetry reviews, however, stands out both for the author's lasting importance and for Smollett's critical acumen in immediately recognizing it: that of James Macpherson's Ossianic epic, *Fingal* (De '61, 405–18 and Ja '62, 45–53). As scholars have noted, Smollett's review in the *Critical* was—of all contemporary critical responses to *Fingal*—"foremost in giving Macpherson a welcome," in an appraisal that was "extravagantly favourable."[20] Although Smollett mistakenly credited Macpherson's claim that *Fingal* was a genuine translation of an ancient Scottish epic, he skirted the authenticity issue to concentrate on the special qualities of the poem itself. Undoubtedly moved in part by Scottish national pride, Smollett acclaimed *Fingal*—in one of the longest reviews ever devoted to a work of poetry in the *Critical*, some twenty-one pages—as an epic comparable to those of Homer and Virgil and even "in many places superior" (De '61, 410). By contrast, the *Monthly* reviewer found more fault with it and concluded, with an oblique glance at Smollett's review, that comparing *Fingal* with Homer and Virgil was like placing "the statue of a dwarf beside the Colossal

Apollo of Rhodes."[21]

Some of the terms of Smollett's critique show that he "was attempting," as Spector aptly puts it, "to fit *Fingal* into the framework of a neoclassical design."[22] At least as interesting, however, is how Smollett attempted to explain the power and beauty of a work that departed from neoclassical orthodoxy in ways that strained his critical vocabulary and that eventually made it an inspirational favorite of Goethe, Blake, and so many of the romantics. Smollett declared that "it would be as absurd to examine this poem by the rules of Aristotle, as it would be to judge a Lapland jacket by the fashion of an Armenian gaberdine" (De '61, 410). Despite his proceeding to show how *Fingal* nonetheless fulfilled the basic Aristotelian criteria, Smollett also resorted to what were for him unusual kinds of critical language. He stated that *Fingal* "abounds with such poetical images, such flights of fancy, such interesting characters, pathetic touches, and sublime sentiments, as cannot fail to excite the admiration of taste, while they wake the soul of sensibility" (De '61, 405). In places his response to "Ossian" seems more like that of Goethe's romantic hero Werther than the controlled, rational Augustan critic we so often expect him to be. For example, Smollett describes Macpherson's use of setting and landscape as

> altogether wild and romantic, generating a silent attention in the mind, and preparing the imagination for extraordinary events: an extended heath, with deer feeding at a distance; a rock with a prospect of the sea; a dusky mountain; a misty vale; a verdant hill; a torrent, a river, and a fountain; a waving wood, a solitary oak, and the moss-clad tomb of a warrior. (De '61, 413)

In *Humphry Clinker*, it becomes obvious that for Smollett, as for young Werther, Ossian not only displaced Homer in his esteem, but permanently affected his imagination. While the Bramble party is roaming the Scottish countryside, Jeremy Melford is moved to write:

> These are the lovely hills of Morven, where Fingal and his heroes enjoyed the same pastime: I feel an enthusiastic pleasure when I survey the brown heath that Ossian wont to tread; and hear the wind whistle through the bending grass—When I enter our landlord's hall, I look for the suspended harp of that divine bard, and listen in hopes of hearing the aerial sound of his respected spirit—[23]

One might compare this passage with Werther's journal entry for 12 October, which begins: "Ossian has replaced Homer in my heart, and what a world it is into which this divine poet leads me!"[24] Both Jeremy and Werther feel the Ossian poet's power to transport them imaginatively, to transform the world around them, processes more reminiscent of Wordsworth and Keats than of the creator of "old square-toes," Matthew Bramble. But the point again here is that Smollett's personal and formal responses to Macpherson's *Fingal* reveal something both about his own sensibilities and, as with his review of Warton's *Essay on Pope*, about the heights to which his critical perceptions could rise on occasion.

What emerges in general from Smollett's poetry reviews is that, whatever the specific merits of his critical analyses, he was gaining respect as a judge and patron of poetical talent. It was for this reason that Cibber had urged Reed to submit his work to Smollett for approval.[25] Similarly, William Kenrick had sent in a copy of his *Epistles* in hopes of a favorable review, according to Smollett, who later had to deal with the poet's disappointment: "If the authors of the Critical Review have such mean abilities, and so little reputation, as this gentleman [Kenrick] mentions, we are surprised that he should have taken the pains to write a letter of compliment to them, with a present of the book, when it was published" (Fe '59, 161). Smollett's close personal and literary friendship with William Huggins grew out of a similar contact, initiated when Huggins sent him a copy of his *Orlando Furioso* in 1756, which Smollett reviewed favorably (My '57, 385–98), and then continued as he solicited Smollett's advice and cooperation in other literary endeavors.[26] The most memorable example is that of the young James Boswell in his pre-Johnson years who, in one of his first overtures to the London literary world, wrote Smollett in 1762 to seek approval and encouragement for an early poetical effort: *A Collection of Original Poems, By Scotch Gentlemen*.[27] Smollett wrote him an encouraging reply, according to Boswell, and in his review of the *Collection*, while finding it largely undistinguished, allowed that pieces in it showed some promise, especially the poems contributed by young "J. B. Esq." (Jn '62, 495–99). Despite the kind mention, Boswell was probably disappointed. This episode may have been one more contributing factor to what at first seems a strange gap in Boswell's literary friendships, for Smollett would seem a natural for him to have cultivated. But this episode together with Boswell's conscious avoidance of excessive Scottish company and what Smollett, who was fiercely proud, would have seen as Boswell's toadying manner, as well as the fact that Smollett left the London literary world just as Boswell was entering it, in 1763, all combine to make it more understandable in retrospect that a close friendship between Smollett and Boswell was almost impossible.

The *Critical*'s reviews of fiction, especially because of Smollett's connection, have attracted considerable scholarly attention, including at least one major study.[28] But despite those efforts, any comprehensive discussion of Smollett's fiction reviews still founders on one fundamental problem: identifying Smollett's reviews.[29] For these reasons, the discussion here is confined to a few general points about those reviews that can be attributed to Smollett with reasonable confidence.[30]

Although he ignored the novel completely in 1756, thereafter Smollett directed at least some attention to current fiction, including (but not limited to) such celebrated books as *Candide* (Jn' 59, 550–54 and Au '61, 131–38) and *Tristram Shandy* (Ap '61, 314–17). Among the minor novels he examined, two were connected with his friend Cleland. In the case of the anonymous *Intriguing Coxcomb* (Fe '59, 184), Smollett briefly denounced it as a plagiarism of Cleland's *Coxcomb*, which he had reviewed favorably years earlier while writing for the *Monthly*. Interestingly—and perhaps suggestively—Smollett mentioned again in this review that Cleland's *Coxcomb* was never finished. He also quietly but warmly endorsed Cleland's *Romance of a Day* (Se '60, 241–42) and encouraged a sequel, which Cleland in fact went on to provide in his *Romance of a Night* in 1762. Smollett was apparently taking more interest than any of his contemporaries in Cleland's post-*Fanny Hill* literary career; it is significant that during the years of Smollett's supervision, Cleland's works invariably received approval in the *Critical*, but after his departure, the reviews could be cold and even hostile on occasion.[31]

Smollett's fascination with Shebbeare—here evident in his review of Shebbeare's political novel *History of the Sumatrans* (My '62, 392–97 and Mr '63, 209–10)—has been examined thoroughly by James Foster.[32] Two points are most significant in this context. First, from Shebbeare's novel (along with other sources) Smollett formed the idea of writing a satirical political novel in an oriental guise, from which his *Adventures of an Atom* resulted in 1769. Second, Smollett exhibited both good nature and critical integrity by heartily applauding Shebbeare's novel in this review, despite having condemned so many of Shebbeare's earlier works and in turn having experienced Shebbeare's resentment. Smollett actually seemed to enjoy the opportunity to reverse his former strictures, noting that Shebbeare was "a writer whom we have formerly censured with freedom, and we now applaud without reserve, because he has selected a subject perfectly suited to his talents" (My '62, 397). And in fact Smollett's whole attitude towards Shebbeare seems to have softened, as can be seen in his mild and balanced treatment of Shebbeare's political writings in the *Continuation* (2:408).

Smollett's review of *The Peregrinations of Jeremiah Grant* in 1763 is of interest primarily because it contains his fullest discussion of the novel since his prefatory discourse in *Ferdinand Count Fathom* (1753). He emphasizes three elements of the novel: structure, verisimilitude, and moral. "This kind of romance," he writes, "is a diffused comedy unrestrained by the rules of the drama, comprehending a great variety of incident and character, referring, however, to one principal action and one particular personage, whose fate must interest the reader, and whose importance must not only engage our attention and esteem, but also unite the whole concatenation of scenes and adventures" (Ja '63, 13). On the proper subject matter of fiction, he observes that "modern romance deals chiefly among familiar scenes of life and brings to the view characters which we every day observe in nature" (Ja '63, 14). Thus he approves of the realism in *Jeremiah Grant* because the hero's adventures "are such as we believe may have happened to many young Creoles, who come over to England" (Ja '63, 15). But it is also the novelist's duty "to regulate the morals of the piece" and "avoid impropriety," on which count he faults *Jeremiah Grant* chiefly because the hero is rewarded far beyond his deserts. In this firm defense of poetic justice and the need for didactic fiction, we can see a shift in emphasis on Smollett's part: he was perhaps still haunted by the negative reception of *Ferdinand Count Fathom* ten years earlier, in which Fathom's career of villainy is abruptly and unconvincingly forgiven in the final chapter. Smollett was to bring Fathom back in *Humphry Clinker*, to demonstrate the genuineness of Fathom's conversion (after sixteen years of extra-textual atonement and penance), and thus compensate for his earlier neglect of the moral imperatives of good fiction. But in the intervening years, these ideas had also become part of his public voice as a critic reviewing novels like *Jeremiah Grant* in the *Critical*.

Given these criteria for fiction, it is not surprising that Smollett found fault with *Candide* and *Tristram Shandy*.[33] In his view, both novels lacked artistic form and moral content. *Candide* seemed to Smollett an intolerable "satire upon the Creator of the Universe" (Jn '59, 550) and *Tristram Shandy* was rife with "gross expressions, impure ideas, and a general want of decorum" (Ap '61, 317). The irregularity and improbability of both novels also bothered Smollett: "There is not such a character in nature as that of his *Candide*" (Jn '59, 551), while *Tristram Shandy*, like *Candide*, "seems to have been written without any plan" (Ap '61, 316). But Smollett's critical criteria did not blind him completely. Although it is a credit more to his honesty of response than to his critical theory, Smollett discerned signs of genius in both. *Candide*, he wrote, "is enlivened with a thousand flashes of brilliant wit, genuine humour, manly sense, and animated satire" (Au' 61, 138); similarly, *Tristram Shandy* "abounds with pertinent observations on life and characters, humourous incidents, poignant ridicule, and marks of taste and erudition" (Ap '61, 316). Indeed, Smollett claimed credit for having been the first to recognize Sterne's brilliance: "While the two first volumes of Tristram Shandy lay half-buried in obscurity, we, the Critical Reviewers, recommended it to the public as a work of humour and ingenuity, and, in return, were publickly reviled with the most dull and indelicate abuse" (Ap '61, 316). With volumes 3 and 4, Smollett took the posture of *Tristram Shandy's* defender against a capricious public who were now condemning them "as unworthy of the first." It is ironic to see Smollett adopting this stance on behalf of a novelist who was not only to surpass him in reputation in the long run, but who would contribute directly to the decline of his reputation with his caricature of him as Smelfungus in the *Sentimental Journey*.

It was to history, however, that Smollett increased his attention most
sharply after 1756. Of the reviews attributable to him, thirty-two treat works
of history, totaling more than four hundred pages.[34] This shift was largely
due to Smollett's connection with the *Universal History*, in which he was a
major compiler and editor. As Martz has demonstrated, Smollett reviewed at
least a dozen volumes of that colossal publication as they appeared, as well as
various other histories used in compiling it.[35] Smollett's basic opinions about
history writing have been discussed above (chap. 5), but further issues and
problems arise in these reviews.

An extraordinary breadth of historical knowledge is suggested by his
reviews. His articles on the *Universal History* were largely quotation and
abstract, but he treated other histories more critically and authoritatively.
Among them were books on the history of Sweden, Poland, Portugal, and
Ireland, as well as histories of the East Indies and of the Arab world.[36]

The most prominent historians he reviewed were Hume and Voltaire,
about whom Smollett had very different things to say. Hume he continued to
applaud, finding the next volume of his *History of England* superior to
previous ones (Ap '59, 289). Voltaire, however, he considered more an entertaining anecdotalist than a real historian: of his *General History of Europe*,
Smollett wrote that "his book is a collection of portraits, not a concatenation
of events: a conversation piece, rather than a history" (No '57, 387). But,
among other saving graces, Smollett believed that Voltaire was "less biassed
by national prejudices, than any other French historian" (No '57, 385) and
despite the methodological flaws in his historical writings, Smollett obviously
found them too valuable in other ways to leave out of his edition of Voltaire's
Works (1761–65).

The least accomplished but most controversial historian Smollett reviewed
was Archibald Bower, the former Jesuit, now ardent Protestant and anti-
Papist. Bower's mysterious background and his dubious claims to having
witnessed atrocities in the Inquisition made him the center of controversy in
the 1750s; the pamphlet war between Bower and those who sought to expose
him inevitably involved the *Critical* in the dispute. Although Smollett made it
clear that he had not reviewed Bower's earlier pamphlets (Mr '61, 231–32),
he did intervene when Bower began to cast aspersions on both the *Critical*
and himself. In reviewing Bower's *History of the Popes*, Smollett defended
himself and the *Critical* from Bower's insults and then, obviously drawing on
the knowledge he had acquired in compiling the history of Italy for the *Universal History*,[37] went on to expose Bower's shortcomings as a historian (Ja
'59, 40–47 and Mr '61, 217–33). What is most significant about these reviews,
however, is the way Smollett assumed the role of a critical arbiter, conducting
a comprehensive review of the whole controversy and evaluating the arguments on both sides. This episode was typical of the many in which Smollett
seemed to feel compelled to intervene, either to offer his judgment on a pub-

lic controversy or to settle a squabble between an angry author and a member of his staff. In this regard, Smollett took seriously the responsibilities of his position as editor-in-chief.

Some of Smollett's history reviews raise questions about his objectivity. It appears that he reviewed both Comber's *Vindication of the Great Revolution* (Se '58, 226–39), an extensive and severe critique of Smollett's own *History*, and Tindal's *Continuation of Rapin's History of England* (Jl '59, 44–54 and Se '60, 186–94), an aggressive rival to Smollett's *Continuation* with which Smollett's publishers were conducting a running battle in the newspapers.[38] His pride piqued, Smollett thoroughly excoriated Comber's book in his review. Although this gesture might be explained as typical of the times and perhaps justified by the rough tenor of Comber's attack, it was excessive and self-defeating, for it debased the *Critical*'s professed editorial standards and tarnished as much as vindicated Smollett's reputation. With Tindal's *Continuation*, Smollett was more restrained, explaining Tindal's lack of success as the misfortune of "a middling writer [who] appears to uncommon disadvantage by succeeding one of superior talents" (Se '60, 186). But again, even if his negative appraisal of Tindal was justified, Smollett was placed in a compromising situation that inevitably reflected badly on him and his journal. And in such instances anonymity was no protection, for the public assumed Smollett's responsibility for any article that touched on his interests and for most others too.

By far the greatest instance of apparently self-interested reviewing was Smollett's series of reviews on the *Universal History*: at least seventeen long articles promoting the various volumes as they appeared.[39] Martz has described Smollett's reviews as essentially "advertisements," noting with amusement the unqualified praise given especially to volumes Smollett had compiled.[40] Smollett took a very serious interest in the success of the *Universal History*, although his reviews extolling its virtues were not as blatant or cynical a case of "puffing" as they might at first seem. Smollett's name was nowhere publicly attached to the compilation, he had no proprietary share in what was in fact a syndicated booksellers' venture, and he was only one of a large team of compilers. In his review of the first volume, Smollett revealed the larger context in which he saw this project's achievement:

We are astonished, when we reflect that a set of private booksellers could be found to engage in such an enterprize; and still more amazed, that they should find authors to execute their plan with any degree of uniformity and precision. Let it then be remembered, for the honour of the undertakers, that they have atchieved a work not unworthy of the most eminent and learned academy that ever flourished in Europe; that they have extracted the essence of all that has been written on the subject; and produced one composition, that, in some measure, has rendered all other histories extant, useless and unnecessary. The Antient and Modern Universal History,

is in itself a complete library, calculated for the conveniency of those who
have neither time, nor inclination, to read every individual book from
which this is compiled; who perhaps know not where to find those books,
or if they did, can neither read nor purchase them. (Ja '59, 1–2)

Here was an encyclopedic project comparable to those of the academicians in
Europe, and clearly Smollett associated it with the same kinds of ideals and
aspirations he had earlier invested in his unsuccessful academy scheme. A
second virtue, equally valuable to him, was its design to accommodate and
encourage that growing segment of the reading public who would otherwise
be barred by limitations of education, income, or daily occupation from
pursuing the study of history. Again here Smollett was catering, as in his
own readable serial *History of England* and in the pages of the *Critical* itself,
to the needs of the emerging middle-class public.

Smollett's seriousness about the *Universal History* was genuine. Although
his reviews were predominantly favorable, he often remarked on its blemishes: signs of hurry and carelessness, the narration sometimes "embarrassed
with useless disquisitions" (Ap '60, 245) and frequently flawed by "prolixity,
and too great minuteness" (De '62, 401). In private letters to Richardson,
who was coordinating the printing and production, Smollett complained of
exactly the same flaws; in editing one batch of copy, for example, he had
had to expunge "many needless notes" and abridge "the text in diverse
places," but was still left with an irreducible bulk owing to "a certain spungi-
ness of expression."[41] Smollett held the proprietors responsible for these
problems. He chafed at the pressures and conditions they imposed on the
compilers, communicating his dissatisfaction to them indirectly but (he
hoped) persuasively through his reviews in the *Critical* and more bluntly
through Richardson, even sending a memo to the proprietors suggesting revisions in the plan.[42] Eventually, when commercially motivated haggling broke
out among the proprietors, Smollett threatened to quit.[43] All this was typical
of the frustrations Smollett felt in trying to organize major publishing projects that served national interests but received no support from the government and therefore always fell to commercial publishers and private citizens.

One other of Smollett's history reviews deserves notice for several reasons:
that of John Curry's *Historical Memoirs of the Irish Rebellion in the Year 1641*
(Fe '61, 116–22). First, it brought Smollett into contact with Edmund
Burke. According to Burke's friend, Charles O'Conor, Burke and John
Ridge met with Smollett and presented him with a copy of Curry's *Memoirs*,
"and from that event proceeded the judgment published in the Critical
Review."[44] Smollett reviewed the book favorably, expressing remarkable
sympathy for the Irish cause, and from about this time—perhaps also in
connection with Smollett's interest in writing a history of Ireland himself[45]—
the *Critical* displayed a sympathetic interest in other books on Ireland, in-

cluding one by the Earl of Egmont, father of Burke's friend Lord Egmont.[46] Finally, as Burke had sought Smollett's help in promoting Curry's book, it may be more than coincidence that the one contention of Curry's (about a massacre of Roman Catholics on the island of Magee) that Smollett thought "the author has not clearly ascertained" (Fe '61, 121) is the very same that Burke later advised Curry to rewrite and bolster with further evidence. In preparing the second edition of his book in 1765, Curry wrote Burke to tell him that he had done so: "From the hint You Gave me, when here Concerning the Massacre in the Island of Magee, I have made a further Search."[47] If Smollett's review was indeed what prompted Burke's advice to Curry, then this incident demonstrates the kind of influence a critic could have on an author and attests to the respect Burke had for Smollett as a historical and critical authority.

iii. ART, SCIENCE, AND POLITICS

The feature on contemporary works of art that Smollett had started so ambitiously in 1756 was continued thereafter, but on a reduced and more irregular basis. An average of two articles a year appeared (as opposed to five in the *Critical*'s first five issues in 1756), concentrating on domestic artists almost to the exclusion of any foreign coverage. Of the fourteen or fifteen brief articles on contemporary works of art that appeared in the *Critical* between 1757 and 1763, the following can be identified as written or edited by Smollett:

My '57, 479	Robert Strange, engraving of *Belisarius*.
Mr '58, 265–66	Samuel Scott, engravings of London Bridge and Westminster Bridge.
Fe '59, 170–71	Richard Paton, paintings of two sea battles against the French, Cape Francois, 21 October 1757, and Carthagena, 28 February 1758.
Ap '59, 375–77	Robert Strange, three engravings: "The Choice of Hercules" (after Nicholas Poussin); "Venus Attired by the Graces" (after Guido Rheni); "St. Agnes with her Lamb" (after Guido Rheni).
Ja '60, 70–71	Richard Paton, painting of sea battle against the French at Montserrat, 3 November 1758.
Mr '60, 231	Richard Houston, mezzotint engraving of Joshua Reynolds's portrait of the Marquis of Granby.
My '60, 399–400	Robert Strange, engravings after Carlo Maratti of his "St. Cecilia" and "Madonna with a sleeping Pargoletto."
My '60, 400	Thomas Frye, several unnamed and forthcoming works; with additional remarks on such artists as

	Kneller, White, Smith, Faber, Houston, and M'Ardel.
Ap '61, 331–32	Thomas Frye, twelve mezzotint engravings after Piazzeta.
Ap '61, 332	Simon Ravenet, engraving of Casali's "Gunhilda." Richard Wilson, two landscape paintings. [?] "Smith," two landscape paintings. William Woollett, engravings in progress.
Oc '61, 312–13	William Woollett, engraving of Richard Wilson's *Niobe*. Thomas Frye, mezzotint engravings of two unidentified female portraits.
Mr '63, 224	[?] "Cooper," engraving of Vandyke's portrait of Charles I and Family. "J. Ryland," engraving of Ramsay's portrait of Lord Bute. "J. Ryland," engraving of George III.[48]

A full discussion of these articles and the works they describe is beyond the scope of this study, but a few points should be made briefly here.

First is the range of artists covered that, although no sculptors receive notice after Wilton (My '56, 387), includes more than a dozen different painters and engravers. Smollett's references to them and their works are sometimes so brief and casual that it becomes difficult to identify the more obscure artists. But others, such as Strange, Reynolds, and Ramsay, were well known then and remain fixtures in British art history today. Smollett's remarks on Reynolds's portrait of the Marquis of Granby, as engraved in mezzotint by Richard Houston, may well be the earliest comments in a monthly periodical about any Reynolds painting (Mr '60, 231). Smollett has nothing but praise for the "excellent picture [by] Mr. Reynolds, whose portraits are universally admired" and goes on to particularize virtues in the work that result as much from Reynolds's talent as from the engraver Houston's: "The resemblance [to Granby] is very happy and striking; the attitude soldierly, and at the same time elegant, and the execution altogether masterly."

The several short art reviews offer various glimpses into the workings of the art world of the time. When the Society of Artists' exhibitions began in 1760, for example, the *Critical* did not review the exhibitions as such. But some of the journal's art reviews and comments are based on its writers' having seen the specific painting or engraving at the exhibition, and the articles often refer readers to other works on display there (My '60, 400 and Ap '61, 331–32). Sometimes we get oblique hints about what the Society of Artists' exhibitions were like: "That we are arrived to great perfection in painting, engraving, and metzotinto [*sic*], the multitudes that flocked to the late exhibition were eye-witnesses" (My '60, 400) or, alluding perhaps to the exhibition crowd's preferences, Smollett mentions a Smith landscape that "so agreeably attracted the eyes of the spectators, during the time of the exhibition" (Ap '61, 332). Smollett's art reviews also continue to refer to works in progress and, on occasion, to direct readers to an artist's gallery where more works can be seen (My '60, 400). There are tidbits of biographical information about artists, such as the news, in May 1760, that currently Strange "is roaming abroad, like an industrious bee, rifling the sweets of Italy, in order to enrich his native land" (400) and sometimes news about prizes, such as the "liberal premium" bestowed by the Society for the Encouragement of Arts on a Ravenet engraving (Ap '61, 332). Some of the articles report the locations of major paintings in private collections (e.g., Ap '59, 375–77), usually the originals on which new engravings were based, although of course with the general public the news might serve only to raise curiosity to see them that could not be satisfied. There are even clues about how history paintings of battle scenes were executed: in his report on two recently begun Richard Paton paintings of victories by Admiral Boscawen off Cape Lagos and by Admiral Hawke off Bellisle, Smollett stresses that Paton is painting these battle scenes based on accounts "from the best authority"—presumably eye-witness accounts, oral or written—and that when finished they will immediately be engraved and published as prints (Ja '60, 71). Here one is reminded that such painters also served a function analogous to that of photojournalists and newsreels in the twentieth century, providing images of the war for general consumption.

Throughout these articles, Smollett chose to notice only works of art that he liked, and then discussed them in uniformly laudatory terms. Not a word of criticism or reservation slipped in and his nationalistic boosterism was frequently evident as, for example, in his remarks on Paton's paintings of sea battles: "the finest prints of that kind ever yet attempted in any nation" (Ja '60, 70). Smollett was particularly enthusiastic about Strange's achievement, which stood out even in an age when the arts were beginning to flourish: "Not to mention the progress which has lately been made by our countrymen in statuary, painting, and music, we can congratulate this age and island, upon having produced one of the best engravers that ever appeared in England" (Ap '59, 375). Smollett used Strange's success as a pretext to editorialize on the need for public support for the arts. He lamented, "Amidst the degeneracy, want of taste, trifling pursuits, and dissipation of the present age, we find many instances of uncommon genius, in all the different branches of the liberal arts, shooting up as it were without culture, and even unheeded, like a number of delicate flowers on a common overgrown with weeds, heath and brambles." Smollett continued to try to help young artists still struggling to get established. Richard Paton, for example, he praised as "an ingenious sea-painter . . . who has not yet had sufficient opportunities of shewing his abilities" (Fe '59, 170). Many of the artists covered in these reviews come in for a mention in Smollett's *Continuation*, where he offers a summary account of the arts under George II: "The British soil, which had hitherto been barren in the article of painting, now produced some artists of extraordinary merit" (4:131). Among some fourteen artists he goes on to mention, at least eight—Hogarth, Wilton, Strange, Rysbrack, Reynolds, Ramsay, Scott, and Smith—are reviewed somewhere in the *Critical* art section.

Beyond providing information and encouragement, Smollett also continued to express occasional moments of powerful response to individual works of art. He wrote of an engraving by Strange: "Venus appears almost naked, reclining on a couch, displaying all the attractions of female beauty, with her eyes turned up, as if she was dissolved into all the languishment of pleasure. It is impossible for a spectator of sensibility to view this figure without admiration even to rapture" (Ap '59, 377). In another engraving, a portrait of Saint Agnes, Smollett saw "an unspeakable sweetness of expression"—precisely the phrase he would utter years later in his *Travels* when responding to Titian's *Venus*, a "sweetness of expression . . . not to be described" (Letter 28, 229). This interest in art, all this excitement about and support for art, are a continuous thread in Smollett's career that somehow disappeared from our inherited image of him but one that now, with these art reviews, can be restored to view. They provide a background against which all the fragmentary references to art in his novels, his *History*, *Travels*, and other works, begin to make sense in a new way.

They also reveal Smollett's role during a transitional period in British art history. Fundamental changes were taking place: the first public exhibitions, the formation of institutions like the Society of Artists (later to become the Royal Academy), and the self-conscious development of a British school of art. For all of these, the *Critical*'s art reviews expressed support and helped to raise awareness in the general public. That Smollett was the driving force behind this arts feature is confirmed not only by his authorship of most of the articles, but also by the fact that very shortly after he left the *Critical* in June 1763 the arts section nearly disappeared altogether. Very occasional articles appeared (such as in October 1763, April 1764, then September 1768),[49] but the impetus was gone. Increasingly, as far as the post-Smollett *Critical* was concerned, the newly reorganized art world was left to fend for itself.

In the area of science and medicine, Smollett continued to bear a large share of the workload; in fact, after Armstrong's departure in 1757, Smollett was the only writer on the staff known to be contributing during this period who was trained in medicine.[50] The full extent of his reviewing in the field, if discovered, may prove to be far greater than the sixty or more reviews attributed to him in appendix A. Three basic points about this mass of reviews should be mentioned.

First, Smollett in general criticized works in this field more strictly— perhaps because of his medical background—than in any other. While of course he found many to be of great value, he seems to have taken onto himself a larger share than elsewhere of mediocre publications. He often editorialized on the redundancy and empty ostentation of many medical works: "We have observed that almost every medical author of these days, thinks it incumbent upon him to display his erudition, by filling up one half of his dissertation with notes, extracted from all the writers who have treated on the same subject" (De '59, 448). Overall, the high proportion of useless tracts made him feel that his labors, "like those of *Sisyphus*, are never ending, ever beginning" (Jn '59, 529).

Second, in his annual encounters with the *Philosophical Transactions*, he grew steadily more impatient with their great bulk and unedited contents. His tone became abusive and this, among other things, hardened Thomas Birch's ill-will toward him.[51] When Smollett left the *Critical* in 1763, a marked change in policy became evident: the reviewer of the *Philosophical Transactions* in 1764 abstained from any critical commentary, explaining that "as the learned editors of the Philosophical Transactions do not pretend to give their own opinions as to the merits of the publications they usher into the world; neither shall we" (Oc '64, 303). This policy would have been anathema to Smollett. Although less likely to give offense to the scientists, such a policy rationalized a reduction in critical effort by the reviewer and with it a decline in service to the general reader.

Third, from 1757 on Smollett increasingly tended to intervene in scientific disputes, as if to fill the role of a central authority that none of the learned bodies such as the Royal Society could or would take on. It was, of course, a presumptuous and ultimately thankless task. Moreover, in one of the most publicized controversies, between Drs. Hunter and Monro, Smollett consistently took his friend Hunter's part, a policy which even if warranted by the facts inevitably carried the stigma of personal favoritism.[52] Other instances reflect more favorably on Smollett. For example, when the accomplished scientist Robert Dossie was standing for the secretaryship of the Society for the Encouragement of Arts, Manufactures, and Commerce, Smollett—who had reviewed appreciatively Dossie's books on chemistry (Oc '59, 292–96 and No '59, 341–52)—used his reviews in the *Critical* to expose the machinations of a faction who were writing pamphlets to discredit Dossie as a scientist and foil his election (Mr '60, 237–39). Ultimately Dossie was elected. But Smollett, by repeatedly adopting such an authoritative posture, albeit with the best of intentions and sometimes very useful results, brought onto himself resentment as well as respect. These wrangles fueled his frustration with what he perceived as the lack of a powerful central authority to promote, coordinate, and supervise activity in the arts and sciences, the same that led him to condemn the Royal Society as ineffectual and that had orginally impelled him to propose his own plan for an academy.

In the end, it was the *Critical*'s treatment of political publications that brought Smollett the most troublesome consequences. Although relatively few political articles contain enough distinctive signs of his authorship to be attributed to him, it seems probable, based on the nature of those few (including the disastrous Knowles review) and on the record of his reviewing in 1756, that Smollett wrote or supervised most of the political reviews from 1757 through at least 1760.[53] Even in a brief survey, several features of these reviews can be illuminated.

There is, as has been argued elsewhere, a traditional sense of the *Critical's* connection with politics that is badly exaggerated. In 1763, a pamphlet typical of many depicted the *Critical* as if it were primarily a political journal, stating that "the design of [it] now is, and of late has been, to indiscriminately condemn all pieces which are wrote on the behalf of the English liberty, constitution or interest, and to applaud with rapture whatever has a tendency to the promotion and establishment of arbitrary power and Scottish aristocracy, or defends Lord Bute and abuses the English nation."[54] And, as Spector reports, the review journals inevitably became involved in politics because of the political pamphlets they were obliged to review, although his contention that between 1756 and 1763 "the chief subject . . . for almost all the periodicals was the [Seven Years] war itself" is open to dispute.[55]

Certainly the *Critical* must be exempted from this generalization because, in fact, no species of literature was given a lower priority or less attention (quantitatively) in the *Critical* than political publications. Under Smollett's editorship, political publications very rarely received attention in full review articles, usually being relegated to the "Monthly Catalogue," and only once in all those years was a political work reviewed in the lead article of an issue (No '57, 377–85). A typical example can be seen during the Sackville controversy: at its height, in September 1759, one issue of the *Critical* contained notices of eighteen political pamphlets, but confined them to a total of fifteen pages of text in the "Monthly Catalogue". In other words, half of the thirty-six publications reviewed that month were on political issues, yet they were accorded only a sixth of the text and all of that at the back of the issue.[56] These are not the signs of a journal that is primarily, or even significantly, political in orientation; rather, they represent the continuation of Smollett's practices in 1756, based on an aversion to, and de-emphasis of, political topics.

Thus it was in many ways ironic, although not accidental, that Smollett's short remarks on a pamphlet by Admiral Knowles in 1758 should bring humiliation in the form of a trial and conviction for libel, followed by a fine and three months' imprisonment. This ordeal has been described in detail by Alice Parker and Knapp,[57] and the offending review itself has been brilliantly analyzed by Boucé for its stylistic and psychological reflections on Smollett.[58] What is most significant here is its effect on the conduct of the *Critical*. As Boucé has discovered, the libelous paragraph of Smollett's review was deleted from later reprintings of the *Critical*,[59] undoubtedly a condition of his sentence. Reissuing the original review would have amounted to repeating the libel. Even before Smollett's case had actually come to trial, however, the furore surrounding the case had caused the *Critical* to soften its stance on Knowles: for example, a very mild and noncommittal review of a second Knowles pamphlet had appeared in June 1759 (Jn '59, 554–55).

Naturally, Smollett's enemies taunted him about his libel conviction, including, ironically, his old antagonist Ralph Griffiths who had himself been prosecuted on various occasions for seditious libel and pornography.[60] But others viewed it more sympathetically, seeing Smollett's conviction as a serious blow to the freedom of the press. Upon hearing the decision, George Faulkner, the Dublin printer, declared that "the press hath received a fatal wound through the sides of Dr. Smallet."[61] The premise of Smollett's defense was, as Spector has stated, "that truth was not libelous—an advanced theory of journalistic practice, which was not challenged by the decision."[62] But he was convicted nonetheless and as a consequence the *Critical* became noticeably more cautious. In 1763, for example, one reviewer (obviously harking back to Smollett's experience with the law) opened a review by writing: "We have not consulted our standing counsel learned in the law, (for no set of men have more reason to retain counsel than the Reviewers have) whether it is safe for us to criticize [this] performance" (Se '63, 227–28).[63] Thus in the wake of Smollett's conviction, the *Critical* was less inclined than ever to enter the arena of political issues and personalities or, especially, to take strong positions about them.

Smollett himself remained deeply concerned about libel law and its application in England. One of the first things he wrote after returning from the Continent in 1765 was a review of *A Digest of the Laws Concerning Libel* (Jl '65, 45–49). Among the objections he raises against current libel law are the fact that truth is no defense when the aristocracy or government officials are involved and yet, on the other hand, a prominent citizen of good reputation (i.e., Smollett himself) has such difficulty defending his name from the mudslinging tactics of Grub Street hacks. Moreover, Smollett is annoyed with this particular writer because while he makes sure to list Smollett's own libel conviction in his summary list of cases, he does not discuss it in his text or do anything to dispel the impression that Smollett was simply a malevolent libeler who got convicted (Jl '65, 49). This seemed to be the one topic about which Smollett, who was mellowing noticeably in the 1760s, remained bitter and adamant. Leaving aside the *Adventures of an Atom*, where it was of course mentioned, the topic of libel also resurfaced in *Humphry Clinker*, where Matt Bramble dwells on it for some three pages of his letter of 2 June (102–4). It seems reasonable to conclude that of all Smollett's experiences as a writer— frustrations, quarrels, poverty, embarrassments—the libel conviction that resulted from his review of Knowles's pamphlet in 1758 was the bitterest and most permanently scarring.

One last point about the *Critical*'s apolitical tendencies should be made by contrasting it with Smollett's overtly and vehemently political periodical, the *Briton*. Smollett's political opponents often tried to connect the two periodicals, depicting them both as mere tools of the pro-Bute faction. "The *Briton*," wrote the author of the *Patriot* in 1762, "I am afraid, if he was to march out in propria persona, would be little more respectable than a *Critical Reviewer*."[64] Certainly the *Critical* displayed a preference for Bute over his opponents, but beyond that, any resemblance to the *Briton* ends. The *Briton* was exclusively political in content and violently partisan in purpose and made no pretense otherwise. It is noteworthy, for example, that whereas Wilkes and his *North Briton* were the objects of relentless vituperation in the *Briton*, the *Critical* occasionally contained praise for Wilkes, referring to him in one issue, for example, as "that elegant writer" of the *North Briton* (Ja '63, 68–69). On another occasion, a political pamphlet, the wisdom of which was praised in highest terms throughout most of an issue of the *Briton* (5 June 1762), received only three sentences of mildly worded approval in the *Critical* (My '62, 438). Similarly, in that same issue of the *Briton*, a second pamphlet was violently condemned that in the *Critical* had received a mixed review with the closing compliment that it "seems to have been written by some person of shrewd parts, and extraordinary intelligence" (Mr '62, 263–64). If indeed Smollett wrote both the *Briton*'s and the *Critical*'s remarks on these pamphlets, it is a remarkable example of editorial voice control. But whether or not he did, the point is that the *Critical* maintained its distance from partisan politics even at a time when Smollett, in other contexts, was most actively engaged in them.

This is one policy that continued even after Smollett left the *Critical* and the Seven Years War was ended. The editorial preface to volume 19 of the *Critical*, in 1765, devoted several pages to reaffirming its disinterest in politics and carefully explaining how it was that so many political publications came to be discussed in its contents (preface, Ja '65, ii–iv). Reviews continued to expose political machinators: "That this is a party publication," wrote one reviewer in 1765, "were there no other evidence, appears from the very moderate price it bears" (Fe '65, 231). In fact the editors who succeeded Smollett on the *Critical* were so sensitive about political controversy that they even delayed reviewing the final volume of Smollett's *Continuation* for several months in 1765. They knew that because it contained discussion of recent events, no matter how they were presented, old political arguments would inevitably break out again (Oc '65, 271).

iv. EDITORIAL ROLE

Smollett seems to have retained editorial control of the *Critical* from 1756 until about mid-1763, when he left for the Continent. During this period, the pool of contributors he was drawing on grew considerably. Although Armstrong left the staff sometime in 1757, Derrick and Francklin continued as regular contributors for several years, Derrick probably at least until he became Master of Ceremonies at Bath in 1763[65] and Francklin for more than twenty years, at least until 1778 and probably later, according to Percival Stockdale.[66] The most important addition to the regular staff was Oliver Goldsmith who, having left the *Monthly*, began reviewing for the *Critical* in January 1759.[67] Other regular contributors included the distinguished botanist Philip Miller,[68] the needy young author Archibald Campbell,[69] and the historian and miscellaneous writer William Guthrie.[70] Several illustrious names figure among those who were occasional contributors to the *Critical* during this period, including Samuel Johnson, David Hume, William Hunter, and William Robertson, as well as lesser figures such as Edward Watkinson and James Ferguson.[71] The arguments for John Cleland's involvement as a *Critical* reviewer between 1757 and the mid-1760s have been made elsewhere, as has the allegation that James Macpherson, whose Ossian poems were reviewed so favorably by Smollett, had become a *Critical* reviewer at least by the 1770s.[72] Patrick Murdoch continued to contribute as a foreign correspondent,[73] George Macaulay was an occasional contributor,[74] and it is quite possible that Smollett's friends Samuel Richardson and Alexander Carlyle contributed to the *Critical* as well as to the *British Magazine*; Carlyle, at least, is known to have helped solicit and coordinate occasional contributions to the *Critical* from among his extensive circle of friends in the Scottish intelligentsia and literati, which included not only Robertson and Hume (both known contributors to the *Critical*), but also Adam Smith, John Home, Adam Ferguson, Hugh Blair, Robert Wallace, and William Wilkie—some or all of whom very probably contributed too.[75] Although there is no evidence to support the alleged participation of Griffith Jones or David Mallet, there were other contributors identified only by initials: "W. F." (Mr '59, 259), "H. R." (Se '57, 280), "M. N." (My '59, 453), and "Dr. W—" in Paris (Jl '57, 362).[76] Still other anonymous contributors and correspondents remain completely unidentified (e.g., Fe '59, 89).

One explanation for this wide range of correspondents and occasional contributors was precisely that feature of the *Critical*'s editorial policy that most distinguished it from the *Monthly*: a relatively relaxed central authority that granted independence to the reviewers, in contrast to Griffiths's practice of screening every submission and amending or rejecting those that failed to conform with *Monthly* policies. Nangle has shown that this policy was continued until the end of the century, by which time Griffiths's son, who had become managing editor, had taken it a step further:

> By a further extension of the theory that the writer for the *Monthly* spoke
> not as an individual but as an unidentified member of a group who spoke
> with one voice, he [young Griffiths] insisted with an intensity which
> approached obsession that not only must all contributors write undis-
> tinguishable—and undistinguished—prose, but that they must also be
> consistent with each other in their opinions, theories, and attitudes con-
> cerning all matters.[77]

Nangle suggests that this long-standing policy must have alienated some staff
writers and prospective contributors, and that the pervasive cautiousness and
old-fashioned tone that resulted eventually put the *Monthly* at a disadvantage
when the innovative, more provocative journals such as the *Edinburgh* and
the *Quarterly* emerged.[78]

But the *Critical*, at least in the years of Smollett's editorship, followed a
very different policy. As Smollett had insisted in 1759: "The Critical Review
is not written by a parcel of obscure hirelings, under the restraint of a bookseller and his wife, who presume to revise, alter, and amend the articles occasionally. The principal writers in the Critical Review are unconnected with
booksellers, unawed by old women, and independent of each other" (Fe '59,
151). In practice, Smollett's adherence to this policy meant several things.
First, reviewers were free to differ from each other and to contradict or ignore
past opinions expressed in the *Critical*. In 1762, for example, the reviewer of
John Ogilvie's *Poems on Several Subjects* recalled that various of Ogilvie's
poems had earlier been reviewed separately in the *Critical*, but because he
had not seen those reviews, the reviewer declared that he would "venture to
pass his own judgment, without regard to what may have been advanced by
his colleagues, which, at present he has no opportunity of consulting" (Oc
'62, 294). In another case, concerning the issue of whether authors should be
granted a formal copyright on their works, a reviewer acknowledged that
earlier publications in support of a copyright law had been reviewed in the
Critical with approval by "some of our colleagues," but nevertheless went on
to endorse the pamphlet before him that opposed such a measure (Jn '62,
523). Perhaps the most notable example is the *Critical*'s treatment of the
well-known philanthropist Jonas Hanway, towards whom they performed an
apologetic about-face in 1761:

> When we reflect upon the meek forgiving spirit of our philanthropical
> author, and that unbounded benevolence which marks every line of the
> performance now in review, we are ready to blame ourselves for having
> been seduced to turn some of Mr. Hanway's serious well-meant lucubra-
> tions into ridicule. . . . [Hanway] has, perhaps, more reason to resent our
> conduct, than half the dunces that have been damned to oblivion by a
> single stroke of the pen. (Jn '61, 442–43)

Thus even when the *Critical* reviewers displayed a sense of editorial continuity and referred to earlier opinions, they did not regard them as binding. Indeed, sometimes—as in the case of Hanway—previous opinions were overturned quite deliberately.

Second, Smollett's editorial policies were more inviting and accommodating toward occasional contributors and correspondents, especially those who wrote to correct or rebut an earlier review. It was in this way that David Hume became involved with the *Critical*. He wrote, in 1759, to respond to an unfavorable review of Wilkie's *Epigoniad*, diplomatically prefacing his article with some general remarks on "the great advantages which result from literary journals" and paying a handsome compliment to the *Critical* in particular: "The public has done so much justice to the gentlemen engaged in the Critical Review, as to acknowledge that no literary journal was ever carried on in this country with equal spirit and impartiality; yet I must confess, that an article published in your Review of 1757, gave me great surprize, and not a little uneasiness" (Ap '59, 323). Hume then went on to offer a detailed vindication of *The Epigoniad* from the *Critical*'s harsh initial treatment of it. In his decision to print Hume's article, Smollett was undoubtedly influenced by Hume's stature and the fact that he was a friend (although the article appeared anonymously); but Smollett did not lose the opportunity to point the letter to the *Critical*'s advantage in the eyes of the public: "By perusing the following article, the reader will perceive, that how subject soever we, the Reviewers, may be to oversights and errors, we are not so hardened in critical pride and insolence, but that, upon conviction, we can retract our censures, and provided we be candidly rebuked, kiss the rod of correction with great humility" (Ap '59, 323). However hyperbolic this claim of editorial "humility" might seem, the opportunity to express dissenting opinions was not denied writers less important than Hume. Occasionally an author's own reply to a review was printed, such as "Dr. Wilson's Remarks upon some Passages of the *Critical Review*, for October 1761" (Mr '62, 274–84) or J. Randall's indignant self-vindication from *Critical* comments in 1765 (Mr '65, 240). Other times the response seemed to come from a member of the general public, as in the case of "H. F." in 1762 (Au '62, 158–60). Correspondents often used the *Critical* to exchange literary news and notes, and at least one author used it to print a retraction of some harsh words on a public figure, explaining that publishing his retraction in the *Critical* was "the most proper method that occurs to me" (Jl '61, 80).

This policy was of course attended with several disadvantages. Using the *Critical* even in a small way as a kind of forum for debate attracted such important contributors as Hume, William Hunter (No '57, 437–39 and Oc '58, 315–16), and James Ferguson (My '63, 329–43; Jn '63, 409–21; No '63, 339–52), but it also attracted unwanted contributions from malcontents, cranks, and self-seekers. The brief replies to correspondents at the end of most issues were often full of rejection notices to such characters.

Smollett's frequent efforts to solicit contributions from such friends as Samuel Richardson and William Robertson could result, if successful, in valuable additions to the *Critical*'s contents. But they could also backfire. Samuel Johnson seems to have been proof against one such solicitation and perhaps even offended by it, according to Boswell: "He [Johnson] said the Critical reviewers, on occasion of he and Goldsmith doing something together (i.e., publishing each a book at the same time, Mr. Johnson the *Idler*) let them know that they might review each other."[79] Boswell reported that "Goldsmith was for accepting the offer," but Johnson squashed the idea, saying, "No; set Reviewers at defiance." A little more than a year later, however, in April 1763, Johnson contributed the first of three reviews in the *Critical* known to be his, although what induced him to do so is still unknown.[80]

Granting independence to reviewers on the staff created other problems. Perhaps unavoidably, but no less embarrassingly for Smollett, instances of unflattering treatment for his friends continued to occur. One reviewer took the opportunity of reviewing a poem about Garrick to criticize his acting technique (Ap '60, 303), while another thoroughly condemned a novel despite elaborate recommendations by Richardson printed in its preface (Ap '60, 318–19), of which the reviewer defiantly took note as he damned the book anyway. Reviewers made mistakes and stirred up controversies for which Smollett had to answer. When *The Rosciad* was first reviewed, for example, not only did the reviewer mistakenly attribute it to George Colman and disparage Colman's character, he also treated the poem so severely that he angered the real author, Charles Churchill. As a result, Smollett found himself privately asking Garrick to explain matters to Colman, atoning in print with a generous review of Colman's *Jealous Wife* (Fe '61, 131–41), arranging a review of the third edition of *The Rosciad* (reviewing later editions being an unusual step itself) just to publish a correction, and then reviewing Churchill's own angry satire, *The Apology, Addressed to the Critical Reviewers* (My '61, 409–11). Such were the joys of editorial responsibility.

Sometimes the personal quarrels of his staff writers also entangled him. Francklin treated Murphy so scathingly in his *Dissertation on Ancient Tragedy* that Murphy responded heatedly in his *Poetical Epistle to Samuel Johnson, A. M.*, attacking both Francklin and the *Critical* in bitter terms. Again Smollett intervened, taking the review of Murphy's *Epistle* onto himself (Oc '60, 319–20). Obviously tired of the whole affair and feeling trapped in the middle, Smollett chastised both authors for their excesses and then, with a generous compliment to Johnson, tried to pass off the quarrel to that literary lion: "We wish, for the sake of both, they would refer it to the decision of that gentleman [i.e., Johnson] to whom this epistle is inscribed; a gentleman whose candour is as universally acknowledged as his genius" (Oc '60, 320).

Despite the relative independence of the reviewers, however, it comes as no surprise that books written by the reviewers themselves were invariably reviewed favorably in the *Critical*. Works by Francklin (Jl '60, 340–41), Armstrong (My '58, 380–86), Philip Miller (Jl '60, 76) and Edward Watkinson (Ja '62, 80 and Au '62, 160), among others, as well as all of Smollett's, received high praise in the *Critical*. Such "logrolling" was commonplace in the publishing world of the time and needed no editorial authority to organize or enforce it. Indeed, writers of the day saw it not as a breach of ethics, but a routine courtesy to review a colleague's book favorably. It must have caused a flap on those occasions when courtesy broke down, as it did with Watkinson's *Exhortation to Beneficence*, which received a terse dismissal in the *Critical* despite his having written for it since 1761 (Ja '66, 80). What is interesting is that the writers on the *Critical* seemed to be sensitive to the problem of appearing prejudiced, as the reviewer of Smollett's *Continuation* made clear in 1761 before saying a word on the book:

> The share which the public hath thought proper to assign the author of the Complete History of England [Smollett] in our periodical labours, is productive of considerable embarrassment to the Reviewers. In treating a performance supposed to be written by a colleague, they are sensible their praises will be wrested into flattery, and their censures regarded as baits to delude the credulous into an opinion of their integrity. (Oc '61, 283–84)

This dilemma notwithstanding, there are some very interesting signs scattered among these reviews that suggest that even in treating works by central figures like Smollett and Francklin, the *Critical* reviewers exercised a critical freedom that would certainly have been curtailed by a more domineering editor than Smollett. In a discussion of Francklin's *Dissertation on Ancient Tragedy*, for example, Francklin was criticized by the *Critical* reviewer for making unwarranted personal attacks on other writers: "The ingenious author has unhappily blended passion and prejudice against certain contemporary writers, who deserve well of the public" (Jl '60, 41). The reviewer of Smollett's *Continuation* presumed to differ with him on one of the issues about which he felt most strongly—the Admiral Byng affair. Had Smollett been exercising close editorial control, the reviewer's remarks would never have found their way into print: "Doctor Smollett will excuse us should we observe, that from his account of Byng's conduct in the engagement of Minorca, we think that admiral justly merited the punishment which his country loudly demanded, though the doctor regards him as a scapegoat" (Oc '61, 292). Doctor Smollett certainly would not have excused them! Although these honest criticisms of works by colleagues are few and scattered, they nevertheless suggest that a certain license to write candidly constituted a real part of the *Critical*'s editorial policy.

Under Smollett's editorship, the *Critical* was often accused of being quarrelsome and fiercely self-interested. Running battles with Grainger, Kenrick, Shebbeare, Comber, and especially with the *Monthly Review* resulted in some very unseemly articles appearing in the *Critical*, many by Smollett himself. One can only laugh at the ludicrous animosity displayed, for instance, in Smollett's review of Grainger's *Letter to Tobias Smollett, M. D.* (Fe '59, 141–58) or in his editorial "To the Old Gentlewoman Who Directs the Monthly Review" (No '57, 469–72). Between 1756 and 1759, there were periods when scarcely a month passed without an exchange of fire between the *Critical* and *Monthly*.

The actual scale and significance of these hostilities, however, may easily be exaggerated. By about 1760, the quarreling between the *Monthly* and the *Critical* had begun to give way to a sense of shared enterprise and collegiality. As one *Critical* reviewer pointed out in 1760, their judgments were often the same and therefore so were their enemies (Mr '60, 214), a point that is corroborated dramatically by the very high incidence of printed works that attack *both* reviews, rather than one or the other.[81] Another reviewer echoed this opinion in 1761 in dismissing one such pamphlet: "Let us for once join issue with the Monthly Reviewers, and agree with them and all mankind, in declaring this paultry production the most impotent attack ever" (No '61, 399). Despite the fierce feuding, Griffiths's publications were often reviewed favorably in the *Critical*.[82] Relations got warmer over the years. In 1765, for example, a *Critical* reviewer defended John Langhorne, "whom," the reviewer wrote, "our author supposes to be concerned in the *Monthly Review*," from charges levied by the attacker that he had been unfairly treated in the *Monthly* (Ja '65, 88–89). In 1767 a *Critical* reviewer actually cited a *Monthly* opinion of Johnson's *Rambler* essays ("an excellent performance") as part of a defense of Johnson from the furious accusations in Campbell's *Lexiphanes* (Ap '67, 264). Interestingly, even during a time when the two reviews were publicly reviling each other, their proprietors were still able quietly to do business with each other. Griffiths routinely hired different printing shops to reprint back issues of the *Monthly*; in 1757, according to Griffiths's own business records, he hired Hamilton's printing shop to reprint the March 1753 issue of the *Monthly Review*.[83] In 1768, Smollett and his publishers arranged to distribute four-page advertisements for his forthcoming *Present State of All Nations* in issues of Griffiths's *Monthly Review*.[84] These are striking reminders that in Grub Street, behind all the public posturing and feuding, profit still took precedence over any other principle.

A balanced view of the *Critical*'s editorial behavior must record not only the editorial outbursts and wrangles that have given it a colorful reputation, but also the examples of disinterested and even generous reviews that lie quietly unnoticed in its thousands of pages of contents. The *Critical* quarreled with some rival periodicals such as the *Monthly* and the *Universal Visiter*, but others it treated with respect. The short-lived *Philological Miscellany* (founded in 1761) threatened, with its extensive coverage of foreign publications, to rival the *Critical's* own foreign coverage, yet it was welcomed and recommended in the highest terms by the *Critical* (My '61, 341–47). Similarly, Edmund Burke's *Annual Register*, although greeted initially with disapproval (My '59, 469–70), was soon receiving consistently high praise in the *Critical*, even for its book review section that might have been regarded as a serious competitor. As one reviewer wrote in 1763, after describing the *Annual Register's* other good features: "The volume concludes with an account of books for 1762, which we cannot be so partial to ourselves as not to recommend" (Jl '63, 69). Perhaps here too was another manifestation of Smollett's good relations with Burke and his circle, which had been nurtured at least partly through Smollett's role as editor of the *Critical*.

Despite all the logrolling on behalf of Smollett's publications, the *Critical* was not used to pursue his own interests as single-mindedly and ruthlessly as it might have been. For example, on the very eve of the appearance of Smollett's translation of the works of Voltaire in the 1760s, the *Critical* published very favorable reviews of translations by other writers of individual works of Voltaire such as his *Semiramis* (Au '60, 154–57) and his *Critical Essays on Dramatic Poetry* (De '60, 430–34). Conversely, when the author of a long poem entitled *The Retort* tried to ingratiate himself with Smollett by dedicating it to him and devoting part of its contents to a defense of Smollett's achievement, the poem was nevertheless found wanting by its *Critical* reviewer. The poet was advised to follow another profession and "wean himself from the nipple of poetry" (No '61, 400).

Given the number of provocations by antagonists, the *Critical* responded in kind to relatively few. As the lists of printed attacks on the *Critical* compiled by Jones, Spector, and this author reveal, the *Critical* might have spent all its time fighting paper quarrels.[85] Many of these attacks were simply ignored. The *Literary Magazine*, for example, for a period in 1757 printed almost monthly attacks on the *Critical*, yet not a word of response appeared in the *Critical*.[86] Some works that attacked the *Critical* were nonetheless reviewed favorably; Murphy's *Ode to the Naiads of Fleet-Ditch*, for example, despite its many barbs at the *Critical*, was credited with having "a considerable share of poetical merit, replete with all the poignancy of satire" (Jn '61, 495).[87] The reviewers often wore their virtue ostentatiously, as with the author of *Tyburn to the Marine Society*: "Notwithstanding the sarcastic freedom with which this author has treated us Reviewers . . . we cannot, without forfeiting that character of impartiality, which we have resolved to maintain, with-hold our approbation of the piece, in which we meet with abundance of arch irony and manly satire, a good deal of wit, and a great deal of humour" (My '59, 465). On one occasion, Smollett noted with amusement that the author of the work before him (Molyneux's *Conjunct Expeditions*) had printed an attack on him in the newspapers after an earlier review, even though that review had been favorable. Nevertheless, Smollett went on to approve of the second book also (Jl '59, 28).

With regard to the treatment of individual publishers, the *Critical* by and large remained impartial. Newbery probably received more favorable notice in the *Critical* than any other single publisher, but this was the result of his genuine prominence as a publisher and his popularity throughout the publishing world, rather than any special treatment by the *Critical*.[88] Newbery publications were by no means exempt from criticism. For example, a *Critical* reviewer found one of his publications—Mason's *Lectures upon the Heart, Lungs, [etc.]*—to contain nothing of interest and concluded: "nor, indeed, do we see any necessity there was for publishing the lectures" (My '63, 399–400). In the same way, other publishers who might have expected favored treatment—such as Baldwin, under whose imprint the *Critical* was first published, and Payne, one of the publishers of Smollett's *British Magazine*—also saw books of theirs damned in the *Critical*.[89] Conversely, as has been shown, many of the archrival Griffiths's publications were reviewed favorably, and at least one book published by Noble, whose lowbrow publications were regularly abused in the *Critical*, received high praise in a long review in 1760 (Oc '60, 280–90). No doubt this impartiality resulted in part from the decentralized editorial control and from the absence of a bookseller-publisher's interests pressing on the proprietors. Smollett's success at keeping the *Critical* free from any detectable commercial interests was a small but important moral victory.

Toward the publishing industry in general, however, the *Critical* was a good friend, supporting a wide range of literary and publishing activity, including anything it felt was for the benefit of the reading public. At various times, writers on the *Critical* recommended individual foreign books to be translated into English (Au '59, 121; Jl '61, 71); criticized authors for using foreign quotations in their books because "they render the book in a manner useless to common readers" (Jn '58, 450); and even resorted to translating some foreign articles themselves because "there are many, who may prefer a faint copy which they understand, to the original they may be imperfectly acquainted with" (Jn '60, 484). They encouraged the publication of rare archival material for the benefit of the general reading public, as was done by the author of *Pièces Fugitives, pour servir à l'Histoire de France* (Ja '61, 62). They supported proposals for public lending libraries such as the Rev. Mr. Hanbury's *Plan for a Public Library at Church-Langton, in Leicestershire* (Mr '60, 244). They encouraged the widespread use of serial publication, in the belief, as they said of one such book project, that "the method the proprietors have chosen of publishing it in weekly numbers, enables all ranks of people to become purchasers" (Oc '60, 323). They were, in short, friends of the "common reader," that educated but not learned reader whom Johnson immortalized in his remarks on Gray's *Elegy* in his *Lives of the Poets* (1781), but whom both Johnson and the *Critical* reviewers had been discussing (and catering to) since the 1750s.[90]

The *Critical* reviewers endorsed proposals for a wide variety of academies and societies and, in the best traditions of the Enlightenment, they also approved of almost every kind of encyclopedic compilation:

> There is scarce any branch of knowledge, which in the present age has not been inculcated under the form of a dictionary; and this has become necessary, from the immense extension of all kinds of history and science. . . .
>
> We are therefore inclined to look upon every epitome, of the nature of that which now lies before us, in which the outlines of every great character are justly preserved, to be not only amusing for the present, but the most likely method of transmitting the accounts of the great to posterity. (Jn '60, 445)

The work under review was Thomas Flloyd's *Bibliotheca Biographica: A Synopsis of Universal Biography* that, like the *Universal History*, was made possible by a syndicate of publishers who pooled capital and shared risks—procedures that were also highly approved of by the *Critical*. In addition, the *Critical* endorsed a similar reference work on geography (Oc '61, 237–50); various proposed dictionaries—including a pronouncing dictionary (Fe '62, 160–61) and a schoolboy dictionary (Au '61, 159–60); a compilation of medical cases in England such as the French Academy published (No '58, 377–86); and a project aimed at publishing engraved prints of every important painting in England (Jn '63, 483–84).

The most difficult and perhaps ultimately the most significant question about editorial policy during Smollett's tenure is whether the reviewers saw themselves shaping or following public opinion. For a journal with the *Critical*'s avowed standards and goals that still had to depend on a wide readership for success, it was a genuine dilemma. The reviewers repeatedly drew the distinction between popular acclaim and artistic achievement; with Lyttelton's *Dialogues of the Dead*, for example, the reviewer wrote: "It is a presumptive, but not a direct proof of the merit of these dialogues, that they have so rapidly attained a second impression. In general the multitude is swayed by a few individuals of superior taste; but there are many instances where books of the least merit rise to the highest vogue, merely from caprice" (My '60, 390). The reviewers were acutely conscious of the position in which they placed themselves: "The Critical Reviewers are too frequently reduced to the disagreeable necessity of combating the opinions of the multitude, and exposing the applause, misplaced by caprice, on writers of no merit" (De '61, 452). Accordingly, they were relieved when the commercial success of a book seemed to confirm their judgment because it also obviated any accusation of prejudice: "It is with pleasure we hear that our judgment of the ingenious Mr. Hume's historical abilities is confirmed by the public approbation; and that, although we recommended with warmth, we have not been accused of partiality" (Fe '62, 81). On several occasions, and perhaps with justification, the reviewers were pleased to call attention to their influence with the public. They took credit, for example, for the success of Paton's paintings, having recommended them before the voice of "The Town" had been heard (Ja '60, 70), and for recognizing the value of Sterne's *Tristram Shandy* when it still lay undiscovered in the literary undergrowth (Ap '61, 316).

At the same time, however, Smollett and his staff were becoming equally concerned about catering to the demands of the public. In addition to the usual pressure to produce a periodical that would sell, they also received a steady stream of specific suggestions from their readership about everything from what books to review to how much quotation to include. Smollett obviously tried to please his readers by responding to their suggestions, but by about 1760 he had received so many pieces of conflicting advice that he prefaced a review with a long editorial statement about the problem:

> There cannot be imagined a situation more irksome than that of a Reviewer, whose imagination is constantly on the stretch to furnish out entertainment for the great variety of different palates. Eager in the pursuit of honest fame, and equally sensible of the sting of reproach, and titillation of applause, his delicacy meets with a thousand shocks and galling disappointments. The opposite tastes, humours, and dispositions of his readers, and frequently the dearth that falls out in point of variety, baffle his utmost endeavours to please all in the same degree. (Se '60, 161)

Instead of seeking to resurrect critical standards and to reform the public taste, as he had when the *Critical* was launched in 1756, here he seems to look to the public for guidance, as if they were the true arbiters of taste. His complaint is that the public espouses such a wide variety of irreconcilable but apparently equally valid standards: "What one admires as exquisitely delicious, another condemns as insufferably insipid; and the choice morsel prepared to tickle the palate of the epicure in learning, creates loathing and disgust in the stomach of the supinely ignorant" (Se '60, 161). Smollett also finds his readership divided in its basic preference of either science or the arts:

> Every reader expects, that an article should be treated in the way most agreeable to him. Geometry, for instance, and every work of science, must be skimmed over with exceeding brevity, while the productions of taste and humour ought to employ the whole attention of the Reviewer. Another, of a contrary opinion, insists upon the superior utility of abstracted studies, and demands that our work shall be a repository of new opinions and notable discoveries in science. (Se '60, 161–62)

Moreover, his readers even disagree about what constitutes a proper book review in the first place and whether quotation or criticism should predominate:

> One cries out against the length and dulness of extracts, and another believes, that no just idea of an author can be conveyed without extracts, which ought to be selected less on account of the entertainment, than the utility and instruction they convey. Too often the learning of the critic is termed pedantry, his just severity construed into scurrility, and his ridicule mistaken for buffoonery. (Se '60, 162)

This was the same reading public that Johnson had identified and anatomized so aptly in the *Rambler*:

> Every size of readers requires a genius of correspondent capacity; some delight in abstracts and epitomes because they want room in their memory for long details, and content themselves with effects, without enquiry after causes; some minds are overpowered by splendor of sentiment, as some eyes are offended by a glaring light; such will gladly contemplate an author in an humble imitation, as we look without pain upon the sun in the water. (No. 145, 6 August 1751)

For all these observations reveal about something that is easy to forget—that is, the complex makeup of the mideighteenth century reading public—they did nothing to ease the difficulty of pleasing such audiences for either Johnson or Smollett. Not surprisingly in the face of these conflicting demands, Smollett struck for a middle way. He announced a compromise policy that left room for flexibility:

> Let it suffice for our readers in general, that we shall endeavour to steer a middle course amidst the variety of dissonant and jarring opinions, from a full conviction founded upon experience, that each of these opinions is both right and wrong, according to circumstances; and that the Reviewer, who invariably adheres to either, is unjust to his readers, to his authors, and to his own reputation. (Se '60, 162)

Smollett's editorial remarks are valuable not only for what they reveal about the kinds of demands that the general reading public were making on this new kind of periodical, the literary review, but for the changes they reveal in Smollett's personal outlook. After almost five years in review journalism, Smollett had become less idealistic and assertive, more pragmatic and tractable, and in every way mellower. The signs are everywhere. The same Smollett who had been so prickly toward his rival Fielding in the 1740s and early 1750s, now, in the 1760s, writes eulogistic accounts of his career in the *Con-*

tinuation and defends Fielding's characters as superior to their many imitators (Fe '61, 132–33). The same Smollett who seethed with resentment at the rejection of his *Regicide* for so many years now, in 1761, can write playfully: "After all, we discontented authors, who have had the stage-door thrown in our teeth, may retire to our garrets, and draw the pen of Aristarchus against patentees and happier bards, as much as we please. The manager is certainly the best judge of what will best suit his own interest, that is, the entertainment of the audience" (Fe '61, 132). The same Smollett who was among the earliest to refer publicly to Smart's mental illness ("They wage no war with Bedlam or the Mint," Ap '56, 287) sees to it that a benefit production of *The Guardian* performed for Smart's relief is generously treated in the *Critical* in 1759 (Fe '59, 171–72) and then subscribes for Smart's *Psalms of David* in 1765. And so on. Smollett's tone and manner in the *Critical* become noticeably milder and more accommodating in the 1760s, as they do in his other writings, from *Sir Launcelot Greaves* and the *Continuation* to *Humphry Clinker*.

His change in attitude, tinged with a note of resignation, is reflected also in his private correspondence. Writing to a friend, William Huggins, in 1760 to advise him not to undertake a literary career because of its trials and uncertainties, Smollett spoke in what for him was a rare confessional mode: "For my part, I long eagerly for some quiet, obscure Retreat, where, as from a safe and happy Harbour, I may look back with self gratulation, upon that stormy Sea of Criticism in which my little Bark has been so long and so violently tossed and afflicted."[91] A year later, in the midst of yet another *Critical*-related fracas, Smollett confided in Garrick: "I desire to live quietly with all mankind, and if possible to be upon good terms with all those who have distinguished themselves by their extraordinary merit."[92] Despite the enthusiasm with which he had founded it and the enormous amounts of time and effort he had invested in it, Smollett's experience with the *Critical* seemed, in his own perception, to have brought him little but frustration and disappointment.

Smollett must have noticed, perhaps with a mixture of pride and regret, some of the many changes that marked his departure from the *Critical* in 1763. By 1764 the feature on works of art had all but disappeared. At the same time, the foreign articles section was also discontinued for a while. When it was refounded in March 1764 "at the request of several of our learned readers" (Mr '64, 230), it was as if no such feature had ever appeared in the *Critical* before. Reviews of volumes of the *Philosophical Transactions* became mere summaries rather than critical analyses. Other signs of a break in editorial continuity cropped up, including instances when a book that had earlier been reviewed in the *Critical* was unwittingly reviewed for a second time (e.g., My '66, 350–58). But what Smollett could not realize—because he was

still too close to events and distracted by personal misery—was the considerable impact his review journal had already made on the literary world and the
transformation it had wrought in his own career.

"These Self-Elected Monarchs": The Impact of the *Critical Review* on the Literary World

Despite its failure to fulfill Smollett's highest hopes for it, the *Critical* had achieved considerable success by the time of his departure from England in 1763. Its reception in those first years was far more positive than is usually remembered. Moreover, it had already made a lasting impact on the literary world—on other periodicals, on authors, on publishers, on the reading public, and on the complex relations among them all—much of it in ways that only the passage of time would reveal. It and the *Monthly* had already begun to influence the way English literature was received in other countries, as well as the way new kinds of foreign literary journals emerged, with new and broader readerships, in imitation of the English review journals. These are all aspects of a literary underworld whose terrain is difficult to map but into which, as scholars like Robert Darnton continue to show, some useful exploration can be done.

Of the many measures of the *Critical*'s success, the first is simply survival. The *Critical* was one of forty-nine journals founded between 1750 and 1760, of which only thirteen lasted two years or more and only five were still publishing in 1765.[1] In 1756 alone, six literary journals were started, but of these, only the *Critical* was still alive at the end of 1758. The competition was impressive: Adam Smith, William Robertson, and Hugh Blair on the *Edinburgh Review* (Edinburgh, 1755–56), Samuel Johnson on the *Literary Magazine* (May 1756–July 1758), and Johnson and Christopher Smart on the *Universal Visiter* (January 1756–?December 1756).[2] It is a measure of Smollett's achievement that where such writers as these had tried and failed, he succeeded in establishing a journal that not only flourished in his lifetime, but lasted well into the nineteenth century, perishing in 1817.

In mid-1756, after only six issues of the newly founded *Critical* had appeared, Smollett wrote to John Moore in Scotland that the *Critical* "meets with a very favourable Reception."[3] On what did he base this opinion? Little attention has ever been paid to the possibility that the *Critical* was welcomed in its early years. In fact, mindful of the many angry responses it provoked, scholars have treated Smollett's early optimism with irony. As Knapp wryly observed, "It is doubtful whether after 1756 Smollett always regarded its reception as 'very favorable.'"[4] Such views have dominated our sense of the *Critical*'s reputation. For lack of evidence to the contrary, Knapp felt that the *Critical*'s "immediate reception must be gauged, unfortunately, by the data of hostile attacks" and, basing his conclusion principally on antagonistic articles in the *Universal Visiter* (March 1756) and the *Gentleman's Magazine* (March 1756), found it impossible to discern any "marked success" for the *Critical*.[5]

But a closer look tells a different story. The very first notice taken of the *Critical*, only twelve days after its first issue came out, was highly favorable. The 13 March 1756 issue of the *Repository; or General Review*—a weekly magazine with its own review section—quoted with approval the opening passages of the *Critical*'s manifesto and then, drawing in part on the *Critical*'s own language, offered a paragraph of commendation:

> As we are assured, that the generous motives which urged the gentlemen, who manage this work, to undertake it, were an indignation for seeing the productions of genius and dulness, wit and impertinence, learning and ignorance, applauded without taste, and condemned without distinction, we are in hopes to see the noble art of criticism rescued from the hands of *hirelings*, the fetters of sordid views, avarice, and interest, and flourish under the jurisdiction of Gentlemen who, actuated by the most benevolent principles towards Printers, Booksellers, Publishers and Hawkers in general, are determined to devote so much of their time and labour to the benefit of so useful and necessary a body, for promoting the cause of literature.[6]

Significantly, the editor of the *Repository* immediately recognized that the *Critical* joined the *Monthly* in a new and distinct category of periodical and he paid them the highest compliment in the Grub Street lexicon: he borrowed articles from them for his magazine. The *Repository* proposed to print parallel reviews from the *Critical* and *Monthly* in each issue, adding that "where they may chance to vary in their judgment, we have determined to inspect and compare their records, examine the merits of the case, and investigate all iniquitous practices."[7] In the event, however, the *Repository* never actually juxtaposed *Monthly* and *Critical* reviews of the same work, but did, in its short life of five issues, print a sampling of articles from each—a total of seven from the *Critical* and three from the *Monthly*.[8] In so doing, the editor of the *Repository* started a practice that quickly became commonplace in magazine publishing. By regularly reprinting articles from both reviews, magazine editors signaled that Griffiths's *Monthly* was no longer a unique source of critical opinion, but merely the first of its kind. By reprinting reviews from the *Monthly* and *Critical* rather than writing their own, the magazine editors implicitly acknowledged the expertise and authority the reviewers had assumed for themselves in the world of letters. (They also, of course, saved themselves the trouble of writing original copy.)

There were other signs of the *Critical*'s securing a place for itself in its first year. The author of the *Rhapsodist* (24 January 1757–14 March 1757), in surveying the field of periodical literature, also classed the *Critical* with the *Monthly* and recognized the review as a distinctive type of periodical:

> There are likewise two *Reviews*: the old and motherly one, is called the *Monthly*; the new and spirited one, the *Critical*. The former is under the influence of *Saturn* and gravitates. *Mercurey* presides over the latter; which, like its patron Deity, is by some judged guilty of deviations, censurable before the impartial throne of *Jupiter*. But this reply may perhaps be made; that the ingenious have always thought themselves privileged to dispense occasionally with their own rules.[9]

This appraisal is notable for its defence of the *Critical* on the grounds that some license must be allowed the "spirited" and "ingenious." The *Critical*'s self-presentation as a compaigning reformer seems to have made an impression. Another writer, the anonymous author of *The Theatrical Examiner* (1757), held both the *Monthly* and the *Critical* in such respect for having "evinced taste and impartial judgment in their monthly examinations" that he urged them, in addition to books, to take the theater under their inspection also.[10]

The compliment that must have pleased Smollett most, however, came from George Colman and Bonnell Thornton in their widely respected periodical, the *Connoisseur*. A letter ostensibly from a country correspondent depicts a scene that demonstrates the *Connoisseur*'s popularity among literate rural society: "There is a club of country-parsons, who meet every Saturday at a neighbouring market-town, to be shaved and exchange sermons: they have a subscription for books and pamphlets: and the only periodical works ordered in by them are the *Connoisseur*, and the *Critical* and *Monthly Reviews*."[11] Three points about this sketch should be noted. First, here again, after only seven issues, the *Critical* is being classed automatically with the *Monthly*. Second, this provincial literary society subscribes not to one review or the other, but to both concurrently, which corresponds to the typical pattern of subscription by real literary societies for the rest of the century. Third, the authors of the *Connoisseur* seem at least as honored to be seen in the exclusive company of the reviews as the other way around.

Already then, as today, review journals were being regarded as a highbrow kind of periodical.

There were more such positive reactions to the *Critical* in the years that followed, but they have been totally overshadowed by the vociferousness and sheer numbers of contemporary complainants. Twentieth-century scholars have compiled long lists of printed attacks on the *Critical*: ninety-five separate titles in Jones's list, to which Spector has added many more, and still others are listed for the first time in appendix B of this study.[12] In truth, for two hundred years we have derived from this material our sense not only of the *Critical*'s reputation, but of its policies, its effectiveness, and its influence in the literary world. It is time for a serious reconsideration, because there are many dangers and problems with allowing these works, however numerous or clamorous, to determine the historical importance of the *Critical Review*.

Sheer numbers are the first problem. Faced with these lists of attacks, it is far too easy for us to think, with Sutcliffe, that "it is significant that no collection of similar length can be made up from remarks of the reviewers' friends."[13] But a moment's thought about human nature suggests that it is not at all significant. Authors, as much or more than the rest of humankind, accept praise in silence, as their just desert. Only criticism provokes a response. Moreover, the numbers have been interpreted too narrowly. Johnson had had to come to terms with critical responses to his *Rambler* essays, and we find him already in the tenth issue taking stock of the many letters, hostile and friendly, he has received. His conclusion: "It is no less a proof of eminence to have many enemies than many friends, and I look upon every letter, whether it contains encomiums, or reproaches, as an equal attestation of rising credit" (no. 10, 21 April 1750). The lists of attacks on the *Critical* also imply a false distinction between its reception and that of its counterpart, the *Monthly*. Although Smollett's prominence made him a convenient target, hostile responses from unhappy authors were not unique to the *Critical*'s experience. At least one list has been compiled that contains 115 separately published attacks on the *Monthly* for the years 1749 to 1771 alone.[14] As Griffiths and Smollett learned, and the correspondence sections of the *Times Literary Supplement* and *New York Review of Books* continue to testify today, such wrangles are endemic to book-review criticism.

One must also consider the visibility and effectiveness of such writings. Many sold only a handful of copies and passed virtually unnoticed. In 1757 a *Critical* reviewer, in reply to a pamphlet attack by Archibald Bower, noted that "Mr. B[ower] seems apprehensive that our work may reach those places where his defence may never be read" and facetiously offered, if Bower would supply copies of his pamphlet, to "inclose them, for the benefit of our readers, in our next *Review*" (Fe '57, 190–92). A more graphic example is Grainger's pamphlet *A Letter to the Author of the Critical Review* (1757), of which—according to Strahan's printing records—only twenty-five copies were printed.[15] It undoubtedly gained more publicity from Smollett's angry review of it (Au '57, 149–52) than it could ever have achieved otherwise. In fact, some authors seemed to court abuse from the reviewers in order to gain publicity through controversy. A reviewer refused to humor one such writer in 1767, passing over his book with the remark, "We shall, however, disappoint the author, who seems to hug himself with the thoughts that the Reviewers, by damning his pamphlet, will introduce it to public notice" (Ap '67, 299). In 1764, the *St. James's Magazine* set itself up as the champion of offended authors, offering—because "the circulation of one book or pamphlet, written in defence of another, [is] seldom very extensive"—to publish their complaints against the reviewers to a wider audience.[16] There is in so many of these attacks a motif of authorial impotence, of being unfairly shut out or put down, that it suggests something of a new power structure taking shape in the literary world of the later eighteenth century.

Then too there are the erratic and self-defeating qualities of so many of these pamphlet attacks. Authors who railed against the impudence and illegitimacy of reviewers sometimes turned out to be reviewers themselves: the author of *Anecdotes of Polite Literature* was exposed in this posture (Jn '64, 439), while Goldsmith in *The Vicar of Wakefield* referred to the *Monthly* and *Critical* reviews as "the diffusive productions of fruitful mediocrity," blithely ignoring the fact that he had written for both of them.[17] The *Critical* was sometimes criticized not for being too harsh, but too lenient: at various times, authors accused the *Critical* of being too *un*critical of books on chemistry (Mr '60, 237), too easily persuaded by a theological work,[18] and too easily pleased by various novels (Ap '60, 318–19). An advertisement for Christopher Smart's *Song to David* quoted a favorable passage from the *Critical* in support of the poem, yet elsewhere in the same ad referred to the *Critical* itself as "a scurrilous pamphlet."[19] Another author attacked the *Critical* for its "trifling observations" on his book, observations it could not possibly have made, given that the offending review is alleged to have appeared in 1754, two years before the *Critical* was founded (Au '66, 142–43). Some angry authors wrote with such venom and bombast as to discredit rather than vindicate themselves. The poet William Shenstone was horrified, for example, when he saw his friend Grainger's pamphlet attack on the *Critical*: "I'm quite asham'd of my neglect. Had I known his intention of answering Smollett, I would have us'd my endeavours to dissuade him. The *properest* answer had been convey'd in a few short notes in the next Edition of his Tibullus."[20] In discussing a pamphlet by Kenrick, Smollett contended that such attacks actually served the *Critical*'s interests: "Angry writers of his stamp would do well to reflect, that all their efforts of revenge, their private abuse, their public letters, their pamphlets, and their threats of *bella, horrida bella*, serve no other purposes, but those of propagating their own want of talent and temper and of increasing the demand for the Critical Review" (Fe '59, 167). Here is the truth of the matter. Taken in sum, as Johnson argued, the noisy complaints and venomous attacks are finally as much testimony to the *Critical*'s importance as the praise of any number of friends. They simply proved that authors regarded it and the *Monthly* as forces to be reckoned with, too prominent and influential to ignore.

A thorough assessment of the *Critical*'s impact, however, must take into account more complex and indirect responses than the straightforward criticisms and compliments it received. The emergence of the *Critical* affected the whole landscape of periodical literature. To this the periodicals themselves attest: the imitation of features, the relinquishing of "territory," and the innovations in publishing and advertising techniques are the silent signs of the *Critical*'s impact.

The three periodicals that responded most immediately and antagonistically to the *Critical*—the *Gentleman's Magazine*, the *Universal Visiter*, and the *Literary Magazine*—were also the three whose subsequent conduct demonstrated most graphically the *Critical*'s impact. Within a short time, all three had retreated significantly from the field of literature. The *Literary Magazine*, which through its advertisements had managed to challenge the *Critical* even before it had begun publishing, suffered from competition with the *Critical* (and presumably with the *Monthly* also) in both phases of its brief history. In the first few issues, under Johnson's editorship, there was a literary orientation: essays and book reviews dominated its contents. But with Johnson struggling to compile each issue essentially by himself, his journal could not compete with the coverage of the two reviews, with their staffs of writers and superior organization. After Johnson's departure, it became much more political in emphasis and, coincidentally, much more hostile toward Smollett and the *Critical*, printing a number of attacks throughout 1757.[21] Neither tactic improved its fortunes. It continued to falter—the *Grand Magazine of Magazines* reported in 1758 that the *Literary Magazine* was "not flourishing"[22]— and stopped altogether before the year was out.

Smart's *Universal Visiter* fared even worse. It, too, had skirmished with the *Critical* almost from the beginning. Its hostility fueled by Derrick's unfavorable review (Ja/Fe '56, 85–88), it printed several attacks on the *Critical*, the most spirited of which was a letter "From *Edmund Curl*, to the principal Author of a Thing, called the *Critical Review*."[23] In its first three issues, the *Universal Visiter* offered a modest selection of literary reviews under the heading "Literary Observations." But the fourth issue (April 1756) had no literature section, no book reviews, not even a list of books published. The editor explained unconvincingly that this was due to "few books having been published last month"[24] and promised to continue the feature in the next issue. The literature section never did reappear, however, as the *Universal Visiter* struggled through the year, dwindling in size from fifty-four pages in January to thirty-eight in December, when it died.[25] Its rapid demise, in part owing to Smart's mental illness, underlines the sad irony of the optimism with which it was founded: the proprietors and editors had entered into a formal agreement renewable for up to ninety-nine years.[26]

The response of the *Gentleman's Magazine*, the grand patriarch of magazines, suggests most clearly what was happening. Primarily through the efforts of Samuel Johnson, the *Gentleman's Magazine* had been offering among its contents some literary material, including occasional book reviews and features on foreign publications, in addition to its monthly list of "Books published." About 1754, Johnson signaled his intention to expand the literature section, "to which we shall, perhaps, more frequently allot an extraordinary page than heretofore."[27] Throughout 1754, 1755, and the first two issues of 1756, this expanded literature section maintained a regular size of two to three pages per issue. But suddenly in the issue for March 1756 major changes occurred: the literature section was increased to more than eight pages, including six pages on English publications. The April issue also contained eight pages of the book list "with remarks" and this time with the whole feature moved forward to a more prominent position in the magazine. This expanded section continued in the May and June issues, with eight and four pages respectively. Over the summer, however, it began shrinking again, and by September the *Gentleman's Magazine* had reduced its literary coverage to the simple one-page list of books published, to which it confined itself well into the 1760s.

These changes are significant because they coincide exactly with the publication of the *Critical*'s first issues. The authors of the *Gentleman's Magazine*, who had not deigned to comment at all when the *Monthly* appeared in 1749, made it clear that they had been watching for the *Critical*. They seized the earliest opportunity to damn it by reviewing its first issue:

> The public has been prepared to receive this elaborate work with proper respect, by a long ostentatious advertisement, that, like another Goliath, has come forth "morning and evening, and presented itself more than forty days," with insult and defiance. The authors are said to be gentlemen, and not hirelings or booksellers, who censure and commend without either justice or mercy. But if their abilities to censure and commend the works of others be estimated by their own, perhaps their impartiality may be admitted, without allowing that they are better qualified for their undertaking than those whom they have treated with contempt.
>
> The manner in which their work is executed shews that they either did not know what should be done, or were not able to do it.[28]

The writer then proceeds to condemn the contents of the *Critical*'s first issue in every particular. These hostile comments and the competitive surge of literary coverage show the *Gentleman's Magazine* trying to defend some of its "territory"—unsuccessfully, as it turned out. Its shift after a few months to a simple one-page list of new titles marked its retreat from the field of book reviewing.

This is not to imply that the *Critical* was solely responsible for these developments on the *Gentleman's Magazine*. The death of Cave in 1754, the departure of Johnson after 1755, and the consequent editorial adjustments were more direct causes. But the actions of the *Gentleman's Magazine*, considered in connection with the histories of the *Universal Visiter* and *Literary Magazine*, suggest at the very least that during the short period 1756 to 1758 the field of review journalism had become extremely crowded and competitive, and miscellaneous journals such as these three were conceding areas of literary coverage to the new specialist journals, the reviews. Johnson commented on the sudden proliferation of periodicals in 1756, comparing them to "wolves in long winters [who] are forced to prey on one another."[29] A year later, he observed that the lack of a good literary journal had been "for a long Time, among the Deficiencies of English Literature, but," he added sardonically, "as the Caprice of Man is always starting from too little to too much, we have now, amongst other Disturbers of human Quiet, a numerous Body of *Reviewers* and *Remarkers*."[30]

In this context, the response of the *Monthly* itself to its new imitator and rival is most significant. Unlike the magazines, the *Monthly* did not greet the *Critical* with a hostile review (or indeed with a notice of any kind), but subtler signs of reaction began appearing immediately. The size of each issue of the *Monthly*, which from 1749 to 1755 had been relatively constant at eighty pages, was suddenly increased to ninety-six pages—and then varied between ninety-six and 112 pages throughout 1756. In August 1757, the *Monthly* discovered in itself a concern for accuracy and began soliciting errata from the public, as the *Critical* had been doing regularly from the beginning (*Monthly* 17:192). By 1761, the Monthly had adopted the *Critical*'s practice of advertising itself as "By a Society of Gentlemen."[31]

Other points of competition between the *Monthly* and the *Critical* were more substantive and had broader implications. As discussed in chapter 3, the *Monthly* followed the *Critical*'s lead in promptness of reviewing new titles, improved its format, and regularized its contents each month—all in response to the new competition. Coverage, in terms of the number of books reviewed, continued to be a point of rivalry and was even emphasized in advertisements, such as the following: "The MONTHLY REVIEW For September, 1758. Containing a candid Account of *Fifty-Three* new Books and Pamphlets . . . [etc.]."[32] The standard form of newspaper ads for the *Critical* and *Monthly* was even more graphic, as it listed the titles of all the books reviewed in that issue.[33]

Smollett's new features on art and foreign literature also caused a stir. In 1758, at the request of a correspondent, the *Monthly* briefly introduced a feature on works of art. It appeared only twice, however, both times supplied

by correspondents rather than staff writers, and it ended having covered only
one work of art (Hogarth's *The Bench*).[34] The *Monthly* also imitated the
Critical's section on foreign literature again, tellingly, at the request of its
readers: "A Succinct Account of *Foreign Publications* having been desired by
several Friends to our Review," announced Griffiths at the end of 1756, "we
take this Opportunity of acquainting them, and the Public, that this Task is
undertaken by a Set of learned and ingenious Correspondents" (*Monthly*
15:viii). But according to Griffiths's own file copy of the *Monthly*, many of
these contributions came not from foreign correspondents but from members
of his staff writing under various pseudonyms.[35] In later years, a former
Monthly reviewer revealed that fictitious titles of books had sometimes been
invented and "reviewed" to fill out this section.[36] Griffiths was content to cite
this feature in advertisements for the *Monthly* (perhaps that was the whole
purpose),[37] but it clearly did not have his wholehearted support. He and his
writers sometimes resorted to compiling it from foreign literary journals, but
with a prefatory disclaimer: "The Readers of the Monthly Review will be
pleased to observe, that we are not answerable for the Characters of the Books
mentioned in this, or any future *Catalogue*, extracted from foreign Journalists" (*Monthly* 16:445). Thus while it is evident that Griffiths imitated several
of the *Critical*'s innovations, it was frequently, as Spector observes, "with less
success."[38]

It has even been argued, based on the coincidence between the arrival of
the *Critical* and Griffiths's declaration in 1757 of an intention to offer more
criticism and less summary in reviews, that competition with the *Critical*
added impetus to the transition in book reviewing from abstracts to
critiques.[39] This may be overstating the case. It does seem likely, however,
that with two reviews in existence, the inevitable comparisons would focus
on differences of critical opinion and analysis, rather than on summaries of
books, which tended to be the same, and thus would make the reviewers more
conscious of that aspect of their reviews. In any case it is clear that the competition between them, while not always friendly, was productive: it led to
new features, improved standards, and more service to the reading public.
There is a useful parallel with the history of the *Gentleman's Magazine* and
its rival the *London Magazine*. In analyzing the early years of their rivalry,
Carlson found that "the book lists became one of the main grounds for
competition," with the result that both exhibited "far greater striving for
accuracy."[40]

There was one impact on the *Monthly* that the *Critical* did *not* have. Traditional opinion has it that it damaged the *Monthly*'s circulation and profits,
even forcing Griffiths "to sell a one-quarter share in his periodical to Benjamin Collins."[41] The printing records tell a very different story. Between
1756 and 1758—the first three years of competition with the *Critical*—the
number of copies of the *Monthly* printed actually went up from 2250 to 2500

per month.[42] The figure stayed at about this level until 1768 when it increased to 3000, and then again in 1776 to 3500. Griffiths may have needed to raise capital when he sold Collins a share of the *Monthly*, but it was not because its sales had dropped off. As the scene depicted by the *Connoisseur* showed, subscribers to the *Critical* would often subscribe to it in tandem with the *Monthly*, rather than as a replacement. Again the parallel with the *Gentleman's* and *London* magazines may be enlightening. Sales of the *Gentleman's Magazine* began to rise in 1732 just as the *London* was starting up, and Carlson reasons that the new competition "may have helped to increase interest in the *Gentleman's* and to further its sale."[43] J. L. Haney has argued that the early quarrels between the reviews were also mutually beneficial: "Such literary encounters did not fail to stimulate public interest in both reviews and to add materially to their circulation."[44] The underlying explanation, however, may be simply that the growing reading public had reached a point where it could support, and perhaps even required, two literary reviews.

As did the *Gentleman's* and *London* with the term *magazine*, the *Monthly* and *Critical* brought the word *review* into common usage. It had been used in the titles of periodicals before 1749 but, with one minor exception, always in the sense of a review of political or historical events—as in Defoe's *Review*—rather than a review of publications.[45] After the *Monthly* and before the *Critical*, two journals briefly appeared using the word in their titles.[46] But in the twenty years after the *Critical* appeared, from 1756 and 1775, at least fifteen periodicals were founded that incorporated the word *review* somewhere in their titles.[47] Most of these, and many others that were reviews in substance if not in name, failed within a year or so. Two lasted as long as five years, but they too were derivative and undistinguished.[48] A succession of journals tried to define themselves in opposition to the *Monthly* and *Critical*, declaring themselves alternatives to that dominant pair—among them the *Weekly Magazine and Literary Review* (15 April 1758–29 July 1758), the *St. James's Magazine* (September 1762–June 1764), and the *Literary Annals: or the Reviewers Reviewed* (January 1765)—but they quickly failed also.[49] The *Monthly* and *Critical* stood unrivaled for some thirty years, until the arrival of the *English Review* (1783), the *Analytical Review* (1788), and the *British Critic* (1793), and even then continued to hold their own until well after the *Edinburgh* (1802) and *Quarterly* (1809) were founded.[50]

During these years, the contents of magazines also began to reflect the preeminence of the *Monthly* and *Critical*. It was not entirely flattering to be plundered by the magazines—every available source was—but beyond the *Gentleman's* and *London*, most magazines reprinted material from the reviews, both in occasional articles and regular features. Several followed the pattern set by the *Repository* in 1756, compiling a regular section of excerpts drawn from both. In explaining this practice, the editor of the *Grand Magazine of Magazines* paid tribute to both the *Monthly* and *Critical* which, he states, "have real merit; and tho' their censure and their praise are sometimes directed by prejudice, friendship, or self-interest, yet it must be acknowledged that where neither of these interfere, their judgment seldom misleads the Reader."[51] His magazine became the first actually to juxtapose comments from each review, enabling readers to compare their opinions on a given book; comparative excerpts from the reviews were to remain a staple of magazine contents for much of the rest of the century, as can be seen, for example, in the *London Magazine* and the *Universal Catalogue* in the 1770s.[52] Readers had already come to value this kind of feature by 1760. When the *Imperial Magazine* was not offering one in 1761, a reader wrote to recommend its usefulness and offered to compile one for them, which he did for several issues.[53] The *Scots Magazine* was more selective, only reprinting reviews of special interest to its readership such as those on Robertson's *History of Scotland*.[54] The *Grand Magazine of Universal Intelligence* was also selective, but for a different reason: Griffiths was the proprietor and accordingly only reviews from the *Monthly* were reprinted in it.[55]

Magazine editors were not above altering or trimming excerpts from reviews to suit their own purposes. At various times, for example, the *Critical* was used as a source for "an anecdote of Bishop Burnet" (*Aberdeen Magazine*), an article on "What is Oratory?" (*Grand Magazine*), and the only tolerable passage (purportedly) in the *Annual Register* for 1759 (*Scots Magazine*).[56] The most striking evidence of how heavily a magazine might rely on the reviews for its material lies in the Library of Congress's copy of the *Critical Review*: the first four volumes have been copiously annotated, obviously by an editor who was cannibalizing its contents to make copy for his magazine.[57] Long articles have been subdivided for serialized reprinting with notes to instruct the compositor and others to guide the reader (e.g., "To be concluded in our next"). Quotations have been lifted from reviews and arranged so they appear to come directly from the book itself. Some articles have been fashioned for the magazine so as to avoid giving credit to either the review or the book, such as one entitled "Account of Bornholm" extracted from a review of Thura's *History of Bornholm* (No '57, 453–55).

Newspapers used the reviews in much the same way. Occasionally a newspaper reprinted most of an entire issue of a review in capsule form, as when *Lloyd's Evening Post* for 23 April 1759 presented notices of eighteen different books abridged from the *Critical*.[58] Much more common were single articles relating to current topics, such as the *Critical's* review of the *North Briton* reprinted in the *Public Advertiser* for 2 November 1763, only one day after it was published in the *Critical* (Oc '63, 277–85). Reviews were also reprinted in provincial newspapers such as *Jackson's Oxford Journal* and the *Literary Register* in Newcastle.[59]

All this pirating and reprinting served to extend the influence of the *Monthly* and *Critical* well beyond their immediate readership, albeit via a fragmentary and unsystematic network. Whether or not they openly credited the *Monthly* and *Critical* as their sources, magazine editors acknowledged and furthered their influence in two ways: directly, by transmitting the opinions of the reviewers to a wider audience, and indirectly, by acquiescing in choices the reviewers had made about which books to review, in what detail, and with what passages selected as exemplary quotations. In other words, the contents and opinions of the reviews determined a temporary "canon" of books that were seen and discussed throughout an extended network of the press; books that were not reviewed or were briefly dismissed obviously did not go out on the network or receive any of this secondary attention.

The people most immediately affected by what might be called the rise of the reviews were the authors themselves. That authors read and cared about what reviewers said is manifestly evident. Using ownership records, Roper has assembled an impressive list of authors who subscribed to the reviews during the second half of the eighteenth century.[60] It is noteworthy that even in the infancy of the reviews, during the 1750s and 1760s, writers were already attending very closely to reviews of their works as they appeared. Their public responses—the numerous and emotional published complaints[61]—are one kind of testimony; their private remarks are equally revealing. The correspondence of William Shenstone in the years 1756–62, for example, shows him heatedly discussing recent reviews with his circle of friends, all minor authors themselves: Thomas Percy, James Grainger, Richard Jago, and John Scott Hylton.[62] The group tended to be scornful toward the reviews, the *Critical* especially, but for all their public indignation, there was private apprehension. "When I consider what strange old stuff I have raked together," wrote Percy on the eve of publishing his *Reliques of Ancient English Poetry*, "I tremble for its reception with the fastidious public. What rare hacking and hewing will there be for Mess.rs the Reviewers!"[63]

Thomas Gray's correspondence during the years 1756–70 reveals similar anxiety among his circle of literary friends, including William Mason, Horace Walpole, and Thomas Warton.[64] Mason was so depressed by the reviews of his *Odes* in 1756 that Gray wrote to console him, cheerfully abusing the reviewers as "Man-Midwives & Presbyterian Parsons" and then asking, "[How] can . . . the censure of such Criticks move you?"[65] Walpole was angry about the reviews of his *Catalogue of Royal and Noble Authors* in 1759, but, as he told a friend, he declined publishing a reply "to set them right," adding (in a grudging compliment to Smollett): "Who *Them* are I don't know—the highest I believe are Dr. Smollett or some chaplain of my uncle."[66] To these can be added discussion of the reviews during the 1750s and 1760s in letters between David Hume and Adam Smith, Caleb Whitefoord and William Burnet, George Colman and Thomas Warton, and seemingly every author whose correspondence survives.[67] Concerned as they all were, perhaps none was as eager to see the reviews as Boswell, who records how he and Erskine awaited the critics' verdict on their *Collection of Original Poems* in 1762: "We got a *Review* fresh from London. We contended who should read it first: we quarreled and were reconciled again."[68]

Authors acknowledged the influence of reviewers on many levels. The practice of sending in a review copy of a new book sprang up immediately, as has been shown, and authors often sent along a letter of introduction too (e.g., Ja '65, 17). The surviving correspondence of eighteenth-century publishers is full of letters from their authors planning strategies to get reviewed. With Christopher Anstey writing to Dodsley in 1775, it was "three little packets which I would beg the favour of you to direct and send immediately to the publishers of the Critical, Monthly, and London Reviews"; with Sir John Sinclair writing Cadell and Davies in the 1780s, it was an instruction to send copies to "the Editors of the Monthly & Critical Reviews, & the British Critic," while Sinclair would send one directly to the *Analytical Review* himself.[69] Often it seems, as in these instances, that authors rather than publishers provided the review copies. Tactics didn't stop there. The same archives show authors pointing out favorable reviews and instructing their publishers to quote them in advertisements for their books; other authors expected the publishers to locate and send them copies of reviews and badgered them with repeated requests until they did.[70] Many writers openly spoke of the power of reviews to affect sales. Garrick felt that the review he wrote for the *Monthly* of Hannah More's *Wreath of Fashion* had "revived the sale of the poem very briskly."[71] Clara Reeve, in her *Progress of Romance*, has one character quote a *Critical* opinion about a novel in 1772; the novelist is asked, "Had this mandate any effect upon the sale of your publication?" To which comes the unhappy answer: "Too much so."[72] In his *Apology to the Critical Reviewers*, Churchill had asked rhetorically, incredulously, "How could these self-elected monarchs raise / So large an empire on so small a base?" (11. 83–84). By 1764, some of his defiance had turned to resignation and bitterness at the passivity of his fellow authors:

> Enough of *Critics*—let them, if they please,
> Fond of new pomp, each month pass new decrees
>
> . . . .
> Uncensur'd let them pilot at the helm,
> And rule in letters, as they rul'd the realm.
> Ours be the curse, the mean tame coward's curse,
> (Nor could ingenious Malice make a worse,
> To do our Sense and Honour deep despite)
> To credit what they say, read what they write.
> (*Candidate*, 47–48 and 63–68)

Coming from Churchill, one of Smollett's fiercest antagonists, within eight years of the *Critical*'s commencement, this reading of the contemporary literary scene and its underlying power structure is particularly telling.

Their growing sense of the power of the reviews prompted some extraordinary measures. At least one author, the Rev. William Dodd, wrote privately to an editor to seek a favorable review, but was so anxious not to be exposed in this position that he closed by expressing his hope that "no public Mention will be made of this Note."[73] Johnson's friend Tom Davies, who was both a publisher and an author, also wrote to editors to solicit good reviews, but would then quibble over minor details even when he got them.[74] Another author, Charles Jennens, was so anxious about negative reviews that he reportedly arranged to have his works published on the first of the month to delay any criticism for as long as possible and later berated his publisher for deliberately seeking to have them reviewed anyway (De '72, 476–77). More commonly, authors began the habit of addressing the reviewers in their prefaces and postscripts, sometimes defiantly,[75] but more often with respect or even flattery.[76] These prefatory pleas to the reviewers quickly became so commonplace that already by 1767 a *Critical* reviewer complains about an author using such a "stale" device (J1 '67, 32). But sometimes these tactics worked. One *Critical* reviewer was moved to leniency: "As this author in his preface addresses himself to the monthly reviewers, declaring his design is not a specimen of elegant writing, but a repository of useful knowledge, we shall pass over a few inaccuracies in the stile" (Ja '63, 80). There were also instances of authors demonstrating their gratitude for a favorable review. One author expressed his thanks in a letter to the *Critical* in 1762 that was duly acknowledged but, for reasons of decorum, not printed (My '62, 444). To Johnson's dismay, Lyttleton was similarly grateful for a favorable review of his *Dialogues of the Dead* in 1760. By Johnson's account: "When they were first published, they were kindly commended by the Critical Reviewers, and poor Lyttelton, with humble gratitude returned, in a note which I have read, acknowledgements which can never be proper, since they must be paid either for flattery or for justice."[77] In the 1770s Lord Kames, remembering favorable treatment he had received in the *Critical* years earlier, made up an inscription for a monument to Smollett as (he said) "no more than a just return."[78]

By far the most telling evidence of the power of these "new critics" (and perhaps the most difficult to discover) is the way authors took the reviewers' advice and corrected or amended their works. The *Critical* reviewers pointed out occasional instances of such response. A poet whose *Ode to the Memory at the Duke of Newcastle* had been severely criticized in March 1769 (Mr '69, 235–36), for example, corrected the second edition according to the reviewer's suggestions, for which he was congratulated rather smugly by the *Critical* (My '69, 400). The author of *A Letter to a Great M[iniste]r* (1761) was criticized for displaying excessive "virulence and acrimony" (My '61, 363–69); rather surprisingly, instead of taking offence, he wrote to the *Critical* to publicly retract some of his comments (Jl '61, 80). Horace Walpole, who was no friend of the reviewers, silently incorporated in the second edition of his *Anecdotes of Painting in England* a point of fact (about the engraver Théodore de Brie) that he had lifted from the *Critical*'s review of his first edition. The *Critical* did not miss the chance to reprimand him for the theft (Jl '67, 58). The *Critical* reviewers also claimed partial credit for improvements and personnel changes in Flloyd's *Biographical Dictionary*: they had felt obliged to castigate the style of the first six volumes, but seemed to detect "the hand of a better writer" in later ones (Jl '62, 27–28). But because the *Critical* reviewed only new titles and because authors were not likely to openly admit taking a reviewer's advice, relatively few such instances came to the reviewers' attention.

There are clear signs, however, that their suggestions and criticisms were being heeded by many authors, including some of the major poets of the day. This emerges in authorial revisions of texts. The word *curl* which the *Critical* reviewer (Francklin) had objected to in a line of Mason's "Ode to Memory"—"See, sportive Zephyrs *curl* the crisped streams" (Ap '56, 209)— was altered to *fan* in later editions.[79] Similarly, the poet Edward Jerningham altered his elegy *The Magdalens*: "We are not fond of the epithet 'nun-clad,'" the *Critical* reviewer had said (Ja '63, 76), and accordingly Jerningham changed it to *cloister'd* in the second edition, which appeared later the same year. Despite his professed disdain for the reviewers, Gray also acted on one of their suggestions: a specific Greek motto that the *Critical* reviewer of his *Odes* had suggested "the author might, with great propriety, have added" (Au '57, 167) was indeed added in 1768 to his collected *Poems*. Even the proud and defiant Churchill quietly amended his most celebrated poem, *The Rosciad*, according to criticisms leveled by the *Critical*. An eight-line passage that the *Critical* had described as "gross and illiberal, and such language as a polite writer would never condescend to make use of" (Mr '61, 209) was omitted from subsequent editions, as was another couplet the reviewer had decried as containing "two of the baldest lines in the whole performance" (Mr '61, 211). Some recently discovered revisions in Johnson's *Dictionary* were the direct result of an article by Smollett himself, in which he pointed out Johnson's errors in the entries for *aloft*, *dab-chick*, and *Sabaoth* in the first edition (Fe '59, 155–56). Johnson quickly corrected them in the 1760 and 1765 editions, but not without expressing his annoyance at Smollett's criticism.[80]

All these are minor emendations compared with the revisions Burke made in his *Essay on the Sublime* to accommodate and answer his reviewers, among whom the *Critical* featured prominently. As a meticulous study by H. A. Wichelns has demonstrated, Burke rewrote and added large passages to later editions very much according to specific points raised by the reviews, seeming to treat the author-reviewer relationship as one of dialogue or debate.[81] Further bibliographical studies like Wichelns's, working with the kind of evidence provided above, would help to illuminate the complex pattern of authorial response to reviews and the consequent effects on literary texts. The available evidence suggests that despite the private grumbling and public hostility, authors were guided in their revisions by reviewers' comments to a greater extent than is usually recognized. By extension, one can see that authors had begun to shift their gaze from the amorphous and unpredictable public to the review critics, who functioned as mediators between writers and readers, not only shaping public opinion by their authority, but also providing a signal back to authors of the predominant tastes and expectations of the public.

The rise of the *Critical* and *Monthly* in the 1750s also had a visible impact on the publishing industry, especially on its advertising techniques. Whatever their private opinions, the pragmatic publishers soon learned to use the reviews to their commercial advantage. During the 1750s, and increasingly so after the foundation of the *Critical*, a quotation from a favorable review became a standard feature of advertisements for new books. Griffiths himself seems to have started the trend in 1750, using quotations from the *Monthly* in newspaper advertisements for one of his own publications, *The Revolution of Genoa*.[82] But however convenient that arrangement was for him, the reviews were an open resource for all publishers and others quickly followed suit. Some publishers watched the reviews so closely that a supportive quotation might begin appearing in advertisements within days: a reference to a review in the *Critical* of May 1759 (459–60) appeared in advertisements for the Marchioness de Sévigné's *Letters* only five days after the review was published.[83] Such acuteness of response suggests that other publishing decisions may have been affected. It seems that publishers could be persuaded to begin advertising a book, or to step up advertising already under way, by the appearance of a favorable review. Moreover, reviews may also have affected decisions about whether or not to plan a second edition and what kinds of new works to commission, especially in cases of easily imitated compilations or of foreign works the reviewers recommended for translation.

The enterprising booksellers were not overly scrupulous about how they used excerpts from reviews. Some were not actually reviews of the book being advertised, but of its original in another language[84] or of other works by the same author.[85] One bookseller continued using the same excerpts from reviews to advertise later editions at least thirteen years after the books had first been reviewed; a second publisher, who used the same review excerpts for at least fourteen years after first publication, added a preface to boast that he had hired an editor to amend the text of a novel strictly in accordance with the original reviewer's criticisms.[86] Later in the century it emerged that publishers sometimes altered or even invented favorable review notices to use in advertisements.[87]

The booksellers employed this technique in the provincial press also, quoting reviews in advertisements for books in the local newspapers of Oxford, Gloucester, Bath, Salisbury, and presumably elsewhere as well.[88] Booksellers in America also quoted the reviews in advertisements: for example, an ad in the *Pennsylvania Journal and Weekly Advertiser* for 4 January 1770 quoted both the *Critical* and *Monthly* in support of Catherine Macaulay's *History of England*. The Dublin bookseller James Hoey relied on this tactic very heavily: nine of fifteen books he listed in an advertisement bound into *The Ladies Complete Letter Writer* (Dublin, 1763) are bolstered by review excerpts, as are four of five in another of his lists bound into *The Orientalist* (Dublin, 1764). If Hoey's practices are at all typical, they suggest that perhaps the reviews were considered to carry more weight the farther removed readers were from London, where they had less access to literary news and information.

Comprehensive information is difficult to compile, but there is at least one case that shows that in this context, the *Critical* was treated with the same respect as the *Monthly* from the very beginning. The Bodleian's long run of *Jackson's Oxford Journal*, complete from its foundation in 1753 through 1765, makes possible an illuminating survey. In those thirteen years of weekly issues of *Jackson's Oxford Journal*, London publications were advertised regularly. In that period, twelve book advertisements appeared that used supportive quotations from the reviews: eleven cited articles in the *Critical* and four in the *Monthly* (three cited both). This is not to imply any real differences—that the *Critical* was somehow more quotable because more prestigious, for example, or more generous with praise—because the booksellers drew no such nice distinctions, if there were any. But this limited survey does show the ways the reviewers' influence could penetrate even the marketing of new books in the provincial trade. Books could always be ordered through provincial booksellers, and sometimes, as a service to their readers, provincial newspapers ran lists of new titles, compiled (the *Shrewsbury Chronicle* announced) according to those "which are taken notice of in the different reviews" (15 June 1776). That booksellers began citing reviews in advertisements suggests their respect for the authority of the reviews. That they continued the practice and increased its use until it became routine or even requisite, however, is the strongest proof we have that their readers were actually moved by the reviewers' opinions.

The question of influence with the reading public brings us to more uncharted ground. As the behavior of both authors and publishers attests, the *Critical* rapidly achieved considerable influence both in its own right and in cooperation with the *Monthly*. Not all of its effects can be traced. It would be interesting to know, for example, whether its arts feature moved readers to visit artists' galleries or whether its foreign section stimulated sales of foreign books. Nevertheless, one can find many concrete indications of its impact on the reading public.

The first is circulation. At the beginning of 1757, one *Critical* reviewer claimed it was "three or four thousand" per month (Fe '57, 192). This was probably an inflated figure. Exact numbers are unavailable, but there is no reason to believe that its circulation in the 1750s and 1760s differed much from the *Monthly*'s: roughly two thousand to twenty-five hundred.[89] This level may not have been reached immediately, but the *Critical* was doing well enough by the end of 1756 to justify introducing "an elegant new type" (Au '56, preface, [ii]) and was already claiming "great Success" for itself in its advertisements.[90] By 1759 several back issues had sold out and had to be reprinted,[91] and in 1763 its advertisements boasted of a "constant Increase in its Sale."[92]

Geographically its circulation—like the *Monthly*'s—was both nationwide and international. The reviews were advertised throughout the provincial press and sold both in local bookshops and by home delivery.[93] Interestingly, although Benjamin Collins in Salisbury was a proprietor in the *Monthly*, he printed detailed advertisements for the *Critical* in his own *Salisbury Journal* and noted that it was for sale in his shop.[94] The reviews may have been more expensive to readers at a distance from London: Miller's bookshop in Edinburgh was charging fourteen pence a copy—two pence above the London price—in 1759.[95] Of course the reviews also circulated in Ireland, although overseas distribution—even for such a nearby country—posed special problems: a letter from the Dublin bookseller James Hoey to Ralph Griffiths reports that contrary winds had hampered shipping so that as of 5 March 1760 neither the November or December (1759) issues of the *Monthly* had yet arrived.[96] Booksellers in the American colonies also sold the reviews, but with less success, according to Benjamin Franklin, because most readers subscribed directly to London dealers for their copies.[97] The reviews were on sale in German bookshops as early as the 1750s and at least one German bookseller, Johann Wendler in Leipzig, found it worth-while to advertise them.[98] John Doughty, who sold books on consignment in Calcutta, reported to Ralph Griffiths in 1763 that the *Monthly Review* was one of his best sellers.[99] Doubtless the *Critical*, with one longtime India veteran either on its staff or at least friends with its editor (John Cleland) and one former *Critical* reviewer posted to India in 1763 (Archibald Campbell), made India part of its distribution network also.[100] Clearly there were booksellers and individuals taking the reviews throughout Europe and the colonies; as one *Critical* reviewer wrote in 1772, "Wherever commerce can sail, our monthly publications attend it" (De '72, 479).

Individual subscribers had various social and professional backgrounds. Largely "upper- and middle-class," as Roper concluded from the list he assembled, they included "landowners great and small; clergymen (including two bishops) and scholars; professional men and commercial men."[101] For those outside London, the reviews were an important link with the literary world, as one can see in the addresses of so many regular writers of letters to the editor. Individual subscribers' copies were often read by more than one person, as was the case when Boswell and Erskine quarreled over who would read the new review first, and joint subscriptions were common.[102]

The widest readership, however, was reached through institutions and societies. Roper has compiled a long list of university libraries, academies, literary societies, book clubs, and circulating libraries that subscribed to the reviews.[103] The *Critical* itself claimed an extensive circulation of this kind: "The Reviews are purchased by almost all the literary societies at present established; one of which, at least, subsists in every town of note" (De '72, 479). The reviews seemed to be in demand among readers. The Aberdeen bookseller Alexander Angus made sure that his circulating library subscribed to both the *Monthly* and the *Critical* from the moment it opened in 1764. But this wasn't just a provincial phenomenon: the same was true with the London Library when it was founded in 1785, where the *Critical*, *Monthly*, and *Analytical* were all taken.[104] In advertisements for his circulating library, in 1759, the Edinburgh bookseller William Gray was careful to note that the reviews could be borrowed for a penny per night.[105] The Signet Library in Edinburgh also allowed the reviews to circulate, as did the circulating libraries of booksellers John Burnett and Alexander Brown in Aberdeen, although both of them limited circulation of the most recent issues to one night.[106] The borrowing records of a community library in the Scottish town of Innerpeffray reveal that between 1747 and 1800, the *Monthly* and *Critical* were among the library's most frequently circulated works.[107] In a composite study of the borrowing records of twelve provincial English book clubs, Paul Kaufman has determined that the reviews commanded the most interest.[108] In the American colonies, too, libraries and societies subscribed to the reviews: the Library Company of Philadelphia, for example, subscribed to both the *Critical* and the *Monthly* from the 1750s on. Similarly, in Germany, as Bernhard Fabian has shown, many of the more than four hundred eighteenth-century "reading societies" subscribed to the two English reviews.[109]

This reliance on the reviews affected acquisitions and thereby shaped collections. Roper suggests that especially in provincial reading societies, the reviewers' opinions "could greatly influence the members' choice of purchases."[110] This would have been true from remote Innerpeffray in Scotland to major English towns such as Ely, where the Ely Pamphlet Club took the *Monthly* and *Critical* at various times in the 1760s and 1770s, "and used them," reports John Feather, "as an aid in book selection."[111] The best example of how directly the reviews could shape a library collection is the history of the Liverpool Library, founded in 1758. Liverpool's was the first proprietary library (wherein members owned shares in the society's stock) in England and typical of the many that followed: Warrington in 1760, Manchester 1765, Leeds 1768, Sheffield 1771, Hull 1775, and Birmingham 1779.[112] From the beginning, the *Monthly* and *Critical* played an important part in acquisitions decisions because members relied on them for information about new books; when the committee met to discuss titles suggested by members, M. Kay Flavell tells us, "the review notice [in the *Monthly* or *Critical*] formed the basis for committee discussions."[113] Within a few years, it had become *required* that members proposing new titles cite the appropriate *Monthly* or *Critical* review article in the suggestion book. In nearby Warrington, the governing committee of the Warrington Circulating Library met once a month to decide on acquisitions and brought copies of the *Monthly* and *Critical* to the meetings as the basis for their discussions. The impact that these policies might have can be suggested statistically, using the Liverpool Library as an example. Its membership was already 140 in 1758, grew to three hundred by 1770 and by 1799 to more than four hundred, among them many of the most influential citizens of the town, all of whom depended directly or indirectly on the two reviews as guides to what they read. Between 1758 and 1800, the library acquired an average of almost two hundred books per year, amounting to a collection of more than eight thousand by 1801, the composition of which, both for contemporaries and for posterity, was largely determined by Churchill's "self-elected Monarchs," the reviews. If one multiplies this effect by the number of societies and libraries starting all over Britain and throughout its colonies during these decades, the implications about influence are tremendous.

A similarly provocative example can be shown in the international context: the case of the University Library at Göttingen. In deciding what books to order from England, the Göttingen librarians were guided largely by the opinions of the *Monthly* and *Critical*; in their eighteenth-century acquisition records (recently investigated by Fabian), they regularly entered references to the specific reviews that had influenced their decisions.[114] In this case, too, the reviews exerted influence not only on individual readers' choices of and preconceptions about what they read, but on the extent and composition of the collection available to them. In the international context, as Fabian suggests, this could have significant effects on the reception and influence of a foreign literature.[115] When one thinks specifically of the importance of English literature to German culture in this period and the number of Germans becoming acquainted with English literature through the Göttingen collection, the possible implications are intriguing.

Evidence of how ordinary individuals reacted to the reviews is extremely rare. John Moore reported to Smollett in 1758 that "a friend of mine was so much enraged at some criticisms in that Review [the *Critical*], that he continued to take it for no other purpose than that he might read all the publications censured by it, and none of those which it praised."[116] Not all were so whimsical. George Ridpath, a Scottish parson, recorded in his diary his preference for the *Monthly* although he felt that in the *Critical* "there is more vivacity and even a greater show of learning than in the *Monthly Review*."[117]

One finds that eighteenth-century readers early adopted the habit of inserting clippings or transcribing quotations from the reviews into their own copies of the books, although it is impossible to say with certainty whether this indicates a causal relationship between review and purchase or merely an illuminating commentary superadded after the book had been bought.[118] Undoubtedly there were as many different responses to the reviews as there were readers, something Smollett discovered to his consternation in trying to reconcile the various conflicting suggestions he received in letters to the editor in 1760 (Se '60, 161–62).

Considering readers in the aggregate, however, contemporary observers almost universally agreed that they were influenced by what they read in the reviews. In Boswell's view the reviews had become "so much the arbiters of literary merit, as in a considerable degree to influence the public opinion."[119] The editor of the *Critical* in 1767 confidently appealed to "every disinterested reader . . . Whether he knows any work [to] subsist, in a tolerable degree of reputation with the public, after having been condemned by the authors of this Review?" (Ja '67, preface, iii). In explaining to the public why he felt compelled to publish a counteropinion to the *Critical*'s of Wilkie's *Epigoniad*, an anonymous writer from Oxford offered his perception of the subtle but inexorable ways that readers' opinions are formed: "If we reflect how much we are influenced by the opinions of our companions, by the judgment of the public, and even by the verdict of those, who, on the first day of every month, have assumed a right of pronouncing sentence upon the productions of their contemporaries, we shall find that we seldom sit down to read with that freedom from prejudice, which a judge ought to possess."[120] David Hume gave a similar rationale for writing his long defence of the *Epigoniad* and publishing it in the *Critical*: because "no literary journal was ever carried on in this country with equal spirit and impartiality," he reasoned diplomatically, "the authority which you possess with the public makes your censure fall with weight" and thus made it all the more imperative for Hume to write at length to correct this rare lapse on the *Critical*'s part (Ap '59, 323–24).

Even the reviewers' enemies conceded their influence over readers. One of Churchill's recurrent themes was the extraordinary degree to which readers immediately subjected themselves to the reviewers' authority and acquiesced in their opinions:

> Our great Dictators take a shorter way—
> Who shall dispute what the Reviewers say?
> Their word's sufficient; and to ask a reason,
> In such a state as theirs, is downright treason.
> True judgment now with them alone can dwell.
> Like Church of Rome, they've grown infallible.
> Dull, superstitious readers they deceive,

> Who pin their easy faith on critics' sleeve,
> And, knowing nothing, everything believe.
> But why repine we that these puny elves
> Shoot into giants?—we may thank ourselves:
> Fools that we are, like Israel's fools of yore,
> The calf ourselves have fashion'd we adore.
>
> (*Apology to the Critical Reviewers*, 93–105)

Another disgruntled poet described his dilemma more plainly:

> Indeed I cannot dread these Lurkers Frown,
> Or Court their Smiles, and yet 'tis plain the Town
> Are much inclin'd to favour or condemn,
> As these *confed'rate Wits* will suffer them.[121]

Whether his lack of success owed more to his bad reviews or his bad verse, this poet's sense of the public's susceptibility to reviewers' opinions was widely shared. A sketch in the *St. James's Magazine* depicted a character regarded as all too typical of review readers who interrupts a circle of friends discussing a recent poem to refute their consensus: "I can by no means agree to this, exclaimed a gentleman, who had hitherto sat in silent dignity, for those oracles of reason the *Reviews*, both of which I always carry in my pocket, declare the contrary."[122] He proceeds to read aloud passages from the *Monthly* and *Critical*, after which, reports the writer, "he closed those awful registers of merit, with evident marks of veneration, and sat down again." Unshakeable in his adherence to the reviewers' opinions, he is dismissed by the group as "impossible to convert" because "he neither saw with his own eyes, nor heard with his own ears, nor understood with his own head." Such were the worst fears writers had about reviews and their readers.

Through his efforts for the *Critical*, Smollett contributed to developments with implications far beyond influencing readers' opinions, writers' reputations, and publishers' sales. From the 1750s on, the circulation of the *Monthly* and *Critical* throughout the nation and throughout the ranks of literate society fostered a higher level of literary awareness and information; it also helped make the arts and sciences more accessible and more intelligible to ordinary readers who might otherwise be barred by geographic distance or by a lack of education, money, or time. As a result, the genuinely learned, such as William Warburton, were not always satisfied. Thomas Davies addressed this point in his retrospect on the years 1750 to 1780: "Dr. Warburton affected to despise the learning of Magazines and Reviews. He might, perhaps, receive no addition to his acquirements by perusing them; but the good people of England, I will presume to aver, have been much improved, within these twenty or thirty years, by that variety of literature and science which has been everywhere disseminated in these vehicles."[123] Or, as Goldsmith wrote in 1761 in vindication of the so-called cheapening of learning effected by periodicals: "Though these performances may justly give a scholar disgust, yet they serve to illuminate the nation."[124] Smollett had wanted to establish an English academy in conjunction with the *Critical* and in this he was disappointed. But he had also wanted to reach the general reader—the same reader at whom he aimed his popular history, his encyclopedic compilations, and his serial publishing methods—and in this he had been effective, if only as one particularly vigorous and productive contributor among many.

Another of Smollett's founding hopes for the *Critical* was through it to advance the reputation of British arts and sciences internationally. Here too his efforts, if not precisely as he had envisaged, proved effective. In France, for example, the *Journal étranger* regularly printed translated excerpts from both the *Critical* and the *Monthly*; in one remarkable instance they reprinted from the *Critical* an article on a French publication, Rousseau's *La Nouvelle Héloise*.[125] When the *Journal étranger* ceased in 1763, the government-sponsored *Gazette de France* added English books to its coverage, relying for its material exclusively on the *Monthly* and *Critical* reviews, which were sent to the editors by a French diplomat in London.[126] In Germany, the first review journals were founded in the late 1750s and modeled almost entirely on the *Monthly* and *Critical*: the *British Bibliothek* (Leipzig, 1756–67) and the *Bibliothek der schönen Wissenschaften und der freyen Künste* (Leipzig, 1757–67).[127] They also relied heavily on the *Monthly* and *Critical* for their contents: in the case of the *Bibliothek der schönen Wissenschaften*, for example, of the eight hundred articles published under its first editor, about 740 can be traced back to the *Monthly* and *Critical*.[128] At least one Italian journal also seemed to be modeled on the English reviews: the *Frusta Letteraria* (1763–65), edited by Johnson's friend Giuseppe Baretti.[129] There seems to have been a similar influence in Russia, where review journals carrying notices of English books also began appearing in the 1760s.[130] Indeed, with their comprehensive coverage and prompt reviewing, the *Monthly* and *Critical* had made themselves the natural avenue of approach for any foreign readers interested in English literature and culture.

Smollett's sense of the connection between review journals and national prestige was borne out by the emergence of review journalism in America at the end of the century. Before the American Revolution, the colonies had depended entirely on the English reviews: what few American periodicals there were did no reviewing of their own, instead borrowing material from London periodicals.[131] Indeed, one Boston correspondent of the *Critical* in 1773 was so eager to have it review American publications that he offered to send them copies of all the books and pamphlets published in the colonies (Au '73, 160). (The offer was declined.) But after independence, the rise in national consciousness led to calls for specifically *American* journals to promote *American* literature and culture. The result, beginning in the 1780s, was a sudden proliferation of review journals and other literary periodicals, many bearing suitably patriotic titles, such as *The United States Magazine*, the *American Magazine*, the *Columbian Magazine*, and the *American Museum*.[132]

Smollett was too close to events to see it fully, but the connections among culture, nationalism, political autonomy and international prestige were emerging more clearly as the century wore on. Meanwhile he had become involved in a literary periodical of an entirely different—and less serious— stripe, the *British Magazine*, into which he was to invest great amounts of imagination and innovation from 1760 to 1763, as will be seen.

Before Its Time: Smollett's Innovative
British Magazine

The *British Magazine* is often treated as a mere footnote to Smollett's career. Knapp, for example, devotes only three pages to it in his definitive biography of Smollett, despite the fact that Smollett founded it, edited it, and contributed voluminously to it for more than three years.[1] Although a very different kind of periodical from the *Critical* (its miscellaneous contents and light manner aimed at a broader and more casual readership), it constitutes an important part of Smollett's activity and achievement. Moreover its operations were closely connected with those of the *Critical*. Not only was Smollett compiling the *British Magazine* while still supervising the *Critical*, but he was using the same printer and many of the same writers who were involved with the *Critical*. Among its contents were a regular review of books, frequent articles on drama and works of art, and assorted pieces of poetry, history, biography, and criticism, as well as the feature for which it is best remembered, Smollett's serialization of *Sir Launcelot Greaves*. As one studies its pages, Smollett's inventive genius shines through, for many of its features anticipate the staples of nineteenth- and twentieth-century periodicals.

Smollett's immediate reasons for founding the *British Magazine* remain a mystery. Not having published a novel since *Ferdinand Count Fathom* in 1753, he may have felt the urge after a seven-year hiatus to turn some of his energies back to creative writing. Then, too, compiling a miscellaneous magazine, its contents drawn from a large number of willing contributors, must have seemed light work compared to the drudgery of editing the *Universal History* and the sometimes disagreeable duties involved in the *Critical*. His experience as an editor and his many contacts among authors and publishers put him in good stead to launch such a venture. His overriding motive, however, was profit. One anonymous pamphleteer speculated that Smollett had decided to found a magazine as an alternative to the *Critical*, "thinking, Cobler like, he should make both ends meet better by laying up all the loose Hints that occur to him in a Sort of Repository, which he is now compiling and digesting in Conjunction with his old Crony Timothy *Crabshaw*."[2] These conjectures were well-founded. Smollett was a proprietor and copyright holder in the *British Magazine* from the outset and "his old Crony Timothy Crabshaw" was indeed his old friend and business partner Archibald Hamilton with whom he had founded the *Critical* and with whom (as will be shown) he had arranged to print the *British Magazine*.

The best account of the publishing arrangements has been given by Albert Smith, who shows that a succession of booksellers was connected with the *British Magazine* in its early stages.[3] The prepublication advertisements listed it as "printed for James Rivington and James Fletcher, at the Oxford Theatre, and H. Payne in Pater-noster Row."[4] Payne may have had the leading part, as a manuscript note in Jackson's office copy of the *Oxford Journal* shows that Payne ordered and paid for the advertisements in that paper at least.[5] Rivington and Fletcher went bankrupt in January 1760, leaving Payne's name alone on the title page. By April 1760, the Dublin bookseller P. Wilson had become involved, as his name appeared with Payne's from then on. In August, Payne took on a partner and became "Payne and Cropley." At some point in its history, John Newbery also acquired a share in the magazine. This was probably in the early stages also, because advertisements for his publications begin appearing on the covers of the *British Magazine* as early as the June 1760 issue. Newbery's participation would help to explain the presence of several contributors who had connections with him, including Goldsmith, Johnson and William Dodd.

The fact that Smith was unable to discover, and that clarifies how the magazine could weather without a trace this ever-shifting team of proprietors, was the identity of the printer.[6] This can now be established, based on a clue buried in the poetry section of the April 1760 issue. In answer to a rebus (a kind of word puzzle) set in March, the following was printed:

> Your Rebus, sir, seems to convey me a hint,
> That it may be the person concern'd in this print:
> For if, in locality, I'm not mista'en,
> *Arch. Hamilton* lives now in Chancery-Lane.[7]

By printing these lines, the editors acknowledged their accuracy; indeed, setting Hamilton's name as the answer corresponds to the use of "Launcelot Greaves," "William Huggins" (a contributor), and other names associated with the magazine as rebus answers in other issues.[8] It is surprising that Hamilton's involvement with Smollett's *British Magazine* has not been conjectured sooner: in view of his experience printing a periodical, his business acumen, and their continuing partnership on the *Critical*, he was the natural figure for Smollett to turn to when planning such a project.

That Smollett was the organizer and the controlling partner of the *British Magazine* is evident from his petition to the government in January 1760 for a license to protect his interests in it:

> To the Kings Most Excellent Majesty The humble Petition of Tobias Smollett of Chelsea in the County of Middlesex, Doctor of Physick.
>
> Most humbly Sheweth, That your Majesty's Petitioner hath been at great Labour and Expence in writing Original Pieces himself, and engaging Learned and Ingenious Gentlemen to write other Original Pieces, which have been published in a Work Entitled "The British Magazine, or Monthly Repository for Gentlemen and Ladies."
>
> Your Majesty's Petitioner therefore, in Consideration of such his Great Labour and Expense, most humbly prays your Majesty to grant him your Royal License for the sole printing and publishing and vending the said Work. And your Majesty's Petitioner shall ever pray &c
>
> Tobias Smollett[9]

Smollett's license was promptly awarded, and, beginning in February, its text was reprinted in full on the covers of the magazine.[10] It was also featured in newspaper advertisements for the magazine.[11] Some criticized Smollett's royal license as a hollow and pretentious ploy: Griffiths's *Grand Magazine* mocked it publicly in February, while Shenstone sneered at it in private, and years later Walpole decried it as the illicit return for Smollett's having dedicated his *History* to Pitt.[12] But in fact, as R. M. Wiles has shown, this was neither an empty nor an extraordinary gesture: many periodicals and books flourished licenses as a necessary protection against piracy.[13] Among them were several magazines that had advertised their licenses in the months and weeks just before the *British Magazine* began, including the *London*, *Royal*, and *Royal Female* magazines.[14] What *was* unusual in Smollett's arrangement was that he rather than a bookseller owned the copyright for the magazine and all its contents.

In addition to soliciting contributions and engaging "learned and ingenious" writers, Smollett handled the actual editing of each issue. This can be demonstrated by comparing passages from his correspondence with unsigned editorial notes in the magazine. In a letter to Huggins in February 1760, apparently responding to Huggins's inquiries about the *British Magazine*, Smollett described his editorial labors:

> At present I am so enveloped in a variety of perplexing Schemes and Deliberations that I have neither Time to consider, nor Leisure to explain my sentiments of the manner in which the new Magazine is to be executed and Improved. *A great number of Essays both in prose and verse are sent to us from different parts of the Kingdom, but we have neither time to arrange them properly*, nor give them that degree of alteration which we apprehend may be

requisite to *fit them for the public*, and in all probability we shall be obliged to disappoint and give offence to some of our Correspondents [italics added].[15]

Five weeks later the same phrases appear in an editorial address to the readers of the *British Magazine*:

The Proprietors of the *British Magazine* having received *a great number of original Pieces in Prose and Verse from different Parts of the Kingdom*, those who have favoured us with their Correspondence will please to take Notice, that *we have not yet had time to arrange them properly*, and to distinguish between those that are, and those that are not *fit for Publication* [italics added].[16]

It seems reasonable to assume that Smollett wrote most or all of the editorial notes for the magazine, at least in its first year or two, including the editorial appeal to the "learned and ingenious of every Denomination" (i.e., the public) for contributions even before the first issue had appeared.[17]

Among the contributors who have been identified, several were also (or would become) contributors to the *Critical*. Samuel Derrick contributed several poems under his own name and perhaps other pieces anonymously.[18] Edward Watkinson offered several short essays on medical and moral topics.[19] James Ferguson, who had insisted on signing his articles in the *Critical*, donated at least one to the *British Magazine*.[20] Knapp is probably right in conjecturing that Philip Miller contributed occasional pieces, and Smollett's friend Carlyle may well have contributed also.[21]

Several other minor authors can be identified. The Scottish polymath, John Gray, who was later to become close friends with Smollett, contributed an article on a new kind of plough.[22] Another Scottish acquaintance of Smollett's, Prof. William Richardson, seems to have contributed at least one essay, signing himself "W. R. of Glasgow."[23] According to John Nichols, Griffith Jones added his "anonymous labours" to the magazine.[24] Arnold Whitridge states (without citing his source) that the Rev. William Dodd, who compiled Newbery's *Christian's Magazine* beginning in 1760, was also a contributor to the *British Magazine*; at least one Dodd article, an excerpt from his "Visitor" essays in the *Public Ledger*, was reprinted in the *British Magazine* (April 1761) and its source acknowledged, which may be a sign of Dodd's cooperation if not active contribution.[25] In the poetry section, there were contributions by John Huddleston Wynne, John Cunningham, and William Huggins. Smollett had written to ask Huggins to contribute something but had carefully stipulated to his ambitious friend that his contributions be "detached Pieces which you think will gratify the general Taste of Magazine Readers."[26] Huggins complied with a specimen of his translation of Dante's

Divine Comedy, which appeared in the April 1760 issue.[27] Undoubtedly with Smollett's assistance, arrangements were made for an edition of Huggins's translation to be published with Payne (one of the *British Magazine* proprietors), and the work was advertised on the inside cover of the next issue of the *British Magazine*.[28] The edition never appeared, however, because too few subscribers came forward, with the result that the specimen printed in the *British Magazine* is the only surviving fragment of Huggins's translation.

The *British Magazine* played a more productive part in the careers of Wynne and Cunningham, and their experiences suggest valuable ways that the increasing number of magazines could serve aspiring young poets. Wynne, who was still in his twenties when his poems began appearing in the *British Magazine* in 1760, went on to become a moderately successful poet and children's book writer and editor of the *Lady's Magazine: or Entertaining Companion for the Fair Sex* (1770–?).[29] Cunningham was a member of a traveling theater company and thus found the magazine a convenient way to publish his poems. He was given special encouragement in the *British Magazine*, where his first offering—a short lyric entitled "Morning"—was printed with an editorial note: "We shall be much obliged to this ingenious gentleman for the continuance of his favours."[30] Cunningham acknowledged the favor by sending in more poems that were also published. Matters developed from there. Later in 1760 the *British Magazine* proprietors Payne and Cropley became Cunningham's first London publishers of a book of poetry when they published his *Elegy on a Pile of Ruins*. In 1762 they published another of his works, *The Contemplatist*, and, according to later accounts, offered him steady employment in London.[31] This was the kind of path to a literary career that Johnson had followed with the *Gentleman's Magazine*;[32] toward the end of the century, a magazine would also be a source of encouragement to William Wordsworth when, at the age of sixteen, he saw his first poem published in the *European Magazine*.[33] By encouraging talent such as Cunningham's and (as will be seen) Goldsmith's, Smollett was following the example set by Edward Cave with the *Gentleman's Magazine* of serving literature while serving his own interests, through shrewd editorial policies and plain good judgment.

Smollett also tried to involve more famous authors in his magazine. He appealed to Samuel Richardson for a contribution in 1760: "I should think myself happy if you would favour our Magazine with any loose essay lying by you which you do not intend for another sort of publication."[34] No contribution by Richardson has yet been identified, but there is a letter in the April 1760 issue of the *British Magazine* that could well be his and, if so, may be connected with this request from Smollett for a more formal contribution. The evidence is largely circumstantial. The letter appears in the *British Magazine* at a time when Richardson and Smollett were working closely with each other on the *Universal History*,[35] and it opens with generous praise for

Smollett: "When I first understood that an author of distinguished abilities had submitted himself to the task of furnishing out a monthly magazine, it gave me great pleasure."[36] As one might expect of Richardson, the letter writer is especially appreciative of the fiction on offer in the magazine, declaring that "the history of Omrah is happily extravagant and oriental; and the adventures of Sir Launcelot Greaves promise a rich fund of entertainment." After politely taking issue with an article on "The Different Schools of Musick" in the last issue, the letter writer signs himself "S. R."[37] Finally, although further proof is needed to attribute this particular piece to Richardson, it seems unlikely that after Smollett's direct request he would have failed to donate something to the new magazine, thus disappointing Smollett at a time when he was anxious to keep him happy in his labors editing the *Universal History*.

One equally famous writer is known to have contributed: Samuel Johnson. Some arrangement with Johnson must have been made in late 1759 because in the premier issue of the *British Magazine* appeared one of his recent *Idler* essays (no. 89), which Smollett proudly introduced with the following note: "The reader, we imagine, will not be displeased to learn that we propose to enrich every number of the *British Magazine* with one paper from the *Idler*, by permission of the Author, whose great genius and extensive learning may be justly numbered among the most shining ornaments of the age."[38] (Clearly Smollett had not taken personally, or had not seen, Johnson's mockery of Minim's academy plan in *Idler* 61.) Smollett's arrangement with Johnson, who together with his publishers had been expressing publicly their concern about unauthorized reprintings of the *Idler*,[39] extended beyond permission to reprint the celebrated essays. Johnson also contributed to the first issue an original essay on "The Bravery of English Common Soldiers."[40] The details of how Smollett enlisted Johnson's help are unknown, but it seems probable that it was in part a gesture of gratitude for Smollett's help in securing the release of Johnson's servant Frank Barber from the Navy.[41] As Greene has observed: "Johnson's gratitude would have been suitably expressed by this offer of one good essay, to help the new periodical get on its feet, but need not have extended itself to the point of contracting to become a regular contributor to it."[42] It seems correct to assume that Johnson's involvement was not extensive—it could hardly have escaped the notice of contemporaries— although Greene has elsewhere detected signs that Johnson may have contributed three other pieces in 1760 under the guise of a "Weekly Correspondent."[43] In any case, Johnson's presence is a further credit to Smollett's editorial prowess, as well as a sign of their growing respect for each other in the 1760s.

One previously unnoticed contributor to the *British Magazine* may have been Johnson's and Smollett's mutual friend, David Garrick. Again the evidence is circumstantial, but there was obviously a strong connection between the magazine and Garrick. Smollett and Garrick were friends and correspondents during this period,[44] and Garrick was enjoying very favorable treatment in the *Critical*, even on occasion eliciting Smollett's exertions on his behalf by sending him complimentary copies of his plays (discussed above in chap. 5). In the *British Magazine*, one of the first in a regular series of drama reviews was devoted to an account of Garrick's *Enchanter* as performed at Drury Lane in December 1760.[45] Thereafter, the *British Magazine* served essentially as a Drury Lane journal: with very few exceptions all the drama reviews that appeared in its pages from 1760 until Smollett's departure in 1763 (a total of nineteen) were devoted exclusively to covering performances at Garrick's theater.[46] Garrick almost certainly did not write any of the reviews himself—most seem to be reprinted from newspaper accounts—but in light of this evidence of a strong connection with the magazine, it seems very probable that he is the author of at least one anonymous piece, submitted in 1760 as a letter on "The Difficulty of managing a Theatre."[47] If indeed Garrick was the author of this or other pieces, it suggests the order of Smollett's aspirations for the *British Magazine* and distinguishes it as the one journal to publish original articles by Smollett, Goldsmith, Johnson, Garrick, and perhaps Richardson—five of the century's most important literary figures— in the course of a single year. It is unlikely that any other literary periodical of the eighteenth century (or the nineteenth either) ever drew on such a constellation of talent in a single year.

Of all Smollett's contributors, it was Goldsmith who played the most important role. Goldsmith had been reviewing regularly for the *Critical* since January 1759, and Smollett now enlisted him on his new magazine, giving him so much work that his reviews in the *Critical* fell off to a trickle.[48] Exactly how many and which articles Goldsmith contributed has been disputed by editors and bibliographers for almost two hundred years.[49] The main controversy surrounds a body of twenty-seven articles from the *British Magazine* attributed to Goldsmith in a collection of Goldsmith's *Essays and Criticisms* published in 1798.[50] The editor of that collection, Isaac Reed, explained the authority for ascribing these essays to Goldsmith in his preface:

> The late Mr. *Thomas Wright*, Printer, a man of literary observation and experience, had, during his connection with those periodical publications, in which the early works of Dr. *Goldsmith* were originally contained, carefully marked the several compositions of the different writers, as they were delivered to him to print. Being therefore, it was supposed, the only person able to separate the genuine performances of Dr. *Goldsmith* from those of other writers, in these miscellaneous collections . . . Mr. *Wright* was- . . . prevailed upon to print the present Selection, which he had just completed at the time of his death.[51]

But subsequent editors have questioned and rejected most of Wright's attributions from the *British Magazine*: Arthur Friedman, in compiling the definitive edition of Goldsmith's *Works*, was willing to accept Wright's attributions from the *Critical Review* and the *Westminster Magazine* because it was known that Wright had been involved in printing those journals, but he rejected (as had Tupper and Crane) the attributions from the *British Magazine* because, as he wrote, "there appears to be no evidence other than this statement [by Isaac Reed] that Wright had any connexion with the *British Magazine*."[52] As a result, Friedman felt confident in listing only ten articles from the *British Magazine* as Goldsmith's. Five of these had been included in the Reed-Wright collection of 1798, but these five were accepted by Friedman on the basis of entirely separate evidence.[53]

With the discovery that Archibald Hamilton's shop printed the *British Magazine*, the authority for Wright's attributions can be established. From 1758 to 1766, which includes the first six years of the *British Magazine*, Wright worked in Hamilton's shop.[54] Moreover, according to Nichols, Hamilton was often absent, leaving the actual managing of the printing business to his "very able assistants—among whom [was] . . . Mr. Thomas Wright."[55] Nichols goes on to report that Wright was "a well-educated sensible man" who, in the hopes of compiling literary memoirs like Nichols's own, had formed the habit of carefully marking the authorship of anonymous articles in the journals he printed. As a foreman or manager for Hamilton, he would have had to do this anyway as part of the business record-keeping. In short, these attributions to Goldsmith come from the most authoritative source: the man to whom manuscript copy was handed by the author and who then supervised its printing and kept careful records of its authorship for payroll purposes.

The addition of Wright's attributions would more than treble the number of *British Magazine* articles in Goldsmith's canon. It would add the fourteen installments of the series "On the Belles Lettres," running from July 1761 to January 1763,[56] and fifteen other pieces, all rejected by Friedman, listed below (with the volume and essay number from the Reed-Wright 1798 edition on the left and the *British Magazine* issue in parentheses):

Reed/Wright

2, 1   "A Parallel between the Gracchi and the Greatest Man of the Present Age" (January 1760).

2, 2   "The History of Omrah, the Son of Abulsaid. An Oriental Tale" (January, 1760, continued in February and March).

2, 3   "Igluka and Sibbersik, a Greenland Tale," (5 [April–May], 1760).

2, 4   "The History of Alcanor and Eudosia" (May 1760).

3, 2   "A Parallel between Mrs. Vincent and Miss Brent" (June 1760).

2, 5   "On the Proper Enjoyment of Life" (August 1760).

2, 12 "Reflections on National Prejudices" (August 1760).
2, 6   "On Pride" (August 1760).
3, 7   "On the Imprudent Fondness of Parents" (August 1760).
2, 8   "An Essay on Physiognomy" (September 1760; continued as "Observations on Physiognomy" in October).
2, 7   "An Essay on Instinct" (December 1760).
2, 9   "An Essay on Fascination. Translated from the *Spanish* of the celebrated *Padre Feijoo*" (December 1760).
3, 8   "On the Approaching Coronation" (December 1760).[57]
2, 10 "Essay on National Union" (December 1760).
2, 11 "Proposals for Augmenting the Forces of Great-Britain" (January 1762).

These articles extend Goldsmith's known connection with the *British Magazine* from 1760 to the beginning of 1763, a period of Goldsmith's career about which exact information is scanty, save the famous story of Johnson's relieving Goldsmith's distress by arranging the sale of the *Vicar of Wakefield* manuscript. But evidently Smollett was also quite instrumental in keeping Goldsmith afloat during these years, as Goldsmith's connection with both the *Critical* and *British Magazine* demonstrates. The variety of these contributions to the *British Magazine* is typical of Goldsmith (short fiction, a serialized oriental tale, moral essays, political satire, criticism and aesthetic theory), and they reveal the degree to which Smollett relied on—or gave rein to—Goldsmith's whimsical creativity.[58]

Goldsmith's work for the *British Magazine* demonstrates once again how journalism could provide a young author with encouragement, income, and the opportunity to experiment in print. Smollett's confidence in Goldsmith's talent is evident in the placement of his long oriental tale "Omrah" as the lead article in the first issue (January 1760). Goldsmith's fanciful "Essay on Physiognomy" (September 1760) received so many compliments from readers that a sequel was offered the next month.[59] Most importantly for Goldsmith's career, a story he wrote for the *British Magazine*—"The History of Miss Stanton"—contained the germ of an idea (the fallen woman story) which he later elaborated in *The Vicar of Wakefield*.[60] Perhaps here is an example of an author gauging public taste by the response to a magazine story and then catering to it in a novel. It may also suggest ways that the magazine-reading public's taste for sentimental fiction was contributing to the emergence of the sentimental novel as the dominant form in the second half of the eighteenth century.

Its remarkable staff of contributors aside, there were several other features of the *British Magazine* that distinguished it from the crowd of magazines publishing in the 1750s and 1760s. Although its basic format was the same established by the *Gentleman's Magazine* thirty years earlier and followed by scores of imitators, it was clear from the outset that Smollett aimed to present new and imaginative features to his readers. His advertisements for the first issue—which by appearing on the first day of the month rather than at the end was itself breaking with convention[61]—promised an impressive array of offerings:

> *The British Magazine. . . . Consisting of the* Political State of Europe and America, the Transactions of the Powers at *War*, and the Connections, whether Natural or Politic, that subsist among the several States upon the Continent.
>
> Together with *Tales, Allegories*, and *Essays*, Humorous, Oriental, and Moral: Distinguished Characters, Ancient as well as Modern, Represented separately, or compar'd together in the most interesting Points of View.
>
> Discoveries in Natural Philosophy, Agriculture, Medicine, Mechanics, Navigation, and all the Arts and Sciences.
>
> A succinct and critical Detail of the most remarkable New Books, foreign and domestic. With a Description of those Productions in Painting and Sculpture, which may appear in this or any other Country, Curious Questions, Problems, and Paradoxes in Mathematics, Geography, &c. Original Pieces in Poetry and Music. Occurrences of the Month, &c.[62]

Smollett was at pains to emphasize that his magazine was composed of original articles, not reprints or piracies. His petition for a license and the terms of the license itself stressed that he had "been at great Labour and Expence in writing Original Pieces himself, and engaging learned and Ingenious Gentlemen to write other Original Pieces."[63] In his newspaper advertisements he explained, "We have not distinguished any of our Articles [i.e., those written by the staff] by particular marks, as the Reader will perceive that they are almost all Originals."[64]

One of its most innovative features was the book review section, which appeared in an entirely new form. It was neither a bare list of books published, like that in the *Gentleman's Magazine*, nor a section of full or partial reviews reprinted from the review journals, such as the *Imperial Magazine* and others were using, but it had elements of both. Pithy comments were attached to each of the fifteen or twenty books listed, as the following examples from the issue for February 1761 illustrate:

> *Modern Universal History*, Vol. XXVI. Price 5s. Miller. Contains the history of Italy, industriously compiled.
>
> Burnet *On Education*. Price 1s. 6d. Wilson. Rude and broad, yet sensible.
>
> *The Jealous Wife*. A Comedy. Price 1s. 6d. Here is a little wit, a good portion of humour, a great deal of good sense, and plenty of entertainment.
>
> *The Life and Adventures of an Animal, &c*. Price 2s. Very dull, and very obscene.[65]

This one-page feature, essentially new-books-at-a-glance, did not repeat the opinions of the review journals and was clearly aimed at a different kind of reader, one too busy or uninterested to read full review articles, but whose curiosity might be satisfied (or interest aroused) by a terse one-sentence characterization. Often witty, always trenchant, these little capsules of comment made entertaining reading and may have incidentally imparted to casual literary dabblers seeking amusement a measure of literary awareness they would not otherwise have acquired. (The feature also anticipated the many tabular or capsule-style review sections of the second half of the twentieth century, such as "Movies at a Glance" in the *New Yorker* or the best-seller list in the [Sunday] *New York Times Book Review*). It is noteworthy that even these squibs were used by booksellers in advertising new books, perhaps because of Smollett's growing reputation as a critic. The Dublin bookseller James Hoey, for example, invoked the *British Magazine* in his advertisement for Mrs. Woodfin's novel *Harriot Watson*: "The character given of this work in Dr. Smollett's magazine, is conceived in these few words, 'Chaste, entertaining, and moral.'"[66]

How this review section was compiled is unclear. That Smollett was responsible for it, as editor or writer, is suggested by the fact (as Robert Mayo noticed) that it disappeared with his departure in 1763.[67] It would have been senseless, of course, for the compiler actually to read all the books covered only to distill his opinions down to a line or two. In some cases it is evident from the order of the listings that the most recent issue of the *Critical* has been used as a guide. In the November 1760 issue, for example, seventeen books are noticed in exactly the same order that they were reviewed in the *Critical* for October 1760.[68] But in many cases the order of the listings bears no apparent relation to the *Critical*, the *Monthly*, or any discoverable source. Moreover, never do these pithy comments quote the exact language of articles in the review journals. Apparently, then, the reviews were often consulted but the compiler formulated his own comments.

On many occasions, books were noticed in the *British Magazine* in the same month's issue as in the *Critical*: five of the six entries in the issue for March 1760, for example, were reviewed in the February issue of the *Critical*, which appeared on the same day.[69] This suggests that the compiler from the *British Magazine* had access to the *Critical* articles in proof or in manuscript; but with Smollett in charge and both being printed in Hamilton's shop, this was easily arranged. There remain, however, those perplexing instances where the *British Magazine* noticed a book a month or more before it was reviewed in the *Critical*. In February 1761, for example, the *British Magazine* reported on two books a month before the *Critical* and a third two months before it.[70] These may be instances where the same writer was reviewing the book for both journals and entered a one-line comment in the *British Magazine* while his detailed analysis for the *Critical* was still in preparation. Whatever the procedure, it is noteworthy that unlike Griffiths's *Universal Magazine* with its regular citations from the *Monthly*, the *British Magazine* was not used to publicize its stablemate, the *Critical*: nowhere in its pages is the *Critical* ever mentioned by name.

Another innovative idea that Smollett carried over from the *Critical* was to offer reviews of recent works of art. This feature had been promised in the advertisements and it duly appeared, although on an irregular basis. The first issue of the *British Magazine* offered a description of some recent engravings by Strange that Smollett also reviewed in the *Critical*, but for some reason not until four months later.[71] During the course of the year, other articles examined a new print of the Duke of York and Frye's designs for a series of mezzotints, and at least the latter seems to be by Smollett himself.[72] No art reviews appeared in 1761, but in 1762 there was an "Essay on the Fine Arts" and "An Explanation of Mr. Hogarth's New Print [*The Times*]," and in 1763 a "Description of [Hayman's] Picture at Vauxhall Gardens."[73] The coincidence of so many of the subjects of these art reviews—works by Strange, Hogarth, Frye, and Hayman, all favorite subjects of Smollett's in the *Critical* and elsewhere—makes it very likely that Smollett wrote most or all of these pieces about art for the *British Magazine* himself. It was very probably this well-advertised feature in the *British Magazine* that impelled the *Imperial Magazine* to offer a similar one, beginning a month after the *British Magazine*.[74] It is this *Imperial Magazine* arts feature that art historians have pointed to as the historic breakthrough in art reviewing, but again Smollett had anticipated it, although of course the *British Magazine*'s art coverage was simply a spin-off from that of the *Critical*. If, as has been suggested, the readership of magazines was broader and perhaps less sophisticated than that of the reviews, then this feature may have offered certain classes of readers their first exposure (albeit a limited one) to contemporary British art. It is another instance of what might be called the "democratization of culture" throughout this whole period. Here as in the *Critical*, however, this feature and its extraordinary potential were foreshortened by Smollett's departure. It ceased after 1763, further confirmation that he had been its inventor and guiding genius.

A third distinctive offering, obviously designed to capitalize on public interest generated by the war with the French in North America, was the serialized "History of Canada." It too began with the first issue of 1760 and trailed off uncompleted in 1763. Based on this coincidence and considerable internal evidence, Martz has argued persuasively that Smollett either compiled or edited it.[75] Like Smollett's *Continuation*, it was written as popular rather than formal history, concentrating on accounts of Indian battles, massacres, captivities and other sensational events. The passage below, describing an Algonquin woman's escape from captivity, illustrates the style in which it was written:

She was stripped stark naked, fettered with cords, and confined to a hut, where she lay surrounded by her enemies. In the middle of the night, perceiving them all fast asleep, she made shift to untie the ropes with which she was bound: then rising softly, she seized a hatchet, with which she slew at one blow the Indian who lay between her and the door; and, going out of the hut, concealed herself in the hollow of a tree, which she had observed the preceeding day. The people of the hut were waked by the groans of the dying man, and in an instant the whole village was alarmed . . . [etc.][76]

Such was the historical background readers were getting about the present conditions in Canada: vividly narrated but thin in terms of substantive history, it read more like a serialized adventure story than a historical tract. Indeed, as Martz has shown, Smollett incorporated episodes and characters from it in the Lismahago scenes of *Humphry Clinker*.[77] What is most significant about this "history," however, is that its style reflects Smollett's sense of what kinds of readers made up his audience and how best to reach them. If it is true, as Martz has argued so effectively,[78] that Smollett's years of writing and editing history affected his later writing style, it is also evident that Smollett's history writing (here as in the *Continuation*) was becoming steadily more journalistic. This is turn suggests that Smollett's work in journalism, with its month-to-month interaction with a popular audience, was another and perhaps equally important influence on the style of his later works.

Despite obvious signs of catering to public interest in current affairs, Smollett kept the *British Magazine* well clear of politics. It printed a regular "History of the Present War," compiled entirely from the *Gazette* and other newspapers, but avoided political essays and discussion. During the *Briton-North Briton* controversy, the *British Magazine* published excerpts from both and from the *Monitor*, but with no commentary and no signs of partiality.[79] Whatever Smollett's motives in engaging to write the *Briton* on behalf of Bute, he did not allow political interests to intrude on the smooth and profitable course of the *British Magazine*.

The full extent of Smollett's own contributions to the magazine remain unknown. In later years, many pieces were ascribed to him indiscriminately, chiefly because his name was so prominently connected with the magazine.[80] He may have had a hand in compiling the "Compendious History of France," which his experience on the *Universal History* would have made relatively easy. H. S. Buck has identified four poems that Smollett contributed to the poetry section in 1760: "Ode to Blue Ey'd Ann" (April 1760), "Ode to Sleep" (June 1760), "Ode to Mirth" (July 1760), and a song, "To fix her—'twere a task as vain" (August 1760). Buck also tentatively attributes four others, including a "Pastoral Ballad" (October 1760), "The Junto" (5 [April–May], 1760), "Morning in Spring, a Fragment" (5 [April–May], 1760), and "Ode to the Late Gen. Wolfe, written after the reduction of

Louisburg" (February 1760).[81] These are mostly casual poems, written years earlier and resurrected only to serve as filler. Smollett is also the probable author of the short lyric "On Signor Tenducci's Singing *Jubal's Lyre*" (January 1761), as it is signed "By a Prisoner in the King's Bench" and appeared while Smollett was serving his term there for libel.

By far the most distinctive and lasting contribution Smollett made to the *British Magazine* was his serialized novel *Sir Launcelot Greaves*. No attempt will be made here to provide a comprehensive discussion of this remarkable novel. It has attracted at least one full-length study, Richard Lettis's useful dissertation, "A Study of Smollett's *Sir Launcelot Greaves*."[82] It has also received brief but excellent attention from Mayo on its place in the history of magazine fiction, from Smith on its bibliographical background, and from Boucé on its literary qualities and its relation to Smollett's other novels.[83] The present discussion will be confined to touching briefly on a few points about its particular connections with Smollett's activities in journalism.

As Mayo has documented, Smollett was far from the first to present serialized fiction in a magazine. There were dozens of precedents.[84] Still, Smollett's was an outstanding innovation in several ways. It was the first time an original novel of anything approaching this length (eighty-five thousand words) had been serialized in a magazine, and it was the first novel consciously planned and written for publication in installments. Moreover, it was the first time a novelist of Smollett's stature, having already published successful novels in volumes, had turned from conventional methods to serialization. Even the illustrations were significant. Although there were only two (February and August, 1760), they were the first illustrations ever to appear in a work of fiction in a magazine.[85]

The structure and style of *Sir Launcelot Greaves* show that Smollett was consciously tailoring it to the serial format, both to meet its special demands and to capitalize on the possibilities it presented. Each installment had to stand on its own as a piece of self-contained entertainment, yet each episode also had to form part of a continuous and coherent narrative with cumulative integrity and effect. Smollett gave his readers their money's worth each month: as Mayo points out, the chapters in *Sir Launcelot Greaves* are on average forty percent longer than the chapters in his first three novels.[86] In the early going, Smollett seemed to be feeling his way, aware of the need for substantial monthly installments, but sensitive to the possibility of overtaxing his readers. Chapter 3, for example, closes with an apology: "But as the reader may have more than once already cursed the unconsionable length of this chapter, we must postpone to the next opportunity the incidents that succeeded this denunciation of war."[87]

At the same time, Smollett needed to engage the reader in his story from the outset and then keep him coming back month after month. There had to be a "hook." This explains, as Boucé observes, "the extraordinary density of information conveyed in the opening lines of the novel."[88] It also helps to explain the lively pace of the action in some passages, the careful staging of scenes to sustain dramatic excitement, and the interpolated narratives that engender multiple levels of interest even when the action is suspended.

The most striking feature is the suspense Smollett skillfully creates with his chapter endings. Several of his chapters (especially the early ones) end with a sudden interruption of the action at a crucial juncture. In chapter 4, for instance, an argument has broken out between Ferret and Tom Clarke, interrupting Tom's narrative; Ferret becomes insulting, in response to which (says the narrator),

> Tom smiled contemptuously, and had just opened his mouth to proceed, when the company were disturbed by a hideous repetition of groans, that seemed to issue from the chamber in which the body of the squire was deposited. The landlady snatched the candle, and ran into the room, followed by the doctor and the rest; and this accident naturally suspended the narration. In like manner we shall conclude the chapter, that the reader may have time to breathe and digest what he has already heard.

This narrative device teases the reader two ways. It naturally excites a curiosity which can only be satisfied, after a month in suspense, by purchase of the next issue. But Smollett also seems to delight in misdirecting his readers and confuting their expectations. In the passage above, he has charged the language with sinister overtones: overtly, with the phrase "hideous repetition of groans," and more subtly, with ambiguous words such as "body" and "accident." The result is an anticipation of violence and foul play. After living under this misapprehension for thirty days, however, Smollett's readers opened the next issue to learn that when the landlady ran into his rooms, "she found the squire lying on his back, under the dominion of the night-mare, which rode him so hard, that he not only groaned and snorted, but the sweat ran down his face in streams."[89] Having set his readers up, Smollett explodes their apprehensions with a ludicrous spectacle; this narrative playfulness is a new twist in his comic technique made possible only by the serial method of publication.

To a greater degree than in his other novels, there is a sense in *Sir Launcelot Greaves* of Smollett self-consciously addressing his audience. Boucé has suggested very plausibly that the course of the novel may have been affected by reactions from readers.[90] There is no concrete proof that it did, but various bits of collateral evidence make it very likely. Certainly Smollett received many letters from correspondents and contributors each month, as he had on the *Critical*. Moving the novel forward to the position of lead article in the second issue (a prominence it enjoyed in many subsequent issues) and printing the letter from "S. R.," with its opening compliment on "Sir Launcelot Greaves" in the April issue, may both be signs that Smollett had received very favorable feedback about the first installments.[91] He also began to feature the novel in advertisements for the magazine.[92] It has been established that Smollett composed the novel gradually over the two years, sometimes even dashing off an installment only as the deadline drew near.[93] Thus he had the opportunity to act on readers' suggestions and comments; his sensitivity to public opinion in other contexts (notably the *Critical*) makes it very unlikely that he would be unaffected by comments from friends or readers who wrote in. Moreover, there is a suggestive analogue in the decision to publish a sequel to Goldsmith's "Essay on Physiognomy" because of favorable reactions from the public.[94] But finally, unless some lost cache of letters to the editor turns up, the question of reader influence must remain provocatively open.

The significance of Smollett's other striking innovation—the introduction of illustrations into magazine fiction—is difficult to interpret. The illustrations may have been intended to stimulate interest in the novel they accompanied. If so, the fact that they ceased after the ninth installment may indicate that the novel was succeeding well enough for him to drop the illustrations and save the extra cost they entailed. On the other hand, the decision to print them may have been prompted by the success of the novel's first installment and then stopped for other reasons. After all, most magazines carried illustrations in every issue and so the decision each month was where to allocate the illustrations, not whether to have any. In either case, although only two were printed, their use implies a perception of typical magazine readers as marginally less serious or less purely cerebral than typical novel readers, in that the former had a taste for pictures with their reading. In this way Smollett may have been experimenting with a kind of novel that anticipated the subgenre of illustrated novels mastered by Dickens and Thackeray in the nineteenth century. As Michael Steig has argued, "The non-intellectual, largely middle-class audiences to whom the publishers hoped to sell the novels of Dickens, Lever, Ainsworth, Thackeray, and Trollope found the illustrations especially attractive as a supplementary form of visualization, whereas more intellectual novelists such as Eliot and Meredith did not require illustrations for their particular audiences."[95]

Thus Smollett's landmark illustrations ultimately have more significance for the history of the novel than for that of the magazine. Illustrations of all kinds (portraits, landscapes, maps, diagrams) were a staple of the magazine and a point of competition among them, while in the novel of the 1760s they were still very rare and virtually nonexistent (*Tristram Shandy*'s pictorial antics notwithstanding) in first editions. Again it may be that the magazines fostered among the reading public certain tastes and expectations that spread their influence to popular fiction. It was only partially a result of *Sir Launcelot Greaves* and its two illustrations, but certainly by the end of the century, illustrated novels were becoming commonplace.[96] These, too, may have been instrumental in transforming and enlarging the audience for fiction, even as they functioned initially as competitive marketing tactics among publishers.

In addition to technical and stylistic innovations, *Sir Launcelot Greaves* exhibits signs of what were for Smollet new kinds of material and new emphases in its contents. Mayo has described it as a "species of topical novel, which draws serious attention to the workings of country justice, the absurdities of parliamentary elections, the quality of life in the new King's Bench Prison, and the abuses of private madhouses."[97] Martz has also remarked on the high proportion of topical materials in this novel and used it to draw a distinction between *Sir Launcelot Greaves* and Smollett's earlier novels:

> Instead of concentrating upon the adventures of his hero, in these parts Smollett seems interested in giving a set picture of contemporary conditions. He had, of course, used such topical materials in his earlier novels, but seldom with such concentration, such overtly topical aims. These incidents point the way to the distinctive content of Smollett's later creative period: topical, historical materials.[98]

Martz goes on to argue convincingly that history writing was the chief influence on the form and style of Smollett's later novels. To that vein of influence must also be added, especially now that the actual mass of Smollett's journalistic writings is more evident, the many connections between Smollett's work in journalism and the distinctive content of his later novels, especially *Sir Launcelot Greaves*.

In the first place, the very fact that Smollett was writing for a magazine audience had to influence his selection of topics and materials. Readers looked at magazines in a different frame of mind and with different expectations from those with which they opened a multivolume novel. But at another level, both the topical subject matter and the underlying seriousness about contemporary conditions in *Sir Launcelot Greaves* grew out of Smollett's recent experience in review journalism. Specific connections with Smollett's book reviews are numerous, and source after source can be traced. Smollett drew on Battie's *Treatise on Madness*, for example, for material for the scenes on madness and madhouses. The whole character of Ferret is based on the prolific pamphleteer John Shebbeare whose various works Smollett had reviewed. The extended satire on contemporary politics harks back to the innumerable political pamphlets Smollett reviewed with such reluctance.[99] The influence of Hogarth, whose works Smollett had also reviewed, is everywhere evident, a point to which we will return momentarily. The point here is that the topical issues that Mayo and Martz identify in *Sir Launcelot Greaves* were the subjects of the books Smollett had been reviewing in large numbers for the *Critical*; these were issues that had filled his mind and moved his pen on a monthly basis for four years before he began writing *Sir Launcelot Greaves*.

Launcelot Greaves is himself much the same kind of moral idealist in society at large as Smollett had been in the republic of letters when he founded the *Critical*, attentive to every cause, every issue and controversy. During what Martz aptly called his "fallow years," the late 1750s, the vast numbers of books Smollett read and reviewed and the vistas they opened on contemporary society provided an important part of the imaginative replenishment he needed to produce another novel.

The influence of Hogarth on *Sir Launcelot Greaves* should be pursued for a moment, as it is a striking example of the way Smollett's close attention to works of art in recent years had begun to inform his creative imagination. Smollett inserted a straightforward compliment to "the inimitable Hogarth" in chapter 12 and borrowed another detail from the penultimate plate of Hogarth's *Idle Apprentice* in chapter 22, where the "conjuror" (Ferret) prophesies that Crabshaw will one day be hanged at Tyburn and advises him "to appear in the cart with a nosegay in one hand, and the Whole Duty of Man in the other"—exactly as the condemned Tom Idle had in Hogarth's plate.[100] In other places Smollett's debt amounts to wholesale appropriation of Hogarth's iconography. The madhouse in *Sir Launcelot Greaves* (chap. 23), for example, has among its occupants a "pope," a "king," a religious fanatic (Methodist), and a mathematician calculating the longitude, all of whom have exact counterparts in plate 8 of Hogarth's *Rake's Progress*. Hogarth had also included a melancholic lover, who in Smollett's version becomes Launcelot himself, "foaming like a lion in the toil" when he hears Aurelia's voice. One of the only characters entirely original to Smollett in this scene is Dick Distich, the bellicose and drunken poet who is in fact based on Charles Churchill and thus represents another fictional detail derived from Smollett's review criticism of the late 1750s.[101]

In addition to the madhouse scene, Smollett's depiction of a country election in chapters 9 and 10 of *Sir Launcelot Greaves* also originates in Hogarth's art, specifically his "Four Prints of An Election" published serially from 1755 to 1758. By 1760 Smollett had devoted at least two articles to Hogarth in the *Critical*, the second of which dealt with *A Poetical Description of Mr. Hogarth's Election Prints* (Ap '59, 274–75) and showed Smollett's familiarity with those prints in particular. Even bearing in mind that Smollett and Hogarth were satirizing actual historical conditions that they both had observed, one sees detail after detail of correspondence between Hogarth's *Election Prints* and Smollett's country election scene. Both take as their theme the corruption, rancor, and violence of party politics. The anti-Semitism of Hogarth's crowds, who bear banners reading "No Jews" (plate 1), is expressed in the narrative description of one of Smollett's election candidates, Isaac Vanderpelft, whose ancestry (it is feared) is "not without a mixture of Hebrew blood" (chap. 9). Another banner in Hogarth's first plate, "Liberty and Property," becomes "Liberty and the Landed Interest" on a banner in Smollett's scene. In Hogarth's second plate a drunken barber argues politics with a drinking companion; in Smollett's story, the village barber argues and then fights with poor Crabshaw during the election fracas. Both Hogarth and Smollett focus ridicule and abuse on John Shebbeare: in Hogarth's third plate he appears, manacled, surreptitiously prompting an idiot how to vote, while in Smollett's version he features as a charlatan selling quack medicine and ranting about politics to the crowds (chap. 10). The blue insignia, ribbons, and flags ("True blue") of Hogarth's third and fourth plates are elaborated into a full political color scheme in Smollett's version, with one faction flourishing blue cockades in their hats and blue silk in their banners, the other orange insignia throughout.

Dickens, it should be noted, seems heavily indebted to these chapters in *Sir Launcelot Greaves* for his sketch of the "Election at Eatanswill" in the *Pickwick Papers* (chap. 13). Both the basic story frame, in which a party of innocents stumble into the midst of a hotly contested country election (with predictably comic results), and specific details, such as the blue and orange party colors which become the "Blues" and the "Buffs" in Dickens, are very similar. If it can be argued, as one critic has, "that Dickens inherited Hogarth's mantle as the great English comic and satiric artist," it seems equally evident that much of Hogarth's influence reached Dickens through the mediation of Smollett.[102] This kind of influence was casually but astutely suggested more than thirty years ago by Alan McKillop, as he noted the topicality and "high visualization" of so much in *Sir Launcelot Greaves*.[103] With the discovery of Smollett's art reviews and his specific attention to Hogarth (including a later article in the *British Magazine*, in September 1762 [3: 492]), one can demonstrate and trace more clearly the adaptation and interplay of these sister arts, the visual and verbal media, in Hogarth, Smollett, and Dickens.[104]

It has usually been assumed that Smollett wrote *Sir Launcelot Greaves* to promote sales of the *British Magazine*;[105] the possibility that his design worked the other way around has been completely ignored. There are, however, many reasons why Smollett, feeling the imaginative materials for a novel building up in him, might have deliberately chosen a magazine as his preferred vehicle. First, the serial method obviated the need to sit down and write the whole novel in advance of publication. In 1747–48, by devoting himself exclusively to the task, Smollett had written *Roderick Random* in eight months. But in 1759–60, Smollett's numerous other commitments made it impossible to set aside time for that method of composition. He could also realize income from his novel as he wrote it, rather than having to wait for the completion of the whole manuscript before receiving a penny. Another advantage was that he could minimize risks by adjusting its length. If the novel proved unsuccessful in the early going, he could cut his losses by foreshortening it—perhaps a significant consideration, in view of *Ferdinand*

Count Fathom's poor reception in 1753.[106] Moreover, Smollett enjoyed a certain flexibility afforded by the gradual method of composition. At one point, for example, he was able to make a journey to Scotland and still keep pace with the novel by sending his installments through the post.[107]

It was also ultimately a less painful way to make a book. Smollett may have taken a lesson from the successful periodical essayists such as Johnson with his *Rambler* and *Idler*, which showed that a two-year run of periodical pieces could later be gathered into a viable and profitable book. That Smollett had something like this in mind is suggested by the carefully planned two-year run of *Sir Launcelot Greaves* (January 1760 – December 1761). Also, less text was required. When *Sir Launcelot Greaves* was published in two volumes in 1762, its overall length of eighty-five thousand words made it the shortest in Smollett's canon, far shorter than *Roderick Random* (over 200,000) or *Peregrine Pickle* (over 300,000), or even *Ferdinand Count Fathom* (155,000).

Publishing a novel in a magazine automatically gave it a wider readership. Exact circulation figures for the *British Magazine* are unknown, but those of other magazines suggest an approximate scale. In the mid-1750s, the *Gentleman's Magazine* reportedly sold ten thousand copies a month and the *London Magazine* about eight thousand.[108] The *Royal Magazine* was claiming sales of eleven thousand in 1760, while in 1762 the editor of the *Library* estimated that the average magazine sold five thousand copies a month. The *Town and Country Magazine*, which was in a sense the successor to the *British Magazine* because it was founded by Archibald Hamilton's son (and probably with the senior Hamilton's help) twelve months after the *British Magazine* ended, enjoyed a circulation of more than ten thousand per month almost from its inception in 1769.[109] It seems safe to assume, therefore, a figure of about three thousand is a very conservative estimate of the *British Magazine*'s circulation and thus of the readership of *Sir Launcelot Greaves*. This compares favorably with the first printings of *Roderick Random* in 1748 and (more significantly) *Humphry Clinker* in 1771: both were two thousand.[110] Moreover, novels in bookshops sold gradually, while the magazine put *Sir Launcelot Greaves* in the hands of readers instantly. Of course, if a novel sold well, it was reprinted one or two thousand copies at a time. But magazines were also reprinted, both as issues sold out and, later, to make up back volumes for new subscribers. As Smith has shown, the first issue of the *British Magazine* was being reprinted within months of its first publication, suggesting that sales were brisk.[111]

Smollett may also have suspected that it could be more profitable to publish a novel this way. If *Sir Launcelot Greaves* had instead been published in volumes, then based on a hypothetical first printing of two thousand copies sold at six shillings each, the gross revenue generated would have been about six hundred pounds. By contrast, based on an estimated monthly sale of three thousand copies of the *British Magazine* (at six pence each) for the twenty-five issues in which *Sir Launcelot Greaves* appeared (an extra issue was published in 1760), then the gross revenue generated by the magazine would have been three times greater, about £1875. Even if three thousand copies of the novel were sold (raising gross revenue to nine hundred pounds), it is still less than half of that from the magazine. It is no wonder that Smollett arranged to control the magazine copyright. Of course, this does not take into account the costs of other copy in the magazine (although a large portion of it was supplied by voluntary contributors) or other possible differences in the costs of printing and distribution. Still, these rough calculations suggest that Smollett had learned how profitable serial publication could be (probably from the success of his *History* and *Continuation* in numbers) and applied the lesson in publishing to *Sir Launcelot Greaves*.

The critical reception of *Sir Launcelot Greaves* is often characterized as "disappointing."[112] Just after its first installment, Goldsmith inserted a puff for it in his "wow-wow" sketch, which appeared in the *Public Ledger* of 16 February 1760. When it was published in volumes in 1762, there were favorable but brief notices in the *Library*[113] and (of course) the *Critical* (My '62, 427–29), as well as a noncommital single sentence in the *Monthly* (26:391). Too much has been made of this quiet critical reception. It must be remembered that the novel's method of publication had preempted criticism. By the time *Sir Launcelot Greaves* appeared in volumes, criticism was pointless: by then it was effectively the second edition of a novel from which passages had appeared in the periodical press every month for two years. The public had already expressed its approval by continuing to buy the *British Magazine*.

This must also be taken into account when one considers the number and frequency of later editions and what they reflect about the novel's popularity. Smith observes that the 1762 edition—the first in book form—"did not sell very quickly," noting that copies were still unsold in 1764.[114] But in fact from 1762 until the end of 1767, when the *British Magazine* ceased, copies of the novel were being reprinted and sold as part of every set of back volumes the magazine sold to new subscribers who wanted to make up the set, which was a common practice. This helps explain the apparent absence of new editions before 1770 and the steadily increasing numbers of them thereafter, of which Smith lists ten published in London alone before 1800.[115] With a new edition appearing every three years (on average) during that period, *Sir Launcelot Greaves* can hardly be categorized as unpopular or unsuccessful.

A more significant measure of the novel's success may be its influence on subsequent writers. There was a small wave of imitation just after *Sir Launcelot Greaves* started publishing in January 1760. Charlotte Lennox's novel *Sophia* began appearing as a serial in the *Lady's Museum* in March 1760.[116] The *Royal Female Magazine* began a serial novel of its own, "The Fortune-Hunter," in July 1760.[117] The *Imperial Magazine*, a constant rival to the *British Magazine* during these years, presented the first installment of

"Belmour and Amanda" in October 1760, with a promise that it would be continued.[118] (It never was.) The *Universal Museum* also tried a serial novel, "The Disasters of Tantarobasus," in 1762, but it too was undistinguished, according to Mayo.[119] Overall, Mayo expresses surprise that *Sir Launcelot Greaves* was not more widely and obviously influential, although he does conclude that from this point on, serial fiction in the magazines becomes much more common.[120] In the long run, Smollett may have simply overleaped his contemporaries, for it was in the nineteenth century that his new method would become standard.

Measuring the success of the *British Magazine* itself is a simpler matter. It survived until 1767, filling eight volumes, in the midst of numerous and aggressive competitors. That it was respected by other periodical writers is evident from their customary expression of regard: piratical reprintings. Although *Sir Launcelot Greaves* was never reprinted by other periodicals (it was too conspicuous to borrow from safely), other pieces were frequently reprinted in the newspapers and other magazines.[121] It was heavily pilfered by the *Aberdeen Magazine*, which in its one-year life (January–December 1761) averaged one article a month from the *British Magazine*, including at least one instance where it reprinted the book review section in its entirety.[122] These literary recyclings could carry on for years. A story from the *British Magazine* of 1760, for example, was reprinted in the *Gentleman's and Lady's Museum* more than seventeen years later, although of course with a new title to obscure its origins.[123]

The *Scots Magazine*, published in Edinburgh, seems to have had a special relationship of some kind with the *British Magazine*. Not only did it frequently reprint its contents, on many occasions the same articles appeared in issues of the *Scots Magazine* and the *British Magazine* published on the same day. For example, in the *Scots Magazine* for December 1759 (published 1 January 1760), there are two essays and two short articles that also appear in the *British Magazine* for January 1760 (published 1 January 1760).[124] The simultaneity of publication in London and Edinburgh precludes either's reprinting from the other. At least some of the material is original and therefore could not have been borrowed from a common source. This leaves only the possibility of dual submissions by contributors or, more probably, some form of cooperation between the compilers of the two journals. Smollett had many connections in Scotland but exactly who may have been the link with the *Scots Magazine* and how their connection worked remain to be discovered.

The *British Magazine* also had at least one foreign admirer, the *Journal encyclopédique*. In its issue for 15 March 1760, it greeted the first issue of the *British Magazine* with a short notice:

The British Magazine. Le Magasin Britannique. C'est Mr. Smollet célèbre par son *Histoire d'Angleterre*, qui est à la tête de ce bon Ouvrage périodique. Il s'est associé plusieurs Gens de Lettres bien dignes de le seconder, & qui travaillent avec le plus grand succès.[125]

Thereafter the *British Magazine* served as its favorite English magazine: the *Journal encyclopédique* reprinted articles from its contents more frequently than from any other. Moreover in 1761 the *Journal encyclopédique* began to print long summaries and excerpts in translation from *Sir Launcelot Greaves*, apparently with the aim for a time to present the public with what was essentially an abridged version of the whole novel.[126] The installments were later stopped, but initially at least this must have been one of the first attempts to present a serialized novel (certainly a serialized *English* novel) to the French reading public. Whether there were any personal or business connections between the proprietors of the *Journal encyclopédique* and the *British Magazine* is unknown but very likely. Back in the early days of the *Critical*, when its first issue was delayed in expectation of foreign articles, it proved to be articles from the first issue of the *Journal encyclopédique* they had been awaiting.[127] Perhaps Smollett had reached an agreement with the authors of the *Journal encyclopédique* that they would serve as reciprocal correspondents between it and the *Critical*, and perhaps this favoritism for Smollett's *British Magazine* beginning in 1760, and especially for his serial novel as published in it, resulted from that continuing correspondence. For now the matter remains a mystery. But these signs of an underground correspondence between Smollett in England and his fellow literati in France, even in the midst of the Seven Years War, suggest another of the ways in which Smollett constantly tended to rise above the routines of Grub Street and to contribute to the literary and intellectual history of his time.

After Smollett's departure in the summer of 1763, the *British Magazine* continued to have a strong literary orientation, as Mayo has noted.[128] But several of its features dropped off, including the "History of Canada," the innovative book review section, and the occasional articles on works of art. It also became steadily more derivative, reprinting material from all sorts of other published works.[129] Here, as in the *Critical*, Smollett's withdrawal was telling. Although he had founded the *British Magazine* with decidedly less idealistic aims, he brought to it the same energy, imagination, and editorial skill that had distinguished the *Critical* from other journals. As a result of the talented personnel he assembled and the innovations he introduced, Smollett's *British Magazine* deserves a place of permanent importance in literary history.

[10]

"Who Killed John Keats?": Smollett and the New Critical Establishment

In 1763, after more than seven years of review and magazine journalism, Smollett's writing career was wrenched from its course. That spring his health and happiness collapsed. The illnesses that had for so long drained his strength and periodically confined him to his house now grew worse. His involvement as author of the *Briton* in the Bute-Wilkes political controversies of 1762–63 had embroiled him in ugly and unpopular political wars from which he emerged, when the *Briton* stopped publishing in February 1763, scarred and embittered. Then on 3 April, his only child and cherished companion, Elizabeth, died at the age of fifteen. Smollett and his wife Anne were devastated. About ten weeks later, having settled his affairs and canceled his many writing commitments, the Smolletts departed for France with little expectation of ever seeing England again.

For the next two years, Smollett lived and traveled in France and Italy, resting and recuperating. Gradually he succeeded in recovering his health and spirits, as well as gathering material for his next book, his *Travels Through France and Italy*.[1] In early summer 1765, he returned to England. He stayed in London for several months, preparing the final volume of the *Continuation* of his *History* (published in late 1765) and the text of his *Travels* (published in May 1766) for the press. Soon his ill health recurred, driving him to the spas at Bath and Bristol in search of relief. Apart from a long journey to Scotland in the spring and summer of 1766, he seems to have moved only between London and Bath during his last three years in England. During this period he also compiled *The Present State of All Nations* (8 vols., 1768) and wrote his scathingly satirical political novel, *The History and Adventures of an Atom* (1769), which was actually published shortly after he left England for the last time, in late 1768. He lived the final two years of his life in Italy and it was from there that he sent to London the completed manuscript of his finest novel, *The Expedition of Humphry Clinker* (1771).

He scarcely lived long enough to read its reviews. He died near Livorno ("Leghorne") in the middle of September 1771, aged fifty.

Throughout those last eight years from 1763 to 1771, although his name was sometimes publicly associated with the *Critical* (especially by disappointed authors), Smollett was in fact quite detached from it and from the *British Magazine*. A few months after his return to England in 1765, Smollett explained to John Moore, "I gave up all connection with the Critical Review and every other literary system before I quitted England," although in the same letter he goes on to acknowledge a slender but continuing link as an occasional contributor: "Since my return I have writt a few articles merely for amusement; but I have now no concern in the work."[2] No longer "tied down to the stake" by editorial and proprietary concerns, Smollett retired into the role of contributing editor emeritus—at the age of forty-four. Among the "few articles" Smollett wrote between 1765 and 1768 in the *Critical*, the handful that can be identified (see appendix A) do seem to have been primarily "for amusement." They fall into Smollett's greatest areas of interest: medicine, science, art, literature. Only one, on *A Digest of the Laws Concerning Libel* (Jl '65, 45–49), carries the old Smollettian anger and indignation, but libel was the one subject on which Smollett seemed unable to get much comic distance even as late as *Humphry Clinker* (2 June, 102–4). Five of the articles are on medical books, among them Wilson's *Remarks Upon Disorders of the Bowels* (Au '65, 149–52), Memis's *Midwife's Pocket Companion* (Se '65, 184–88), an anonymous *Treatise on Mineral Waters in England* (Oc '65, 281–88), and a quack-medicine treatise, *Observations on the Baume de Vie* (Oc '65, 310–11). Two articles are devoted to reviewing the Royal Society's *Philosophical Transactions for 1764*, which is done with Smollett's characteristic mix of thoroughness and comic flare (Se '65, 257–65 and No '65, 348–58). Another is devoted to the subject of art: a review of *The English Connoisseur*, a book whose aim Smollett applauded even as its execution faltered, for it set out to catalog and describe major English collections of art for the general public (Jn '66, 407–9). Finally, there were works of literature that captured Smollett's attention: William Stevenson's *Original Poems* (Au '65, 124–34), Sayer's translation of Montesquieu's *Temple of Gnidus* (Au '65, 152–53), George Colman's comedy *The English Merchant* (Mr '67, 214–16), and an anonymous (and bad) collection of verse, *Miscellanies* (Se '67, 226).

But more important than these lighthearted book reviews of Smollett's later period is the change in his literary character that they help to mark. By the early 1760s, Smollett had undergone a transformation. Gone are the angry young men and anxious outsiders of his early works—the fierce, unforgiving voices of his satires, *Advice* (1746) and *Reproof* (1747), the proud, hotheaded protagonists of *Roderick Random* (1748), *Peregrine Pickle* (1751), and *Ferdinand Count Fathom* (1753), who spent their time not only exposing ignorance and pretense, but taking revenge on those who blocked their paths, the elite and powerful, the insiders, the men with success and influence. In the post-1760 fiction one instead finds main characters like Sir Launcelot Greaves and Matthew Bramble who hold positions of social responsibility, who exercise reason and benevolence, and who provide care and comfort even to those who don't seem to deserve it. The satire in their novels is ultimately a forgiving, or at least a self-inclusive, mockery of human foibles. The railing of the outsider gives way to the voice of authority and confidence not only in the novels but in the history writing and encyclopedic compilations of Smollett's later career.

At the center of this transformation in Smollett's tone and outlook is his intense seven-year stretch as a literary journalist, from 1756 to 1763. During those years, by coincidence precisely the span of the Seven Years War, Smollett could not have appreciated fully the prominent role his journals were playing, and would continue to play, in shaping the history of journalism and of literature generally. But he must have sensed something of it. Known first as a popular novelist and translator, by the end of the 1750s Smollett had begun to gain respect—largely through the *Critical* and his *History*—as an eminence in the world of letters. Not only was he (as Knapp and Spector have said) "the leading reviewer in London for the period from 1756 to 1763,"[3] but his role became that of literary arbiter and spokesman. All the writers, both aspiring and established, who sought his influence; all the disappointed authors who cringed or railed at his journal's opinions; all the editors who imitated the *Critical* or reprinted its articles; all the readers who received its opinions or experienced its influence through so many different channels: all these wittingly or unwittingly acknowledged his achievement. Smollett the angry outsider had become a pillar of the literary establishment.

Perhaps one passage in his writings best represents his rise to this stature. When Smollett decided to bring his *History of England* down to the 1760s by writing the *Continuation*, his roles as journalist and historian merged. He became a commentator on his own times. At the close of his account of events during the reign of George II, he provided a twelve-page summary of the progress of the arts and sciences.[4] It was in essence a "state of the arts" address, for which his years of reviewing publications in so many fields— literature, science, history, politics, and the arts—had amply prepared him. In this three-thousand-word sketch, he summarized developments and listed important figures in every field: religion and philosophy, metaphysics and medicine, agriculture, literature, history, music, painting, sculpture, architecture, and science. Many of his friends and acquaintances, including Hunter, Richardson, and Garrick, were among those he praised most generously, but so were some former rivals and adversaries such as Fielding, Johnson, and Monro. Garrick, it should be noted, was moved to write Smollett a letter of thanks for being so honored.[5]

What is most striking about this sketch, however, is its style. It has the grand sweep and generous outlook, the confident manner and authoritative tone of a statesman of letters. Smollett was just turned forty when he wrote this volume but, even allowing for the differences between fiction and historical prose, how changed are the underlying attitudes expressed here from the slashing satire of his twenties and early thirties. Only direct quotation can fully convey the new tone and manner. In one paragraph, for example, Smollett surveys that field about which he claimed to know little but always showed keen interest, the fine arts:

> The British soil, which had hitherto been barren in the article of painting, now produced some artists of extraordinary merit. Hogarth excelled all the world in exhibiting the scenes of ordinary life; in humorous historical designs. Hudson, Reynolds, and Ramsay, distinguished themselves by their superior merit in portraits; a branch that was successfully cultivated by many other English painters. Wooton was famous for representing live animals in general; Seymour for race horses; Lambert and the Smiths, for landscape; and Scot for sea-pieces. Several spirited attempts were made on historical subjects; but little progress was made on the sublime parts of painting. Essays of this kind were discouraged by a false taste, founded upon a reprobation of British genius. The art of engraving was brought to perfection by Strange and laudably practised by several other masters; and great improvements were made in mezzotinto, miniature, and enamel. Many fair monuments of sculpture or statuary were raised by Rysbach, Roubilliac, and Wilton. Architecture, which had been cherished by the elegant taste of a Burlington, soon became a favourite study; and many magnificent edifices were reared in different parts of the kingdom.

Rarely would one expect to find such a confident overview of the contemporary art scene, especially by a writer without any artistic training or talent, who had only his experience as an amateur art critic on which to draw.

A second excerpt shows Smollett surveying a more familiar field: literature. He begins by mentioning those writers who had flourished earlier but lived on into the reign of George II, which began in 1727:

> Swift and Pope we have mentioned on another occasion. Young still survived a venerable monument of poetical talent. Thomson, the poet of the Seasons, displayed a luxuriancy of genius in describing the beauties of nature. Akenside and Armstrong excelled in didactic poetry. Even the Epopoes did not disdain an English dress, but appeared to advantage in the Leonidas of Glover, and the Epigoniad of Wilkie. The public acknowledged a considerable share of dramatic merit in the tragedies of Young, Mallet, Home, and some other less distinguished authors. Very few regular comedies, during this period, were exhibited on the English theatre, which, however, produced many less laboured pieces, abounding with satire, wit, and humour. The Careless Husband of Cibber, and Suspicious

Husband of Hoadley, are the only very modern comedies that bid fair for reaching posterity.

Then, after cataloging and complimenting the greatest actors of the age—Garrick, Quin, Susannah Cibber, and Hannah Pritchard—Smollett moves on to the major writers of more recent literary history. Considering not only genres of literature but categories of authors, Smollett bestows laurels on more than twenty contemporary worthies:

> That Great Britain was not barren of poets at this period, appears from the detached performances of Johnson, Mason, Gray, the two Whiteheads, and the two Wartons, besides a great number of other bards who have sported in lyric poetry, and acquired the applause of their fellow citizens. Candidates for literary fame appeared even in the higher sphere of life, embellished by the nervous stile, superior sense, and extensive erudition of a Corke; by the delicate taste, the polished muse, and tender feelings of a Lyttelton. King shone unrivalled in Roman eloquence. Even the female sex distinguished themselves by their taste and ingenuity. Miss Carter rivalled the celebrated Dacier in learning and critical knowledge; and Mrs. Lennox signalized herself by many successful efforts of genius, both in poetry and prose. The genius of Cervantes was transfused into the novels of Fielding, who painted the characters, and ridiculed the follies of life with equal strength, humour, and propriety. The field of history and biography was cultivated by many writers of ability, among whom we distinguish the copious Guthrie, the circumstantial Ralph, the laborious Carte, the learned and elegant Robertson, and above all the ingenious, penetrating, and comprehensive Hume, whom we rank among the first writers of the age, both as an historian and philosopher. Nor let us forget the merit conspicuous in the works of Campbell, remarkable for candour, intelligence, and precision. Johnson, inferior to none in Philosophy, philology, poetry, and classical learning, stands foremost as an essayist, justly admired for the dignity, strength, and variety of his stile, as well as for the agreeable manner in which he investigates the human heart, tracing every interesting emotion, and opening all the sources of morality. The laudable aim of inlisting the passions on the side of virture, was successfully pursued by Richardson, in his Pamela, Clarissa, and Grandison; a species of writing equally new and extraordinary, where, mingled with much superfluity and impertinence, we find a sublime system of ethics, and amazing knowledge, and command of human nature.

In addition to those mentioned in the excerpts quoted here, another forty names are singled out for special mention by Smollett in his personal version of an Academy Awards program.

But these were public pronouncements, not private opinions, and thus what becomes interesting is the extraordinarily wide reception his pronouncements enjoyed. First issued in late 1761 in a serial installment of his *Continuation*, which was then selling over ten thousand copies weekly and would sell more than twenty thousand copies by 1765, this sketch reached an immediate audience that was vast in itself. But editors quickly saw its special appeal for other readerships. Within days the sketch was lifted and reprinted as a separate article in London's largest-selling newspaper, *The Public Advertiser*, where it was introduced as "The State of Commerce, Arts, and Science, in the Reign of George II, from Smollett's *Continuation of the Complete History of England*." Days after that it was reprinted in at least two Scottish newspapers, the *Caledonian Mercury* (14 October 1761) and the *Edinburgh Evening Courant* (17 October 1761), and then in several magazines, including the *Imperial Magazine* in London and the *Edinburgh, Aberdeen*, and *Scots Magazines* in Scotland.[6] It even reached a foreign audience. The *Journal encyclopédique* reprinted the full passage, with additional complimentary remarks, in its issue for 15 November 1761; later it appeared in French again, as part of Jean-Baptiste Targe's multi-volume translation of Smollett's *History*, published in Orleans in 1759–64. And of course encyclopedic compilations and derivative histories pirated and continued to recirculate Smollett's sketch for the rest of the century, often, as in the case of Thomas Mortimer's *British Plutarch* (1762), without crediting the source.[7] Until the publication of Johnson's *Lives of the Poets* in 1779–81, no such comprehensive critical retrospect would be as widely read and accepted. By virtue of numbers alone, Smollett's had become the standard, if not definitive, assessment of the state of the arts and sciences, and he himself the de facto spokesman for his age.[8]

Smollett had indeed come into his own. And in the course of realizing his own transformation as a literary figure, his inclusion and rise within the literary establishment, he had also been contributing to the transformation *of* that establishment, that network of relations among authors, publishers, and readers which somehow determined what got published, what prospered, what perished. We are used to thinking of review criticism as central to our literary culture—pervasive, essential, powerful. We think of Hardy's decision to abandon novel writing after the harsh reviews of *Jude the Obscure* (1896), or, more happily, of George Eliot's intellectual development as a reviewer for the *Westminster Review* in the 1850s; we remember Coleridge's discursive (and perhaps penitential) passages about review critics in his *Biographia Literaria* (1817) and Byron's heroic rage in *English Bards and Scotch Reviewers* (1809). Examples are legion. Even Matthew Arnold's classic study, "The Function of Criticism at the Present Time," takes as its starting point some of Wordsworth's fulminations against review critics.

At the beginning of the nineteenth century, review critics began to assume almost mythic stature, as they became the archfiends of our folklore about artistic genius. "Who killed John Keats?" asked Byron in a short poem, and then provided his own half-angry, half-ironic answer: "'I,' says the *Quarterly*,

/ So savage and tartarly; / 'Twas one of my feats.'" Here was the Romantic myth of the poet, martyred by critical abuse and neglect, shut out to suffer and die by an unthinking, unfeeling critical establishment. Of course tuberculosis, not depression, killed Keats and like most myths, this one was attractive for its symbolic rather than factual truth. Yet it was shared in by Wordsworth, Shelley, Hunt, Hazlitt, and generations of others. Partly because the romantics succeeded in fashioning from their critical disappointments this self-dramatizing myth of persecution, we have inherited a particularly strong impression of review critics and their power arising just at the beginning of the nineteenth century.

Scholars have long acknowledged the influence of reviewers on individual writers: Newman White's *The Unextinguished Hearth* (1938), for example, dispelled the myth of Shelley's critical neglect in his own day, and Edgar Shannon's *Tennyson and the Reviewers* (1952) analyzed their influence on a poet of whom it has been said that he never left a line unaltered that had been criticized by a reviewer. But again here as always our notions of review criticism are centered in the nineteenth century. John Gross speaks for many when, in his discussion of "The Rise of the Reviewer," he says: "It was only at the beginning of the nineteenth century that a review emerged as a really powerful institution, a major social force."[9] Or again, Elaine Showalter's landmark study, *A Literature of Their Own*, traces the roots of "The Double Critical Standard" back only to 1800: "Gentleman reviewers had patronized lady novelists since the beginning of the nineteenth century . . . ."[10]

It is hoped that the mass of information assembled and examined in this study will help to relocate the rise of the review, with its attendant effects on literary history, back in the middle of the eighteenth century. Johnson himself, whose overarching eminence made his perhaps the last literary period to be labeled with one man's name, traced the rise of the review. He, who had lamented the lack of a good English literary journal in the early 1750s, tried and failed to start one of his own in 1756, and scoffed at the sudden surfeit of "Remarkers and Reviewers" in 1757, had by 1763 actually written reviews for the *Critical* and in 1767 found himself discussing the relative merits of the *Monthly* and *Critical* in conversation with King George III. Johnson's cautious remarks to the King ("the Monthly Review was done with most care, the Critical upon the best principles") gave way ten years later, when the subject again came up in conversation, to Johnson's famous jest about the *Monthly* reviewers as "duller men . . . glad to read the books through" and, more importantly, his staunch defense of both reviews: "I think them very impartial: I do not know an instance of partiality."[11]

What is important here is not which of the two reviews Johnson preferred, or for what reasons, but the fact that in the 1760s, in an impromptu conversation between two people of such disparate intellectual gifts and social ranks as George III and Samuel Johnson, the two review journals should provide the topic on which they could converse most easily. It is in so many ways symbolic of the centrality of the reviews in English cultural life already at that date. Within only a decade or two there had been in the world of literature a fundamental realignment of the relations among readers, writers, and publishers, with anonymous review critics now mediating among them all. A new machinery was in place—impersonal, powerful, and inescapable.

How writers approached this new literary establishment is best exemplified in the career of one of Johnson's young friends and protégées, Fanny Burney. Her attitudes are typical. "No hackneyed writer [or] half-starved garretteer," as she herself said, she came from a family of means, education, and literary sophistication. Thus it is all the more telling that when she made her literary debut with *Evelina* in 1778, she ushered that first novel into the world with a long formal dedication, "To the Authors of the Monthly and Critical Reviews." Just as her heroine Evelina makes her "entrance into the world" under the authority and protection of proper guardians, so does the author seek admission to a world regulated by these critical authorities. Such had been Boswell's approach and Warton's and that of scores of others before Burney (many of them discussed above in chap. 8), and such would be her concern throughout her career. Her diaries and letters bespeak continuing sensitivity to what the review critics said. Perhaps most tellingly of all, as Edward and Lillian Bloom have demonstrated, her extensive revisions of *Camilla* in the late 1790s were based meticulously on criticisms by reviewers in the *Monthly* and elsewhere.[12] Once again it is a pattern we have seen before, a pattern of response that had become characteristic of authors since the rise of the reviews in the 1750s and 1760s. A generation or two after Fanny Burney, when Byron, Shelley, and the others created the myth of critical martyrdom—such as Keats's—they were actually rebelling against institutions and powers that had existed in the literary world for some seventy years.

Few have remembered that Smollett was a founding father of this new critical establishment. Once or twice a late eighteenth century writer in the *Critical* would refer to Smollett as "our predecessor in this work" (Jn '87, 421) or mention a feeling for him of "filial reverence as our great ancestor" (Jl '91, 356), but it was a faint memory. In general, the curtain of anonymity hid the extent of his work as critic and editor from his contemporaries and insured that it would quickly sink from sight thereafter. By pulling aside that curtain, however slightly, we can now restore to view an enormous volume of writing and work and open an important new dimension in Smollett's career. We can also better understand the significance of the nearest thing to straight autobiography that Smollett left us: the memorial he wrote for himself in the form of a self-portrait in his valedictory novel, *Humphry Clinker*. There, looking back on his turbulent but productive career, Smollett chose to depict himself not as a novelist, or a historian, or a physician, but as the respected and influential editor of a literary journal.[13] Smollett builds a full comic episode around the Sunday lunch for authors and other literati at his Chelsea home, to which Matt Bramble and Jerry Milford come along. For all its comedy, however, the sketch presents Smollett as an eminence: "a man of character in the literary world" (131), "one of those few writers of the age that stand upon their own foundation" (124), and "courted by such a number of literary dependants" (132)—the last phrase uttered in the novel by an author who had himself applied to Smollett for favorable treatment in the *Critical* but, although his book was "treated civilly," he felt (so typically) dissatisfied and resentful. The same character asks the question that Smollett had so often asked himself during his years as *Critical* editor: "What advantage or satisfaction [can] he derive from having brought such a nest of hornets about his ears?"

But it was in this role that Smollett chose to present himself to posterity, a role that for all the hardship and frustration it had brought him clearly had also provided unique satisfactions. His work as critic and journal editor was an integral part of his own sense of importance and now can be seen as a major part of his literary achievement. Smollett was the first man of letters really to fill the role of review journal editor, inventing and defining it as he went along, and as such he is a forefather of all the review critics and editors since.

Appendix A
A List of Smollett's Articles in the *Critical Review* 1756–1767 and the Evidence for Their Attribution

The list below is offered as a preliminary effort to establish a canon of Smollett's contributions to the *Critical* from 1756 through the late 1760s. Following the checklist, the balance of the appendix is devoted to brief summaries of the evidence for each attribution.

The majority of the articles for 1756 come from Archibald Hamilton's records in his annotated file copy of the *Critical*. The authority and reliability of his records of authorship are discussed above, in chapter 3. To avoid repetition and save space, Hamilton's ascriptions are marked with an asterisk (★) and listed here without further elaboration. All the rest, including a few articles in 1756 that Hamilton left unannotated but which seem to be by Smollett, are attributed to Smollett on the basis of various kinds of evidence, ranging from Smollett's explicit acknowledgment of some to compelling circumstantial and internal evidence for others. Every effort has been made to be as rigorous and cautious as possible, undoubtedly with the result that many Smollett articles have been left out. These must await the discovery of new evidence before they can be added to the list.

PART I—SMOLLETT'S ARTICLES

Volume 1	(*January to July 1756*)
(pages)	
[i–ii]	★"Preface."
10–23	★James Grieve, trans., *Of Medicine*, by A. Cornelius Celsus.
41–53	★Thomas Birch, *The History of the Royal Society of London.*
56–65	★William Borlase, *Observations on. . . the Islands of Scilly.*
74–75	Samuel Pegge, *A Series of Dissertations on. . . Anglo-Saxon Remains.*
78–82	★Arthur Murphy, *The Apprentice, A Farce.*

83–85   *Samuel Foote, *The Englishman Return'd from Paris.*
88–90   *[John Shebbeare], *A Third Letter to the People of England.*
94–96   *"Performances in *Painting* and *Sculpture*" [works by Hamilton, Strange, and Rysbrack].
96   *"To the Public" [editorial note].
97–106   *Richard Rolt, *A New. . . History of South America.*
106–14   *Francis Home, *Experiments on Bleaching.*
144–45   *Charles Marsh, *The Winter's Tale. . . Alter'd from Shakespeare.*
146   *[Henry Dell], *The Spouter; or the Double Revenge.*
169–70   *Charles Lucas, *An Appeal to the Commons and Citizens of London.*
170–71   *A Fair Representation of His Majesty's Right to Nova Scotia.*
172–75   *Robert Taylor, *Oratio Anniversaria in Theatro Collegii Regalis Medicorum Londinensium.*
181–84   *"A Letter from Monsieur de Voltaire to the French Academy" [and] "A Second Letter from M. de Voltaire to the Same."
184–85   *"A Letter from an Englishman to the Authors of the Journal Encyclopédique."
192   *"Articles of Correspondence."
220–26   *[Fulke and Frances Greville], *Maxims, Characters and Reflections.*
226–40   *[Joseph Warton], *An Essay on the Writings and Genius of Pope.*
242–46   *Richard Manningham, *Aphorismata Medica.*
246–48   *Hydrops, Disputatio Medica.*
248–53   *Letters on Mr. Hume's History of Great Britain.*
258–59   *The Occasional Patriot.*
259–60   *The Important Question Concerning Invasions.*
262–63   *John Duncombe, *Poems.*
263   *The Manner of Securing. . . Buildings from Fires.*
263–65   *Deliberate Thoughts on. . . Our Late Treaties.*
265–66   *An Address to the Great.*
276–79   *Frances Brooke, *Virginia, a Tragedy.*
287–88   *"To the Public" [editorial note].
321–45   *Charles Lucas, *An Essay on Waters.*
387   *"Sculpture" [works by Joseph Wilton].
389–409 *Patrick Browne, *Civil and Natural History of Jamaica.*
409–19   *Essays and Observations, Physical and Literary.*
438–43   *[Thomas More Molyneux], *The Target, a Treatise upon Art Military.*
457–58   *A Plain Account of the Cause of Earthquakes.*
459–62   *M. Mooney, *A Dissertation on. . . the Venereal Disease.*
479–80   *"Painting" [William Hogarth's triptych altar painting of "The Ascension" for St. Mary Redcliffe in Bristol].
482–83   *Essays Pastoral and Elegaic.*

from 4: 130).

332–38   [John Shebbeare], *The Occasional Critic, or the Decrees of the Scotch Tribunal in the Critical Review Rejudged.*

376   [Untitled editorial notes.]

377–85   *The Monitor; or, the British Freeholder*, vol. 2.

385–95   Voltaire, *The General History and State of Europe*, Parts 5 and 6.

431–36   "Article VIII" [editorial notes subjoined to an exchange of letters between Drs. Monro and Hunter].

469–72   "To the *Old Gentlewoman* Who Directs the Monthly Review."

504–9   William Bromfield, *An Account of the English Nightshades and their Effects.*

509–16   William Battie, *A Treatise on Madness.*

523   [Footnote to "A Letter from Dr. Donald Monro, to the Authors of the Critical Review".]

546   [Charles Lucas], *Letters of Dr. Lucas and Dr. Oliver.*

Volume 5   (*January to June 1758*)

79   [John Shebbeare], *A Sixth Letter to the People of England.*

136–44   Abbè de Marigny, *The History of the Arabians.*

177–88   Abbè de Marigny, *The History of the Arabians* (cont. from 5: 144).

196–98   [John Gilbert Cooper], *The Call of Aristippus, Epistle IV.*

199–206   [John Cleland], *Tombo-Chiqui: or, the American Savage.*

224–28   [John Monro], *Remarks on Dr. Battie's Treatise on Madness.*

265–66   "Painting, & c." [Two prints by Samuel Scott].

346   Jacques de la Perrière, *The Mechanism of Electricity.*

380–86   [John Armstrong], *Sketches: or Essays on Various Subjects.*

438–39   Admiral Charles Knowles, *The Conduct of Admiral Knowles on the Late Expedition Set in a True Light.*

476–91   *Philosophical Transactions*, vol. 50, part 1.

Volume 6   (*July to December 1758*)

17–25   Theophilus Cibber, ed., *The Insolvent*, by Aaron Hill.

33–46   *Philosophical Transactions*, vol. 50 (cont. from 5: 491).

62–65   A. Sutherland, *The Nature and Qualities of Bristol Water.*

100–118   John Entick, *A New Naval History.*

226–39   Thomas Comber, *A Vindication of the Great Revolution in England . . . as Misrepresented by the Author of the Complete History of England.*

280–85   Charles, Lord Whitworth, *An Account of Russia [in] 1710.*

312–17   Alexander Monro, *Observations, Anatomical and Physiological, Wherein Dr. Hunter's Claim to Some Discoveries Is Examined* [and] Mark Akenside, *Notes on . . . [Monro's] Observations.*

345–46   *A Bone for the Chroniclers to Pick.*

439–53   [William Kenrick], *Epistles Philosophical and Moral.*

475–82   James Grainger, *A Poetical Translation of the Elegies of*

63–64   Giampetro Cavazzoni Zanotti, *Avertimenti . . . par lo Incamminamento di un Giovane alla Pittura.*

72–73   *Eulogium Medicum, sive Oratio Anniversaria Harvaeana.*

73–75   [John Armstrong], *A Day: An Epistle to John Wilkes.*

81–91   *The Modern Part of an Universal History,* vol. 26.

99–103   George Harris, trans., *The Four Books of Justinian's Institutes.*

103–8   Gilbert Burnet, *Thoughts on Education.*

116–22   [John Curry], *Historical Memoirs of the Irish Rebellion in the Year 1641.*

131–41   George Colman, *The Jealous Wife.*

217–33   Archibald Bower, *The History of the Popes,* vol. 5.

314–17   Laurence Sterne, *Tristram Shandy,* vols. 3, 4.

331–32   [Untitled article on Thomas Frye mezzotints.]

332   [Untitled article on engraving by Ravenet, landscape paintings by Richard Wilson and "Smith" (unidentified), and engravings by William Woollett.]

409–11   Charles Churchill, *The Apology, Addressed to the Critical Reviewers.*

449–59   *Philosophical Transactions,* vol. 51, part 2.

Volume 12   (*July to December 1761*)

81–103   *The Modern Part of an Universal History,* vol. 31.

131–38   Voltaire, *Candid: or, All for the Best.*

161–78   *The Modern Part of an Universal History,* vol. 32.

182–86   John Perceval, Earl of Egmont, *The Question of the Precedency of the Peers of Ireland in England.*

237–50   Anton Friedrich Büsching, *A New System of Geography.*

278–83   John Hill, *The Vegetable System,* vol. 2, part 1.

312–13   "Engraving" [William Woollett engraving of Richard Wilson's *Niobe* and two Thomas Frye mezzotints].

321–35   *The Modern Part of an Universal History,* vol. 33.

390–92   l'Abbé Coyer, *Histoire de Jean Sobieski, Roi de Pologne.*

405–18   James Macpherson, *Fingal: An Antient Epic Poem.*

477–78   *A Seventh Letter to the People of England, Occasioned by a Late Resignation.*

Volume 13   (*January to June 1762*)

45–53   James Macpherson, *Fingal* (cont. from 12:418).

107–20   *The Modern Part of an Universal History,* vol. 34.

121–29   *Medical Observations and Inquiries, by a Society of Physicians in London,* vol. 2.

135–38   William Whitehead, *The School for Lovers.*

157–58   David Garrick, *Florizel and Perdita; or, The Winter's Tale.*

161–63   *The Defects of an University Education . . . and [the] Necessity of Electing at Glasgow, an Academy.*

222–26   *Medical Observations and Inquiries* (cont. from 13:129).

272   *The Rosciad of C[o]v[e]nt G[a]rd[e]n.*

346–47   Samuel Ingham, trans., *The Diseases of the Bones*, by
         DuVerney.
381–92   *The Modern Part of an Universal History*, vol. 35.
392–97   [John Shebbeare], *The History of the. . . Sumatrans*, vol. 1.
418–27   William Hunter, *Medical Commentaries*, part 1.
495–99   [James Boswell, et al.], *A Collection of Original Poems*, by
         Scotch Gentleman.
504–12   Daniel Peter Layard, *An Essay on the Bite of a Mad Dog*.

Volume 14   (*July to December 1762*)
75–76   Charles White, *A Particular Narrative [about] . . . a Paper*
         Published in the 51st Volume of the Philosophical Transactions.
107–18   Solomon de Monchy, *An Essay on the. . . Diseases in Voyages to*
         the West Indies.
122–30   [Patrick Murdoch, ed.] *The Works of James Thomson*.
241–49   *The Modern Part of an Universal History*, vol. 36.
321–36   *Philosophical Transactions*, vol. 52, part 1.
401–10   *The Modern Part of an Universal History*, vol. 37.

Volume 15   (*January to June 1763*)
13–21   *The Peregrinations of Jeremiah Grant, Esq; the West-Indian*.
120–26   *A Critical Dissertation on the Poems of Ossian, the Son of Fingal*.
200–209 James Macpherson, *Temora, an Antient Epic Poem*.
209–10   [John Shebbeare], *The History of the. . . Sumatrans*, vol. 2.
224   "Engraving" [Engravings by Cooper, of Vandyke's "Charles I
         and family," and by Ryland, of Allan Ramsay's portrait of
         Lord Bute].
399–400 H. Mason, *Lectures upon the Heart, Lungs, [etc.]*.
401–3   *Considerations on the Present Dangerous Crisis*.

[From mid-June 1763 to late June 1765 Smollett was abroad and contributed
nothing to the *Critical Review*. From July 1765 until late fall of 1768 he was
back in England, but made only occasional contributions to the *Critical*
"merely" (he said) "for amusement," of which the following can be identified
as his:]

Volume 20   (*July to December 1765*)
45–49   *A Digest of the Laws concerning Libels*.
124–34   William Stevenson, *Original Poems on Several Subjects*.
149–52   Andrew Wilson, *Short Remarks upon. . . Disorders of the*
         Bowels.
152–53   John Sayer, trans. *The Temple of Gnidus [by] Montesquieu*.
184–88   John Memis, *The Midwife's Pocket Companion*.
257–65   *Philosophical Transactions. . . vol. 54, for 1764*.
281–88   *A General Treatise on Mineral Waters in England*.
310–11   *Observations on the Baume de Vie*.
348–58   *Philosophical Transactions. . . vol. 54, for 1764* (cont. from

20: 265).

465–66   "Dr. J. S———," *A Letter to J. K———, M.D.*.

Volume 21   (*January to June 1766*)
407–9   *The English Connoisseur: an Account of Painting, Sculpture, etc. [in] England.*

Volume 23   (*January to June 1767*)
214–16   George Colman, *The English Merchant.*

Volume 24   (*July to December 1767*)
226   *Miscellanies. The Lion, Cock, and Peacock; a Fable.*

PART II—THE EVIDENCE FOR ATTRIBUTION

The following is a summary of the evidence for each of the attributions listed above:

Volume 1   (*January to July 1756*)
[i–ii]   "Preface" [to Volume 1, published ca. 1 July 1756]. Smollett is known to have written other editorial addresses in 1756 (see "To the Public," 1: 287–88, and "Reply to a Letter," 2: 188–92). As editor-in-chief, Smollett naturally would have written most if not all of such articles. The tone, themes, and even phraseology echo those in his "Proposals" for the *Critical* (quoted above, chap. 2). The emphasis on charitable reviewing—"They have treated simple dulness as the object of mirth or compassion . . . and never, without reluctance, disapproved, even of a bad writer, who had the least title to indulgence"—parallels Smollett's statement in the April issue that they "have leaned towards the side of mercy" in reviewing poor writers (1: 287). The writer here claims the *Critical* has received "public favour," similar to Smollett's observation to Moore in August 1756 that the *Critical* "meets with a very favourable reception" (*Letters*, 46).

74–75   Samuel Pegge, *A Series of Dissertations on . . . Anglo-Saxon Remains.* The reviewer's sarcastic treatment of antiquarian discoveries—Pegge's work "chiefly tends to establish a fact of great importance to the curious collectors of our English Antiquities, to wit, *that our Saxon ancestors had amongst them some coined gold*"—conforms exactly with Smollett's sarcasms on antiquarians such as Ward (1: 536 and 2: 29–30) and with his satirical account of an antiquarian mistaking a worn farthing for a Roman coin in *Peregrine Pickle* (chap. 103, 662–65). Like Smollett, the reviewer closely criticizes neologisms and gallicisms; the latter, he asserts, "inervate" the English language, much as Smollett in a review known to be his criticized the introduction of gallicisms because it "relaxes the nerves and destroys the uniformity of our language" (1:221). Both the authoritative tone and satirical style point to Smollett.

96   "To the Public" [an editorial note]. See evidence for the preface to Volume 1 above (1:[i–ii]). Moreover, this note solicits contributions to the *Critical*; presumably only Smollett would be in a position to make such an editorial appeal.

192   "Articles of Correspondence." See the discussion of editorial notes above (1:[i–ii]). Moreover, one note announces the rejection of "Mr. R——'s" submission, an editorial decision Smollett would have made. Another is a response to criticism of a review that Smollett wrote: that of Shebbeare's *Third Letter* (1:88–90). It should be noted that Smollett almost certainly wrote all the replies to correspondents himself in 1756: see 1:288, 484, 572, and 2:96, 188–92, 288, 384, 482. Smollett's role as editor is further clarified by the fact that, according to Hamilton's own annotations, Hamilton himself contributed nothing to the *Critical*, even the minor notes that in other periodicals were usually written by the printer or publisher.

Volume 2   *(August to December 1756)*
[i–ii]   "Preface" [to Volume 2]. See discussion of editorial writings above (1:[i–ii]).

48–51   Theophilus Cibber, *Two Dissertations on the Theatres*. Smollett reviewed most of the works on drama in 1756, Cibber was a friend of his, and the work attacks Garrick, with whom Smollett was concerned to curry favor in 1756 as he hoped to stage his *Reprisal* at Drury Lane. The reviewer softens and deflects Cibber's criticism of Garrick, but otherwise endorses his views; this is consistent with Smollett's position at the time. In a review known to be by Smollett in 1761, he digressed on the memory of Cibber and discussed Cibber's appeals to the public, of which these *Dissertations* are typical (11:223–24).

277–78 *Reasons Humbly Offered to Prove that the Letter Printed at the End of the French Memorial. . . Is a French Forgery*. Smollett reviewed most political works himself in 1756: of approximately twenty-nine such reviews for which Hamilton's annotations provide authors, twenty-three are Smollett's, six Derrick's, and none is by Murdoch, Armstrong, or Francklin. The reviewer here, exactly like Smollett, criticizes the author's Scotticisms: "We should judge it to be the production of some North-briton from several peculiar modes of expression, such as *these* for *those*, *stand disculpate*, . . . *succumb* and *Phenomenon*, and many other Scotch idiotisms." *Succumb* is one of the Scotticisms Smollett derided in a review known to be his, that of Hume's *History* (2:394).

281   *Impartial Reflections on the Case of Mr. Byng.* Smollett reviewed all the other pamphlets on the Byng case in 1756,
according to Hamilton's record, nine in all. The reviewer
expresses views on the case very similar to those Smollett
expressed in other reviews: urging moderation, impartiality,
and an end to pamphleteering.

473–74   *A Modest Remonstrance to the Public. . . about Admiral Byng.*
See discussion of Byng pamphlets above (2:281). The reviewer's facetious treatment of the pamphlet writer is characteristic
of Smollett's reviews.

474   [David Garrick], *Lilliput, A Dramatic Entertainment.* Smollett reviewed several other farces and comedies in 1756, including all those published by the most eminent comedians such
as Murphy and Foote. The reviewer approves of the play's
classical style of burlesque and its didacticism, attitudes that
Smollett held about comedy. The special praise for Garrick
—"the prologue by Mr. *Garrick* abounds with the fire and
pleasantry so peculiar to that author"—suggests that Smollett
was returning the favor that Garrick had just done him by
accepting his play for production (*Letters*, 50–51).

474–75   [John Shebbeare], *An Answer to a Pamphlet Called, The Conduct of the Ministry Impartially Examined.* Smollett reviewed
most political pamphlets himself; see above (2:277–78). The
reviewer detects Shebbeare's authorship based on a familiarity with his other writings, all of which Smollett had reviewed
earlier in 1756; see *Critical* 1:88–90, and 2:35–44, 279–80. See
also Foster's similar conclusion in "Smollett's Pamphleteering
Foe Shebbeare," 1077, n. 90.

480–81   *The Fatal Consequence of the Want of System in. . .Public
Affairs.* See above (2:277–78). The reviewer makes a characteristically Smollettian mockery of the author's proposal for
the creation of a system of public boards, dismissing them as
unnecessary and adding: "But if ever it should be found need-
ful to establish a *board of perplexity*, he may command all our
interest towards his being elected president."

Volume 3   *(January to June 1757)*
1–20   Edward Lisle, *Observations in Husbandry.* The reviewer refers repeatedly and knowledgeably to the contents of the *Journal œconomique*, from which Smollett had translated thirty-
nine essays for publication in 1754. He urges "men of learning
and fortune" to contribute to this field, as Smollett had in a
review in 1756 (1:227). He refers to the "late progress of experimental philosophy," especially chemistry, applied to "the
mechanic arts" just as Smollett had commended the same development in reviewing Home's *Bleaching* (1:106). He singles
out Dr. Stephen Hales for special praise: "No person. . .

deserves such applause [as Hales for the] practical observations and improvements which he hath recommended to his
countrymen"; Smollett had praised Hales in the same terms
elsewhere (2:132). Philip Miller, a friend of Smollett's and
sometime reviewer for the *Critical* (see *Letters*, 74), is called
"that judicious and learned botanist"; Smollett referred to
him in another review as "that accurate botanist" (2:26). The
reviewer, like Smollett, is evidently an experienced physician,
for he notices with regret the inclusion of medically valuable
plants in the author's "catalogue of weeds." In a characteristic
phrase (and perhaps drawing on personal experience like Smollett's), the reviewer urges doctors to take up other fields rather
than "starve in a tie-wig at London." Finally, Smollett shows
familiarity with Lisle's *Husbandry* in *Humphry Clinker* (11 Oct,
327).

24–30   John Woodward, *Select Cases, and Consultation in Physic.*
Like Smollett's other writings, this review contains extensive
scatological humor—with some cause, apparently, as throughout these cases "the constant effect of the Doctor's prescription
was a discharge of wind and stools, slimy, frothy, green and
stenchy." A favorite Smollett joke about flatulence is included:
"We could venture to lay a wager that Dr. *Woodward* was particularly fond of a loin of veal with butter sauce"; Smollett uses
the same joke verbatim in a letter to Wilkes in 1759, describing
a task as being "almost as disagreeable as that of dining with
our friend Armstrong, when the wind blows from the East, on
a Loin of Veal roasted with Butter sauce" (*Letters*, 80).

62–74   *A New History of the East Indies.* History was one of Smollett's special areas of interest. The reviewer criticizes the author's Scotticisms, among them the word *adduce* (69); Smollett
had cited *adduce* among other Scotticisms in a review known to
be his in 1756 (1:228). The reviewer closely scrutinizes and
corrects the translation from the French, a common feature of
Smollett's reviews. The reviewer notices that the author has
borrowed (without crediting the source) his account of Portuguese discoveries from "Ossorius" (Osorio), translated by
"Mr. Gibbs"; Smollett was very familiar with Osorio, as Martz
has demonstrated (*Later Career*, 31), having used Gibbs's edition as the source for his own articles on Vasco da Gama and
Cabral in the *Compendium* (1756).

92–93   Claude du Choisel, *A Method of Treating Persons Bit by Mad
Animals.* Smollett reviewed most medical works in 1756. The
reviewer points out that Choisel's treatment is the same
"recommended in a pamphlet expressly written on the subject,
by the late Mr. *John Douglas*, surgeon in *Westminster*, about
eighteen years ago"; "eighteen years ago" (i.e., 1739) is exactly
the year Smollett had come to London as a young doctor,

which might explain the precision of the reviewer's recollection. Smollett knew Douglas, moved in his circles, and perhaps even studied under him; he was certainly familiar with his works (see Knapp, *Tobias Smollett*, 21, 41, and 47–48).

96   [Untitled editorial notes.] In 1756, Smollett had written most editorial material, including responses to critics and correspondents (see above, 1:[i–ii] and 192). One of these notes is written to defend a review Smollett had written himself (2:315–26). The second concerns a review written by Francklin (2:331–40); this editorial note apologizes to the correspondent for aspects of that review, which Francklin himself almost certainly would not have done, and which only Smollett had the authority to do concerning reviews written by others.

107–13   Francis Home, *The Principles of Agriculture and Vegetation*. Smollett knew Home and took a close interest in his writings (see *Letters*, 38). The reviewer refers to an earlier review of Home's *Bleaching*, which Smollett had written (1:106–14). The reviewer also indicates that he had reviewed Lisle's *Husbandry*; that review can be demonstrated on its own to be by Smollett (see above, 3:1–20). The reviewer notes with approval the support given Home by a "society" in Edinburgh and endorses Home's proposal that a committee be established to perform experiments in agriculture and publish their findings in periodical newspapers; both are ideas that Smollett repeatedly supported in various contexts throughout his reviews.

124–36   Thomas Birch, *The History of the Royal Society*, vols. 3 and 4. Smollett had reviewed the first two volumes of Birch's *History* in 1756 (1:41–53). Here the reviewer refers to that review and shows familiarity with it, noting that "in the two volumes before us, [Birch] has not been so studious to entertain his readers . . . as in the two former volumes." The same points are made here that Smollett had made in reviewing the first two volumes: that the injudicious and undiscriminating editing of materials published, "instead of procuring to the learned and illustrious society that honour which it deserves, will expose it to contempt and ridicule." The reviewer applauds in particular an account of a new technique in painting on marble and states that "it would be a means of perpetuating the performances of our excellent artists in painting"; Smollett had already devoted considerable attention to the works of Britain's "excellent artists" in 1756 (1:94–96, 387, 479–80) and would continue to do so (see chaps. 6 and 7 above).

153–57   *Four Pieces, Containing a Full Reply of . . . the Empress-Queen of Hungary and Bohemia, to . . . the King of Prussia.* Smollett had reviewed the work to which this publication is a reply (2:315–26). The reviewer here shows a detailed knowledge of that first pamphlet and uses points from it to refute arguments in the work under review. The reviewer's tone of impartiality and fatigued resignation to political pamphlet wars suggests Smollett's attitude in early 1757, after he had reviewed most of the political pamphlets in 1756 (see above, 2:277–78).

185   *Admiral Byng's Defence, as Presented by Him.* The reviewer is evidently the same who reviewed the Byng pamphlets in 1756, referring authoritatively to them and stating that all in this pamphlet was contained in those (see above, 2:281). Moreover, the reviewer adopts the same stance as Smollett had in defending Byng: "We cannot help thinking the admiral did his duty to the best of his understanding."

323–38   [William Fawcett, trans.], *Reveries or Memoirs upon the Art of War*, by Field-Marshal Count Saxe. Smollett reviewed two books on the military arts in 1756 and the structure and style of this review are similar to those (1:438–43 and 2:244–51). Smollett later showed detailed familiarity with this book: one of the passages selected for approval in this review is also incorporated into Smollett's *Travels*, as Felsenstein has shown (*Travels*, 61 and n. 18). The reviewer seems to be a doctor, as he comments closely on the medical sections and even contributes a medical opinion of his own.

383–84   "Advertisement" [Editorial response to a newspaper attack]. See discussion of Smollett's editorial writing above (1:[i–ii], 96, and 192). A phrase in this review—"the day-labourers of Messieurs N[oble], who never paid to any author for his labour a sum equal to the wages of a journeyman taylor"—echoes one of Smollett's in *Peregrine Pickle*: "booksellers, who . . . oppress and enslave their authors . . . by limiting men of genius to the wages of a journeyman taylor" (*Peregrine Pickle*, chap. 102, 645). The authoritative and derisive tone resembles Smollett's, especially in the more colorful phrases of abuse: "chimney sweep," "spider in a neglected privy," and "wipe the posteriors of his scurrility."

385–98   [William Huggins, trans.], *Orlando Furioso*, by Ariosto. Smollett explicitly stated that he was reviewing the work in a letter to Huggins in April 1757: "I have begun to read the Translation of Ariosto as a Critick, and perceive I shall make a very favourable Report of it to the Public" (*Letters*, 55).

474–75   *Evident Proofs; or, An Answer to the Memoirs Raisonnè of the Court of Berlin.* The reviewer refers, apparently from memory, to having reviewed "some time ago" the King of Prussia's pamphlet justifying his invasion of Saxony: Smollett wrote that review (2:315–26). The reviewer shows a detailed knowledge of the contents of that pamphlet. Moreover, the reviewer criticizes the translator's "inaccuracies" and unfamiliarity with various idioms of both French and English; Smollett, an experienced translator, habitually criticized these matters in his reviews.

479   "Engraving" [Strange's *Belisarius*]. Smollett had reviewed Strange's drawing of Belisarius in 1756 (1:95); thus he would know, as this reviewer points out, that it had been some time in appearing as an engraving: "Mr. *Strange* has at length published his *Belisarius*." Smollett's high praise for the drawing— "the accurate elegance, and delicacy of the drawing, are almost inconceivable" (1:95)—accords with this reviewer's appraisal of the engraving: "by far the most elegant and best finished print that any artist of this nation ever produced." The reviewer's statement here that "we need not now envy other countries their Edelinck, Nenteuil, [etc.]" echoes Smollett's statements in his art reviews: "Our neighbours on the continent, will no longer reproach us with want of talent for the arts of Painting, Engraving, Sculpture" (1:387) and his praise of Strange, "with whom very few engravers in *Europe* can come in competition" (1:95). Smollett was to write in the *Continuation* 4 (1761), 131, in George II's reign "the art of engraving was brought to perfection by Strange."

479–80   [Untitled editorial notes.] The writer is responding to criticism of past reviews, something Smollett usually did (see above, 1:192 and 2:188–92). The writer displays a familiarity with Hunter's, Sharp's, and Douglas's medical experiments, lectures, and publications of "a good many years ago"—all of which were well known to Smollett, who had moved in those medical circles since 1739. Moreover, the writer reveals that in the work under discussion (Pott's *Treatise*) the author had failed to mention his private consultations with Hunter, a fact that could have been learned only from Hunter himself, with whom Smollett was close friends and whose interest Smollett was supporting (see below, 4:35–45 and 223–27). The second note deals mockingly with the Nobles' threat of a lawsuit, in language typical of Smollett's responses to such attacks.

536–47   *Medical Observations and Inquiries, by a Society of Physicians in London.* The reviewer treats favorably this book that contains medical cases by several of Smollett's friends, including George Macaulay, John Clephane, and William Hunter. The reviewer presents a case-by-case abstract, the same technique that Smollett used in his reviews of such works. The reviewer makes a scatological joke typical of Smollett, suggesting the possible utility of an "electrical apparatus" introduced into the furniture of the "c[loaca]l chamber." This review is continued in the July issue (4:35–45) where there is further evidence of Smollett's authorship.

550–52   *The Iliad*, by Homer [a new edition published by Glasgow University]. Smollett was a loyal friend to Glasgow University and maintained many ties with members of its faculty (see *Letters*, 30–31, 58–59, 72–73, and 105) and with his good friend "honest Robin [Robert] Urie," printer of this book, who was an eminent Glasgow printer closely attached to the university (Knapp, *Tobias Smollett*, 20, 162, 270). This would explain both the reviewer's sustained panegyric on the university and the extensive inside information he discloses about the forthcoming publications and editorial procedures of that press. The reviewer inserts special praise for the mathematician, Dr. Robert Simson, who may have been Smollett's instructor at Glasgow (see Knapp, 17) and whose son was a friend of Smollett's (*Letters*, 131); Smollett had lauded Simson's essays in mathematics in 1756 (2:13–14).

Volume 4   (*July to December 1757*)

35–45   *Medical Observations and Inquiries* (cont. from 3:547). See above (3:547). Here the reviewer uses a long footnote (4:42–44) to defend William Hunter from a recent attack in the *Monthly*; that Smollett wrote this is evident from Hunter's letter of 23 August 1757, in which he thanks Smollett for this defense as an "instance of warm friendship" and expresses fear that "future trouble" with this *Monthly* reviewer (James Grainger) lies ahead (letter quoted in Knapp, *Tobias Smollett*, 203).

83–85   Marchese Torquato Barbolani, *Orlando Furioso. . . in Versi Latini*. The reviewer contrives to mention approvingly Huggins's "accurate translation of this great poet" and refers the readers to the review of it that Smollett had written (see above, 3:385–9). The reviewer's survey of the state of literature in England, France, Italy, and Germany is typical of Smollett's style and opinions. The reviewer's ambivalence about "rules" versus "imagination" in literature—he finds Homer more regular but Ariosto more pleasing to the fancy—conforms with views Smollett expressed in his review of Warton's *Essay on Pope* (1:226–40).

94   *An Account of. . . the Loss of Minorca, by the Monitor*. Smollett had reviewed most of the Byng pamphlets himself (see above, 2:281). Here the reviewer refers to the drudgery of reviewing the long succession of pamphlets: "The task of a reviewer is like that of Sisyphus in hell. No sooner has he rolled up one heavy performance to the public view, than another tumbling down, requires an incessant repetition of his labour." As Smollett often did, the reviewer uses a medical simile to disparage Shebbeare's many works, most of them reviewed by Smollett (see 1:88–90; 2:35–44, 279–80, 474–75, and below, 4:332–38), in a ridiculing fashion much like Smollett's: "Why had not the author borrowed a few faggots of political fuel from his clamorous brother Dr. S[hebbeare], which, like half-dried hemlock, fumes, and frets, and spits, and stinks, and crackles in the flame?"

121–30   John Rutty, *A Methodical Synopsis of Mineral Waters*. Smollett took a special interest in works on mineral waters, having written his own pamphlet on the subject and reviewed in 1756 two others (1:321–45 and 2:97–109). In 1757, he had a particular interest in Rutty's works; he was to edit one of them for publication by Strahan in October (*Letters*, 62). The reviewer criticizes the lengthy title as a bookseller's ploy, exactly as Smollett had in a review in 1756 (2:432). The close criticism of inaccuracies in language and of the tedious prose style are also typical. The review is continued in October, where there is further evidence of Smollett's authorship (see below, 4:242–56).

130–49   *Philosophical Transactions*, vol. 49, part 2. Smollett reviewed earlier volumes of the *Transactions* in 1756 (1:528–36, and 2:13–35 and 126–35); here the reviewer uses the same method, summarizing and evaluating the contents article by article. Like Smollett, the reviewer laments the mixture of "crude and trivial essays" with valuable ones, and the resulting damage to the Royal Society's reputation. The reviewer approves highly of discoveries at Herculaneum, as Smollett had in 1756 (2:15–19); he is also similarly facetious about seemingly useless reports, such as one about sea coral on the ocean floor, where "it might have remained until the day of judgment, for all the service the knowledge of it will ever do the public." The reviewer uses a favorite Smollett expression: "What entertainment or instruction can be fished up from such troubled waters?" (4:137); in 1756, Smollett called Lucas "a turbulent partisan, who wanted to fish in troubled waters" (1:170) and he had used the phrase "fishing in troubled waters" in chapter 30 of *Ferdinand Count Fathom* (141). The review is continued in the September issue (see below, 4:205–22).

149–52   [James Grainger], *A Letter to the Author of the Critical Review*. Smollett's friend, William Hunter, reported that he had heard Smollett was preparing to review this pamphlet and encouraged him in a letter in August 1757: "I understand that you propose taking notice of a letter to the author of the Critical Review" (quoted in Knapp, *Tobias Smollett*, 203). Grainger's pamphlet was a response to remarks in the *Critical* (4:42–44, evidently by Smollett; see above); the reviewer here acknowledges himself the author of that review. The reviewer seems to know Grainger personally, as Smollett is known to have done (Knapp, *Tobias Smollett*, 182 and 207). As Smollett regularly did, the reviewer speaks authoritatively and disdainfully of Grainger's attack as typical of offended authors. He speaks with knowing confidence about Smollett's reaction: "The gentleman at whom you level your leaden arrows, is malice-proof."

160–62   Charles Lucas, *An Analysis of Dr. Rutty's Methodical Synop-*

sis. The reviewer defends Rutty from Lucas's attack, using inside information about the history of publication of Rutty's book; Smollett had a source for such information: William Strahan, who printed Rutty's publications and for whom Smollett was to edit another Rutty pamphlet in 1757 (see above, 4:121–30). The reviewer shows a detailed knowledge not only of Rutty's *Synopsis*, but of Lucas's *Essay on Waters*; Smollett had reviewed the latter in 1756 (1:321–45). The reviewer uses a phrase that closely parallels one used in another review attributable to Smollett. Here the reviewer writes, "He foams, and fumes, and frets, and bounces, and crackles" (4:161); in the earlier review it was written that Shebbeare's writings are like fuel that "fumes, and frets, and spits, and stinks, and crackles in the flame" (see above, 4:94). Again like Smollett, the reviewer quotes a passage from Lucas on the combustion of flatus, and then comments: "This is indeed a very high flavor'd joke, and very natural from a wit whose profession has obliged him occasionally to examine the posteriors of his fellow creatures."

205–22   *Philosophical Transactions*, vol. 49, part 2 (cont. from 4:149). See above, 4:149. The reviewer makes a mocking allusion to Dr. Parsons whom Smollett had discussed, with a similar mockery, in 1756 (2:25 and 188–92). The reviewer mocks an account of weather as a specious pretense of science, exactly as Smollett had in 1756 (1:530). He refers in detail to articles in the last volume of the *Transactions* by Hales and Miller; Smollett had reviewed that volume, extending special praise to Hales and Miller for their articles (2:25–26; see also above, 3:1–20). He also refers knowledgeably to "a former paper" on population by Brakenridge that Smollett had reviewed with approval in 1756 (2:126–29).

223–27   Alexander Monro, Jr., *De Venis Lymphaticis Valvulosis*. The reviewer methodically refutes Monro's claim to a discovery by demonstrating that William Hunter had discovered the same thing years earlier. His refutation is based on information "communicated to us by a person of probity," i.e., Hunter or a member of his circle. Smollett maintained ties with Hunter and Hunter's letters to him and to Cullen reveal that Smollett was conducting his defense in these articles in the *Critical* (Knapp, *Tobias Smollett*, 203–5). The reviewer also offers information about the Hunter brothers' experiments and lectures in the winter of 1755–56 and how the artist Reemsdyk sketched them in May 1756 "in presence of many pupils and occasional visitants"—all pointing to Smollett.

242–56   John Rutty, *A Methodical Synopsis of Mineral Waters* (cont. from 4:130). See above, 4:121–30. The reviewer criticizes Rutty for failing to describe the waters nearest London and their uses; this kind of information was the only redeeming feature Smollett had found in Lucas's *Essay* in 1756 (1:326). The reviewer takes most exception to Rutty's observations on the medicinal uses of water, precisely the chief area of Smollett's interest.

332–38   [John Shebbeare], *The Occasional Critic, or the Decrees of the Scotch Tribunal in the Critical Review Rejudged*. Shebbeare wrote this in response to the critical treatment he had received in articles written largely (or entirely) by Smollett (see 1:88–90; 2:35–44, 279–80, and 474–75). Smollett referred to this work in a letter to Moore of 2 January 1758, where he complains of the *Critical* being "abused as a *Scotch Tribunal*" (*Letters*, 65), obviously remembering it distinctly. The reviewer here shows familiarity with many of the opinions Smollett had expressed in his reviews of Shebbeare's works. He uses many of the same phrases: "like a quack in medicine" (used by Smollett in 2:35) and "a desperate incendiary" (2:44). The derisive and condescending tone—"poor man"—echoes Smollett's treatment of Shebbeare as "the poor creature" in 1756 (2:280). The reviewer speaks authoritatively about the *Critical*'s staff—stating that only one reviewer is a Scot—in a way that suggests only Smollett as editor-in-chief could have written it.

376   [Untitled editorial notes.] At least the first note is evidently by Smollett, as it deals with a letter about the "Occasional Critic's Lucubrations," referring to a review attributable to Smollett in its own right (see above, 4:332–38). The review contains a Smollettian quip about how Shebbeare's pamphlet might be used in preference "to the neck of a goose so warmly recommended by Pantagruel"; the reviewer of the *Occasional Critic* (shown to be Smollett above, 4:332–38) had suggested that Shebbeare might vend his pamphlet printed on "brown paper" at street corners, obviously for the same purpose (4:333).

377–85   *The Monitor; or, British Freeholder*, vol. 2. The reviewer appears to be the same who reviewed the first volume of the *Monitor*—Smollett himself (2:343–48)—referring to what "we have said of the former volume" apparently from memory, without citing specific references. He evinces familiarity with the prose style of the first volume, contending the second is better on that count. Also like Smollett in his earlier review, the reviewer agrees with the *Monitor*'s antiministerial position while urging restrained and reasoned rhetoric and criticizing the writer's "hackneyed" topics and flawed language.

385–95   Voltaire, *The General History and State of Europe*, parts 4 and 5. History and the works of Voltaire were both special interests of Smollett's. The reviewer faults Voltaire as a historian for his "vanity" and his "affectation of singularity in his way of thinking," calling this "the greatest fault that can be charged upon an historian." Smollett had used the same phrases in reviewing Hume's *History*, objecting to the practice of "reflecting" or "dogmatizing" (elsewhere he called it "philosophizing") that serves "to fix upon the historian the charge of vanity, singularity, and affectation" (2:386). The reviewer criticizes Voltaire's omission of battles, affirming that "to the generality of readers, the description of battles is the most entertaining part of history" (4:387). Smollett made exactly the same point about Hume: "Nothing is more agreeable to an *English* reader, than a battle well told" (2:394). The reviewer displays his familiarity with the historian Barre, whom Martz has shown to be one of the sources for Smollett's "History of Germany" in the *Universal History* and an authority Smollett cites in other reviews (see below, 7:337–56, and see Martz, "Smollett and the *Universal History*," 6 and n. 24). Similarly, the reviewer singles out Voltaire's section on England—Smollett's area of greatest expertise—for close commentary and correction of "anachronisms," "inaccuracies," and misinterpretations. The reviewer comments authoritatively on the impossibility of one man's doing such a work alone or completing it in only twenty volumes—points that Smollett, then editing the *Universal History* with teams of writers, would readily make.

431–36   "Article VIII" [editorial notes added to an exchange of letters between Monro and Hunter]. Smollett had been handling the Hunter medical controversies (see above, 3:479–80; 4:35–45, 149–52, and 223–27). The reviewer insists on his impartiality and his esteem for both Monro and Hunter; Smollett praised both in his *Continuation* (4:124), citing them as the two greatest researchers in anatomy. The reviewer notes that printing these letters is a breach of the *Critical*'s policy; presumably only Smollett could authorize such an exception. The reviewer tactfully takes Hunter's side against Monro, another sign of Smollett's hand.

469–72   "To the Old Gentlewoman Who Directs the Monthy Review." The writer is responding to the *Monthly*'s endorsement of Shebbeare's attack on Smollett and the *Critical* in his *Occasional Critic* (which Smollett reviewed; see above, 4:332–38), something that affected Smollett directly. The writer was evidently one of the founding *Critical* reviewers, as he refers repeatedly to the time "when the Critical Review was first published" and characterizes editorial policy over the whole period since its foundation. The writer professes familiarity with Griffiths's staff—"We know what sort of doctors and authors you employ"—as Smollett (perhaps alone of the *Critical* staff, as Goldsmith had not yet defected) could, both from his brief stint as a *Monthly* reviewer in 1751–52 and through his friends

Cleland and Cibber who were also on Griffiths's staff. The mockery of incorrectness in language and condescending tone are also typical of Smollett.

504–9   William Bromfield, *An Account of the English Nightshades and their Effects.* Like Smollett, the reviewer is evidently an experienced physician, at one point refuting a medical opinion not "from argument and analogy" but from "fact and experience." The reviewer again uses the image of a street vendor hawking "slips of brown paper," which appeared in an earlier review attributable to Smollett (see above, 4: 332–38 and 376). The reviewer expresses concern about cruelty to experimental animals and points out the connection between humanity in the laboratory and humanity with patients—points that Smollett had made vigorously in 1756 (1: 414–15 and 2: 32–33).

509–16   William Battie, *A Treatise on Madness.* It has been shown by Hunter and Macalpine that Smollett knew this work intimately and borrowed a passage from it for use in *Sir Launcelot Greaves* (chap. 23, 187); it is a passage that the reviewer singles out to disagree with, while in the novel Smollett puts it in the mouth of a quack doctor (see Hunter and Macalpine, "Smollett's Reading in Psychiatry," 409–11). The reviewer is evidently a doctor, citing Mead and Van Swieten to dispute Battie's clinical opinions. The reviewer, like Smollett, has a high opinion of the medical virtues of cold baths: "The cold bath will perform wonders." (See for examples *Humphry Clinker*, 126 and 183, and *Letters*, 119.)

523   [Footnote to "A Letter from Dr. Donald Monro, to the Authors of the Critical Review".] See above, 4: 431–36, for evidence of Smollett's supervision of the Hunter-Monro controversy.

546   [Charles Lucas], *Letters of Dr. Lucas and Dr. Oliver.* Smollett had reviewed two works by Lucas in 1756 (1: 169–70 and 321–45). Here the reviewer treats Lucas as Smollett had, criticizing especially his "knotty expressions" and unintelligible prose style (see 1: 169–70 and 321–24). The reviewer repeats a favorite Smollett expression: Lucas "will not find his account in thus continually fishing in troubled waters"; Smollett accused Lucas of wanting to "fish in troubled waters" in 1756 (1: 170) and used the same phrase in *Ferdinand Count Fathom* (141).

Volume 5   (*January to June 1758*)
79   [John Shebbeare], *A Sixth Letter to the People of England.* Smollett reviewed most or all of Shebbeare's writings (see above, 2: 474–75 and 4: 322–38 and 376). The reviewer refers to Dr. Battie as an expert on madness; it can be demonstrated independently that Smollett reviewed Battie's *Treatise on Madness*, to which this is a reference (see above, 4: 509–16). See

also Hunter and Macalpine, "Smollett's Reading in Psychiatry," 409–11.

136–44   Abbé de Marigny, *The History of the Arabians*. The reviewer refers knowledgeably to the contents and authorship of a volume of the *Universal History* that was not to appear for almost a year; Smollett, as an editor in that project, had such inside information (*Letters*, 78–79 and 87–92). In a later review that can be attributed to Smollett in its own right, he indicates that he had also reviewed this work (see below, 7:2). The review is continued in the next issue by the same reviewer, where there is further evidence of Smollett's authorship (see below, 5:177–88).

177–88   Abbé de Marigny, *The History of the Arabians* (cont. from 5:144). The reviewer quotes a passage from Barre's *History of Germany*; for Smollett's familiarity with Barre's works, see above 4:385–95. Typical of Smollett, the reviewer detects the omission of a relevant episode in English history, Smollett's special province (5:187–88).

196–98   [John Gilbert Cooper], *The Call of Aristippus, Epistle IV*. The reviewer refers familiarly to the recent editorial article "To the Old Gentlewoman Who Directs the Monthly Review," which Smollett had apparently written (see above, 4:469–72). The reviewer's high praise for Akenside conforms with Smollett's opinion of him, expressed in the *Continuation* (4:126); Smollett refers playfully to Cooper's "wrong-headed" poetry in a letter in 1759 (*Letters*, 79). The reviewer's suggestion that one of Cooper's images would be a useful idea for "any modern sculptor, who had skill enough to execute this design," accords with Smollett's continuing attention to contemporary British artists, some of whose works he reviewed in 1756 (1:94–96, 387, and 479–80).

199–206   [John Cleland], *Tombo-Chiqui: or, the American Savage*. This favorable and substantial review of a mediocre play (it was never staged) suggests that here Smollett was doing a favor for his old friend Cleland of the same kind they had done when reviewing each other's books for the *Monthly* a few years earlier (Knapp, *Tobias Smollett*, 120–21; 134; 245, n. 109; 296; and Epstein, *John Cleland*, 112 and 116–20). Smollett seems to have reviewed other works connected with Cleland (see below, 7:184 and 10:241–42); significantly, during the years that Smollett directed the *Critical*, Cleland's works were treated favorably (8:325; 9:417–19; 10:241–42 and 455–61), but thereafter they were not (14:319; 20:301–5; 25:284–94). Like Smollett in his drama reviews of 1756, the reviewer is pleased to see "the rules of the drama well preserved." He urges that the play be staged—it would succeed "under the conduct of a Garrick"—and gently suggests suitable revisions in the text, both of which point to Smollett's discreetly mediating between his friends.

244–48   John Monro, *Remarks on Dr. Battie's Treatise on Madness.* Smollett seems to have reviewed Battie's *Treatise* (see above, 4: 509–16); here the reviewer shows detailed knowledge of that work in analyzing Monro's critique. The reviewer's mixed opinions of Battie conform with those of the earlier review. The reviewer makes an editorial aside on the number of recent "medical quarrels," an observation that Smollett, having handled the Hunter controversies and others (see above: 4: 35–45, 149–52, 223–27, 431–36, and 523), would be likely to make.

265–66   "Painting & c." [Two prints by Samuel Scott]. Smollett had taken charge of the art reviews from the beginning (see his art reviews in 1756: 1: 94–96, 387, and 479–80) and may well have written or edited all the art reviews in the *Critical* up until June 1763 (see discussion of Smollett art criticism and support for the arts above, chaps. 6 and 7). Here the reviewer offers high praise for Scott's prints of London Bridge and Westminster Bridge, with Smollett-like enthusiasm and national pride: he refers to Scott as "the only ship-painter of any note or eminence now living" and "no way inferior to the celebrated . . . Vanderveld and Monamy." Note the verbal parallel with Bramble on the young painter in *Humphry Clinker*: "the best landscape-painter now living" (19 May, 76). Smollett ranked Scott among the best painters in the reign of George II in his *Continuation* 4 (1761), especially "for sea-pieces." Like Smollett, the reviewer lightens the article with a joke, expressing a hope that the British admirals will give Scott a chance to exercise his talents to depict "what we have almost forgot, a *victory at sea.*"

346   Monsieur [?] Perrière, *The Mechanism of Electricity.* The reviewer shows familiarity with the poor prose style of Lucas's works, calling Perrière "the Dr. Lu[ca]s of Paris" for his "hard words" and "new modes of expression." Smollett had reviewed Lucas's works in earlier volumes and commented in detail on the same features (1: 169–70 and 321–45; see above 4: 160–62 and 546).

380–86   [John Armstrong], *Sketches: or Essays on Various Subjects.* This highly favorable review is obviously written by a friend of Armstrong's, who quibbles facetiously with Armstrong's preference for mutton over venison and flounder over turbot, calling this "a downright solecism in eating, on which we should be glad to hold a practical conference with Mr. Launcelot Temple" (i.e., Armstrong). Smollett and Armstrong were close friends and presumably dined together often (*Letters*, 80). The reviewer uses a favorite metaphor of Smollett's to describe the difficulty of certain words that "may indeed do some injury to decayed teeth in the pronunciation"; Smollett, in his review of Warton, had described a "sentence which no man can pronounce with safety to his teeth" (1:233). Other signs of Smollett's authorship include the close discussion of neologisms and versification and the warm, personal tone of the closing compliments to Armstrong.

483–89   Admiral Charles Knowles, *The Conduct of Admiral Knowles on the Late Expedition Set in a True Light.* Smollett acknowledged that he wrote this review during his trial for libel (Knapp, *Tobias Smollett,* 213–14).

476–91   *Philosophical Transactions,* vol. 50, part 1. The style and tone of the review exactly resemble those of Smollett's reviews of earlier volumes of the *Transactions* (1:528–36; 2:13–35 and 126–35; 4:130–49 and 205–22). The reviewer refers to those past volumes familiarly, finding this one less defective by contrast. The reviewer interjects a comment about diseases among the "negroes in Jamaica"; Smollett had visited Jamaica in the Navy, married a Jamaican lady, and continued, through her property, to own slaves there (*Letters,* 85–87). The approval of reports on Herculaneum (484–85), the mockery of reports on weather (485, 487) and antiquarianism (488–89), and the minute correction of grammatical errors, "for the honour of the Society" (484), all conform to Smollett's reviewing traits. The review is continued below (6:33–46) where other signs of his authorship appear.

Volume 6   (*July to December 1758*)
17–25   Theophilus Cibber, ed., *The Insolvent,* by Aaron Hill. Cibber was a friend of Smollett's: significantly, the reviewer distinguishes between Hill's dramatic writing, which he finds affected, stiff, and uncouth, and Cibber's talents, which he finds (in contrast to the "rawness" of Cibber's fellow actors) worthy of applause. A special editorial plea is made on behalf of Cibber and, as in the review of an earlier play by a Smollett friend (see above, 5:199–206), the play is recommended as stageworthy, while the reviewer gently suggests appropriate revisions of the text. Smollett was to discuss Cibber again in a review in 1761 (11:223–24).

33–46   *Philosophical Transactions,* vol. 50 (cont. from 5:491). See above, 5:491, for evidence of Smollett's authorship. Here the reviewer refers knowledgeably to works by Hunter and Monro that Smollett had almost certainly reviewed (see above, 4:223–27), using details from them to demonstrate the uselessness of one article (39). The reviewer also repeats the assertion that Hunter had been lecturing on certain matters years before Monro or anyone else, information of a kind Smollett got from his friend Hunter. A mild joke at the expense of Dr. Parsons (43) and support for Brakenridge's researches into measuring population (44–46) echo opinions in Smollett's earlier reviews (2:25, 126–29, and 188–92).

62–65   A. Sutherland, *The Nature and Qualities of Bristol Water*. The reviewer complains of the large number of recent works on mineral waters, implying that he has had to review them himself; Smollett can be shown to have reviewed several between 1756 and 1758 (1:321–45 and 2:97–109; see above, 4:121–30, 160–62, and 546). The reviewer's detection of Sutherland's omission of Rutty from his authorities and his mockery of Lucas also point to Smollett's authorship.

100–118   John Entick, *A New Naval History*. The reviewer authoritatively criticizes errors of fact, poverty of style, and neglect of sources; he also refers knowledgeably to several works that render the present one unnecessary and detects various borrowings by Entick from earlier writers. All this is consistent with Smollett's expertise in English history and his reviewing methods. Moreover, the reviewer uses a phrase that distinctively echoes Smollett: "Other modern historians have piqued themselves upon retrenching the superfluities of their predecessors"; in the "Plan" of Smollett's *History*, he wrote that "his aim is to retrench the superfluities of his predecessors" (*History* 1:[iii]; quoted also in Knapp, *Tobias Smollett*, 191).

226–39   Thomas Comber, *A Vindication of the Great Revolution in England . . . as Misrepresented by the Author of the Complete History of England*. Much of the reviewer's information could only be provided by Smollett: that Dr. John Hill had alternately praised and abused Smollett "for these ten years [seven years before the *Critical* began]" (277); that Smollett "has not deigned" to write a pamphlet in reply to Comber (227); that Smollett had considered but decided against taking legal action (231); that in compiling his *History*, Smollett had deliberately left out a piece of scandal reported by Burnet "because it was unsustained by proper historical evidence" (235); that Smollett was personally unacquainted with Comber (238). Other information was unlikely to be remembered or collected by any one person other than Smollett: the catalog of Smollett's enemies—Shebbeare, Hill, Griffiths and his staff; the occasions and contents of their printed attacks; intricate details of the facts and arguments contained in Smollett's *History*; the fact that the proprietors of Rapin's *History* had been printing newspaper attacks on Smollett's *History*; the fact that sales of Smollett's *History* in serial numbers had passed ten thousand per week. The reviewer's extensive familiarity with Hume's *History* (Smollett reviewed it in 1756, 2:385–404) and the facts of English history itself, together with his many confident descriptions of Smollett's opinions, motives and intentions, further demonstrate Smollett's authorship.

280–85   Charles, Lord Whitworth, *An Account of Russia [in] 1710.* The reviewer informs the reader about some editorial decisions that presumably would have been made by Smollett: that *The Lives of Royal and Noble Authors* (sic) had not escaped notice on its first publication, but that it was decided not to review it out of respect for "the modesty of the ingenious writer"; now that the author is known, the reviewer announces an intention to review it as soon as the second edition appears. The reviewer evinces familiarity with the works of other authorities on Russian history; as Martz has shown, Smollett was familiar with such sources, including Voltaire and Büsching (Martz, "Smollett and the *Universal History*," 14; see also below, 13: 381–92).

312–17   Alexander Monro, *Observations, Anatomical and Physiological, Wherein Dr. Hunter's Claim to Some Discoveries Is Examined* [and] Mark Akenside, *Notes on. . . [Monro's] Observations.* Smollett had been handling the Hunter-Monro quarrels (see above: 3: 479–80; 4: 35–45, 149–52, 223–27, 431–36, and 523; 6: 33–46). The reviewer recounts the history of their exchanges, showing such detailed familiarity with their pamphlets as Smollett would have had from reviewing them. The reviewer's defense of Hunter and his other opinions repeat exactly Smollett's comments in earlier reviews.

345–46   *A Bone for the Chroniclers to Pick.* The reviewer sympathizes with this rejected playwright: "We cannot help sympathizing with our brother in his affliction, as we ourselves have not so long exercised the same profession, without having felt the pangs of theatrical miscarriage." Smollett's bitter disappointment over the *Regicide* and his subsequent reconciliation with Garrick are well known, but the reviewer also defends Garrick sympathetically—"a manager has humours like other men"—and advises the writer to abandon his satirical attacks; all this is consistent with Smollett's experience and current attitudes.

439–53   [William Kenrick], *Epistles Philosophical and Moral.* A manuscript annotation in the University College London copy of the *Critical* assigns this review to Smollett. Although the annotator is unidentified and this is the only review to which he assigns an author, his reliability is suggested by the fact that elsewhere in the volumes he ascribes authors to anonymous books under review with unfailing accuracy. In a review in the February 1759 issue (7: 160–67) that also seems to be by Smollett, he acknowledges himself author of this review. The reviewer here criticizes the poet's "little ungrammatical idioms" in detail, pinpointing examples of grammatical errors and "vulgarisms" in the verse; similarly, Smollett had criticized a poem in 1756 condemning instances where grammar was "sacrificed to *poetry*" (2:470). Other signs of Smollett's authorship include his comments on Voltaire (440) and his insistence that society must be based on hierarchical authority (447–48).

475–82   James Grainger, *A Poetical Translation of the Elegies of Tibullus*. In defending this review from Grainger's follow-up attack in 1759, the reviewer of Grainger's *Letter to Tobias Smollett, M.D.* repeatedly acknowledges that Smollett wrote this review (see especially 7: 142–44, 146, 148, 151, and 155–56). Internal signs of Smollett's authorship include: a quotation from *Gil Blas* (which he had translated in 1748), detailed objections to sacrificing grammar to meter in the verse (see above, 6:439–53), the detection of gallicisms and Scotticisms, and the rejection of certain neologisms that "we are afraid the public will reject as not sterling" (Smollett used the same metaphor to denounce neologisms in 1756, 1:75). A favorite Smollett image about pronunciation is repeated here: "Reader, beware of your teeth . . . in pronouncing this that follows"; in reviewing Warton, Smollett noticed "a sentence which no man can pronounce with safety to his teeth" (1:233).

495–500   *The Gardener's New Kalendar*. The reviewer editorializes on the pernicious practices of booksellers who use hack writers to compile faulty, plagiarized works on any topic; this is typical of Smollett (see 1:97–98). The reviewer detects and denounces several plagiarisms from Philip Miller's book on gardening; Miller was Smollett's friend and sometime contributor to the *Critical*; Smollett probably consulted with Miller in preparing this review, as he is known to have been consulting with him about various other books and reviews at just this time (*Letters*, 74).

501–6   Claude Adrien Helvétius, *De L'Esprit*. The reviewer's prefatory discourse on the state of the arts and sciences in the various countries of Europe is typical of Smollett's style and approach not only in his reviews but in his *Travels* (106 and 290) and his *Continuation* (4:120–32). Moreover, the reviewer disputes the thesis of Helvétius and others that the arts and sciences prosper most under conditions of liberty, arguing— exactly as Smollett had in his review of Warton (1:233)—that history affords many examples like France where they thrive under tyrannical regimes. A habitual Smollett criticism is voiced: Helvétius displays "an affectation of singularity," as did Hume and Voltaire (see 2:386 and above, 4:385–95). The announcement that further notice of this work will be taken in a "future number" suggests an editorial decision that Smollett would make.

506–8   William Huggins, *Part of Orlando Furioso*. Smollett had reviewed Huggins's *Orlando Furioso* in 1757 (see above, 3:385–98) in the same glowing terms of approval. The explanation of

Huggins's motivations in publishing this addendum suggests a personal connection between reviewer and author; as Smollett's letters show, he was a friend and admirer of Huggins and corresponded with him regularly (*Letters*, 50, 54–55, 59–60, 67–68, 70–71, etc.). That Smollett was aware of this work and was discussing it with Huggins before it was published is revealed in a letter of 2 July 1758 (*Letters*, 70).

516–17   William Baylies, *An Historical Account of the Rise, Progress, and Management of the . . . Hospital of Bath*. Smollett dealt with medical topics and with controversies (e.g., the Hunter-Monro conflict) and this book concerns both. Knapp has attributed it to Smollett on persuasive grounds (*Tobias Smollett*, 149) and the reviewer's opinions here, especially on the dismissal of Dr. Archibald Cleland in 1743, are exactly like Smollett's in his *Essay on the External Use of Water* (1752; repr. 1935, ed. Jones, 72). The reviewer's dislike for those who inflame public opinion against competent professionals is very similar to Smollett's view, expressed in an angry letter of 1753 (*Letters*, 21–26).

Volume 7   (*January to June 1759*)
1–14   *The Modern Part of an Universal History*, vols. 1, 2, 3. In his article, "Tobias Smollett and the *Universal History*", Martz has assembled evidence that persuasively demonstrates Smollett's authorship of this review and eleven others dealing with volumes of the *Universal History*: 8:189–99; 9:161–77; 10:81–90, 161–78; 11:5–18, 81–91; 12:81–103, 161–78, 321–35; 13:107–20, 381–92. Based on connections among reviews and on material in Smollett's works and letters, Martz's demonstrations are scholarly and reliable; in the interest of brevity, they will not be repeated here. Only corroborative evidence above and beyond Martz's findings will be cited in this and the articles on the *Universal History* that follow. It should be noted that in two of the reviews shown to be Smollett's, the reviewer implies his regular involvement in reviewing the *Universal History*. In one (8:189), he announces a plan "to take notice" of each of the future volumes as it is "ushered to the public." In the other (10:90), he explains that the readers must not expect every month such a copious article as he has just given because that "would render the fatigue of the month insupportable." In this first review, there is an echo of Smollett's stated historical method. In reviewing Rolt, Smollett had said that a historian had "to form and digest a proper plan of history; compile materials, . . . compose and polish the style, and complete the execution of the work" (1:97–98); here it is stated that the author has taken too little care in "digesting the materials, composing the history, polishing the style, or rendering

the work entertaining" (14). Other signs of Smollett's authorship include his disapproval of trivial antiquarian findings (see above, 1:74–75) and his opinion that all French historians except Montesquieu and Voltaire are biased against foreign writers; earlier Smollett had described Voltaire as "less biassed by national prejudices, than any other French historian" in 1757 (4:385).

22–26   *The Monitor,* vol. 3. Smollett had reviewed the first volume of the *Monitor in 1756* (2:343–48) and the second in 1757 (see above, 4:377–85). The reviewer's opinion that with Pitt "at the helm of government. . . faction and opposition are, in a manner, annihilated" is exactly the same as Smollett expressed in a private letter a few months later: "Mr. Pitt is so popular that I may venture to say that all party is extinguished in Great-Britain" (*Letters,* 87). Some characteristically facetious metaphors, including Smollett's favorite about using the *Monitor's* issues as toilet paper, also suggest his authorship.

40–47   Archibald Bower, *The History of the Popes,* vol. 4. Smollett is known to have reviewed vol. 5 of Bower's *History* (see below, 11:217–33). Here, as in that review, he refers knowledgeably to Bruys' *History of the Popes,* which was, as Martz has shown ("Smollett and the *Universal History,*" 10), one of the sources used in compiling the "History of the Popes" in the *Universal History,* also apparently written by Smollett. There is also a long facetious comparison of Bower with the mythical Pope Joan, which in structure and tone closely resembles a similar device comparing Bower with Cibber in Smollett's review of Bower's next volume (11:224).

88   [Untitled editorial notes.] For evidence that Smollett wrote most of this material, see above, 1:192 and 3:96. Besides the tone of editorial authority, other signs of Smollett's authorship include the defense of a review Smollett had written (see above, 6:475–82) and the criticism of neologisms and barbarisms even in Shakespeare and Milton; the latter's language "is stiffened all over with foreign idioms," a criticism Smollett often voiced (e.g., 1:221–23).

141–58   James Grainger, *A Letter to Tobias Smollet, M.D.* The reviewer clearly acknowledges both that Smollett reviewed Grainger's *Tibullus* and that this review is written by the same hand, i.e., Smollett's (see 142–44, 146, 148, 151, and 155–56 and see above, 6:475–82). The reviewer also seems to be the same who reviewed Huggins's *Ariosto*—again, Smollett (see above, 3:385–98). Much of the reviewer's information could only be provided by Smollett: that "Dr. Smollett has been congratulated by some of his best friends on this attack"; that Smollett's surname had been burlesqued in Hill's pamphlet attacks (published before the *Critical* began); that Smollett had

not used Broekhusius as a source in his review of Grainger;
that Smollett had not written another recent article that Grainger attributes to him; that Grainger had been a guest at Smollett's house; that "Dr. Smollett does not value himself upon
being a great poet"; and that "a very large impression" of
Peregrine Pickle had been sold. Numerous other signs confirm
Smollett's authorship: reference to Grainger's reputed insan-
ity, something Hunter had communicated to Smollett in a
letter (see Knapp, *Tobias Smollett*, 203); the phrase "a groupe
worthy of Hogarth's pencil," used by Smollett in *Roderick
Random* (283) and *Humphry Clinker* (144); the comparison of
Grainger with Shebbeare, Smollett's old enemy; the rejection
of barbarisms and uncouth words, especially *opinionatre*, a
variant of which Smollett had specifically derided in a review in
1756 (1:75); the defense of "high flavoured" humor in Smollett's novels on the grounds that Cervantes, Rabelais, and Swift
had used even more (exactly Smollett's arguments in *Ferdinand
Count Fathom*, 7–8).

160–67   William Kenrick, *A Scrutiny; or the Critics Criticised*. Smollett usually handled such pamphlet attacks on the *Critical* (e.g.,
7:141–58). This pamphlet is a response to a review Smollett
can be shown to have written (see above, 6:439–53); the reviewer here explicitly acknowledges himself as the same who
wrote that review. The reviewer mentions having "already
sustained the resentment of Dr. Sh[ebbea]re"; Smollett had
reviewed all the Shebbeare publications and dealt with
Shebbeare's subsequent "resentment" (see above, 4:332–38).
A favorite Smollett metaphor is used: the reviewer likens the
Critical to a ship that has "weathered many a storm" and "will
still continue its course, without being overset by this sudden
squall"; a few months after this, Smollett was to write in a
private letter that he longed for a respite from "that stormy Sea
of Criticism in which my little Bark has been so long and so
violently tossed and afflicted" (*Letters*, 95). Finally, in addition
to the characteristic Smollettian claims of leniency toward the
book's faults, independence of any government influence, and
imperviousness to praise or criticism from authors, there is a
close verbal echo: in 1758 Smollett had used the phrase, "This,
we conceive, is a downright solecism in eating" (5:381); exactly the same construction is used here—"This, we apprehend,
is downright self-contradiction" (165).

168   Comte de Caylus, *Dissertation sur le Papyrus*. Smollett is
known to have borrowed Philip Miller's copy of this book in
the weeks just before this review appeared (*Letters*, 74 and n.
3). Significantly, the letter in which it is mentioned is devoted
exclusively to arranging reviews for the *Critical*.

170–71   [Two paintings of sea battles by Richard Paton.] For evidence that Smollett wrote or edited most of the art reviews until mid-1763, see above, 3:479 and 5:265–66 and see chapters 6 and 7. Here the reviewer remarks authoritatively on the painter's accuracy, especially in distinguishing English and French ships, and observes that the painter's "education in the royal navy" made possible his authentic composition; Smollett was himself a Royal Navy veteran and had experienced sea battles against the French, so could speak with such authority. Also, the reviewer takes the tone of encouraging rising merit— "an ingenious painter... who has not yet had sufficient opportunities of shewing his abilities "—very like Bramble's support for the young painter in *Humphry Clinker* who "will make a capital figure, as soon as his works are known" (19 May, 76).

184   *The Intriguing Coxcomb.* The reviewer notices that this novel is plagiarized from Cleland's *Memoirs of a Coxcomb*; Smollett knew that novel well, having reviewed it for the *Monthly* in 1751 (5:385–87). Moreover, here the reviewer mentions that *Coxcomb* "was published some years ago, but not finished"; Smollett in his 1751 review of *Coxcomb* had made the same point, noting that the unfinished story left the reader "impatient" for its completion.

274–75   *A Poetical Description of Mr. Hogarth's Election Prints.* Smollett's close attention to Hogarth's works is evident in his review of Hogarth's altar painting in 1756 (1:479–80) and throughout his books (see Moore, *Hogarth's Literary Relationships*, 162–95). A favorite Smollett phrase is used: "would have required a pen equal to the pencil of Mr. Hogarth" (see above, 7:141–58), which frequently appears in his novels too. The reviewer's exposure of the author's imposition on Hogarth, obviously drawing on private sources of information (such as Smollett had) to affirm that Hogarth did not authorize the work and that he highly resents it, also suggests Smollett's authorship.

289–303   David Hume, *The History of England, under the House of Tudor.* The reviewer seems to be the same who reviewed Hume's *History of Great Britain*, noting that what was said there regarding Hume's style and method applies to this volume also and need not be repeated; Smollett wrote that earlier review (2:385–404). Other signs confirm Smollett's authorship: several other references to that volume of Hume's *History*, the detection of specific Scotticisms and neologisms, and the correction of minute points of historical fact.

337–56   Walter Harte, *The History of the Life of Gustavus Adolphus, King of Sweden.* Martz had demonstrated Smollett's authorship of this review ("Smollett and the *Universal History*," 6 and n. 24). Other evidence includes: the use of a Spanish saying; a reference to *Don Quixote*; evident familiarity with the historical writings of Puffendorf and Voltaire; and especially the extended discussion of barbarisms—his prose is "interlarded with foreign words and idioms" and "if we thus naturalize foreign words and foreign subjects, our blood, our manners, and our language, will be soon alike adulterated," both typical of Smollett (see above, chap. 4, and specific reviews such as 1: 221–23 and 2: 393–94).

375–77   "Engraving" [Three prints by Strange]. Smollett's earlier reviews of Strange express the same opinions in the same panegyrical language as in this one (see 1: 94–95 and see above, 3: 479). The summary tribute to the progress of the arts in Britain and the image of genius blooming like a delicate but neglected flower occur repeatedly in Smollett's reviews (1: 94–96, 276, and 387). The reviewer refers knowledgeably to Strange's "former productions" (which Smollett had reviewed); he also reveals that he has seen these still unfinished prints, a privilege that Smollett—who knew Strange and was then employing him to engrave prints for his *History*—would presumably have.

399–409   Edward Barry, *A Treatise on the Three Different Digestions and Discharges of the Human Body*. Not only is the reviewer a physician, but he mentions cases he himself has observed in the West Indies and in long sea voyages, all experiences Smollett had had. Also like Smollett, he emphasizes the value of the Bath waters, quoting a long passage on them, and mentions having observed a dissection by "the best anatomist of the age"—Smollett's friend Hunter. Smollett displays detailed familiarity with this book in *Humphry Clinker* (18 April, 18).

529–34   Francis Home, *Medical Facts and Experiments*. The review begins with a discourse on the plight of the reviewer such as Smollett habitually included. A favorite Smollett image is repeated: the reviewers' monthly labors, "like those of *Sisyphus*, are never ending, ever beginning" (see above, 4: 94). Other signs of Smollett's authorship include a quotation from Horace, the careful distinction between condemning an author's work and respecting his character, and the deft mockery of the author's more trivial findings.

550–54   Voltaire, *Candide*. Smollett had reviewed other works by Voltaire (see 1: 181–84 and above 4: 385–95); he was planning and may have already begun his translation of Voltaire's *Works*. His objections to *Candide* are based on standards exactly like those Smollett held: it lacks "plan, contrivance, character, argument, or philosophy"; the characters are unrealistic, the incidents improbable, and the plot unorderly (see the dedication to *Ferdinand Count Fathom*, 2–3). The reviewer objects to Voltaire's unfounded exaltation of Moslem culture over Christian, a penchant of French writers that Smollett had objected to in reviewing Marigny's *Arabians* (see 5: 137).

As Klukoff has shown, the use of the rare word *Galemathias* that Smollett had also used in a review of 1756 (2:189) and close parallels with passages of Smollett's notes in his edition of Voltaire's works confirm his authorship (see Klukoff, "Smollett and the *Critical Review*: Criticism of the Novel," 123ff.).

Volume 8 (*July to December 1759*)

16–28 *An Inquiry Concerning the Cause of the Pestilence.* The reviewer refers knowledgeably to points in Pringle's *Diseases of the Army*; Smollett had reviewed that book in 1752 (*Monthly*, 7:52–56). Evidently a physician with shipboard experience (as Smollett had), the reviewer writes authoritatively on conditions and diseases among the troops below decks; he cites as one of his examples "the British forces on the Carthagena expedition," the very expedition on which Smollett had sailed as surgeon's mate. Other evidence includes the detailed familiarity with episodes in English history and the allusion to Boerhaave as "the Dutch Hippocrates," an epithet used in other Smollett reviews (e.g., 7:400).

28–31 Thomas More Molyneux, *Conjunct Expeditions.* The reviewer indicates that he is the same who reviewed Molyneux's *Target* in 1756, i.e., Smollett (1:438–43).

31–44 *Philosophical Transactions*, vol. 50, part 2. Smollett appears to have reviewed the earlier volumes (1:528–36 and 2:13–35 and 126–35; see above 4:130–49 and 205–22; 5:476–91; and 6:33–46); in structure and tone this review exactly resembles his earlier ones. The prefatory disquisition on the decline of the Royal Society and the "faulty good nature" of the editors who fail to weed out the essays of "pseudo-philosophers," together with special praise for the mathematician Simson (Smollett had praised him generously in 1756, 1:528 and 2:13–14) point specifically to Smollett's authorship.

44–54 Nicholas Tindal, *The Continuation of Mr. Rapin's History of England*, vol. 20. Smollett's authorship is evident in his detailed arguments on points of English history and especially his long critique of Rapin's account of the Battle of Carthagena, correcting points about topography, troop deployment, and battle action in a way that suggests eyewitness authority; Smollett had witnessed that battle and written the account of it that appeared in the *Compendium* (see Martz, "Smollett and the Expedition to Carthagena, 428–46). The reviewer's avowal of candor regardless of "whatever provocation we have received" seems to be an allusion to the printed attacks on Smollett's *Continuation* by Tindal's publishers; Smollett had referred to them in other reviews (see above, 6:226–39). Smollett appears to have reviewed the next volume of Tindal also (see below, 10:186–94).

82–83   *An Impartial Estimate of the Rev. Mr. Upton's Notes on the Fairy Queen.* The signs of Smollett's authorship are: the long, spirited defense of Smollett's friend Huggins and his *Orlando Furioso* (see above, 3: 385–98; 6: 506–8); the attack on Griffiths and the threat to expose past impostures by *Monthly* reviewers, knowledge Smollett had had the opportunity to acquire working for Griffiths in 1751–52; and the reference to Pope Joan, whom Smollett had been discussing in other recent reviews (7: 42).

121–37   Claude Adrien Helvétius, *De L'Esprit: or, Essays on the Mind.* The reviewer acknowledges that he is the same who reviewed *De L'Esprit* in the original (6: 501–6)—evidently Smollett (see above, 7: 501–6). Other signs include: slurs on booksellers' schemes and on the *Monthly* ("our *mother-critic*"), and the methodical refutation of abstract theory with common sense and experience.

148–54   Robert Maxwell, *The Practical Husbandman.* This review repeats the points Smollett made in earlier reviews on husbandry: the value of classical authorities, citing Varro, Cato, Virgil, and Columella (3: 2); the need for the learned to apply themselves to the field (3: 1–3), especially in applying the science of chemistry (3: 107–13); and the exemplary success of the newly formed Edinburgh Society for the Improvement of Arts and Manufactures (3: 107). Other signs include: praise for European academies, the writer's disavowal of expertise in husbandry, and the call for a clearer prose style.

160–6   *A Letter to a Late Noble Commander of the British Forces in Germany.* The *Critical*'s treatment of the numerous pamphlets on the Lord George Sackville case exactly parallels that of the Byng controversy, which was conducted entirely by Smollett (discussed above in chap. 4; see also above, 2: 277–78 and 281). It is likely, as Klukoff argues ("Smollett and the Sackville Controversy") that Smollett reviewed most or all of the pamphlets on the Sackville episode. Internal signs of Smollett's authorship here include a typical attack on Griffiths, a general slur on unscrupulous booksellers, the call for an end to inflammatory pamphlets, the defense of the accused against prejudicial rumors, and the reviewer's claims of absolute impartiality. See also below, 8: 162.

162   *A Seasonable Antidote against the Poison of Popular Censure.* In addition to the evidence that Smollett reviewed all the Sackville pamphlets (see above, 8: 160–62), here the Byng case (which Smollett had covered in the *Critical*) is invoked as a tragic precedent—"We wish the blood of the innocent may not be now crying for vengeance"—and a close verbal parallel with a known Smollett review occurs: "Let us not give way to a rash prejudging spirit of prejudice, or unfounded resentment"; in

1756, Smollett had written, "Let us not, at such a crisis, be hurried into rash and dangerous resentments" (2:44).

189–99 *The Modern Part of an Universal History,* vol. 9. For evidence, see above, 7:1–14. An additional sign of Smollett's authorship is the reviewer's familiarity with and esteem for "Ossorius" (Osorio), an important source for Smollett's *Compendium* (see above, 3:72–74).

271–76 John Hill, *The Vegetable System.* The introductory disquisition on the aims and problems of the reviewers suggests Smollett, as do the references to a long-running feud with Hill; Smollett's paper quarrels with Hill extended back to 1751 (see Knapp, *Tobias Smollett,* 117–18 and 216 n. 81) and were often mentioned in reviews by Smollett (see above, 6:226–39 and 7:141–58). Two Smollettian verbal echoes occur: the usual admonition to rid the language of "all stiffness and affectation" and the observation that in his hack writing, Hill had had to "model his capacity *invita Minerva*"; the latter had been used by Smollett a few months earlier in a private letter, describing his work as "writing dull Commentaries *invita Minerva*" (*Letters,* 79).

292–96 [Robert Dossie], *Institutes of Experimental Chemistry.* The summary comments on the present state of learning, on the rise and progress of science under the Royal Society, and on the value of chemistry as an applied science all suggest Smollett (see 1:41–53, 106; 2:31–32, 97–109; and see above, 3:1–20). The stated decision to review the book in more detail in the next issue is the kind that, as editor, Smollett would make. See below, 8:341–52.

338 *A Short Answer to . . . Queries . . . [on] the Hospital of Bath.* The reviewer here and in the following brief notice indicates that he is the same who reviewed Baylies's earlier book, who seems to have been Smollett (see above, 6:516–17). The reviewer speaks with editorial-sounding authority about his "reluctance" to "intermeddle in such disputes," although he is obliged to because "of the plan we have laid down for reviewing new literary publications." Other evidence of Smollett's voice: the denunciation of "illiberal" and "personal" abuse, the avowed impartiality, the quotation from Horace, and the cautious agreement with Baylies that Bath Hospital "is too much influenced by a medical cabal." Knapp also provides evidence of Smollett's involvement as a reviewer in the Baylies-Bath dispute (*Tobias Smollett,* 148–50).

338 William Baylies, *A Full Reply to . . . A Short Answer.* The evidence that Smollett also reviewed this pamphlet, which is a response to the preceding title, is presented above (8:338).

341–52 [Robert Dossie], *Institutes of Experimental Chemistry* (cont. from 8:296). The prefatory remarks on the difficulty of re-

viewing books without incurring censure and resentment and
especially the expression of relief at reviewing an anonymous
work—thereby precluding accusations of prejudice—suggest
Smollett's authorship. The half-apologetic admission that the
article is aimed only at interested specialists foreshadows Smollett's editorial in 1760 on the difficulty of pleasing all readers
(see below, 10:161–78). See also below, 9:237–38 and 238–39.

448–52   Richard Guy, *An Essay on Scirrhous Tumours, and Cancers.*
The reviewer generalizes about the labored style of "almost
every medical author of these days"; Smollett could do this,
having reviewed most of the medical works for the *Critical*
since 1756 (see above, appendix A, passim). Other signs of his
hand include: the facetious tone, a quotation from *Gil Blas*
(which Smollett had translated in 1748), the disapproval of
ostentatious parades of quoted authorities, and the emphasis
on case reports over abstract theory. The discussion here of
Plunkett's remedy is referred to in a later Smollett review (see
below, 10:446–50).

Volume 9   (*January to June 1760*)
59–65   Edmund Stone, *The Construction and Principal Uses of Mathematical Instruments.* The reviewer's definitive pronouncement
that "since the commencement of our periodical labours, none
of Mr. Stone's works have passed through our hands" points
directly to Smollett who, since Armstrong's departure in
1757 (see chap. 3), was left the only founding staff member
who covered science. Supporting evidence emerges in the reviewer's protestations of impartiality (a recurrent note in Smollett's reviews) and especially his indignation at the nation's
failure to reward this great scientist's achievement: "The great
ought to blush for their neglect" (see similar opinions in 2:433
and in the *Continuation* 4:125 and 128–30).

70–71   [Untitled article on Richard Paton paintings of a sea battle.]
For a summary of the evidence that Smollett wrote or edited
most of the art reviews from 1756 to 1763, see above 5:265–66
and chapters 6 and 7. Additional evidence of Smollett's authorship includes: the nationalistic pride ("the finest prints of
that kind ever yet attempted in any nation"), the call for the
public to support this worthy artist, and the information (as
was Smollett's habit) provided about works in progress and
plans to publish them as prints.

81–92   *The Modern Part of an Universal History*, vol. 14. For evidence of Smollett's many other reviews of these volumes, see
above, 7:1–14. The reviewer reveals inside knowledge such as
only an editor (i.e., Smollett) could have, announcing the
writers' plan to include Malta with Europe in a future volume
rather than in this one. Moreover, the reviewer describes the

authors' plan "to fill up the chasm" between sections, exactly the colloquial phrase Smollett used in complaining to Richardson in 1759 about his task "of filling up a chasm of fifteen or sixteen sheets" in the *Universal History* (*Letters*, 78).

161–77   *The Modern Part of an Universal History*, vol. 15. For evidence, see above, 7: 1–14.

187–97   Elizabeth Nihell, *A Treatise on the Art of Midwifery*. The reviewer's thorough defense of Smellie's opinions, publications, and methods of teaching, partly based on personal observation, points to Smollett, for he had known Smellie well at least since 1750, had edited Smellie's three books on midwifery, and was familiar with his opinions and practices (Knapp, *Tobias Smollett*, 135 and 137–40). Other evidence includes: a typical joke based on the "expulsion of wind"; a mocking allusion to "Prester John, cham of Tartary" (mentioned by Smollett in a review in the same issue; see 9: 170 and above, 9: 161–77); the sustained mockery and derision; and the detection of a long list of "foreign idioms, uncouth and affected words." (See also Klukoff, "Smollett's Defense of Dr. Smellie in the *Critical Review*").

197–205   Daniel Webb, *An Inquiry into the Beauties of Painting*. As Felsenstein has shown, a passage from this review, summarizing Webb on Raphael, appears in paraphrase—with close verbal parallels—in Smollett's *Travels* (284 and n. 1). The long disquisition on how even men "of sensibility and erudition" may not, despite Webb's precepts, acquire a discerning taste in art resembles Smollett's self-effacing remarks about his artistic judgment in the *Travels* and *Humphry Clinker* (discussed above in chap. 4).

231   [Untitled article on a Richard Houston mezzotint of Joshua Reynolds's portrait of the Marquis of Granby.] For a summary of the evidence that Smollett wrote or edited most of the art reviews from 1756 to 1763, see above, 5: 265–66 and chapters 6 and 7. Additional evidence here is the unreserved, almost extravagant, style: Houston is the "ingenious artist," Reynolds's portraits are "universally admired," etc., much like the praise Smollett had lavished on Hogarth, Wilton, Strange, and others. Smollett ranked Reynolds among the three painters most distinguished "by their superior merit in portraits" in the *Continuation* 4 (1761), 131.

237–38   *Remarks on Mr. Robert Dossie's Institutes of Experimental Chemistry*. The reviewer reveals he is the same who reviewed Dossie's *Institutes*; that review seems to be by Smollett (see above, 8: 292–96 and 341–52).

238–39   [Robert Dossie], *A Refutation of the Remarks on the Institutes of Experimental Chemistry*. The reviewer is evidently the same as the one who reviewed the pamphlet above (see above,

9:237–38), as well as Dossie's *Institutes* (see above, 8:292–96 and 341–52).

245–60   *The Modern Part of an Universal History*, vol. 16. For evidence of Smollett's reviews of other volumes, see above, 7:1–14. The reviewer seems to be the same who reviewed the last volume (see above, 9:161–77). Other evidence includes: a detailed review of the faults of previous volumes, here remedied; the reviewer's sympathy for the "tedious and laborious" work of compilation; and his detailed discussion of the compilers' plan and method, with suggestions for improvement.

399–400   "Engraving" [Two engravings by Strange of paintings by Carlo Maratte]. Smollett had reviewed more of Strange's works than any other artist's (see 1:94–95 and above, 3:479 and 7:375–77). The extravagant praise—"one of the finest figures we have seen"—and personal information about Strange's travels accord with Smollett's earlier opinions and with his known connections with Strange.

400   [Untitled article on Thomas Frye mezzotints and the state of British art.] For a summary of the evidence that Smollett wrote or edited most of the art reviews from 1756 to 1763, see above 5:265–66 and chapters 6 and 7. Here the reviewer exudes nationalistic pride like Smollett's: "What a rapid progress we make in the polite arts" and "we are arrived to great perfection in painting, engraving, and mezzotinto" and "particularly in mezzotinto we may be justly said to excel every other nation." Smollett noted that "great improvements were made in mezzotinto" during George II's reign in the *Continuation* 4 (1761), 131. The reviewer urges readers to see Frye's works at his studio in Hatton-Garden, as Smollett had with Wilton and others in 1756 (see chap. 6).

417–19   [John Cleland], *The Times. A Second Epistle to Flavian*. For evidence of Smollett's reviews of other Cleland works, see above, 5:199–206 and 7:184. The review stands out as unusual because although the reviewer admits the poem is bad— "delivered in so unpoetical a manner"—he commends highly its "strong sense and good satire." This, together with a compliment to "the ingenious writer" and a recommendation that the letter rewritten in prose "would make a most spirited and manly composition," suggest Smollett again supporting his old friend Cleland.

470–79   *Philosophical Transactions*, vol. 51, part 1. The opening remarks on the decline of the *Transactions*, the mixture of valuable and trifling papers, and the culpability of the undiscriminating editors all resemble exactly Smollett's opinions on former volumes (see 1:528; 2:135; and above, 4:130–49 and 205–22; 5:476–91; 6:33–46; and 8:31–44). The reviewer upholds an opinion of Rutty's over previous findings to the contrary, as Smollett would do. The review is continued by the same reviewer below, 10: 20–26.

Volume 10	(*July to December 1760*)
1–19	*The Modern Part of an Universal History*, vol. 19. For evidence of Smollett's reviews of other volumes, see above, 7: 1–14. The reviewer detects the repetition of an incident that had been recounted in the volumes on the Arab world; Smollett had reviewed those volumes (see above, 7: 1–14). The reviewer of the next volume—shown below to be Smollett—indicates that he also wrote this review (see below, 10: 161–78).
20–26	*Philosophical Transactions*, vol. 51, part 1 (cont. from 9: 479). The repeated complaints about trivial essays, the compliment for Brakenridge, and the closing injunction to the editors to reduce the size of the volumes all point to Smollett. See above, 9: 470–79.
70–72	*Yorick's Meditations upon Various. . . Subjects.* As Foster has shown, ("Smollett's Pamphleteering Foe Shebbeare," 1099), the passage about quacks quoted by the reviewer seems to have been the model for a scene in *Sir Launcelot Greaves* (79–81). Among other resemblances is a close verbal echo: the reviewer quotes Yorick's speech containing the line, "There are quacks in the law, quacks in divinity, and scribbling quacks"; Smollett has Ferret say, "We have quacks in religion, quacks in physic, quacks in law, [and] quacks in politics" (*Sir Launcelot Greaves*, 79). The coincidence in publication dates is significant: the review appeared in the July issue (published ca. 1 August 1760), while this part of *Greaves* appeared only two months later (ca. 1 October 1760).
81–90	*The Modern Part of an Universal History*, vol. 20. For evidence, see above, 7: 1–14.
111–18	*An Essay on the Autumnal Dysentery.* Like Smollett, the reviewer appears to be an experienced doctor, familiar with authorities and with cases. The long list of "new and difficult words" indicated by the reviewer, his concerns with style and organization, and his closing objection to the author's "affectation of philosophizing" all echo Smollett's usual criteria and phraseology (see above, 4: 385–95 and 6: 501–6).
161–78	*The Modern Part of an Universal History*, vols. 21, 22. For evidence, see above, 7: 1–14. In addition, the reviewer peevishly notes the difficulty of summarizing two volumes, which "the proprietors have thought fit this month to publish"; this terse criticism of the proprietors' publishing strategy was fully articulated in Smollett's "Hints for the Consideration of the Proprietors of the Universal History," a memo he forwarded to the proprietors through Richardson only twelve days after this review appeared (*Letters*, 91 and n. 3).

186–94   Nicholas Tindal, *The Continuation of Mr. Rapin's History of England*, vol. 21. The reviewer seems to be the same as in the review of the preceding volume, where Smollett's hand is evident (see above, 8:44–54). The detailed critique of Tindal's style, the correction of points of fact in English history, and particularly the objection to Tindal's "coldness" in describing battles (see above, 4:385–95) all point to Smollett.

241–42   [John Cleland], *The Romance of a Day*. For evidence of Smollett's other reviews of Cleland, see above: 5:199–206; 7:184; and 9:417–19. The reviewer claims to recognize the author of this anonymous novel by his style; this Smollett (perhaps alone of the *Critical* staff) could do, having reviewed Cleland's *Coxcomb* in 1751 (*Monthly* 5:385–87). As a friend of Cleland's perhaps he learned directly from the source. The reviewer's suggestion that the novel be continued is exactly the same as Smollett had made in reviewing *Coxcomb* and may reflect Smollett's knowledge that Cleland was already planning the sequel, *Romance of a Night* (1762).

319–20   Arthur Murphy, *A Poetical Epistle to Mr. Samuel Johnson, A.M.* The reviewer displays thorough and privileged knowledge of the authorship of past reviews in the *Critical*, exculpating Francklin of responsibility for one and explaining an error made by its real author; this information and the editorial tone suggest Smollett, who elsewhere had clarified issues concerning identities of reviewers (see 7:151) and occasionally acknowledged errors by reviewers (3:96). The closing compliment to Johnson may have been partly to atone for an earlier review that Smollett knew had offended Johnson (see *Letters*, 77) and partly a gesture of thanks for Johnson's contributions to Smollett's *British Magazine* (see above, chap. 9).

372–85   Henry Augustus Raymond, *The History of Gustavus Ericson, King of Sweden*. Martz has thoroughly demonstrated Smollett's authorship of this review ("Smollett and the *Universal History*," 7–8).

446–50   [Robert Dossie], *Theory and Practice of Chirurgical Pharmacy*. Like Smollett, the reviewer is a doctor. He also shows familiarity with Dossie's *Institutes*, which Smollett seems to have reviewed (see above, 8:292–96 and 341–52). The reviewer's familiarity with the story of Plunkett's cancer medicine connects this review with an earlier one that also seems to be Smollett's, in which Dr. Guy's acquisition and use of Plunkett's remedy is discussed at length (see above, 8:448–52).

473–78   [?Thomas Holland], *A Most Circumstantial Account of that Unfortunate Young Lady Miss Bell*. Extraordinarily long for a "Monthly Catalogue" entry, this review parallels exactly the "Remarkable Story of Miss Bell" that Smollett relates in the *Continuation* (4:16–19), published shortly after this review.

The same sympathy for Miss Bell, outrage at her accused murderer, and suspicion about the coroner's findings occur in both. The reviewer's comment that her case represents "one of the most flagrant outrages ever offered to public justice and humanity" parallels Smollett's decision to include it as the most representative episode of a period of unprecedented "luxury" and moral depravity (*Continuation*, 4:16).

Volume 11   (*January to June 1761*)
1–2   "Preface." Klukoff has presented convincing evidence of Smollett's authorship ("A Smollett Attribution in the *Critical Review*"). The resemblance to Smollett's earlier editorial pronouncements is complete; see 1:[i–ii], 2:[i–ii] and above, passim.
5–18   *The Modern Part of an Universal History*, vol. 25. For evidence, see above, 7:1–14.
25–29   William Battie, *Aphorismi de Cognoscendis & Curandis Morbis*. The reviewer appears to be the same who reviewed both Dossie's *Pharmacy* (see above, 10:446–50) and Battie's *Treatise on Madness* (see above, 4:509–16): i.e., Smollett. Additional evidence includes: comments on the use of Latin to protect decency and facilitate communications with foreign scholars and a note on the "peculiar concinnity and neatness required in aphorisms," exactly like Smollett's stated standards for maxims in 1756 (see 1:222).
36–45   *Authentic Memoirs Concerning the Portuguese Inquisition*. In a later review that is definitely Smollett's (see below, 11:217–33), he indicates that he had also written this one (11:232). This is confirmed within the review by his evident familiarity with several authorities on papal history and with Bower's *History of the Popes*; the latter Smollett reviewed (see above, 7:40–47, and below, 11:217–33), while the former he knew from compiling the volume on Italy in the *Universal History* (see Martz, "Smollett and the *Universal History*," 9–13).
63–64   Giampetro Cavazzoni Zanotti, *Avertimenti. . .par lo Incamminamento di un Giovane alla Pittura*. Smollett could read Italian (*Letters*, 84). His authorship here is suggested by his familiarity with the *Critical*'s original plan to review Italian books regularly and his knowledge of how the scheme was interrupted and why; that scheme had been Smollett's, he had commenced it, and he later discussed the problem of maintaining such channels of foreign correspondence in an editorial address in 1756 (1:[ii]).
72–73   *Eulogium Medicum, sive Oratio Anniversaria Harvaeana*. Smollett had reviewed at least one of these annual orations previously (1:172–75). Here the reviewer refers knowledgeably to past orations, expressing relief at seeing the College of

Physicians "rescued at length from the direction of that sordid spirit, which endeavored to hang the trammels of monopoly about the neck of learning and ingenuity." Smollett had argued the same point, in the same language, in 1756, railing against efforts to make the college "the great monopoly of medicine" (1:173); he had also ridiculed the xenophobic and unfounded elitism of English-trained physicians in *Ferdinand Count Fathom* (252–53).

73–75   [John Armstrong], *A Day: An Epistle to John Wilkes.* The generous praise for Wilkes and Armstrong (both Smollett's close friends) and the insinuation about the avarice of Millar (with whom Smollett had recently quarreled; see *Letters*, 64, 66–67, and 89) point to Smollett. A phrase from a passage of the poem quoted here in the review is also quoted in *Humphry Clinker*: "the mind's elbowroom" (13 July, 199). Jokes about Scotland and about Armstrong's gastronomic preferences (see above, 5:380–86) as well as the characteristic phrases "hobbling measure" (1:230) and "chasms" (*Letters*, 78), are further evidence. Smollett had earlier reviewed Armstrong's *Sketches* (see above, 5:380–86).

81–91   *The Modern Part of an Universal History*, vol. 26. For evidence, see above, 7:1–14.

99–103   George Harris, trans., *The Four Books of Justinian's Institutes.* The reviewer announces an editorial decision to break with policy and review the second edition of this work, as the first "preceded the commencement of our periodical labours"; this points to Smollett. The reviewer's evident knowledge of legal systems in several European countries may reflect knowledge Smollett acquired in compiling and reviewing the *Universal History* (see Martz, "Smollett and the *Universal History*," 1–14); the reviewer's introduction of a detailed account of the 1674 campaign against Holland by Louis XIV to illustrate a point accords with Smollett's area of expertise in compiling the section on France in the *Universal History* (Martz, "Smollett and the *Universal History*," 3–4); the same campaign is treated in detail by Smollett in a review in the last issue (11:10–12; see above, 11:5–18).

103–8   Gilbert Burnet, *Thoughts on Education.* The reviewer's extensive familiarity with Burnet's historical works suggests Smollett, who had used Burnet as a source for his own *History* (*Letters*, 61). The detection of various gallicisms and Scotticisms is further evidence; one gallicism—*opinionatre*—had been singled out in earlier reviews by Smollett (1:75 and above, 7:141–58). Other signs include a verbal echo—the phrase "interlarded . . . with French words" (see above, 7:337–56)— and a characteristic joke about poor Scottish hygiene (see 1:106).

116–22   [John Curry], *Historical Memoirs of the Irish Rebellion in the Year 1641*. According to Edmund Burke's friend Charles O'Conor, Burke and John Ridge personally presented Smollett with a copy of Curry's *Memoirs*, "and from that event proceeded the judgment published in the Critical Review" (quoted in Knapp, *Tobias Smollett*, 243–44, n. 96). The reviewer's familiarity with various English historians, his defense of the Scots from Clarendon's account, and his reference to a line from a Foote comedy (a favorite of Smollett's) are further evidence.

131–41   George Colman, *The Jealous Wife*. The reviewer's general remarks on the state of the theater, his praise for Garrick's judicious management and selection of plays, and his reference to himself as a playwright who had had "the stage-door thrown in our teeth," all indicate Smollett's authorship. Several verbal echoes occur: "It foams, and screams, and slobbers, and whoops, and hollows" (see above, 4:160–62 and *Letters*, 60); "a few ill-chosen French words, with which his language is insipidly interlarded" (see above, 11:103–8) and, most significantly, "we have always respected him [Colman] as a man of genius"—Smollett repeated this a few days later in a letter to Garrick about Colman, "whom I have always respected as a man of genius" (*Letters*, 98).

217–33   Archibald Bower, *The History of the Popes*, vol. 5. Smollett stated that he wrote this review in a letter to Garrick (*Letters*, 98).

314–17   Laurence Sterne, *Tristram Shandy*, vols. 3, 4. The general reflections on the various kinds of humor; the astute remarks on Lucian, Rabelais, and Cervantes (see *Ferdinand Count Fathom*, 7–8), and the detailed reference to an ancient history of the East Indies (Smollett had reviewed the East Indies volume of the *Universal History*; see above, 8:189–99) all suggest Smollett. Most tellingly, the reviewer demonstrates the verisimilitude of Sterne's mock writ of excommunication by quoting a papal bull "published against the emperor Lewis . . . by pope Clement VI": Smollett had recently recounted this episode in his review of vol. 26 of the *Universal History* (11:84; see also above, 11:81–91).

331–32   [Untitled article on Thomas Frye mezzotints.] For a summary of the evidence that Smollett wrote or edited most of the art reviews from 1756 to 1763, see above 5:265–66 and chapters 6 and 7. Here the reviewer's notice of continuing improvements in mezzotint technique is reminiscent of Smollett's similar view in the *Continuation* 4 (1761), 131. The freely laudatory manner, the nationalistic pride, and the reviewer's authoritative tone about poetry all point to Smollett. One marked verbal echo: of the engraving arts the reviewer states, "We rejoice to see them brought to such perfection among us" (331), while in Smollett's *Continuation* appear the words, "the art of engraving was brought to perfection by Strange" (4:131).

332   [Untitled article on an engraving by Ravenet, landscape paintings by Richard Wilson and "Smith" (unidentified), and engravings by William Woollett.] For a summary of the evidence that Smollett wrote or edited most of the art reviews from 1756 to 1763, see above 5:265–66 and chaps. 6 and 7. Other details suggest Smollett's authorship: the attention to Ravenet, whom Smollett had employed to engrave plates for his *History* (1757–58) and *Continuation* (1760–61); the favorable mention of the Society for the Encouragement of Arts and its "liberal premiums" for artists, of which Bramble was "extremely fond" in *Humphry Clinker* (5 June, 115); and the direction of readers to Boydell's print shop where Woollett's works can be had, the kind of information Smollett habitually added to his art reviews.

409–11   Charles Churchill, *The Apology. Addressed to the Critical Reviewers*. The reviewer's authoritative statement that Hamilton "never in the whole course of his life wrote one single article in the Critical Review" and that Smollett had not written the review of the *Rosciad* could only come from Smollett. Similarly, he reveals that Smollett had "solemnly declared to the friends of the apologist [Churchill]" that he had not written the review; this Smollett had done in a private letter to Garrick in 1761 (*Letters*, 97–98). A challenge to Churchill to prove any past misdeeds by the *Critical*, an avowal of "excess lenity" toward bad authors, and the image of Churchill as an insect that had begun "to hum and buz and sting like a gad-fly in the dog-days" (see 2:43) all echo earlier Smollett reviews. A favorite phrase of Smollett's used here—"to throw out behind" (410)—is also used in chapter 8 of *Sir Launcelot Greaves*, which appeared about three months after this review.

449–59   *Philosophical Transactions*, vol. 51, part 2. Almost every opinion echoes an earlier Smollett review: the opening criticism of the indiscriminate editing due to the mistaken "good nature" of the editors; the mockery of trivial and foolish essays, particularly those on antiquarian research; the special praise for a Rutty paper on mineral waters; the high proportion of attention to medical cases; the mockery of the "profound Dr. Parson's of whose labours we have had repeated occasions to speak with admiration"; the wry disdain for a grammatical solecism ("inedited"). The review is continued below in the next volume (12:15–26) where, however, there are no distinctive signs of Smollett's authorship and thus it is not yet attributable to Smollett.

Volume 12   *(July to December 1761)*
81–103   *The Modern Part of an Universal History*, vol. 31. For evidence, see above, 7: 1–14. In addition, the reviewer shows familiarity with the volumes on France and Spain, which Smollett had reviewed earlier (see above: 10: 81–90 and 161–78, and 11: 5–18).
131–38   Voltaire, *Candid: or, All for the Best*. The reviewer indicates that he is the same who reviewed *Candide* in the original and is here "continuing [his] analysis"; the earlier review has been shown to be Smollett's (see above, 7: 550–54). A favorite Smollett expression is used: he wishes Voltaire's wit were "seasoned with a greater share of the milk of human kindness"; Smollett had used the same Shakespearean phrase in two earlier reviews (1: 344 and 2: 278) and in *Ferdinand Count Fathom* (7). (See Klukoff, "Smollett and the *Critical Review*," 126–27.) Smollett was at this time well underway with his translation of Voltaire's *Works*, in which *Candide* was included, published from 1761 to 1765.
161–78   *The Modern Part of an Universal History*, vol. 32. For evidence, see above, 7: 1–14. Other evidence includes: the familiar references to past volumes; disclosures about the difficulty of compiling the volumes on Africa (which a mere reviewer could not have known); the reviewer's interest in the history of Ireland (Smollett was considering writing a history of Ireland at this time; see Knapp, *Tobias Smollett*, 243–44); and his intimations about the contents of the volume on Sweden, which was not yet published, but which Smollett himself was compiling (see *Letters*, 87–90, and Martz, "Smollett and the *Univeral History*," 7).
182–86   John Perceval, Lord Egmont, *The Question of the Precedency of the Peers of Ireland in England*. The reviewer has high praise for the "eloquent Egmont," a view Smollett shared, as he showed in contriving to mention Egmont as a model of oratory in *Sir Launcelot Greaves* (chap. 3, 26). Smollett had earlier in this year reviewed a book on Ireland that Burke had asked him to do (see above, 11: 116–22); Burke was the younger Egmont's close friend, he probably helped edit this volume (as he did others of Egmont's works), and he may have been the channel through which it came to Smollett. Smollett was particularly interested in Irish history at this date because he was planning to write a history of Ireland and even to travel to Ireland to gather materials in 1761–62 (see Knapp, *Tobias Smollett*, 243). Other evidence of Smollett's authorship: the reviewer's detailed knowledge of British history, his references to authorities such as Puffendorf and Grotius that Smollett knew well from compiling the *Universal History*, and especially his authoritative tone in explaining that he is bending the

Critical's usual policy in reviewing the second edition of a book first published in 1739.

237–50   Anton Friedrich Büsching, *A New System of Geography*. Smollett's authorship of this review has been demonstrated by Martz ("Smollett and the *Universal History*," 8, n. 33) and supported by Felsenstein, who notes a reference to it in the *Travels* (147–48 and 420, n. 10). In addition, the repeated references to the contents of past volumes of the *Philosophical Transactions* (which Smollett had been reviewing) and one in particular to an essay by Murdoch (his friend and a former reviewer for the *Critical*) also point to Smollett.

278–83   John Hill, *The Vegetable System*, vol. 2, part 1. The reviewer indicates he is the same who reviewed Hill's first volume, i.e., Smollett (see above, 8:271–76). Further evidence includes references to a long-running acquaintance with Hill's works and praise for Lord Bute (Smollett was soon to enter his employ as writer of *The Briton*).

312–13   "Engraving" [William Woollett's engraving of Richard Wilson's *Niobe* and two Thomas Frye mezzotints]. For a summary of the evidence that Smollett wrote or edited most of the art reviews from 1756 to 1763, see above 5:265–66 and chapters 6 and 7. The reviewer exhibits Smollett's national boosterism ("the best of the kind this nation has produced") and his vigorous support for worthy artists (wishing "this truly ingenious artist the encouragement his merit deserves"). The latter is a verbal echo of phrases in other reviews attributable to Smollett, e.g., we "wish him the success his merit deserves" (7:171). The style of the reviewer's description and analysis resembles Smollett's in his known art reviews of 1756 (1:94–96, 387, 479–80).

321–35   *The Modern Part of an Universal History*, vol. 33. For evidence, see above, 7:1–14. Also, the reviewer reveals inside knowledge about the *Universal History*, announcing that a folio edition "is preparing."

390–92   l'Abbé Coyer, *Histoire de Jean Sobieski, Roi de Pologne*. The reviewer displays foreknowledge of the contents of the *Universal History* volume on Poland, a volume that Smollett was involved in compiling (see Martz, "Smollett and the *Universal History*," 8–11). The reviewer's objection to the "rage of philosophizing upon every occurence [which] breaks the texture of the narrative" is the same Smollett had made to the style of Voltaire (see above, 4:385–95) and others; this passage closely parallels one of Smollett's in 1756, where he had objected to the "rage of reflecting. . . [by which] the chain of events is broken" (2:386).

405–18   James Macpherson, *Fingal: An Antient Epic Poem*. Several features point to Smollett: the general observations on the reviewer's predicament; objections to points about English history and the citation of various authorities to support them; the defense of Ariosto's prosody from its critics; and the extensive familiarity with authorities in Danish and Swedish history such as Saxo Grammaticus, on whom Smollett had relied in compiling sections of the *Universal History* (see Martz, "Smollett and the *Universal History*," 7–8). The reviewer discusses the ancient kingdom of Cumbria whose capital was "Alcluyth or Dunbritton" in exactly the same way Smollett had described it in a personal letter of 1756 (*Letters*, 43–44). Above all, the reviewer singles out the word *caraculla* for discussion and corrects Macpherson's etymology of it to include an ancient term for "a garment worn by the barbarians"; in a long discussion of the same word *caraculla* in the *Travels*, Smollett cites Macpherson's etymology and again corrects it to include "the name of a Gaulish vestment" (*Travels*, 234). Smollett also refers feelingly to *Fingal* in *Humphry Clinker*, (3 September, 240). The review is continued by the same writer below (13:45–53).

477–78   *A Seventh Letter to the People of England, Occasioned by a Late Resignation.* Smollett had reviewed most or all of Shebbeare's "Letters" (1:88–90; 2:35–44 and 279–80; see above, 5:79); the tone and style here are similar to those, and the reviewer intimates that he is the same who reviewed those, referring to them familiarly and discerning that this pamphlet is too unlike the others to be Shebbeare's. (See also Foster, "Smollett's Pamphleteering Foe Shebbeare," 1077–79.)

Volume 13   (*January to June 1762*)
45–53   James Macpherson, *Fingal* (cont. from 22:418). The reviewer here is the same as in the first part (see above, 12:405–18), shown to be Smollett. Further evidence includes; the introduction of a detailed account of Edward III from English history and the refutation of various criticisms of *Fingal* that had appeared since the first part of the review was published, both in accord with Smollett's views and expertise.

107–20   *The Modern Part of an Universal History*, vol. 34. For evidence, see above, 7:1–14. In addition: the reviewer's discussion of the origins of distinctive national characters closely resembles views Smollett expressed in 1756 (1:220). He also sympathizes, as Smollett well could, with the compilers over the "length and tediousness" of their labors.

121–29   *Medical Observations and Inquiries, by a Society of Physicians in London*, vol. 2. Smollett almost certainly reviewed the first volume of this work (see above, 3:536–47, 4:35–45). As in those articles, the reviewer here extends particular praise to Smollett's friends Clephane, Hunter, and Macaulay. The preference for case histories over medical theory, wry remarks about Scotland, and the extra attention paid to articles about shipboard diseases, together with the reviewer's evident experience as a ship's doctor, strongly suggest Smollett. The review is continued by the same writer below (13:222–26) where there are further signs of Smollett's hand.

135–38   William Whitehead, *The School for Lovers*. The review opens with a disquisition typical of Smollett on the travails of a reviewer, who suffers endless resentment and personal attack. The sweeping denial of ever having maligned Whitehead, the avowals of esteem for him (Smollett had praised him in the *Continuation* 4 [1761], 227), and the open challenge to any to produce an example of past misdeeds by the *Critical* all suggest Smollett. The reviewer's approval of Whitehead's "preservation of the unities" and the observance of other "proprieties" resemble Smollett's dramatic opinions in 1756 (see above, chap. 5).

157–58   David Garrick, *Florizel and Perdita; or, The Winter's Tale*. Smollett is known to have received a copy of this play from Garrick the month before this review appeared (*Letters*, 103). Internal signs of Smollett's hand include: the reviewer lives "at a distance from the theater" (Smollett lived in Chelsea); both his desire to see the "irregularity of Shakespeare's Winter's Tale" corrected and his feeling that such alterations must be made with "caution" repeat exactly the opinions Smollett expressed in reviewing another adaptation of the play in 1756 (1:144–45); the term *chasms* appears here and in many of Smollett's writings (see above, 11:73–75 and *Letters*, 78).

161–63   *The Defects of an University Education. . . and [the] Necessity of Erecting at Glasgow, an Academy*. The reviewer's defense of the University of Glasgow faculty, their teaching and scholarship, and the method of their selection reflect Smollett's loyalty to his alma mater and personal ties with many of the faculty (see above, 3:550–52). Smollett repeats the opinions of this review almost exactly in *Humphry Clinker* (3 September, 237), most notably the idea that the methods of teaching at Glasgow are superior by comparison with those of other universities. One verbal echo: Glasgow is called a "flourishing city" twice here in the review and twice in the corresponding passage in *Humphry Clinker*. Support for the academy proposal is of course typical of Smollett.

222–26   *Medical Observations and Inquiries* (cont. from 13:129). This is written by the same reviewer as the first part, where there is strong evidence of Smollett's authorship (see above, 13:121–29). Further evidence here: special praise for Dr. Thomas Dickson, another close friend of Smollett's (*Letters*, 36 and 123; Knapp, *Tobias Smollett*, 247) and for a case of William

Hunter's.

272   *The Rosciad of C[o]v[e]nt G[a]rd[e]n.* Smollett had every
incentive to review "Rosciad" publications, as the first (which
he had *not* reviewed) embroiled him in unwanted quarrels (see
Letters, 97–98 and above, 11:409–11). The image of "a poor
babbler in the pack" repeats verbatim a Smollett phrase used
in a review in 1756 (1:227) and in *Peregrine Pickle* (chap. 103,
661).

346–47 Samuel Ingham, trans., *The Diseases of the Bones*, by Du-
Verney. The reviewer indicates that he is the same who
commented on an Ingham case in his review of *Medical
Observations*: i.e., Smollett (see above, 222–26). The general
remarks on the state of the medical profession and the language
("swarms . . . who buz round this metropolis") are characteristic of Smollett.

381–92 *The Modern Part of an Universal History*, vol. 35. For evidence,
see above, 7:1–14. In addition, the reviewer discusses the
unsuccessful efforts of the compilers to contain the *History* in
a smaller compass and he attributes small errors to the "hurry"
of the compilers, both views that Smollett held and further
signs of his intimate connection with this compilation.

392–97 [John Shebbeare], *The History of the . . . Sumatrans*, vol. 1.
The reviewer discerns Shebbeare's hand in this anonymous
book and refers to having reviewed his works in the past;
Smollett had reviewed most or all of Shebbeare's works (see
1:88–90; 2:35–44, 279–80, and 474–75; see above, 4:332–38
and 5:79). The general remarks on political writing, on the
progress of learning and the arts during various reigns down to
the present, and on the condition of the publishing world are
all typical of Smollett, as are the closing protestations of impartiality.

418–27 William Hunter, *Medical Commentaries*, part 1. The reviewer displays intimate knowledge of various matters that only
Smollett could have: of the complicated Monro-Hunter controversy and attendant pamphlets (which Smollett had reviewed; see above, 4:223–27, 431–36, and 523; 5:224–28; and
6:312–17); of the "indefatigable pains" Hunter had taken in
arranging the best plates for his book; of opinions expressed in
earlier reviews in the *Critical*; of Hunter's private opinions and
intentions; of events in Hunter's laboratory; of unpublished
information about Monro received "from Edinburgh."

495–99 [James Boswell, et al.], *A Collection of Original Poems. By
Scotch Gentlemen*. According to Boswell's own report, he had
written to Smollett asking for a kind review of this *Collection*
and Smollett had replied favorably, assuring him that he reviewed "the productions of Scotland *con amore*" (Boswell letter
of 22 January 1762, quoted in Pottle, *James Boswell: The Early*

Years 1740–1769, 475). The reviewer's evident awareness that "J. B. Esq." is a young poet and his mild praise for "some agreeable light pieces by J. B. Esq." accord with this account and, together with the reviewer's scatological and Scottish jokes, confirm Smollett's authorship.

504–12   Daniel Peter Layard, *An Essay on the Bite of a Mad Dog*. The reviewer refers to Choisel's treatise on the subject (which Smollett is shown to have reviewed; see above, 3:92–93) and to John Douglas's methods and publications of "four and twenty years ago," again just the time when Smollett had arrived in London as a newly trained physician and come in contact with Douglas (see above, 3:92–93). Other signs of Smollett include sarcastic comments on trivial observations and special approval for the benefits of sea bathing.

Volume 14   (*July to December 1762*)

75–76   Charles White, *A Particular Narrative [about] . . . a Paper Published in the 51st Volume of the Philosophical Transactions*. The reviewer indicates that he is the same who reviewed the *Philosophical Transactions* in June 1761: i.e., Smollett (see above, 11:449–59). The reviewer's insistence that he is impartial and his concern that a medical quarrel not break out are typical of Smollett's remarks.

107–18   Solomon de Monchy, *An Essay on the . . . Diseases in Voyages to the West Indies*. Smollett's interest in shipboard diseases has been noted above, 13:121–29. Here the reviewer's familiarity with Pringle's works (Smollett reviewed Pringle for the *Monthly*, July 1752) and those of other authorities, his emphasis on using case histories to prove theories, and especially his generous but completely gratuitous praise for Armstrong's *Art of Preserving Health* (several lines of which he quotes) all point to Smollett's authorship.

122–30   [Patrick Murdoch, ed.] *The Works of James Thomson*. The reviewer speaks as if he had known both Thomson and Murdoch personally, which Smollett had (Knapp, *Tobias Smollett*, 82–84). The reviewer's warm praise for Murdoch accords with Smollett's esteem for Murdoch, a founding staff writer in the *Critical* and lifelong friend. The reviewer devotes his article to Thomson's life and his special qualities of character ("overflowing benevolence," "dear to his contemporaries"); in the *Continuation* 4 (1761), Smollett devoted extra paragraphs to Thomson's character in similar terms—"the most benevolent heart that ever warmed the human breast" (129). The reviewer closes with a tribute to the bookseller Millar, who was foregoing his profits to fund a memorial to Thomson, an act "that reflects equal honour on the author and the bookseller" (130); in the *Continuation*, Smollett interjected a similar tribute to

Millar whose self-sacrifices enhanced "the honour of the book-sellers" (129).

241–49   *The Modern Part of an Universal History*, vol. 36. For evidence of Smollett's writing several reviews of volumes of this work, see above, 7:1–14. The reviewer shows inside knowledge of the difficulties the compilers faced in writing the "History of the Italian States"—a section compiled at least in part by Smollett (see Martz, "Smollett and the *Universal History*," 10–11)—and of the project's editorial problems as a whole. Similarly, he detects many repetitions in this volume of material in the volume on Italy; Smollett had reviewed that volume (see above, 11:81–91).

321–36   *Philosophical Transactions*, vol. 52, part 1. The reviewer's general remarks on how the indiscriminate inclusion of trivial essays damages "the honour of the society" repeat Smollett's annual refrain (see 1:528; 2:135, and above, passim); he displays familiarity with those earlier volumes and with the tenor of the *Critical*'s treatment of them. The mockery of antiquarian discoveries ("for which we would not give an English farthing") and those of other pseudophilosophers, and the especially close attention to medical cases all suggest Smollett.

401–10   *The Modern Part of an Universal History*, vol. 37. The reviewer is the same who reviewed the last volume (see above, 14:241–49), where Smollett's authorship is evident. Here also is a detailed critique of the editorial process wherein blame for blemishes is shifted from the writers to the publishers of their project; the reviewer again displays familiarity with the contents of the volume on Italy, which Smollett had helped to compile.

Volume 15   *(January to June 1763)*
13–21   *The Peregrinations of Jeremiah Grant, Esq; the West-Indian.* Klukoff has demonstrated convincingly Smollett's authorship of this review ("Smollett as the Reviewer of 'Jeremiah Grant.'") In addition, Smollettian verbal echoes occur: the author "has interlarded his work with some quotations from the classics," a phrase Smollett used often (see above, 7:337–56 and 11:103–8); the reviewer compares the author's imitation of Smollett "to the wrong side of [a] tapestry, on which the figures do not appear to the best advantage"—an image Smollett used verbatim in his translation of *Don Quixote* and in a private letter of 1767 (*Letters*, 131 and n. 3). The reviewer's assurance that Smollett "will be proud to see himself so taken off" and his defense of the *Critical* against its critics, offering a fifty-guinea reward for any proof of corruption, suggest only Smollett could have written the review.

120–26   *A Critical Dissertation of the Poems of Ossian, the Son of Fing-*

al. The reviewer indicates that he is the same who reviewed *Fingal*; it has been shown elsewhere that Smollett wrote that review (see above, 12:405–18 and 13:45–53). The reviewer discourses on the history of Cumbria, the capital of which was "Alcluyth" or "Dunbritton," exactly the same discussion Smollett had presented in the *Fingal* review (12:408–9) and in a letter of 1756 (*Letters*, 43–44). Another sign of Smollett's authorship is his praise for the author's "elegance and purity of language," unexpected "in the works of a Scotch professor."

200–209   James Macpherson, *Temora, an Antient Epic Poem.* The reviewer indicates that he is the same who reviewed *Fingal*, i.e., Smollett (see above, 12:405–18 and 13:45–53). Supporting evidence includes: the reviewer's Scottish origins (he recalls hearing Highland tales as a child); his familiarity with various Danish historians, including Saxo-Grammaticus (see above, 12:405–18); and his applause for "Ossian's" preservation of the classical unities, while he dismisses—as Smollett had in reviewing *Fingal*—other critical conventions as inapplicable (see 12:410).

209–10   [John Shebbeare], *The History of the . . . Sumatrans*, vol. 2. For evidence that Smollett reviewed the first volume, see above, 13:392–97. The reviewer here seems to be the same who reviewed the first; he is familiar not only with that review, but with the earlier reviews of Shebbeare's works (most or all by Smollett) and with the "pleasure" the reviewer had felt in reversing his former censures of Shebbeare.

224   "Engraving" [Engravings by Cooper, of Vandyke's "Charles I and family," and by Ryland, of Allan Ramsay's portrait of Lord Bute.] For a summary of the evidence that Smollett wrote or edited most of the art reviews from 1756 to 1763, see above 5:265–66 and chapters 6 and 7. Additionally, here the reviewer digresses to include a mention of an earlier work by Strange (that "admirable engraver") in the most favorable terms; Smollett expressed similar views in his several reviews of Strange's work (1:94–96; 3:479; 7:375–77). Here too, like Smollett, the reviewer is uniformly laudatory and echoes the pat phrases of earlier reviews: "ingenious artist," "attained to perfection in the art," etc. The reviewer's choice of Ryland's engraving of Ramsay's *Bute* coincides with Smollett's esteem both for Ramsay (distinguished, with Reynolds, for portraiture in the *Continuation* 4:131) and for Lord Bute, for whom Smollett had been writing the *Briton* in 1762–63.

399–400   H. Mason, *Lectures upon the Heart, Lungs, [etc.].* The reviewer shows familiarity with the contents of *Medical Observations*, a book Smollett has been shown to have reviewed (see above, 13:121–29 and 222–26). Most significantly, he detects Mason's omission of medical precedents established by Hunter, calling Hunter "the best anatomist of the age"—precisely the epithet he frequently applied to Hunter (see above, 7: 399–409).

401–3   *Considerations on the Present Dangerous Crisis.* Evidence includes: the reviewer's defending Bute (as Smollett had done in *The Briton*); his declaration that Bute never pensioned any Scottish writers, although "some of the best writers of the age were born on the north side of the Tweed"; and especially his comment that the "single circumstance of [a man] being a North Britain" is sufficient to damn anyone "in the eyes of an English mob," repeating a complaint Smollett had often voiced (see *Letters*, 65). Among other verbal echoes is the phrase "traduced by faction," similar to Smollett's self-description in Letter 1 of the *Travels*: "traduced by malice, persecuted by faction" (2).

[Mid-June 1763 to late June 1765 Smollett was abroad and made no discoverable contributions to the *Critical Review*.]

Volume 20   (*July to December 1765*)
45–49   *A Digest of the Laws Concerning Libels.* Smollett was back in England by late June or early July 1765 (Knapp, *Tobias Smollett*, 258–59) and admitted to Moore on 13 November 1765 that "since my return I have writt a few articles [in the *Critical Review*] merely for amusement." This effectively counterbalances the statement in the *Critical* thirteen months later (De '66, 433–34) that Smollett "has not, for several years past, had the least concern with the Critical Review." Clearly he *had*. Either the writer was unaware of Smollett's occasional contributions or his notion of having a "concern" was like Smollett's, meaning "editorial or proprietary concern," not merely writing (see *Letters*, 108 and 125).

Smollett had a special interest in libel law, having been prosecuted and imprisoned for a libel against Knowles in 1758–60 (see Knapp, 213–24, 230–33). The reviewer's detailed protests about current libel law, interspersed with wry satiric remarks about the author's more fatuous observations ("telling us that good laws never encourage robbery, with other secrets of the same kind"), both point to Smollett's authorship. One Smollettian symbol recurs here: the reviewer plays on the idea of a painter being sued for libel because someone sees himself in his painting of a monkey; in Smollett's "Apologue" to *Roderick Random* (added in 1755), he allegorizes about a painter who paints a picture in which a monkey is drawing an ass, bear, and owl, and the people who imagine themselves the originals threaten to sue for libel (*Roderick Random*, xxxvii). Verbal echoes of Smollett abound, especially from his reviews of

Shebbeare's works; e.g., "a most villainous incendiary, who . . ." (47) parallels Smollett's repeated epithet for Shebbeare, "a desperate incendiary, who . . ." (2: 44 and 4: 333). Also indicative is the reviewer's use of a quotation from Pope ("Who shall decide when doctors disagree?"), whom Smollett frequently quoted in reviews. Most tellingly, the reviewer criticizes the book for failing to set the record right about Smollett's own libel case and reveals detailed familiarity with that episode which only Smollett could have had (49). Smollett's preoccupation with libel law resurfaced in *Humphry Clinker* (2 June, 102–4), which Smollett began writing within a few months after this review appeared.

124–34   William Stevenson, *Original Poems on Several Subjects.* Smollett known to be contributing to *Critical* in 1765 (see above 20: 45–49). The reviewer reveals himself a good friend of John Armstrong ("our worthy friend Dr. Armstrong") and makes a jest of the author's mistaken notion that Armstrong was dead (124). The reviewer detects borrowings from Thomson, whose works Smollett knew and admired; he remarks, as Smollett habitually did, on Scotticisms and Scottish pronunciation; he talks knowledgeably about the "tedious and severe winters" of Scotland, which Smollett knew well from his youth; he inserts a typically Smollettian anecdote with a chamberpot punchline; and he responds authoritatively and condescendingly to the author's "apostrophe to the Reviewers," again an old Smollett practice. A verbal echo: "a flat poetical contradiction" (125) here repeats the "flat contradiction" usages which occur twice in the review Smollett wrote the previous month (20: 47 and 49).

149–52   Andrew Wilson, *Short Remarks upon. . . Disorders of the Bowels.* Smollett known to be contributing to *Critical* in 1765 (see above, 20: 45–49). The Reviewer shows medical training and expertise, and Smollett was a doctor; the reviewer favors cases over theory, a deep-seated Smollett view; the reviewer shows familiarity with (and makes mild jests about) Scottish medical education and remarks jocularly on the annual waves of new medical publications produced by Scottish doctors, both consistent with Smollett's background and views he expressed in earlier reviews (e.g., 7: 529–34 and 8: 448–52). Like Smollett, the reviewer criticizes the author's stylistic flaws, including Scotticisms; one Scotticism he cites—*these* for *those*—is exactly the same Smollett had cited in earlier reviews (e.g., 2: 277–78).

152–53   John Sayer, trans. *The Temple of Gnidus, [by] Montesquieu.* Smollett known to be contributing to *Critical* in 1765 (see above, 20: 45–49). The reviewer's authoritative tone, wry condescension, and historic perspective on the *Critical* all suggest

Smollett: "Since we undertook the office of Critical Reviewers, we have had frequent experience that it is far more dangerous to tickle an ass than to drub him." The reviewer defends Thomson from Sayer's remarks in phrases very similar in tone and construction to Smollett's: the reviewer defends "our departed friend [Thomson]. . . one of the greatest and *most amiable characters*, both as a poet and a man, *that ever adorned the British nation*"; Smollett's *Continuation* (4:129) praises "Thomson, with *the most benevolent heart that ever warmed the human breast*" (italics added). Another favorite Smollett image is used: "We are apt to indulge the *milk of humanity* by . . ." (152–53) is very like Smollett's frequently used "*milk of human kindness*," found in earlier reviews (1:344; 2:278; 12:131–38) and *Ferdinand Count Fathom* (7).

184–88   John Memis, *The Midwife's Pocket Companion*. Smollett known to be contributing to *Critical* in 1765 (see above, 20:45–49). The reviewer is, like Smollett, a doctor; he emphasizes practice and cases over theory, as Smollett regularly did. The reviewer notices the author's unacknowledged dependence on "Dr. Smellie's first publication," which Smollett was particularly well qualified to do, as he had edited that book for publication in 1750–51 (Knapp, *Tobias Smollett*, 138). Also like Smollett, the reviewer criticizes the author's many Scotticisms, using a Smollettian phase—"absolutely unintelligible on this side the Tweed." See also Noyes (*Letters*, 215–16) who felt this review was "the only piece" from this period he could ascribe with confidence to Smollett.

257–65   *Philosophical Transactions. . . vol. 54, for 1764* (cont. below, 20:348–58). Smollett known to be contributing to *Critical* in 1765 (see above, 4:130–49 and 4:205–22, and passim). During his absence abroad, the reviews of these volumes changed dramatically, from critiques to neutral abstracts (see chap. 8). Here the critical style and themes Smollett had used pre-1763 return: Smollettian sarcasms on trivial reports (e.g., rainfall in Cornwall—"A very important circumstance, truly!") and enjoyment in imagining comic scenes suggested by the reports (e.g., two astronomers who miss the long-awaited celestial event because one gets the tremors, the other watery eyes, at the key moment). The close attention to reports of unwrapping and dissecting mummies accords with Smollett's interest; he adopted the metaphor for himself (needing only "some pitch and painted linen") when he lay dying in Italy (*Letters*, 140). The review is continued below (20:348–58) where there are further signs of his authorship.

281–88   *A General Treatise on Mineral Waters in England*. Smollett known to be contributing to *Critical* in 1765 (see above, 20:45–49). Mineral waters were a special lifelong interest of Smol-

lett's, from his own *Essay on the External Use of Water* (1752)
through *Humphry Clinker* (e.g., Bramble's statement "I have
read all that has been written on the Hot Wells," 20 April, 23).
Here the reviewer refers knowledgeably to a paper on sulphur
water written by Rutty in the *Philosophical Transactions* for
1759, a volume Smollett had reviewed and in which he had
singled out Rutty's paper for particular approval (see above,
9:470–79). The reviewer notes that the author has omitted
Pringle's writings, which had bearing on his topic; Smollett
had reviewed Pringle's *Diseases of the Army* for the *Monthly* in
July 1752 (Knapp, *Tobias Smollett*, 135). The reviewer drily
mocks nonsensical experiments—"so ends this extraordinary
experiment" (283)—much as Smollett habitually did. The reviewer has ties with Scottish science professors and detects a
heavy borrowing here from the lectures of a "very celebrated
professor of chemistry in Scotland," which Smollett's wide
circle of medical and scientific friends in Scotland enabled him
to do.

310–11   *Observations on the Baume De Vie*. Smollett known to be
contributing to *Critical* in 1765 (see above 20:45–49). The reviewer has medical background, as did Smollett, and speaks
authoritatively in exposing quack medicine here as Smollett
did in his *Travels* and in *Humphry Clinker* (e.g., 17–20),
which Smollett began writing in the same year this review
appeared. The reviewer's staunch John-Bull style antigallicism
is consonant with much in Smollett's *Travels*, which he had
just prepared for the press in the summer of 1765 (e.g.,
"French foppery," "French cooks," and "French quackery").
The detailed attention to quackery—"French quackery" and
"our own quacks are equally expert"—is reminiscent of Smollett's frequent use of those terms, as in *Sir Launcelot Greaves*
("quacks in religion, quacks in physic," etc., 79) and in reviews (e.g., 4:332–38).

348–58   *Philosophical Transactions. . . vol. 54, for 1764* (cont. from
20:265). Smollett known to be contributing to *Critical* in 1765
(see above 20:45–49). This is a continuation of a review in
which Smollett's authorship is evident (see above, 20:257–65).
Further evidence of Smollett's authorship includes: the mockery of silly experiments (e.g., on the compressibility of water,
352), criticism of style ("28 pages of the most unintelligible
algebraical jargon," 355), and dry jests about antiquarianism
(e.g., an inscription on an object from Malta "which has so
happily escaped the ravages of time," 358). Like Smollett, the
reviewer complains of the trivial findings and unedited contents and urges the Royal Society to edit these volumes more
carefully, that the Society might "shine forth. . . in the future
annals of literary fame" (358); compare with Smollett's

exhortations to the Society "to have a greater regard to [its] reputation" and see that *Transactions* are "better weeded" before publication (1:528).

465–66   "Dr. J. S———," *A Letter to J. K———, M.D.* Smollett known to be contributing to *Critical* in 1765 (see above 20:45–49). The reviewer seems to be, like Smollett, a physician; he refers knowledgeably to medical authorities, particularly Fothergill and Huxham, whom Smollett frequently cited in his earlier medical reviews. Here both Smollett's long experience of medical quarrels and his style as a comic novelist are evident, as he generalizes about how whenever two doctors settle near each other, "if their tongues do not actually wag, they never fail to act such a pantomime of scandal and malignity, by grinning, nodding, shrugging, and significant reserve"; compare, for example, with the pub scene in chapter 2 of *Peregrine Pickle*, where Hatchway refrained from the conversation but played pranks on Trunnion, "made wry faces" and "cocked his eye at him," enacting a devilish "marine pantomime" (8). The reviewer's insertion of an anecdote about a physician friend from Ireland (perhaps Dr. John Curry, Burke's friend, the Dublin physician whose book Smollett reviewed in 1761, 11:116–22) is also characteristic of Smollett's reviewing style.

Volume 21   (*January to June 1766*)
407–9   *The English Connoisseur.* Smollett's interest in and support for English art is evident in his many art reviews, which are discussed above in chapters 6 and 7. The book under review aims to describe English collections of art and monuments of architecture for the general public, an aim Smollett—like this reviewer—would have applauded: we have "long wished to see a work of this kind" (407). The reviewer chooses three examples to present, ones whose "originals are accessible to every reader": this accords with Smollett's habit in his art reviews of sending readers to view the originals in artists' studios and promoting projects that made art available to the general public. In the *Continuation* (2:414), for example, Smollett lauded the Duke of Richmond for opening a gallery-studio to the public. The reviewer's concern for national prestige also echoes Smollett's views: this project is potentialy "of national importance" and could, if done well, bring "honour to the kingdom" (409). Also, there is a verbal parallel: the reviewer's phrases "capital beauties and defects" and "capital pieces" echo Smollett's use of "capital beauties" and "a capital figure" in a single paragraph about an artist in *Humphry Clinker* (19 May, 75).

Volume 23   (*January to June 1767*)
214–16   George Colman, *The English Merchant.* Smollett reviewed

favorably an earlier Colman play, *The Jealous Wife* (see above, 11:132–41) and told Garrick he "respected [Colman] as a man of genius" (*Letters*, 98), which accords with the reviewer's favorable opinions here. The reviewer casually quotes the *Critical*'s title page motto—"nor set down aught in malice"—a motto Smollett had approved and perhaps even selected when the *Critical* was founded. The reviewer interjects a sympathetic anecdote about "our friend Thomson"; Smollett, who had been a friend and admirer of Thomson's, had warmly praised him in the *Continuation* (4:129) and in a review of his *Works* in 1762 (see above, 14:122–30) and had interjected tributes to Thomson into at least two other recent reviews (see above, 20:124–34 and 152–53). The reviewer shows intimate knowledge of Voltaire's *L'Ecossaise*, which Smollett, who had translated Voltaire's *Works* in 1761–65, could well do. A habitual Smollettian construction is used at the close: "We will venture to say that . . . as in any that ever appeared on the English or any other stage."

Volume 24 (*July to December 1767*)
226   *Miscellanies. The Lion, Cock, and Peacock; a Fable.* The reviewer's authoritative, wry, dismissive tone is like Smollett's: "It will always give us pleasure to be regarded as formidable by the corrupters of taste and enemies of public tranquillity"; compare with Smollett's editorial remarks in the *Critical* 1756 to 1763. The tone is also similar to the disdainful bemusement Smollett expressed in a private letter the month before this review appeared in which he credited "the Stings of my Grub street Friends" with keeping him alive (*Letters*, 133). The book resurrects the political controversies of the period 1760–63; the reviewer objects, much as Smollett would, to the revival of those painful animosities (226). The reviewer cleverly contrives a scatological joke exactly in Smollett's style: the book's dated subject matter moves the reviewer to say that these pieces of verse, because of "their extreme hardness, and the slowness of exoneration, seem to have lain in the author's bowels for a considerable time."

Appendix B
A List of Published Attacks on the *Critical Review* from 1756 to 1771

This list of attacks on the *Critical Review* is offered as a supplement to the lists compiled by Jones and Spector, who between them have discovered about 115 separate attacks on the *Critical* published between 1756 and 1771.* None of the following works is recorded by Jones or Spector, but all of them contain aspersions, mockery, or sustained invective aimed at the *Critical*. All of them either mention the *Critical* by name or otherwise identify it so specifically that it would have been unmistakable to a contemporary reader. (Some bibliographical detail is given only for the most obscure items.)

1755
> *The Public Advertiser*, 25 December 1755: [3], in an advertisement for the forthcoming *Literary Magazine* (to be edited by Samuel Johnson) that quotes and mocks advertisements for the forthcoming *Critical Review*.

1756
> [David Garrick], "A Recipe for a Modern Critic," *The Universal Visiter* 4 (April 1756): 191–92. Reprinted in the *St. James's Magazine* (February 1764): 362–63 and in *Beauties of the Magazines* 3 (March 1764): 106–7.
>
> [George Smith Green?], "To the Author," *Jackson's Oxford Jour-*

---

*See Claude E. Jones, *Smollett Studies* (Berkeley and Los Angeles: University of California Press, 1942), "Appendix B1: Attacks on the *Critical*, 1756–1771," 107–10; Robert D. Spector, "Attacks on the *Critical Review*," *The Periodical Post Boy* (June 1955): 6–7; and these six by Spector, all in *Notes and Queries*: "Further Attacks on the *Critical Review*," n.s., 2 (December 1955): 535; "Additional Attacks on the *Critical Review*," n.s., 3 (October 1956): 425; "Attacks on the *Critical Review* 1764–65, n.s., 5 (March 1957): 121; "Attacks on the *Critical Review* in the *Court Magazine*," n.s., 5 (July 1958): 308; "Attacks on the *Critical Review* in the *Literary Magazine*," n.s., 7 (August 1960): 300–301; "An Attack on the *Critical Review* in *Politcal Controversy*," n.s., 22 (February 1975): 14.

nal, 11 December 1756: [3].

[Samuel Johnson], "Reflections on the Present State of Literature," *The Universal Visiter* 4 (April 1756): 164.

The Literary Magazine 1 (May 1756): 29, in the poetry section in "An Occasional Prologue" by Arthur Murphy and a footnote to it (almost certainly by Johnson).

1757

Archibald Bower, Mr. *Bower's Reply to a Scurrilous Libel, intitled A Full Confutation, &c.* (1757).

———, *Mr. Bower's Answer to a New Charge Brought Against Him in a Libel, Intituled Bower and Tillemont Compared* (1757).

———, "To the Printer," *Gazetteer and London Daily Advertiser*, 5 February 1757.

[George Colman], *A Letter of Abuse, to D——d G——k, Esq.* (1757).

The Literary Magazine 2 (February 1757): 27–31.

The Literary Magazine 2 (March 1757): 75–76.

The Literary Magazine 2 (June 1757): 246–48.

The Literary Magazine 2 (July 1757): 289.

Dr. Thomas M'Donnel, *The Reviewers Reviewed* (1757), Cooke, 6d.

"Sampson Syllogism, a baker" [pseud.], *A Modest Apology in Defence of the Bakers* (1757).

1758

Mr. Bally, *The Day of Judgement, A Poem* (1758).

The Grand Magazine of Universal Intelligence 1 (November 1758): 578–79, in letters from "Philo" and from "E. D.," both apparently reprinted from *Lloyd's Evening Post*.

The Grand Magazine of Universal Intelligence 1 (May 1758): 220–22 in "A Defence of Mr. Worthington's Two Letters" (by Mr. Worthington?).

[George Smith Green?], *Jackson's Oxford Journal*, 13 May 1758, in an advertisement for Green's *Images of the Ancients*.

Owen's Weekly Chronicle, 16 December 1758: 291–92. "To the Author."

[John Shebbeare?], *A Seventh Letter to the People of England* (1758).

1759

An Apology for W[illiam]. P[itt]. Esq; In which the Conduct of L—— G—— B——h is vindicated (1759).

The Black Book; or, a Complete Key to the Late Battle at Minden (1759), 27–28.

[Thomas Comber?], *Owen's Weekly Chronicle*, 2 September 1759: 175, in an advertisement for Comber's *Vindication of the Great Revolution*.

The Gentleman's Magazine 29 (February 1759): 83–84, in a favorable review of Grainger's *Letter to Tobias Smollett*.

The Grand Magazine of Universal Intelligence 2 (May 1759): 261, a favorable review of Grainger's *Letter to Tobias Smollett.*

The Grand Magazine of Universal Intelligence 2 (September 1759): 486–87, "To the Author of the *Grand Magazine.*"

The Edinburgh Chronicle, 26 April 1759: 82–83, in an anonymous letter defending Wilkie's *Epigoniad*, apparently reprinted from *The London Chronicle.*

William Hawkins, *Jackson's Oxford Journal*, 15 September 1759, in an untitled address to the public.

[William Kenrick?], *The General Evening Post*, 25 January 1759, in an advertisement for Kenrick's *Scrutiny.*

"Dr. M'Gripes" [pseud.], *An Answer to that Heterogeneous Letter, Addressed to Dr. Wessels, of St. Mary-Axe* (1759).

1760

The Imperial Magazine 1 (September 1760): 475–76, reprinting Goldsmith's "Essay on Modern Criticism" from *An Enquiry into the Present State of Polite Learning in Europe.*

The Imperial Magazine 1 (October 1760): 519–20, "On the Present State of Literature in England."

1761

The Court Magazine 1 (November 1761): 138 and 177, former in the "Plays" review section and the latter in a letter from "R.T.W." at Bath.

The Library 1 (May 1761): 105, in a favorable account of Churchill's *Apology.*

The Life and Opinions of Bertram Montfichet (1761), 1: 26–27.

Arthur Murphy, *Ode to the Naiads of Fleet-Ditch* (1761).

Robert Lloyd, *An Epistle to Charles Churchill* (1761).

1762

James Boswell, *The Cub at Newmarket* (1762), viii–ix.

Charles Churchill, *The Rosciad* (1762).

A Continuation of the Address to the City of London (1762), Davies, 1s 6d.

The Court Magazine 2 (April 1762): 346 in "Estimate of TASTE and UNDERSTANDING."

[Robert Lloyd], *The St. James's Magazine* 1 (January 1762): 2–3.

————, *Poems* (1762).

The Patriot, 17 July 1762.

[James Ridley], "The Schemer," *The London Chronicle*, 24 August 1762. Reprinted in the collected *Schemer* (1763), 220–22.

[Cuthbert Shaw], *The Four Farthing-Candles, A Satire* (1762).

1763

The Court Magazine 3 (September 1763), in "The TEMPLE of SCANDAL."

[James Elphinston], *An Apology for the Monthly Review; with an Appendix in behalf of the Critical* (1763).

The St. James's Magazine 2 (May 1763): 108ff.

1764

Beauties of all the Magazines Selected 3 (June 1764): 241–43, "Inconsistency of the Reviews."

A Letter to a Young Lady on her Marriage (1764).

Lloyd's Evening Post, 14 January 1764, in a letter from "Crito."

The St. James's Magazine 3 (March 1764): 24–29 ("A Letter to the Editors" from "J. C."), 29 ("The Substance of a Conversation Concerning Churchill's *Gotham*"), and 51–54 ("An Apology to the Critical Reviewers" from "T. T.").

The Salisbury Journal, 26 March 1764, in an advertisement ("To the Public") for *The St. James's Magazine*.

1765

The Genuine Memoirs of Mr. Charles Churchill (1765), 120–21.

John Sayer (trans.), *The Temple of Gnidus: A Poem, from the French of Montesquieu* (1765).

1766

[Thomas Amory], *The Life of John Buncle*, vol. 2 (1766), "Advertisement," iv. Reissued in 1770 in four volumes, the "Advertisement" appears in vol. 3.

James Burges, *An Account of the Preparation and Management Necessary to Innoculation*, 2nd ed. (1766).

Oliver Goldsmith, *The Vicar of Wakefield* (1766), chap. 19.

[William Kenrick], *A Defence of Mr. Kenrick's Review of Dr. Johnson's Shakespeare* (1766), 20–21.

1767

Robert Houlton, *The Practice of Inoculation Justified* (1767).

The Nature of a Quarantine in Italy (1767), in the "Postscript."

The Political Register, and Impartial Review of Books 1, no. 2 (June 1767): 121–28 "The Reviewers Reviewed, in a Letter to the Editor"; continued in no. 3 (July 1767): 184–96 and no. 4 (August 1767): 269–72.

The Trial of England's Cicero (1767).

[Thomas Underwood], *The Impartialist* (1767).

A Very Old Thing, By an Upright Downright Very Odd Fellow (1767).

1768

Cobleriana, or the Cobler's Medley (1768), vol. 1, "Address to the Reviewers."

James Elphinston, in a letter printed in several newspapers, dated 6 December 1768; the text of the letter is reprinted in Elphinston, *The Hypercritic* (1783), 65.

T[homas] Underwood, *Poems & c.* (1768), in the following poems: "Liberty," "The Snarlers," and "An Epistle to a Friend."

1769

[William Kenrick], *Critical Memoirs of the Times*, vol.1 (26 January 1769).

———, *Critical Memoirs of the Times*, vol. 1 (10 February 1769).

Observations on the Review of the Controversy between Great Britain and Her Colonies (1769).

1770

[Richard Griffith], *Posthumous Works of a late Celebrated Genius
. . . The Koran* (1770), vol. 1, chap. 2, "The Critical Reviewers,"
8–10.

The Political Register, and Impartial Review of Books 6 (March
1770): 176, a review of Johnson's *False Alarm* by "M."

1771

The Gazetteer and New Daily Advertiser, 8 January 1771, "To the
Printer."

Appendix C
A Table of *British Magazine* Articles by Smollett, Johnson, Goldsmith, Garrick, and Richardson

The table below lists the articles contributed to the *British Magazine* during Smollett's editorship (1760–63) by five major authors: David Garrick, Oliver Goldsmith, Samuel Johnson, Samuel Richardson, and Smollett himself. (Those for which the authorship is established for the first time in this study are marked by an asterisk [*].)

British Magazine issue:

DAVID GARRICK

no. 5 [April–May], 1760
*"The Difficulty of Managing a Theatre." [Garrick may also have edited or arranged for some of the following favorable reviews of Drury Lane productions: 1 (1760): 709–10; 2 (1761): 86–88, 243–45, 313–16, 365–68, 413–15, 656–58; 3 (1762): 81–84, 132–33, 653–55; 4 (1763): 7–9, 81–84, 171–73.]

OLIVER GOLDSMITH

January 1760
*"A Parallel between the Gracchi and the Greatest Man of the Present Age."
*"The History of *Omrah*, the Son of *Abulsaid*. An Oriental Tale" (continued in February and March).

February 1760
"On the Different Schools of Music" (continued in April).
"A Reverie at the Boar's Head Tavern in Eastcheap" (continued in March and April).

no. 5 [April–May], 1760
*"Igluka and Sibbersik, a Greenland Tale."

May 1760
"The Effect Which Climates Have upon Men and Other Animals."
"A Dream" (The Fountains of Fine Sense and of Good Sense).
*"The History of Alcanor and Eudosia."

June 1760
"The Distresses of a Common Soldier."
*"A Parallel between Mrs. Vincent and Miss Brent."

July 1760
"The History of Carolan, the Last Irish Bard."
"A True History for the Ladies."

284

"A Dream" (The Mansions of Poetry and Taste).

"The History of Miss Stanton."

August 1760 ★"On the Proper Enjoyment of Life."

★"Reflections on National Prejudice."

★"On Pride."

★"On the Imprudent Fondness of Parents."

September 1760 ★"An Essay on Physiognomy."

October 1760 ★"Observations on Physiognomy."

"The Adventures of a Strolling Player."

December 1760 ★"An Essay on Instinct."

★"An Essay on Fascination. Translated from the *Spanish* of . . . *Padre Feijoo.*"

★"On the Approaching Coronation."

★"Essay on National Union."

July 1761 ★"On the Belles Lettres."

August 1761 ★"On the Belles Lettres."

September 1761 ★"On the Belles Lettres."

October 1761 ★"On the Belles Lettres."

December 1761 ★"On the Belles Lettres."

January 1762 ★"Proposals for Augmenting the Forces of Great Britain."

★"On the Belles Lettres."

February 1762 ★"On the Belles Lettres."

March 1762 ★"On the Belles Lettres."

April 1762 ★"On the Belles Lettres."

May 1762 ★"On the Belles Lettres."

June 1762 ★"On the Belles Lettres."

September 1762 ★"On the Belles Lettres."

November 1762 ★"On the Belles Lettres."

January 1763 ★"On the Belles Lettres."

SAMUEL JOHNSON

January 1760 *Idler* essay no. 89 (reprinted here "by permission of the Author.")

"The Bravery of English Common Soldiers" (three further *possible* attributions are discussed by Donald Greene, "Samuel Johnson, Journalist," in *Newsletters to Newspapers*, ed. Donovan H. Bond, 92 and 100).

SAMUEL RICHARDSON

April 1760 ★"To the Author of the *British Magazine*" (a reply to an essay the previous month on "The Different Schools of Musick").

TOBIAS SMOLLETT

January 1760– "The Adventures of Sir Launcelot Greaves" (continued monthly for twenty-five issues, January 1760 to December 1761).

January 1760– "An Account of New Books" (continued monthly from January 1760 to May 1763, some or all compiled by Smollett).

"History of Canada" (translated and edited by Smol-

	lett, continued monthly January 1760 to May 1763).
February 1760	"Ode to the Late Gen. Wolfe."
	*"Engravings by Strange" (Smollett probably wrote some or all of subsequent articles on works of art).
April 1760	"Ode to Blue Ey'd Ann."
no. 5 [April–May], 1760	"The Junto."
	"Morning in Spring, a Fragment."
June 1760	"Ode to Sleep."
July 1760	"Ode to Mirth."
August 1760	"To fix her-'twere a task as vain . . ."
October 1760	"Pastoral Ballad."
January 1761	"On Signor Tenducci's Singing *Jubal's Lyre*."

Notes

CHAPTER 1. GRAND DESIGNS

1. "To John Moore," 3 August 1756, Letter 29, *The Letters of Tobias Smollett*, ed. Lewis M. Knapp (Oxford: Clarendon Press, 1970), 46. All subsequent references to Smollett's letters will be to this edition, cited as *Letters*.

2. Thomas Sprat, *History of the Royal Society* (1667), ed. Jackson I. Cope and Harold Whitmore Jones (St. Louis, Mo.: Washington University, 1958), 39–45; Samuel Johnson, "Life of Roscommon," *Lives of the English Poets*, ed. George Birkbeck Hill (Oxford: Clarendon Press, 1905), 1:232–34; Matthew Prior, *Carmen Seculare for the Year 1700* (1701), stanza 34; Daniel Defoe, *An Essay Upon Projects* (1697), 227–51; Joseph Addison, *The Spectator*, no. 135 (4 August 1711); Jonathan Swift, *A Proposal for Correcting, Improving and Ascertaining the English Tongue* (1712); Voltaire, *Lettres sur les Anglais* (1733), no. 24, translated in Smollett's *Works of Voltaire*, vol. 13 (1762), "On the Royal Society and Academies," 176–83.

3. Sprat, *Royal Society*, 39–45.

4. Walter Graham, *The Beginnings of English Literary Periodicals: A Study of Periodical Literature, 1665–1715*, (New York: Oxford University Press, 1926), 22–59 and 196–207.

5. "To John Moore," 1 March 1754, Letter 20, *Letters*, 32.

6. In only one of the articles does he credit the source.

7. See Raymond F. Birn's useful study, *Pierre Rousseau and the philosophes of Bouillon*, vol. 29 of "Studies on Voltaire and the eighteenth century," ed. Theodore Besterman (Geneva: Institut et Musée Voltaire, 1964), 16 and passim.

8. See, for example, the *Critique désintéressée des journaux littéraires et des ouvrages des Savants* (1730), "par une société de gens de lettres," listed in Eugene Hatin, *Bibliographie historique et critique de la presse périodique française* (Paris: Librarie de Firmin Didot Frères, Fils et Cie., 1866), 42; and Birn, *Pierre Rousseau*, 46.

9. Quoted in Lewis M. Knapp, *Tobias Smollett, Doctor of Men and Manners* (Princeton: Princeton University Press, 1949), 172.

10. Birn, *Pierre Rousseau*, 153.

11. Graham, *Beginnings*, 196–207. As Graham notes, many of these editors were either emigrants from the Continent or closely connected with literary circles there.

12. Uta Janssens, *Matthieu Maty and the Journal britannique 1750–1755* (Amsterdam: Holland University Press, 1975), 19–20.

13. *Journal britannique*, 1:107f., quoted by Janssens, *Matthieu Maty*, 70; see also Janssens, 18–19 and 56–58.

14. Janssens, *Matthieu Maty*, 14 and 54–60.

15. *The True Briton* 4, no. 1:10.

16. Harris, *Observations upon the English language in a letter to a friend* [1752], 13–14, quoted in Allen Walker Read, "Suggestions for an Academy in England in the Latter half of the Eighteenth Century," *Modern Philology* 36 (1938):145–56.

17. [William Whitehead], *The World*, no. 19 (10 May 1753).

18. *Observations on the Importance and Use of Theatres; Their Present Regulation and Possible Improvements* (1759). See also *The Old Maid*, no. 2 (22 November 1755) and no. 4 (6 December 1755); Theophilus Cibber, *Two Dissertations on Theatrical Subjects* (1756); *The Theatrical Examiner* (1757), 88–89; *A Letter of Abuse to David Garrick* (1757), 7; and [James Ralph], *The Case of Authors by Profession or Trade* (1758), 62–63.

19. *The Works of William Collins*, ed. Richard Wendorf, 87–88, 190–94, and 215.

20. *The Covent-Garden Journal*, no. 1 (4 January 1752), ed. G. E. Jensen (New Haven: Yale University Press, 1915), 138. For other opinions Fielding shared with Smollett on the state of criticism, see his views on the following: neglected merit (no. 2:143), taste (no. 4:157), the need for authority to govern literature (no. 5:163–66 and no. 6:169–71), and the usefulness of learned societies and their publications (no. 41:366–68).

21. *Continuation* 2 (1760):414.

22. See *Rules and Orders of the Edinburgh Society for the Encouragement of Arts, Sciences, Manufactures, and Agriculture* (1765); *Letters*, 27; and Knapp, *Tobias Smollett*, 71, 121, and 160.

23. Knapp, *Tobias Smollett*, 168.

24. Read, "Suggestions for an Academy," 145–56.

25. See also: No '58, 386; Ja '59, 1; Oc '59, 323; Ja '60, 9–10; Se '62, 170.

26. "To Francis Hayman," 11 May 1750, Letter 8, *Letters*, 13.

27. Quoted from H. S. Buck, *A Study in Smollett, Chiefly "Peregrine Pickle"* (New Haven: Yale University Press, 1925), 6.

28. *Roderick Random*, 373–97; *Peregrine Pickle*, 637–66; *Ferdinand Count Fathom*, 7–8, 33–34, 247 and 264–65.

29. "To Alexander Carlyle," 1 March 1754, Letter 21, *Letters*, 33.

30. Knapp, *Tobias Smollett*, 167–69; C. E. Jones, *Smollett Studies* (Berkeley: University of California Press, 1942), 81–82.

31. [Joseph Reed], *A Sop in the Pan for a Physical Critick* (1759), 5.

32. "To John Moore," 11 December 1755, Letter 26, *Letters*, 42.

33. Unpublished manuscript letter in British Museum, Br. Mus. Add. MS 39867, ff. 113–113a.

34. Derek Roper, "Smollett's 'Four Gentlemen': The First Contributors to the *Critical Review*," *The Review of English Studies* (February 1959):38–44.

35. Roper, "Smollett's 'Four Gentlemen,'" 38–44.

36. "To Dr. George Macaulay," 6 April 1756, Letter 28, *Letters*, 45.

37. *Letters*, 46.

38. *Universal Visiter*, 1 (March 1756):139–40.

39. Roland B. Botting, "Johnson, Smart, and the *Universal Visiter*," *Modern Philology* 36 (1938–39):293–300.

40. *Old Maid*, no. 4, 6 December 1755.

41. *Old Maid*, no. 22, 10 April 1756.

42. One other interesting coincidence: Smollett's reference in 1754 to a rejected *Virginia* becoming an "old maid" in a gossipy letter to Carlyle (*Letters*, 34), which may have some connection with Brooke's idea for the periodical of that name she started in 1755. If so, then Smollett may have been one of the judges who read her essays in manuscript and encouraged her to publish them (*Old Maid*, no. 2, 22 November 1755).

43. He staged at least three separate presentations: 14 January 1756 at the Haymarket; 28 January at the Lecture Room in the Robin Hood near Temple Bar (Macklin's Coffee House);

and 18 March at the New Wells in Goodman's Fields. See P. H. Highfill, Jr., et al., *A Biographical Dictionary of Actors, Actresses, Musicians, Dancers, Managers and Other Stage Personnel in London 1660–1800* (Southern Illinois University Press, 1975), 3:258.

44. Cibber, *Two Dissertations on Theatrical Subjects* (1756), 61–62.

45. Benjamin C. Nangle, *"The Monthly Review" First Series 1749–1789. Index of Contributors and Articles* (Oxford: Clarendon Press, 1934), 9.

46. *Roderick Random*, 50, 277, and notes.

47. [Reed], *A Sop in the Pan*, 18–19.

48. The review gently chastises Cibber's attack on Garrick, but generally approves the rest; Smollett was hoping Garrick would stage his comedy *The Reprisal* in the coming season.

49. Highfill, *Biographical Dictionary of Actors* 3:258–59. Cibber's ship sank en route to Dublin and he drowned, along with most of the passengers, in October 1758.

50. Advertisements appeared in the *Public Advertiser* on 19 December 1755 and again on 24 and 30 December; they are quoted in full in Knapp, *Tobias Smollett*, 171–72 and below, in chapter 2.

51. Defoe, *Essay Upon Projects*, 250–51.

52. Knapp, *Tobias Smollett*, 196–202 and *Letters*, 52–54, 97–98, 103–4.

53. Birn, *Pierre Rousseau*, 21, and Hatin, *Bibliographie*, 24–27 and 28–32.

54. Birn, *Pierre Rousseau*, 21, n. 2.

55. *Continuation* 2 (1760):412.

56. *Continuation* 4 (1761):128.

57. *Continuation* 4 (1761):129–30.

58. See *Letters*, 85, 92, 95 and passim.

59. Knapp, *Tobias Smollett*, 271–72.

60. See, for example, the front page article "To the Public" in *The Evening Advertiser*, 8 January 1756.

61. Arnold, "Academies," *Cornhill Magazine* (August 1864), rpt. in *Essays in Criticism*, 2nd ed. (London: Macmillan, 1869); Levin, "War of Words," in *Contexts of Criticism* (Cambridge: Harvard University Press, 1957); John Barrell, "Language Properly," *English Literature in History 1730–80: An Equal, Wide Survey* (London: Hutchinson, 1983). See also James G. Basker, "Minim and the Great Cham: Smollett and Johnson on the Prospect of an English Academy," in *Johnson and His Age*, ed. James Engell (Cambridge: Harvard University Press, 1984), 159–61.

CHAPTER 2. THE YOUNG PRETENDER

1. *Lives of the English Poets*, 1:232–33 and 3:16.

2. "The Idler," no. 61. *The Universal Chronicle* 2 (16 June 1759), 185; rpt. in *The Idler and the Adventurer*, ed. W. J. Bate, John M. Bullitt, and L. F. Powell (New Haven: Yale University Press, 1963), vol. 2 of the Yale Edition of the Works of Samuel Johnson, 190.

3. See Smollett's two letters to Wilkes in Johnson's behalf, 16 March 1759 and 1 April 1759, *Letters*, 75–77.

4. Johnson, "Life of Roscommon," 232–34. For a fuller discussion of Smollett's and Johnson's differences on the academy issue, see Basker, "Minim and the Great Cham," 137–61.

5. *Public Advertiser*, 19 December 1755; repeated 24 and 30 December.

6. Knapp, *Tobias Smollett*, 92, 106–7, and 118. See also Albert H. Smith, "The Printing and Publication of Early Editions of the Novels of Tobias George Smollett," (Ph.D. diss., London University, 1976), 2:283.

7. "To John Moore," 19 August 1762, Letter 87, *Letters*, 108.

8. Smith, "Early Editions of Smollett," 2:283–84.

9. Knapp, *Tobias Smollett*, 330–31.

10. *The Public Advertiser*, 25 December 1755.

11. D. J. Greene, "Johnson's Contributions to the *Literary Magazine*," *RES*, n.s. 7 (1956): 367–92; also James L. Clifford, *Dictionary Johnson: Samuel Johnson's Middle Years* (London: Heinemann, 1979), 165–87.

12. *Boswell's Life of Johnson*, ed. George Birkbeck Hill, revised by L. F. Powell (Oxford: Clarendon Press, 1934), 1:284–85. See also Johnson's preface, "To the Public," *Literary Magazine* 1 (1756): [iii–iv].

13. The title "Annals of Literature" may have been suggested by the French journals *Les Cinq années litteraires* (1748–52) and *L'Année littéraire* (1754–90); see Hatin, 44–45. According to the *NCBEL* (*The New Cambridge Bibliography of English Literature*) 2, col. 1291–1301, no English journal with that phrase in its title had yet been published.

14. *Literary Magazine* 1 (1756): 29 and *Universal Visiter* 1 (1756): 164.

15. *London Chronicle*, 1 January 1757.

16. To John Wilkes, 1 April [1759], *Letters*, 77.

17. To John Wilkes, 16 March 1759, *Letters*, 75.

18. Smollett's letters to Wilkes of 16 March, 24 March, and 1 April 1759, *Letters*, 75–7; Johnson's contributions to the *British Magazine* are discussed below, in chapter 9.

19. *Continuation* 4 (1761): 127–28 and Boswell's *Life of Johnson* 5: 366–67.

20. Greene, "Johnson's Contributions to the *Literary Magazine*," 390–92.

21. This has made the *Monthly* and *Critical* invaluable not only to the literary historian, but to every scholar of the second half of the eighteenth century.

22. Knapp, "Ralph Griffiths, Author and Publisher 1746–50," *Library*, 4th ser., 20 (1939): 197–213.

23. The accusation is made by several contemporaries; see [John Shebbeare], *An Appendix to the Occasional Critic* (1757), 32; *The Battle of the Reviews* (1760), 76–77; and Edward Thompson, *The Demi-Rep* (1756 [for 1766]), 5–6.

24. See Knapp, *Tobias Smollett*, 118–19 and 132.

25. The most detailed studies are in Nangle, *"The Monthly Review" First Series 1749–89*, and in W. Denham Sutcliffe, "English Book-Reviewing 1749–1800," (D. Phil. diss., Oxford University, 1942).

26. Edward A. Bloom, "'Labors of the Learned': Neoclassic Book Reviewing Aims and Techniques," *Studies in Philology* 54 (1957): 537–63.

27. Roger Lonsdale, "New Attributions to John Cleland," *Review of English Studies*, n.s. 30 (1979), no. 119: 271 and 276.

28. Per Griffiths's own annotated copy, now in the Bodleian: 3:58 and 189–97. The following notes are based on his copy also.

29. *Monthly* 14:44–49.

30. *Monthly* 5:465–66.

31. *Monthly* 12, following 240 (Harvard copy).

32. Kenrick reviewed his own attack on the *Critical*, entitled *A Scrutiny, or, the Criticks Criticis'd* (1759) in the *Monthly* (20:219–24) and two of his own works of translation: Rousseau's *Eloise* (25:194–214 and 241–60) and Rousseau's *Emile* (27:212–17, 258–69, 342–58; continued in 28:1–14 and 81–96).

33. See the following advertisements in the *Monthly*: 1:79; 2:79–80 and 281; 7, bound in at the end, a list of seventy-one Griffiths publications; 8, bound in at the end, same list as in 7; 9:240; 11, between 160 and 161 is a four-page advertisement (Harvard copy); 13, on verso of last page of "Contents."

34. See Basker, "Tobias Smollett and Literary Journalism, 1756–1763" (D. Phil. diss., Oxford, 1983), appendix C, "Printed Attacks on the *Monthly Review*, 1749–1771," 429–37.

CHAPTER 3. THE MAN OF LETTERS AS REVIEW EDITOR

1. Roper, "Tobias Smollett and the Founders of his 'Review'," *Call Number* (University of Oregon publication) 19 (1957):4–9; revised as "Smollett's 'Four Gentlemen': The First Contributors to the *Critical Review,*" *Review of English Studies,* n.s. 10 (1959):38–44. All references are to the latter version.

2. See Knapp, ed., *Letters,* 46, n. 4, and 52, n. 8, and Paul-Gabriel Boucé, *The Novels of Tobias Smollett* (London: Longman, 1976), 19 and 197.

3. For permission to examine the volumes, I am indebted to the University of Oregon Library, Eugene, Oregon.

4. Griffiths's marked file is in the Bodleian Library; the various abbreviations he used for each author's name are recorded in Nangle, *"The Monthly Review" First Series 1749–89,* 1–47.

5. Boswell reported it: see *The Journal of James Boswell, 1765–1768,* vol. 7 of *Private Papers of James Boswell from Malahide Castle,* ed. Geoffrey Scott and Frederick A. Pottle (n.p.: [privately published], 1930), 189. See also Knapp, *Tobias Smollett,* 173 and n. 7.

6. For Hamilton's handwriting, see British Museum MS Add. 38730, ff. 86 and 104b.

7. John Nichols, *Literary Anecdotes of the Eighteenth Century* (1812), 3:399.

8. D. F. McKenzie, *Stationers' Company Apprentices 1701–1800* (Oxford: Oxford Bibliographical Society, 1978), 154.

9. Andrew Bisset, *Memoirs and Papers of Sir Andrew Mitchell* (1850), 1:37–46; see also the entry for Murdoch in the *Dictionary of National Biography* (*DNB* hereafter).

10. See appendix A.

11. Sutcliffe, "English Book Reviewing 1749–1800," 142–43; quoted by permission of Mrs. W. D. Sutcliffe.

12. "To Philip Miller," 20 January 1759, Letter 57, *Letters,* 74.

13. See appendix A.

14. *Court Magazine* 1 (1761), "Sentiments of different Persons on the Coronation," 1.

15. Alexander Carlyle, *Anecdotes and Characters of the Times,* ed. James Kinsley (London: Oxford University Press, 1973), 172.

16. Nichols, "George Steevens," *Minor Lives,* ed. Edward L. Hart (Cambridge: Harvard University Press, 1971), 53.

17. Daniel Lysons, *The Environs of London* 3 (1795):265, quoted by Knapp, *Tobias Smollett,* 276, n. 63; Nichols, *Illustrations of the Literary History of the Eighteenth Century* (1817) 2:399; *The Memoirs of Percival Stockdale* (1809) 2:57–58; Roper, *Reviewing before the "Edinburgh" 1788–1802* (London: Methuen, 1978), 21–22.

18. Nangle, *"The Monthly Review" First Series 1749–89,* 18–19.

19. *Monthly* 3:366–67.

20. *Monthly* 12:603–4.

21. *Monthly* 12:27–34, 145–46, 156–57, 191–99, 237, 378–79, 392, 395–96, 474–77; 13:78–79, 155, 300–301, 312, 467, 474–75; 14:44–49, 72–73, 76–78, 208–23, 356–59, 453, 579; 15:482–85, 627–29.

22. *Monthly* (Bodleian copy) 12:191–99; 14:208–23; 15:482–85. It is noteworthy that an unusually high percentage of the reviews of Griffiths's own publications are unannotated, fourteen of the twenty-nine. It seems unlikely that he did not know who reviewed so many of his own works; he may well have reviewed others too, forgetting, or not needing, to record his authorship.

23. *Monthly* 24:11–22, 67–73, 276–77, 358, 441–42; 25:146–49, 150–51, 225–26, 315, 394, 466–68, 473.

24. See also, *Critical* Ap '56, 265–66; My '56, 315–16; Jn '56, 481–83; Jl '56, 567–68, 570; Au '56, 87–88; No '56, 357–62, 377; De '56, 480–81.

25. Knapp, *Tobias Smollett,* 330–31.

26. Knapp, *Tobias Smollett*, 80–83; see also *DNB* articles, "John Armstrong" and "Patrick Murdoch."

27. Knapp, *Tobias Smollett*, 178, n. 32; see also *Letters*, 57.

28. "Proposals," *Public Advertiser*, 30 December 1755.

29. These and the following details from the *DNB*.

30. Knapp, "Dr. John Armstrong, Litterateur, and Associate of Smollett, Thomson, Wilkes, and other Celebrities," *PMLA* 59 (1944): 1019–58.

31. "To Alexander Carlyle," 1 March 1754, Letter 21, *Letters*, 36.

32. *DNB*.

33. *Boswell's Life of Johnson* 3:483.

34. [Ralph Heathcote], ed., *The New and General Biographical Dictionary* (1784), vol. 12: 674.

35. *Boswell's Life of Johnson* 1:457.

36. Knapp, *Tobias Smollett*, 178; *Letters*, 57.

37. "To John Moore," 12 May 1757, Letter 40, *Letters*, 57.

38. Roper, "Coleridge and the 'Critical Review'," *Modern Language Review* 55 (1960): 11.

39. Clifford, *Dictionary Johnson*, 166.

40. *Boswell's Life of Johnson* 1:456–57; *Boswell's London Journal 1762–1763*, ed. Frederick A. Pottle (London: Heinemann, 1950), 228 and 327; William Strahan in an unpublished letter to Ralph Griffiths in the Bodleian Library, MS Add. C. 89, f. 343.

41. *Humphry Clinker*, 26 April, 39 and 6 May, 62–63.

42. "To John Moore," 3 August 1756, Letter 29, *Letters*, 46.

43. "The Motives for Writing," *Court Magazine* 1 (1761): 167–69.

44. Knapp, "Griffiths's 'Monthly Review' as Printed by Strahan," *Notes and Queries*, n.s., 5 (1958): 216–17; R. A. Austen Leigh, "William Strahan and his Ledgers," *Library*, 4th ser., 3 (1923): 276.

45. Jones, "Smollett and the *Critical Review*," *Smollett Studies*, 80.

46. C. Lennart Carlson, *The First Magazine: A History of the Gentleman's Magazine* (Providence: Brown University Press, 1938), 241 and n. 1.

47. Although the *Monthly* had standardized these features by 1753, it was not this fully developed at its inception in 1749. For a summary of its early development, see Graham, *English Literary Periodicals* (New York: Thomas Nelson and Sons, 1930), 208–10.

48. The Public Record Office, London, King's Bench 1/14 Affidavits, Trinity Term, 32–33 George II. This copy was preserved as evidence in the Knowles libel case.

49. [John Shebbeare], *The Occasional Critic* (1757), quoted in *Lloyd's Evening Post and British Chronicle* 1 (21 October 1757): 316.

50. *True Briton* 3, no. 1:6.

51. Carlson, *First Magazine*, 53 and 130–32; see also copies preserved with wrappers in the Bodleian Library, Hope Adds. 1167.

52. *General Magazine of Arts and Sciences*, no. 45 (June 1758), preserved in the Bodleian, Vet. A5 d. 781.

53. *Grand Magazine of Magazines* 2, no. 10 (May 1751), in Bodleian Vet. A5 d. 783.

54. *Monthly* 31 (October 1764); single issue in covers, Houghton Library call number *51-2271.

55. Based on an examination of seven complete sets of the *Critical*: those in the University of Oregon Library, the Bodleian, the British Library, Harvard's Widener Library, the Huntington Library, and the Library of Congress, and a set formerly owned by William Dodd, now owned by the author.

56. See Basker, "Smollett and Literary Journalism," appendix D, 438–39, where the May 1758 covers are reproduced. See also references to the covers of the *Critical* in *Lloyd's Evening Post*, 21 October 1757 and the *General Evening Post*, 17 January 1759.

57. "To Samuel Richardson," 12 October 1760, Letter 73, *Letters*, 91–92. See also Smollett's "Hints for the Consideration of the Proprietors of the Universal History," reprinted in the *Monthly Magazine* 47 (1819): 328.

58. Roy McKeen Wiles, "The Relish for Reading in Provincial England Two Centuries Ago," in *The Widening Circle*, ed. Paul J. Korshin (Philadelphia: University of Pennsylvania Press, 1976), 95. After a new duty was passed in 1757, the cost per insertion rose by one shilling.

59. Robert Kerr, *Memoirs of William Smellie* (Edinburgh, 1811), 1: 434.

60. Based on a standard *Critical* advertisement size of about thirty lines and an average of twenty to thirty total insertions per month.

61. Knapp, "Griffiths's 'Monthly Review' as Printed by Strahan," *Notes and Queries*, n.s., 5 (1958): 216–17.

62. Austen Leigh, "Strahan and His Ledgers," 280.

63. James R. Sutherland, "The Circulation of Newspapers and Literary Periodicals, 1700–30," *Library*, 4th ser., 15 (1934): 124.

64. David Foxon, "Letter to the Editor," *Publishing History* 6 (1979): 113–15.

65. John W. Robberds, *Memoirs of the Life and Writings of William Taylor of Norwich* (1843) 1: 130–32; *Boswell's Life of Johnson* 4: 214; and *The Adventures of an Author* (1767) 1: 181–82; all cite two guineas per sheet as the rate. See also a mock account of an author's pay for various bits of journalism, including reviews at four pence each, in the *Court Magazine* 2 (1762): 271–72.

66. *Memoirs of Stockdale* 2: 57.

67. This would have been adding insult to injury for Derrick: as "trash reader," he was reviewing many more works for far less copy space than any of the others. In 1756 he reviewed seventy-four publications, but his longest printed review was only five pages (one-quarter sheet); most were only a page or two and many were only a few lines long.

68. Robberds, *William Taylor*, 1: 130–32.

69. Roper, "Smollett's 'Four Gentlemen,'" 43–44.

70. Armstrong had left by October 1757 at the latest because in that issue, Smollett stated positively that "of five persons engaged in writing the *Critical Review*, only one [i.e., Smollett himself] is a native of Scotland" (*Critical*, Oc '57, 333).

71. "To Dr. George Macaulay," 10 December 1756, Letter 31, *Letters*, 49.

72. "To John Moore," 19 August 1762, Letter 87, *Letters*, 108.

73. Donald D. Eddy, *Samuel Johnson: Book Reviewer in the Literary Magazine; or, Universal Review 1756–1758* (London: Garland Publishing, 1979), 79–81.

74. "To Philip Miller," 20 January 1759, Letter 57, *Letters*, 74.

75. Carlson, *First Magazine*, 149–50.

76. Knapp, *Tobias Smollett*, 183, n. 52. For other information about books for which Smollett subscribed, the writer is indebted to P. J. Wallis, Director of the "Books Subscription Lists Project," School of Education, University of Newcastle Upon Tyne. See also the project's publications, especially F. J. G. Robinson and P. J. Wallis, *A Preliminary Guide to Book Subscription Lists* (University of Newcastle Upon Tyne, 1972).

77. Eddy, *Johnson: Book Reviewer*, 98–99, n. 32.

78. *The Regicide* was first published by subscription "For the Author" and then in a trade edition for J. Osborn and A. Millar in 1749. No list of subscribers survives in any copy of the former and the texts of the two issues are typographically identical, suggesting that subscribers were so embarrassingly few that no list was ever published and the (perhaps considerable) stock of remainders was reissued with a new title page to stimulate sales.

79. According to P. J. Wallis (personal letter, 29 April 1980), and Knapp, *Tobias Smollett*, 183, n. 52, Smollett subscribed for:

James Nelson, *An Essay on the Government of Children* (1753).
Richard Rolt, *The Memoirs of James Lindesay* (1753).
Samuel Derrick, *A Collection of Original Poems* (1755).

80. "To Richard Smith Esq. of New Jersey," 8 May 1763, Letter 90, *Letters*, 113.

81. *Monthly* 12:150.

82. "To William Huggins," 7 December 1756, Letter 33, *Letters*, 50–51.

83. See also Jl '56, 528; Au '56, 88; Se '56, 188; and Oc '56, 280.

84. See also Oc '58, 314–15; Fe '59, 161; Ja '65, 17.

85. Manuscript letters in the Victoria and Albert Museum, 48.G 3/30, MSS 34, 41, and 43. Derrick's letters from Faulkner are published in *Prince of Dublin Printers: The Letters of George Faulkner*, ed. Robert E. Ward (n.p.: University Press of Kentucky, 1972), 49–74.

86. Unpublished letter to Derrick, Victoria and Albert Museum, 48.G 3/30, MS 34.

87. "To Samuel Derrick," 18 December 1759, *Letters of Faulkner*, 58.

88. [Fielding], *Covent-Garden Journal* 1, no. 5, ed. Jensen, 165; [Shebbeare], *Lydia; or Filial Piety* (1755), chap. 89.

89. *True Briton*, 1, no. 3:49–50.

90. John Ginger, *The Notable Man: The Life and Times of Oliver Goldsmith* (London: Hamish Hamilton, 1977), 117–18.

91. The statement appears in a review of *Monody on the Death of Major-General James Wolfe*, one shilling, Thrush.

92. *Critical* Ap '64, 288–89 and Ja '65, 17.

93. Eddy, *Johnson: Book Reviewer*, 79–80.

94. Eight-page advertisement bound in at the end of volumes 7 and 8 of the Bodleian's copy of the *Monthly*.

95. Four pages of advertisements printed in *A General Index to the Monthly Review* (Griffiths, 1760), [vi] and sigs. P3^r and P4^{r,v}.

96. For example, an advertisement for *A New System of Geography* (1764) assured the public of its quality by saying that "the Paper is the best that could be procured [and] the Printing is performed by Mr. *Archibald Hamilton*" (*Salisbury Journal*, 18 June 1764).

97. *Boswell's Life of Johnson* 2:226.

98. "To Dr. William Hunter," 14 June 1763, Letter 91, *Letters*, 114.

99. Knapp, *Tobias Smollett*, 330.

100. See Roper, "Smollett's 'Four Gentlemen,'" 43, and appendix A. Two reviews in the first issue were not assigned authors by Hamilton, but at least one of them was certainly by Smollett.

101. See appendix A.

102. *Public Advertiser*, 2 February 1756, quoted by Knapp, *Tobias Smollett*, 172.

103. Knapp, *Tobias Smollett*, 86–87 and 116–17.

104. It is sometimes difficult to determine what role the author ascribed to foreign articles actually performed, whether he was reviewing a foreign production himself, translating a review sent from abroad or gleaned from a foreign periodical, or merely forwarding some remarks made by one of his friends abroad. All three seem to have occurred.

105. Ascribed by Hamilton. See Roper, "Smollett's 'Four Gentlemen,'" 44.

106. Carlson, *First Magazine*, 149–50.

107. *Monthly* 15, "Advertisement," viii; 16 (February 1757):140.

108. Despite the erroneous title of address—"Dr."—which might have been presumed of a Cambridge professor, the addressee must be Francklin. No works by anyone whose name begins with "F" are reviewed in the March or April issues, nor are there in Hamilton's notes any unannotated reviews in those issues that might otherwise explain the "present" of an "ingenious performance" by Dr. F———.

109. Roper, "Smollett's 'Four Gentlemen,'" 39.

110. Roper, "Smollett's 'Four Gentlemen,'" 43–44. In the June, July, August and September issues combined, Smollett wrote only one article for the "Catalogue," but Francklin wrote fourteen, Derrick twelve, and Armstrong three.

111. Smollett wrote to Moore in 1758: "I consider the Church not as a religious but as a political Establishment so minutely interwoven in our Constitution that the one cannot be

detached from the other . . ." (*Letters*, 73).

112. "To Dr. George Macaulay," 14 December 1756, Letter 34, *Letters*, 52.

113. "To Samuel Richardson," 10 August 1756, Letter 30, *Letters*, 47–48.

114. "To John Moore," 2 January 1758, Letter 48, *Letters*, 65.

115. "To David Garrick," 5 April 1761, Letter 77, *Letters*, 98.

116. "To Garrick," *Letters*, 98.

117. James Prior, *Life of Oliver Goldsmith* (1837) 1:222. See also Thomas Percy manuscript notes, British Museum, Add. MS 42516, cited by Ginger, *Notable Man*, 105 and 337, n. 31.

118. Both letters are printed in Robberds, *William Taylor*, 1:122. See also Sutcliffe, "Book-Reviewing," 166–70.

119. Griffiths's correspondence in the Bodleian, quoted by Sutcliffe, "Book-Reviewing," 167–69.

120. See, for example, Nichols, "Thomas Davies," *Minor Lives*, 246.

121. Roper, "Coleridge and the 'Critical Review,'" 13.

122. For accounts of these working dinners, see Carlyle, *Anecdotes*, 172, and *Humphry Clinker*, 10 June, 124–33.

123. "To?," [?November–December 1757], Letter 47, *Letters*, 64. The editor, Knapp, does not identify the recipient of the letter but it can be shown to be Strahan by internal evidence referring to the printing of the second edition of *Peregrine Pickle* in 1758, which Strahan is now known to have printed. See Albert Smith, "Early Editions of Smollett," 1:173.

124. The supplements to the semiannual volumes were usually published in July and January, although sometimes they were as much as two months delayed.

125. *Gentleman's Magazine* 26:45–47 and 93–95.

126. See also Ja '56, 96; Mr '56, 288; Ap '56, 384; Oc '57, 311.

127. See also Oc '57, 376.

128. See also Au '57, 156; Se '57, 191; De '57, 462.

129. Another reviewer, noting this cycle of publishing seasons, lamented the crop of "literary mushrooms" that comes each winter (*Critical*, Oc '56, 275–76). The *Gentleman's Magazine* noticed the same cycle continuing in 1765 when, in its August issue, it listed only two new domestic publications and resorted to reviewing seven foreign works to make up the difference (25:384–89).

130. *Monthly* 3:375–93, 444–59; 4:70–80.

131. Sutcliffe, "Book-Reviewing," 79.

132. See *Peregrine Pickle*, 661–62; and *Briton*, no. 4:22.

133. Preface, *General Magazine and Impartial Review* 2 (1788):6.

134. A standard phrase in advertisements for supplementary issues to the *Monthly*. See, for example, the *General Evening Post*, 29 January 1759.

CHAPTER 4. A NEW CRITICAL VEHICLE

1. See appendix A.

2. *Critical*, Jl '56, 528–36, Au '56, 13–35, Se '56, 126–35; and *Critical*, Fe '57, 160–81, Mr '57, 227–43, Ap '57, 299–315. Internal evidence shows that, at least in the case of the latter, Smollett wrote the review serially rather than merely dividing a completed article into segments.

3. Per Griffiths's marked set of the *Monthly* (15:261f. and 361f.) in the Bodleian. See Nangle, *"The Monthly Review" First Series 1749–89*, 173–74.

4. *Critical*, Mr '56, 181–85; Ja/Fe '56, 94–96; My '56, 387; Jn '56, 479–80.

5. Editorial addresses: *Critical* Ja/Fe '56, "Preface," [i–ii]; Ja/Fe '56, 96; Ap '56, 287–88; Au '56, "Preface," [iii–iv]; Se '56, 188–92. Replies to correspondence: Mr '56, 192; Ap '56, 288; Jn '56, 484; Jl '56, 572; Au '56, 96; Se '56, 192; Oc '56, 288; No '56, 384; De '56, 482. See also

appendix A.

6. Johnson's reviews in *The Literary Magazine* 1–2 (1756–57) are listed in the *NCBEL*, vol. 2, col. 1141; Goldsmith's reviews in the *Monthly* in 1757 are reprinted in his *Works*, ed. Arthur Friedman (Oxford: 1966), 1: 3–141; Burke's reviews appear in *The Annual Register* 1–8 (1758–65), passim.

7. On Birch, see *Critical*, Ja/Fe '56, 41–53 and *The Literary Magazine* 1: 30–32; on Browne, *Critical*, Jn '56, 389–409 and *The Literary Magazine* 1: 176–85.

8. See *Critical*, Ap '56, 226–40 and *The Literary Magazine* 1: 35–38. It is interesting that in the three examples cited and in general Smollett was able—despite his obligation to cover dozens of works in each issue—to devote considerably more space to each review than was Johnson in the context of his miscellany.

9. *Monthly* 1: 66–67 and Sutcliffe, "Book-Reviewing," 330–32. See also Knapp, *Tobias Smollett*, 134.

10. *Monthly* 2: 250.

11. *Monthly* 16: 402.

12. For further discussion of the epitomizing conventions of early eighteenth-century book reviewing, see Graham, *English Literary Periodicals*, 196–201; Robert D. Spector, *English Literary Periodicals and The Climate of Opinion during The Seven Years' War* (The Hague: Mouton, 1966), 316–17; and Bloom, "Labors of the Learned," 537–50 and 555–58.

13. Roper, *Reviewing before the "Edinburgh" 1788–1802* (Newark: University of Delaware Press, 1978), 20.

14. Sutcliffe, "Book-Reviewing," 349–50.

15. "Proposals," quoted from Knapp, *Tobias Smollett*, 171.

16. Quoted from Knapp, *Tobias Smollett*, 171–72.

17. [Reed], *A Sop in the Pan*, 10.

18. Bloom, "Labors of the Learned," 557.

19. *Anecdotes of Polite Literature*, vol. 2, part 2, 10.

20. Rowland Jones, *The Philosophy of Words* (1769), 45.

21. [John Free], *The Monthly Reviewers Reviewed by an Antigallican* [1755], 5 and 17.

22. Quoted from an advertisement in *The Salisbury Journal*, 26 March 1764.

23. *Critical Memoirs* 1 (1769), 73.

24. Even today, the printing of excerpts and abridgements from recent books, without critical commentary, has not lost its popular appeal—as demonstrated by such successful periodicals as *Reader's Digest* and *Book Digest Magazine*.

25. "Butler Swift" [pseud.], *Tyburn to the Marine Society*, in the "Dedication."

26. James Ralph, *The Case of Authors by Profession or Trade Stated, with Regard to Booksellers, the Stage and the Public* (1758).

27. Clara Reeve, *The Progress of Romance* (Colchester, 1785), 2: 47 and 50–51; Lamb letter to Coleridge, 27 May 1796, *The Letters of Charles Lamb*, ed. E. V. Lucas (London: J. M. Dent & Sons and Methuen & Co., 1935), 1: 1.

28. Johnson, *The Literary Magazine* 1 (1756): 193.

29. Kenrick, *Critical Memoirs* 1 (1769): 73; *Monthly Review* 51: 280.

30. Untitled letter, *London Chronicle*, 20 May 1758, 484.

31. See Louis L. Martz, "Tobias Smollett and the *Universal History*," *Modern Language Notes* 56 (1941): 12–14 for a discussion of Smollett's reviews. See also appendix A.

32. *Peregrine Pickle*, chap. 103, 661.

33. Sprat, *Royal Society* (1667), 38–45; Defoe, *An Essay Upon Projects* (1697); Prior, *Carmen Seculare, For the Year 1700* (1701), stanza 34; Swift, *A Proposal for Correcting, Improving and Ascertaining the English Tongue* (1712); Addison, *The Spectator*, no. 135 (4 August 1711). See also Thomas Tickell, *On the Prospect of Peace* (1713) and Voltaire, "On the Royal Society and Other Academies" (1733).

34. [Reed], *A Sop in the Pan*, 5.

35. See also Se '56, 188; Ja/Fe '56, 75; No '56, 344–45.

36. Spector, *Climate of Opinion*, 324–28.

37. Sutherland, "Some Aspects of Eighteenth-Century Prose," in *Essays on the Eighteenth Century Presented to David Nichol Smith* (Oxford: Clarendon Press, 1945), 107–9.

38. Christopher Wordsworth, *Memoirs of William Wordsworth* (London, 1851), 2:459, cited in Fred W. Boege, *Smollett's Reputation as a Novelist*, Princeton Studies in English, 27 (Princeton: Princeton University Press, 1947), 80.

39. For examples of Smollett's opinion of French manners, see *Peregrine Pickle*, chap. 43, 204–10 and *Travels*, Letter 7, 52–62.

40. John Sekora, *Luxury: The Concept in Western Thought, Eden to Smollett* (Baltimore: Johns Hopkins University Press, 1977), 2–12, 135–37, and passim.

41. For examples, see: *Critical*, Mr '56, 172; Ap '56, 233, 243–44, and 247 (Latin); Oc '56, 280; No '56, 326 (French); Mr '56, 172 (Greek); Mr '56, 100 (Spanish).

42. *Travels*, Letter 21, 181.

43. See also Jl '56, 484; Se '56, 192; Oc '56, 288.

44. Hume, *Political Discourses* (1752). According to the *NCBEL* 2, col. 1874, this list was published separately in 1752 and was frequently included in editions of Hume's *Essays and Treatises on Several Subjects*. It was also reprinted in 1760, with additions by an anonymous correspondent, in *The Scots Magazine* 22:686–87, and again in *The Aberdeen Magazine* 1 (February 1761):104–6.

45. See Hume's letter to Robertson, 8 February 1759, in *New Letters of David Hume*, ed. Raymond Klibansky and Earnest C. Mossner (Oxford: Clarendon Press, 1954), 45.

46. *Boswell's London Journal 1762–1763*, ed. Frederick A. Pottle, Yale Editions of the Private Papers of James Boswell (London: Heinemann, 1950), 177.

47. See Adam Smith, *Lectures on Rhetoric and Belles Lettres*, especially the introduction by the editor John M. Lothian (Carbondale and Edwardsville, Illinois: Southern Illinois University Press, 1963, rpt. 1971), xxxi–xxxix.

48. Knapp, *Tobias Smollett*, 57–59.

49. *The Autobiography of Alexander Carlyle*, ed. John Hill Burton (London and Edinburgh: T. N. Foulis, 1860), 198–99.

50. See Spector, "Eighteenth Century Political Controversy and Linguistics," *Notes and Queries*, n.s. 2 (1955):387–89; Spector, *Climate of Opinion*, 95–99 and 142–45; and Sekora, *Luxury*, chap. 6, "The Politics of Peace: The *Briton* and the *Atom*."

51. O M Brack, Jr., and James B. Davis, "Smollett's Revisions of *Roderick Random*," *PBSA* (*Papers of the Bibliographical Society of America*) 64 (1970):304–305.

52. "To John Moore," 2 January 1758, Letter 48, *Letters*, 65.

53. See also Jl '56, 511; Se '56, 187; No '56, 373–74.

54. See the preface to *The Regicide*; the story of Melopoyn in *Roderick Random*, chaps. 61–63; the college of authors episodes in *Peregrine Pickle*, chaps. 101–2; and the digression on a "needy author" in *Ferdinand Count Fathom*, chap. 8.

55. See [Reed]'s *A Sop in the Pan*; James Grainger's *Letter to Tobias Smollet, M. D.* (1759); Shebbeare's *Occasional Critic*, or various others of the hundreds of attacks identified by Jones, Spector, and the present writer, in appendix B.

56. Not included in this or the following chart are articles in which no opinion is expressed.

57. "To John Harvie," 10 December 1759, Letter 67, *Letters*, 85.

CHAPTER 5. THE REPUBLIC OF LETTERS

1. [John Wilson], *Noctes Ambrosianae* (1829), cited in A. S. Collins, *The Profession of Letters: A Study of the Relation of Author to Patron, Publisher, and Public, 1780–1832* (London: Routledge, 1928), 226–27.

2. *Fathom*, dedication, 2–4 and chaps. 1, 7–8.

3. This and the following six books are mentioned, probably ironically, as works by "our modern authors that are worth reading" in *Fathom*. See 185 and n. 3.

4. Smollett reviewed it for the *Monthly* 5: 385–87.

5. Knapp, *Tobias Smollett*, 154 and n. 22, citing H. R. S. Van Der Veen, *Jewish Characters in Eighteenth Century Fiction and Drama* (Batavia, 1935), 41ff. See also *NCBEL*, 2, col. 997.

6. James R. Foster, "Smollett's Pamphleteering Foe Shebbeare," *PMLA* 57 (December 1942): 1076.

7. Smollett detects a plot device borrowed from *David Ranger* in his review of Murphy's *Apprentice* (Ja/Fe '56, 80).

8. Smollett, *Letters*, 11, and *Peregrine Pickle*, 682; Fielding, *Amelia*, bk. 8, chap. 5, and *Covent Garden Journal*, 7 January 1752.

9. *Monthly* 5: 385.

10. See Buck, *Smollett as Poet* (New Haven: Yale University Press, 1927).

11. Robert Foulis was an old friend of Smollett's, according to Knapp, *Tobias Smollett*, 28, 48, and 102. Most excerpts from works in foreign languages were translated into English; see, for example, Mr '56, 181–84.

12. *Complete History of England* 8: 102n. See also: *Advice*, 21; *Roderick Random*, 424 and 430; *Peregrine Pickle*, 604; *Ferdinand Count Fathom*, 240; *Humphry Clinker*, 94, 119, 596.

13. *History of England* 4: 323. Smollett's early satires *Advice* (1746) and *Reproof* (1747) were modelled on those of Pope (see Knapp, *Tobias Smollett*, 62–66). His novels are laced with allusions to Pope: *Roderick Random*, 75 and n. 3, 95 and n. 3, 195 and n. 3, and 383 and n. 1 (in which Melopoyn tries to emulate Pope's career); *Peregrine Pickle*, 2 and n. 1, 134 and n. 1, 538 and n. 1, 658 and n. 2, 659 and n. 2, 660 and n. 1; *Ferdinand Count Fathom*, 8 and n. 2; *Sir Launcelot Greaves*, 188 and n. 3, and 189 and n. 1; *Humphry Clinker*, ed. André Parreaux (Boston: Houghton Mifflin, 1968), 55 and 89 and notes. In the *Critical* itself, Smollett assumed the manner of Pope to rebuff the *Critical*'s first wave of attacks, borrowing such Popean lines as "dunce meets dunce, and jostles in the dark" and (vis-à-vis Smart and the *Universal Visiter*) "they wage no war with Bedlam and the Mint," (Ap '56, 287).

14. Johnson's review of Warton's *Essay* appeared in the *Literary Magazine* of 15 May 1756, about a fortnight after Smollett's in the April issue of the *Critical*.

15. Joseph Bunn Heidler, "The History, from 1700 to 1800, of English Criticism of Prose Fiction," *University of Illinois Studies in Language and Literature* 13, no. 2 (May 1928): 46–[57].

16. Roper, "Smollett's 'Four Gentlemen,'" 43–44.

17. William Park, "Change in the Criticism of the Novel after 1760," *Philological Quarterly* 46 (January 1967): 40–41.

18. Edward Niles Hooker, "The Reviewers and the New Criticism, 1754–70," *Philological Quarterly* 13 (April 1934): 189–202; Hooker, "The Discussion of Taste, from 1750 to 1770, and the New Trends in Literary Criticism," *PMLA* 49 (June 1934): 577–92; Hooker, "The Reviewers and the New Trends in Poetry, 1754–1770," *Modern Language Notes* 51 (April 1936): 207–14; Jones, "Poetry and the *Critical Review*, 1756–1785," *Modern Language Quarterly* 9 (March 1948): 17–36; Jones, "'The Critical Review's' First Thirty Years (1756–1785)," *Notes and Queries*, n.s. 3, no. 2 (February 1956): 78–80; Jones, "'The Critical Review,' and Some Major Poets," *Notes and Queries*, n.s., 3, no. 3 (March 1956): 114–15; Jones, "Dramatic Criticism in the *Critical Review*, 1756–1785," *Modern Language Quarterly* 20 (March 1959): 18–26, 133–44.

19. Hooker, "The Reviewers and the New Trends in Poetry," 214.

20. Jones, "'The Critical Review's' First Thirty Years," 80.

21. Spector, *Climate of Opinion*, 316–43.

22. "To Samuel Richardson," 10 August 1756, Letter 30, *Letters*, 47.

23. Compare Smollett on Marsh's *Winter's Tale . . . alter'd from Shakespeare* (Mr '56, 144–45) with Francklin on Garrick's *Catharine and Petruchio . . . alter'd from Shakespeare's Taming of the Shrew* (Mr '56, 145–46).

24. See appendix A for evidence of Smollett's authorship.

25. "To John Moore," 2 January 1758, Letter 48, *Letters*, 65.

26. Spector, *Climate of Opinion*, 332–33. That Smollett did not agree with or endorse the review in no way invalidates Spector's argument that it was typical of drama criticism at this time.

27. Northrop Frye, "Towards Defining an Age of Sensibility," *ELH, a Journal of English Literary History*, 23 (June 1956): 144–52, rpt. in *Eighteenth Century English Literature: Modern Essays in Criticism*, ed. James L. Clifford (New York: Oxford University Press, 1959), 311–18.

28. René Wellek, *The Later Eighteenth Century* (New Haven: Yale University Press, 1955), vol. 1 of *A History of Modern Criticism: 1750–1950*, 30.

29. Bertrand Harris Bronson, "When Was Neoclassicism?" in *Facets of the Enlightenment: Studies in English Literature and Its Contexts* (Berkeley: University of California Press, 1968), 3–4.

30. Pope, "An Essay on Criticism," in *The Poems of Alexander Pope*, ed. John Butt (London: Methuen, 1963), 149, ll. 152–53.

31. Johnson, "Preface to Shakespeare," *Johnson on Shakespeare*, 7 in *The Yale Edition of the Works of Samuel Johnson* (New Haven: Yale University Press, 1968), 67.

32. Quoted here as the *Critical* prints it. In later editions, Warton revised the wording; see William Darnall MacClintock, *Joseph Warton's Essay on Pope: A History of the Five Editions* (Chapel Hill: University of North Carolina Press, 1933), 34–70.

33. *Literary Magazine* 1 (15 May 1756): 37.

34. Joan Pittock, *The Ascendancy of Taste: The Achievement of Joseph and Thomas Warton* (London: Routledge and Kegan Paul, 1973), 1.

35. Pittock, *Ascendancy of Taste*, 151.

36. Pittock mentions reviews in the *Monthly* and the *Literary Magazine*, but not the *Critical*; see *Ascendancy of Taste*, 151–54.

37. Knapp, *Tobias Smollett*, 49–57 and 106–8.

38. Including an opera, *Alceste*, and another farce, *The Absent Man*. See Knapp, *Tobias Smollett*, 86–92 and 196–202.

39. Richard W. Bevis, "Smollett and *The Israelites*," *Philological Quarterly* 45 (1966): 387–94, and Basker, "Another Smollett Play?" *Notes and Queries*, n.s. 27, no. 1 (February 1980): 33–34.

40. See appendix A.

41. See also Charles Harold Gray, *Theatrical Criticism in London to 1795* (New York: Columbia University Press, 1931), 154.

42. *Literary Magazine* 1 (15 May 1756): 29.

43. Quoted and discussed in Boucé, 15.

44. See Murphy's attacks on Smollett in his *Poetical Epistle to Mr. Samuel Johnson, A. M.* (1760) and *Ode to the Naiads of Fleet-Ditch* (1761).

45. See Buck, *A Study in Smollett*, 86–94.

46. 'To Dr. Macaulay," 24 November 1756, Letter 32, *Letters*, 50; "To David Garrick," [ca. January 1757], Letter 35, *Letters*, 53.

47. "To David Garrick," 4 February 1757, Letter 36, *Letters*, 54.

48. Knapp, *Tobias Smollett*, 199.

49. "To David Garrick," [ca. January 1757], Letter 35, *Letters*, 53. See also Shebbeare, *Appendix to the Occasional Critic* [1757], 24.

50. Buck, *A Study in Smollett*, 93–94 and Knapp, *Tobias Smollett*, 196–202, 209–210, and 273.

51. *Sir Launcelot Greaves*, 26 and *Continuation* 4 (1761):126.

52. Knapp, *Tobias Smollett*, 198, 236, 273; "To David Garrick," 27 January 1762, Letter 83, *Letters*, 103.

53. George Winchester Stone, Jr., and George M. Kahrl, *David Garrick: A Critical Biography* (Carbondale and Edwardsville: Southern Illinois University Press, 1979), 342.

54. *Peregrine Pickle*, 273–75 and 651–52.

55. [Reed], *A Sop in the Pan*, 18–19.

56. *Maxims* is ascribed by Roper (42) to "Fulke and Frances Greville."

57. See a similar statement in *The Present State of All Nations* 2:215 and a passage in *Ferdinand Count Fathom*, both pointed out by Damian Grant, ed. *Ferdinand Count Fathom*, 101 and n. 2.

58. *Journal encyclopédique*, Tome 1: janvier 1756, 58–61 and 95–97.

59. *Journal encyclopédique*, Tome 1: janvier 1756, 120–22.

60. Smollett and Francklin, eds., *The Works of Voltaire* (1761–65), 35 vols. See also Eugène Joliat, "Smollett, Editor of Voltaire," *Modern Language Notes* 54 (June 1939):429–36.

61. Knapp, *Tobias Smollett*, 186–87.

62. Advertisement, *Pope's Bath Chronicle*, 12 December 1765.

63. Knapp, *Tobias Smollett*, 226–27.

64. Martz, *The Later Career of Tobias Smollett* (New Haven: Yale University Press, 1942), 7.

65. Two other "histories"—Birch's *History of the Royal Society* and Patrick Browne's *Civil and Natural History of Jamaica*—are really books about science and natural history and are treated as such by Smollett in his reviews. See below, chap. 6.

66. Joliat, *Smollett et La France* (Paris: Librairie Ancienne Honoré Champion, 1935), 213–14, cited in Knapp, *Tobias Smollett*, 186.

67. See, for example, Thomas Comber, *A Vindication of the Great Revolution in England . . . as Misrepresented by the Author of the Complete History of England* (1758).

68. See a letter on "The Character of King James I," *The Oxford Magazine* 1 (1768):211 and the ensuing correspondence, 2 (1769):16 and 93.

69. See also Greene, "Smollett the Historian: A Reappraisal," in *Tobias Smollett: Bicentennial Essays Presented to Lewis M. Knapp*, ed. G. S. Rousseau and P.-G. Boucé (New York: Oxford University Press, 1971), 50 and n. 35.

70. See a letter from "S. Watson" of Shropshire, *Gentleman's Magazine* 28 (April 1758):161–63.

71. Greene, "Smollett the Historian," 45–54.

72. Greene, "Smollett the Historian," 25–56.

73. Greene, "Smollett the Historian," 31–39; Priestley, *The Rudiments of English Grammar, adapted to the Use of Schools* (1768).

74. Greene, "Smollett the Historian," 31.

75. "To John Moore," 28 September [?1758], Letter 56, *Letters*, 73.

76. Letter to Andrew Millar, 17 May 1762, *The Letters of David Hume*, ed. J. Y. T. Grieg (Oxford: Oxford University Press, 1932), 1:359.

77. Letter to Andrew Millar, 6 April 1758, *Letters of Hume*, 1:273–74.

78. Letter to William Robertson, 12 March 1759, *Letters of Hume*, 1:302.

79. [To David Hume], 31 August 1768, Letter 103, *Letters*, 136.

CHAPTER 6. "HIS SEVERAL PROVINCES"

1. Roper, "Smollett's 'Four Gentlemen,'" 38–44.

2. Ronald Paulson, *Hogarth: His Life, Art, and Times* (New Haven: Yale University Press, 1971), 231.

3. Although Smollett uses only surnames in discussing these well-known artists of the time, thus obscuring the identities of the less memorable, this list seems correct. For instance, there were several artists called Hamilton but *Gavin* Hamilton was working in London in 1756, painted and drew allegorical scenes, and received the patronage of the Duke of Bedford. See Ellis Waterhouse, *The Dictionary of 18th Century Painters in Oils and Crayons* (Woodbridge, Suffolk: Baron Publishing, for Antique Collectors' Club, 1981), 155. Smollett consistently renders Rysbrack's name as "Riesbach." His mistaken attribution of *Diana and Endymion* to Rysbrack (Ja/Fe '56, 96) is quickly corrected in the next issue (Mr '56, 192) to "Plura," the Italian-born sculptor Giovanni Battista Plura, who had lived in England since the 1740s and died in London in 1756. See Robert Gunnis, *Dictionary of British Sculptors 1660–1851* (Cambridge: Harvard University Press, 1954), 309.

4. See, for example, *Gentleman's Magazine* 3 (1733): 422; 8 (1738): 349; 22 (1752): 379; and *London Magazine* 4 (1735): 390 and 22 (1753): 437.

5. Andrew Shirley, ed., [sic] "Painting and Engraving," in *Johnson's England: An Account of the Life and Manners of His Age*, ed. A. S. Turberville (1933; rpt. Oxford: Clarendon Press, 1952), 2: 49.

6. William T. Whitley, *Artists and Their Friends in England 1700–1799* (London and Boston: The Medici Society, 1928), 1: 167.

7. Whitley, *Artists and Their Friends* 1: 167–68 and Shirley, "Painting and Engraving," 55–56.

8. Gunnis, *Dictionary of British Sculptors*, 434–35.

9. "Proposals," quoted by Knapp, *Tobias Smollett*, 171.

10. "To Dr. Macaulay," 14 December 1756, Letter 34, *Letters*, 52.

11. Whitley, *Artists and Their Friends* 1: 156–66.

12. "To Francis Hayman," 11 May 1750, Letter 8, *Letters*, 13–14.

13. Whitley, *Artists and Their Friends* 1: 165.

14. Laurence Sterne, *A Sentimental Journey through France and Italy*, ed. Gardner D. Stout, Jr. (Berkeley: University of California Press, 1967), 117–18.

15. Frank Felsenstein, introduction, *Travels*, lviii–lxv.

16. Robert Etheridge Moore, *Hogarth's Literary Relationships* (Minneapolis: University of Minnesota Press, 1948), 166.

17. *Travels*, Letter 28, 241.

18. *Humphry Clinker*, 19 May, 76.

19. Boucé, *Novels of Smollett*, chap. 2, "Autobiography and the Novels," 40–67.

20. *Humphry Clinker*, 19 May, 76.

21. *Travels*, Letters 28 and 31–33, 233–41 and 263–92.

22. *Travels*, Letter 28, 238.

23. David Bindman, *Hogarth* (New York: Oxford University Press, 1981), 190–91. See also Frederick Antal, *Hogarth and His Place in European Art* (London: Routledge & Kegan Paul, 1962), 154–55 and, for a negative opinion, Paulson, *Hogarth*, 2: 228–34.

24. Bindman, *Hogarth*, 190. See also Joseph Burke, *English Art 1714–1800* (Oxford: Clarendon Press, 1976), 159.

25. Waterhouse, *Dictionary of 18th Century Painters*, 155.

26. "To Dr. Macaulay," 14 December 1756, Letter 34, *Letters*, 51. It should be noted that this is the same letter in which Smollett asks Macaulay for an article on a work of art.

27. *Humphry Clinker*, 19 May, 76.

28. Moore, *Hogarth's Literary Relationships*, 166–67. Moore's identification of the artist as William Taverner rather than John Taylor does not affect the main point. See Knapp, ed., *Humphry Clinker*, 75 and n. 3.

29. Knapp, *Tobias Smollett*, 164–65, 187, and 227; *British Magazine* 1–3 (1760–62), illustra-

tions passim.

30. *London Evening Post*, 3 August 1754.

31. Knapp, introduction, *Letters*, xxi. See also Knapp, *Tobias Smollett*, 183 and n. 53, and *Chelmsford Chronicle*, 8 November 1771. The portraits by Gainsborough, Reynolds, and the "Voltaire" portrait painter have not been located.

32. Spector, *Climate of Opinion*, 208.

33. *Monthly* 5: 465–66 and 7: 52–56. See also Knapp, *Tobias Smollett*, 135–40.

34. The extent of the curriculum Smollett may have followed is examined in Knapp, *Tobias Smollett*, 14–17.

35. Knapp, *Tobias Smollett*, 135–45 and notes; Spector, *Climate of Opinion*, 208–12 and notes; G. S. Rousseau, "'No Boasted Academy of Christendom': Smollett and the Society of Arts," *Journal of the Royal Society of Arts* 121 (June 1973): 468–75, continued in July: 532–35, and August: 632–38; Rousseau, *Tobias Smollett: Essays of Two Decades* (Edinburgh: T. & T. Clark, 1982), chaps. 1, 7, 8, and 10–12; Richard A. Hunter and Ida Macalpine, "Smollett's Reading in Psychiatry," *Modern Language Review* 51 (July 1956): 409–11; Jane M. Oppenheimer, "John and William Hunter and Some Contemporaries in Literature and Art," *Bulletin of the History of Medicine* 23 (1949): 21–47; and Oppenheimer, "A Note on William Hunter and Tobias Smollett," *Journal of the History of Medicine and Allied Sciences* 2 (1948): 481–86.

36. Rousseau, "'No Boasted Academy of Christendom,'" 472–73.

37. *Continuation* 4: 132.

38. *Continuation* 4: 15–16.

39. Rousseau, "'No Boasted Academy of Christendom,'" 470–72.

40. See "To Samuel Richardson," 4 April 1759, Letter 61, *Letters*, 78.

41. *Travels*, Letter 22, 184.

42. Spector, *Climate of Opinion*, 209 and 211.

43. *Literary Magazine* 1 (1756): 136–40, 30–31, 95–96, 168, and 225–26.

44. *Literary Magazine* 1 (1756): 139 and 229.

45. *Literary Magazine* 1 (1756): 193.

46. *Literary Magazine* 1 (15 August 1756): 193.

47. See appendix A.

48. Greene, "Johnson's Contributions to the *Literary Magazine*," *RES*, n.s. 7 (1956): 390–92.

49. "To John Moore," 3 August 1756, Letter 29, *Letters*, 46.

50. See: Roper, "The Politics of the *Critical Review*, 1756–1817," *Durham University Journal* 53 (June 1961): 117–22; Spector, *Climate of Opinion*, 30–32, 47–48, 84–85, 95–99, and 143–45; Greene, "Smollett the Historian," 49–54; Donald Bruce, "Smollett and the Sordid Knaves," *Contemporary Review* 220 (March 1972): 133–38; Robin Fabel, "The Patriotic Briton: Tobias Smollett and English Politics, 1756–1771," *Eighteenth Century Studies* 8 (Fall 1974): 100–114; Sekora, *Luxury*, 135–238.

51. See, for example, Roper, "The Politics of the *Critical Review*," 117.

52. See especially the articles by Roper, Greene, Bruce and Fabel cited above, n. 50.

53. See also *Candide*, chap. 24, where Candide is horrified at Byng's fate.

54. *Literary Magazine* 1 (1756): 305, 309 and 351.

55. Greene, ed., *Political Writings*, vol. 10 of *The Yale Edition of the Works of Samuel Johnson* (New Haven: Yale University Press, 1977) 213–17. See also Bate, *Samuel Johnson* (New York: Harcourt Brace Jovanovich, 1975), 328.

56. Spector, *Climate of Opinion*, 30.

57. *Continuation* 1: 323; see also 315–39, 457–64, and 470–80.

58. *Continuation* 1: 478.

59. *Atom*, 268–69.

60. *Atom*, 262.

61. Thus the organizing principle of Spector's useful study, *English Literary Periodicals and the Climate of Opinion During the Seven Years' War*; see especially 13–61.

CHAPTER 7. "TIED DOWN TO THE STAKE"

1. "To Dr. Macaulay," 14 December 1756, Letter 34, *Letters*, 52.

2. "To John Moore," 4 June 1757, Letter 41, *Letters*, 58.

3. "To John Moore," 2 January 1758, Letter 48, *Letters*, 65.

4. "To John Moore," 28 September [?1758], Letter 56, *Letters*, 73.

5. See appendix A.

6. Appendix A.

7. Smollett prepared at least two works by other writers for the press in 1757–58, both for William Strahan (*Letters*, 62 and 64).

8. "To Philip Miller," 20 January 1759, Letter 57, *Letters*, 74, and "To John Wilkes," 1 April 1759, Letter 60, *Letters*, 77. In a note to Letter 60, Knapp conjectures that Johnson's complaint was prompted by the review of his *Prince of Abissinia* in the April issue (Ap '59, 372–75), but this is impossible, as that issue would not have appeared until ca. 1 May; Johnson was actually responding to remarks about him in the review of Grainger's *Letter to Tobias Smollet* [sic] (Fe '59, 154–56), written by Smollett himself (see appendix A).

9. "To John Wilkes," 20 April 1759, Letter 62, *Letters*, 79–80.

10. "To William Huggins," 25 February 1761, Letter 76, *Letters*, 96.

11. "To David Garrick," 5 April 1761, Letter 77, *Letters*, 98.

12. "To John Moore," 19 August 1762, Letter 87, *Letters*, 108.

13. "To Richard Smith Esq. of New Jersey, North America," 8 May 1763, Letter 90, *Letters*, 113.

14. Martz, *Later Career of Smollett*, 29.

15. Martz, "Tobias Smollett and the *Universal History*," *Modern Language Notes* 56 (1941): 11.

16. Roper, "Smollett's 'Four Gentlemen,'" 38–44.

17. See appendix A for the following reviews: My '57, 385–98; Jn '57, 550–52; Jl '57, 83–85; Mr '58, 196–98; De '58, 439–53, 475–82 and 506–8; Mr '59, 274–75; Jl '59, 82–83; My '60, 417–19; Oc '60, 319–20; Ja '61, 73–75; My '61, 409–11; De '61, 405–18; Ja '62, 45–53; Mr '62, 272; Jn '62, 495–99; Fe '63, 120–26 and 200–209.

18. [Reed], *A Sop in the Pan*, 19.

19. The exception was Grainger's *Translation of the Elegies of Tibullus* which Smollett treated with unrelenting harshness (De '58, 475–82), fostering a violent paper quarrel between them.

20. Bailey Saunders, *The Life and Letters of James Macpherson* (London: Swan Sonnenschein, 1894), 172. The *Critical*'s reception may have had a lasting effect on Macpherson, if it was true—as an anonymous pamphlet suggested—that by the 1770s he had joined the staff of the *Critical*. See *The Reviewers Reviewed* (1779), 18.

21. *Monthly* 26:141. Ironically, the *Monthly* reviewer was also of Scottish descent: Charles Miller, son of Smollett's friend and occasional reviewer, Philip Miller. See Nangle, *The Monthly Review Second Series 1790–1815* (Oxford: Clarendon Press, 1955), 44–45.

22. Spector, *Climate of Opinion*, 336–37.

23. *Humphry Clinker*, 3 September, 240.

24. Quoted from Catherine Hutter, trans., *The Sorrows of Young Werther*, by Johann Wolfgang von Goethe (New York: New American Library, 1962), 90.

25. [Reed], *A Sop in the Pan*, 18–19.

26. "To William Huggins," 7 December 1756, Letter 33, *Letters*, 50–51. See also their continuing correspondence in *Letters*, 54–56, 59–61, 67–72, 83–84, and 94–97.

27. Frederick A. Pottle, *James Boswell: The Earlier Years 1740–69* (London: Heinemann, 1966), 475.

28. Philip J. Klukoff, "Smollett and the *Critical Review*: Criticism of the Novel" (Ph.D. diss., Michigan State University, 1965).

29. Klukoff, for example, ingeniously but not always convincingly attributes some fourteen reviews to Smollett, almost all of which—perhaps too felicitously—are of major works such as Burke's *Inquiry into the Sublime and the Beautiful*, Johnson's *Rasselas*, Adam Smith's *Theory of Moral Sentiments*, and Rousseau's *Eloisa*. See Klukoff, "Smollett and the *Critical Review*," 96–100, 108–12, 118–30, and 138. However, some of his attributions are based on compelling evidence and are included in appendix A.

30. See appendix A for the following reviews: Fe '59, 184; Jn '59, 550–54; Jl '60, 70–72; Se '60, 241–42; Ap '61, 314–17; Au '61, 131–38; My '62, 392–97; Ja '63, 13–21; and Mr '63, 209–10.

31. See discussion in appendix A, under Mr '58, 199–206. For more detail on the Smollett-Cleland connection, see Basker, "The Wages of Sin: The Later Career of John Cleland," *Etudes anglaises* 40 (1987): 178–94.

32. Foster, "Smollett's Pamphleteering Foe Shebbeare," 1053–1100.

33. Smollett appears to have reviewed *Candide* both in the original and in translation: see appendix A, Jn '59, 550–54 and Au '61, 131–38. Smollett evidently reviewed volumes 3 and 4 of *Tristram Shandy* (Ap '61, 314–17); he may also have reviewed the other volumes, but those reviews lack distinctive signs of his authorship and are not attributed to him in appendix A.

34. See appendix A for the following reviews: Ja '57, 62–74; No '57, 385–95; Fe '58, 136–44; Mr '58, 177–88; Au '58, 100–18; Se '58, 226–39; Ja '59, 1–14; Ap '59, 289–303 and 337–56; Jl '59, 44–54; Se '59, 189–99; Fe '60, 81–92; Mr '60, 161–77; Ap '60, 245–60; Jl '60, 1–19; Au '60, 81–90; Se '60, 161–78 and 186–94; No '60, 372–85; Ja '61, 5–18 and 36–45; Fe '61, 81–91 and 116–22; Mr '61, 217–33; Au '61, 81–103; Se '61, 161–78; No '61, 321–35; No '61, 390–92; Fe '62, 107–20; My '62, 381–92; Oc '61, 241–49; De '61, 401–10.

35. Martz, "Smollett and the *Universal History*," 1–14.

36. See appendix A for the following reviews: Ja '57, 62–74; Fe '58, 136–44; Mr '58, 177–88; Au '58, 100–118; Ap '59, 337–56; No '60, 372–85, Ja '61, 36–45; Fe '61, 116–22; No '61, 390–92.

37. Martz, "Smollett and the *Universal History*," 10–11.

38. For example, see the series of advertisements for Smollett's and Tindal's histories in *Jackson's Oxford Journal* in 1759 (issues for 18 and 25 February and 4, 11, 18, and 25 March) which contain charges, counter-charges, and ever-escalating inducements for buyers.

39. See appendix A, Ja '59, 1–14, and Martz, "Smollett and the *Universal History*," 12–14.

40. Martz, "Smollett and the *Universal History*," 12 and 14.

41. "To ?Samuel Richardson," 1 May 1760, Letter 70, *Letters*, 89.

42. "To ?Samuel Richardson," 12 October 1760, Letter 73, *Letters*, 91 and n. 3.

43. "To ?Samuel Richardson," 12 October 1760, Letter 73, *Letters*, 91–92.

44. Quoted in Knapp, *Tobias Smollett*, 243–44, n. 96.

45. Knapp, *Tobias Smollett*, 243.

46. *Critical*, Se '61, 167 and 182–86; No '62, 360–70; and My '63, 361–67. Smollett endorsed *The Question of the Precedency of the Peers of Ireland in England* (Se '61, 182–86), originally published in 1739 and now republished by the earl's son, the second Earl of Egmont, perhaps with the assistance of Burke who was at this time compiling and editing other pamphlets for him (*The Correspondence of Edmund Burke*, ed. Thomas W. Copeland [Cambridge: Cambridge University Press, 1958], 1: 124 and n. 5).

47. *Correspondence of Edmund Burke*, 1: 201.

48. See appendix A. Three further articles on art that are not by Smollett: Fe '57, 173–74; Jl '59, 70–81; Jn '63, 483–84.

49. Oc '63, 313–14; Ap '64, 298–99; Se '68, 219–22.

50. Jones, "Contributors to *The Critical Review* 1756–1785," *Modern Language Notes* 61 (1946): 433–41.

51. Knapp, "Comments on Smollett by the Rev. Dr. Thomas Birch," *Notes and Queries*, n.s.,

12 (1965): 218–21.

52. For reviews on the Hunter-Monro dispute, see the *Critical*: Au '57, 149–52; Se '57, 223–27; No '57, 431–36; and Oc '58, 312–17.

53. See appendix A for the following: Fe '57, 153–57 and 185; My '57, 474–75; Jl '57, 94; No '57, 377–85; Ja '58, 79; My '58, 438–39; Ja '59, 22–26; Au '59, 160–62 and 162; and De '61, 477.

54. *A Letter to the Right Hon. George Grenville* (1763), 8.

55. Spector, *Climate of Opinion*, 14.

56. Klukoff has suggested plausibly that Smollett wrote most or all of these notices himself; see Klukoff, "Smollett and the Sackville Controversy," *Neuphilologische Mitteilungen* 69 (1968): 618 and n. 2.

57. Alice Parker, "Tobias Smollett and the Law," *Studies in Philology* 39 (1942): 545–58, and Knapp, "*Rex Versus Smollett*: More Data on the Smollett-Knowles Libel Case," *Modern Philology* 41 (1944): 221–27.

58. Boucé, *Novels of Smollett*, 344–47.

59. Boucé, "Smollett's Libel," *The Times Literary Supplement*, 30 December 1965, 1218.

60. Knapp, "Ralph Griffiths, Author and Publisher, 1746–1750," *The Library* 20 (1939): 197–213. Griffiths referred to the Knowles libel case in an attack on Smollett he printed in his *Grand Magazine of Universal Intelligence* 2 (1759): 486–87.

61. A letter from George Faulkner in London to Samuel Derrick in Ireland, 2 December 1760, in the Papers of Samuel Derrick, Victoria and Albert Museum, catalog number 48.g 3/30, ms. 47.

62. Spector, *Climate of Opinion*, 54.

63. For another example of concern expressed about the possible legal ramifications of a review, see the *Critical*, Mr '63, 232.

64. *The Patriot*, 17 July 1762.

65. In an unpublished manuscript note, Derrick listed among his literary productions "Critical Review, one vol[ume] at least." Even at the hectic rate of his submissions in 1756, which produced about nine sheets or a quarter of a volume of copy for that year, it would have taken another three years to amass a full volume. See the Papers of Samuel Derrick, Victoria and Albert Museum, catalog number 48.g. 3/30, ms. 92; also quoted in Knapp, *Tobias Smollett*, 178, n. 32.

66. Stockdale discusses Francklin's reviews of his works in the 1770s in *The Memoirs of the Life and Writings of Percival Stockdale* (1809), 2: 118–19.

67. Friedman, "Goldsmith's Contributions to the *Critical Review*," *Modern Philology* 44 (1946): 23–52.

68. "To Philip Miller," 20 January 1759, Letter 57, *Letters*, 74. See also *Humphry Clinker*, 8 August, 234 and n. 2.

69. Knapp, *Tobias Smollett*, 290–92. Campbell was hired at Smollett's request, but proved to be an ingrate. The fortune he later amassed in India not only brought charges of "gross corruption," but cast a pall over the *Critical* with which his name was associated in the newspapers. See also Jones, "Contributors to *The Critical Review* 1756–1785," 434, where, however, Campbell is mistakenly identified as "*John* Campbell."

70. Knapp, *Tobias Smollett*, 276 and n. 63. Exactly when Guthrie began as a *Critical* reviewer is unknown, but he was a major contributor and editor in the 1760s, he worked with Smollett on the *Universal History* throughout this period, and his initials appeared at the bottom of an article in the *Critical* as early as January 1757 (Ja '57, 87). See also the *Critical*, (Ja '71, 1).

71. Jones, "Contributors to *The Critical Review* 1756–1785," 433–41. Jones lists *John* Hunter, but it was actually his brother *William* Hunter; see Knapp, *Tobias Smollett*, 202–205. In a letter of 15 March 1759 from Robertson to Smollett, a letter perhaps typical of such communications from other authors, Robertson discussed his submission of a book review to the *Critical* on

Lord Kames's *History of Law Tracts*; the review appeared in the *Critical* April 1759, 356–67. See Robert Anderson, *The Life of Tobias Smollett, M. D.*, 5th ed. (Edinburgh, 1806), 187–88.

72. Basker, "The Wages of Sin"; *The Reviewers Reviewed* (1779), 18.

73. See for example an article "from our correspondent at *Berlin*"—undoubtedly Murdoch— in the *Critical* for January 1757 (Ja '57, 78). Murdoch may well have continued as a correspondent for many years; he was still friends with Smollett as late as 1769. See Armstrong's letter to Smollett, dated 10 October 1769, quoted in Knapp, *Tobias Smollett*, 286.

74. Smollett asked Macaulay to contribute an article to the *Critical* in 1756 in a manner that indicated it was not an isolated instance ("To Dr. Macaulay," 14 December 1756, Letter 34, *Letters*, 52).

75. Smollett asked Richardson for a contribution to his *British Magazine* in 1760 ("To ?Samuel Richardson," 1 May 1760, Letter 70, *Letters*, 90) and, although it is unknown whether Richardson obliged him, Smollett often arranged for writers to contribute to both of his periodicals (as did Goldsmith, Derrick, and Watkinson, among others). Carlyle claimed in later years to have reviewed John Home's *Agis* for the *British Magazine* (Carlyle, *Anecdotes*, 182), but as the play was published in 1758, two years before the *British Magazine* was founded, it seems that Carlyle had a confused memory, either mistaking *Agis* for a later play of Home's or mistaking the *British Magazine* for the *Critical*, where Home's *Agis* was reviewed in March 1758 (Mr '58, 233–42). Carlyle's role in arranging contributions by Scottish writers is revealed in Robertson's letter of 15 March 1759 to Smollett, which is printed in Anderson, *Life of Smollett*, 5th ed., 187–88. In *Humphry Clinker*, Matt Bramble gives credit to Carlyle for having introduced him to Hume, Home, Robertson, Smith, Wallace, Blair, Ferguson, Wilkie, and others (8 August, 233).

76. Jones, "Contributors to *The Critical Review* 1756–1785," 433–41. Jones also lists a "T. C.," but in fact "T. C." was the author of a work reviewed, rather than the reviewer (Jn '56, 483).

77. Nangle, *The Monthly Review, Second Series*, xi.

78. Nangle, *The Monthly Review, Second Series*, x–xii.

79. *Boswell's Life*, 5:274 and n. Goldsmith's book was probably the collected *Citizen of the World*.

80. For Johnson's reviews, see the *Critical*, Ap '63, 314–18; Oc '64, 170–77 [for 270–77]; De '64, 458–62.

81. One need only compare the lists of attacks on the *Critical* in appendix A with the list of attacks on the *Monthly* in the same years; see Basker, "Smollett and Literary Journalism," (D. Phil. diss., Oxford, 1983), appendix C.

82. See the following reviews in the *Critical*: Ja '57, 83; Fe '57, 180; De '57, 546; Fe '58, 175; Fe '60, 158; and Ap '60, 323–24.

83. In Griffiths's own copy of the *Monthly*, now in the Bodleian Library, on the first page of the issue for March 1753 he has written: "Re-printed by Hamilton—1757."

84. *Monthly* 38, following index (Harvard copy).

85. See appendix B and n. 1.

86. See appendix B, under 1757.

87. For similar examples, see the *Critical*: Mr '59, 288; No '61, 404; Ja '63, 68–69; Jl '63, 72.

88. The following reviews in the *Critical* all contain warm praise for Newbery and his publications: Se '59, 253–54; De '59, 486–87; Ap '60, 310–14; Mr '61, 255; My '61, 377–81; Ap '62, 312–19; Jl '63, 75–76.

89. For Baldwin publications reviewed negatively, see: Ap '58, 347; My '59, 452–53 and 468–69; Jl '59, 82–83. For Payne's, see De '60, 484–85; and De '62, 471–72.

90. Johnson mentions the "common reader" as early as *Rambler* 4 (31 March 1750), the *Critical* by 1758 (e.g., Jn '58, 450).

91. "To William Huggins," ca. 1760, Letter 75, *Letters*, 95.

92. "To David Garrick," 5 April 1761, Letter 77, *Letters*, 98.

CHAPTER 8. "THESE SELF-ELECTED MONARCHS"

1. *NCBEL* 2, cols. 1198–1302.

2. The three other journals founded in 1756 were: the *Monthly and Critical Review* (January 1756–June 1756), the *Repository; or General Review* (March 1756–May 1756), and the *Literary Miscellany* (1756–57).

3. "To John Moore," 3 August 1756, Letter 29, *Letters*, 46.

4. Knapp, *Letters*, 46, n. 5.

5. Knapp, *Tobias Smollett*, 178–80. See also the *Universal Visiter* 1 (March 1756): 139–40, and the *Gentleman's Magazine* 26 (March 1756): 141–42.

6. *Repository; or General Review* 1 (13 March 1756): [9].

7. *Repository* 1 (13 March 1756), introduction.

8. *Repository* 1 (13 March 1756): 34–48; (27 March 1756): 49–83; (10 April 1756): 139–44; and (24 April 1756): 145–67.

9. *Rhapsodist*, no. 1 (24 January 1757): 3.

10. *The Theatrical Examiner: An Enquiry into the Merits and Demerits of the Present English Performers in General* (1757), 88.

11. *Connoisseur*, no. 139 (23 September 1756); quoted here from *The British Essayists*, ed. Robert Lynam (London: J. F. Dove, 1827), 19: 274.

12. See appendix B and n. 1.

13. Sutcliffe, "English Book-Reviewing," 79.

14. Basker, "Smollett and Literary Journalism," appendix C.

15. Knapp, "Smollett's Works as Printed by William Strahan," 291.

16. Quoted from an advertisement for the forthcoming *St. James's Magazine* in the *Salisbury Journal*, 26 March 1764.

17. *Vicar of Wakefield* (1766), chap. 19.

18. Thomas Patten, *St. Peter's Christian Apology* (1756), 75–76.

19. An advertisement for Smart's *Song to David*, printed in his *Poems* [1763], 21.

20. "To Thomas Percy," 6 June 1759, *The Letters of William Shenstone*, ed. Marjorie Williams (Oxford: Basil Blackwell, 1939), 514.

21. *Literary Magazine* 2 (1757): 27–31, 36–38, 75–76, 246–48, 289, and 426–27. See also chapter 2 above and Greene, "Johnson's Contributions to the *Literary Magazine*."

22. *Grand Magazine of Magazines* 1 (1758): 2.

23. *Universal Visiter* 1 (1756): 139–40; reprinted also in Jones, *Smollett Studies*, 111.

24. *Universal Visiter* 1 (1756): 204.

25. The *Universal Visiter* ceased in December 1756, not 1758 as the *NCBEL* indicates (2, col. 1300). See Botting, "*Universal Visiter*."

26. Botting, "*Universal Visiter*," 293–95.

27. *Gentleman's Magazine* 24 (1754): preface. See also 23 (1753): preface, written by Johnson.

28. *Gentleman's Magazine* 26 (1756): 141–42.

29. *Universal Visiter* 1 (1756): 164.

30. *London Chronicle* 1 (1757): preface, [1].

31. See an advertisement for the *Monthly* in the *London Chronicle* 10 (1761): 118 and 131; quoted in Spector, "The *Monthly* and Its Rival," 159–61.

32. *General Evening Post*, 3 October 1758.

33. See typical advertisements in any of the following issues of the *General Evening Post* in 1758: 1 July, 6 July, 1 August, 5 August, 30 September, 3 October, 7 October, 2 November, 2 December, and 30 December.

34. *Monthly* 19 (1758): 318–20 and 605–7.

35. Griffiths's annotations in the Bodleian copy of the *Monthly* show that Rose, Goldsmith,

Griffiths himself, and perhaps Grainger actually wrote articles that are presented as coming from correspondents in the following issues of vol. 16 (1757): February, 140–41; March, 245–71; and June, 558–63.

36. Disclosed by Kenrick in the *London Review* 1 (1775): 476.

37. *General Evening Post*, 1 July 1758.

38. Spector, *Tobias George Smollett* (New York: Twayne Publishers, Inc., 1968), 30–31.

39. Sutcliffe, "English Book-Reviewing," 331–32.

40. Carlson, *The First Magazine*, 53.

41. Spector, "The *Monthly* and Its Rival," 159; and Spector, *Smollett*, 30–31.

42. Knapp, "Griffiths's 'Monthly Review' As Printed by Strahan," 216–17.

43. Carlson, *The First Magazine*, 63.

44. John Louis Haney, *Early Reviews of English Poets* (Philadelphia: Egerton Press, 1904), xviii–xix.

45. *NCBEL* 2, col. 1291–99. The exception was the *Critick: A Review of Authors and their Productions* (6 January 1718–3 June 1718).

46. The *London Review; or Weekly Entertainer* (14 October 1749–21 October 1749) and the *General Review; or Impartial Register* (May 1752–July 1752).

47. *NCBEL* 2, cols. 1299–1305.

48. The *Political Register: and Impartial Review of New Books* (May 1767–June 1772) and the *London Review of English and Foreign Literature* (January 1775–December 1780).

49. See editorial statements in the following: an advertisement for the *Weekly Magazine* in *Jackson's Oxford Journal*, 15 April 1758 (repeated 22 and 29 April); an advertisement for the *St. James's Magazine* in the same, 10 March 1764; and *Literary Annals* 1 (1765): 30.

50. Roper, *Reviewing Before the "Edinburgh,"* 22–27 and passim.

51. *Grand Magazine of Magazines; or Universal Register* 3 (1759): 250.

52. *Grand Magazine of Magazines* 1 (1758): 114, 171–72, and 293; 2 (1759): 12–14; 3 (1759): 315–16; *London Evening Post*, 2–5 November 1771 and 6–8 October 1772.

53. *Imperial Magazine* 2 (1761): 537; see also 2 (1761): 537–42 and 580–84; and 3 (1762): 16–22.

54. *Scots Magazine* 21 (1759): 77–81 (from the *Critical*) and 126–32 (from the *Monthly*).

55. *Grand Magazine of Universal Intelligence* 2 (1759): 206–13 and 260; see also 3 (1760): 423.

56. *Aberdeen Magazine* 1 (1761): 204–5; *Grand Magazine, or Universal Register* 2 (1759): 269; and *Scots Magazine* 22 (1760): 392.

57. Library of Congress, call number AP4.C9. Unfortunately, it is not clear who the annotator was or what magazine he was compiling.

58. Similar articles appeared in *Lloyd's Evening Post*, 21 March and 20 April 1759, and in the *Whitehall Evening Post*, 3 February 1770.

59. See, for example, *Jackson's Oxford Journal*, 12 June 1760, and the *Literary Register* [supplement to the *Newcastle Journal*] 1–3 (1769–71): passim.

60. Roper, *Reviewing Before the "Edinburgh,"* 24 and n. 68.

61. See appendix B.

62. *Letters of Shenstone*, 460–61, 486–87, 503, 514, 529–30, 547, 552, 556 and 635.

63. Percy to Richard Farmer, 10 February 1765, *The Correspondence of Thomas Percy and Richard Farmer*, ed. Cleanth Brooks (Baton Rouge: Louisiana State University Press, 1946), vol. 2 of *The Percy Letters*, ed. David Nichol Smith and Cleanth Brooks, 82.

64. *Correspondence of Thomas Gray*, ed. Paget Toynbee and Leonard Whibley (Oxford: Oxford University Press, 1935), 2: 466–67, 522–24, 526, 532–33, 616, and 690; and 3: 1025 and 1068.

65. Gray to Mason, 23 July 1756, *Correspondence of Gray*, 2: 466–67.

66. Walpole to John Chute, 2 February 1759, *The Walpole Correspondence*, vol. 35, ed. W. S. Lewis, A. Doyle Wallace, and Robert A. Smith (New Haven: Yale University Press, 1973), 107.

67. Hume to Smith, 12 April 1759, *Letters of David Hume*, 305; *The Whitefoord Papers*, ed.

W. A. S. Hewins (Oxford: Clarendon Press, 1898), 132 and 148–49; John Wooll, *Biographical Memoirs of the Late Revd Joseph Warton* (1806), 258–59.

68. *Early Papers of James Boswell, 1754–1763*, vol. 1 of *Private Papers of James Boswell from Malahide Castle* (Mount Vernon, N.Y.: [privately printed], 1928), 135.

69. Anstey to Dodsley, quoted from Francis Doherty, "Letter of Christopher Anstey to Robert Dodsley," *Notes and Queries*, n.s., 32, no. 2 (June 1985): 237. Sinclair to Cadell and Davies, unpublished letter in Bodleian Library, MS Montagu d. 10 (f.51).

70. Unpublished correspondence in Bodleian Library, MS Montagu d.10 (f.226), (f.229), (f.290), and (f.404).

71. William Roberts, *Memoirs of the Life and Correspondence of Mrs. Hannah More* (1834), 1:73.

72. Clara Reeve, *The Progress of Romance* (Colchester, 1785), 1:82.

73. Unpublished letter from Dodd to the "Authors of the Monthly Review," 17 November 1760, in the Papers of Ralph Griffiths, Bodleian Library, MS Add C.89, f.34.

74. "Thomas Davies," in Nichols, *Minor Lives*, 244–46.

75. For examples, see: Thomas Amory, *The Life of John Buncle*, 2 (1766), iv; *The Adventures of an Author* (1767), 2:203; Richard Griffith, *The Koran* (1770), 1:8–10; see also the *Critical*, Ap '67, 305.

76. Such remarks are noted by reviewers in the *Critical* in many reviews: Ja '63, 80; Au '65, 124–34; No '68, 380–81; Fe '70, 113–17; and Jl '70, 68–71.

77. Johnson, "Life of Lyttelton," *Lives of the English Poets*, 3:452.

78. J. Irving, *Some Account of the Family of Smollett of Bonhill* (Dumbarton: 1859), 22; quoted in Boege, *Smollett's Reputation*, 56.

79. For this and the following three examples of authorial emendation the writer is indebted to the MS annotations (author uncertain) in the University College Library copy of the *Critical Review*.

80. For an account of this episode, see Basker, "Minim and the Great Cham," 151–53.

81. Herbert A. Wichelns, "Burke's *Essay on the Sublime* and its Reviewers," *Journal of English and Germanic Philology* 21 (1922): 645–61.

82. *The General Advertiser*, 14 December 1750 (brought to my attention by Professor Antonia Forster).

83. *British Chronicle*, 6 June 1759 and *Lloyd's Evening Post*, 6 June 1759. See other examples of expeditious borrowing in advertisements in *Lloyd's Evening Post*, 9 April 1759 and *Jackson's Oxford Journal*, 23 March 1765.

84. See an advertisement for a translation of *Magasin des Enfans* in *Lloyd's Evening Post*, 16 December 1757.

85. See an advertisement for Charlotte Lennox's *Lady's Museum* in *Jackson's Oxford Journal*, 23 February 1760.

86. An eleven-page advertisement section in *Magasin des Enfans: the Young Ladies Magazine* (Dublin, 1776): 185–96, published by James Hoey, lists at least five books that are supported by quotations from the *Critical* of 1763. The fourth edition of *The History of Jack Connor*, published in Dublin by Hulton Bradley in 1766, quoted a *Monthly* article of July 1752 at length, and explained how the reviewer's suggestions had been heeded, in "The Bookseller to the Publick," ix–xv.

87. *Monthly* 80:288.

88. See advertisements in: *Jackson's Oxford Journal*, 29 April 1758; *Gloucester Journal*, 24 January 1763; *Pope's Bath Chronicle*, 24 March 1765; *Salisbury Journal*, 30 January 1764.

89. Knapp, "Griffiths's 'Monthly Review' as Printed by Strahan," 216–17.

90. *Jackson's Oxford Journal*, 6 November 1756.

91. Advertisement in *Jackson's Oxford Journal*, 3 November 1759.

92. Advertisement in *Jackson's Oxford Journal*, 26 February 1763.

93. See Roy McKeen Wiles, "The Relish for Reading in Provincial England Two Centuries

Ago," in *The Widening Circle*, ed. Paul J. Korshin (Philadelphia: University of Pennsylvania Press, 1976), 97 and passim. See also typical advertisements in: *Boddely's Bath Journal*, 14 February 1757, and the *Salisbury Journal*, 25 February 1765.

94. *Salisbury Journal*, 20 February 1764.

95. Advertisement in the *Edinburgh Chronicle*, 7 April 1759.

96. Griffiths Papers, Bodleian Library, C.89.f158.

97. Letter from Franklin to William Strahan, 1 May 1764, in *The Writings and Letters of Benjamin Franklin*, ed. Albert H. Smyth (New York: The Macmillan Company, 1905-7), 9:246-47.

98. Bernhard Fabian, "English Books and Their Eighteenth-Century German Readers," in *The Widening Circle*, 141-42.

99. Griffiths Papers, Bodleian Library, C.89.f40.

100. Knapp, *Tobias Smollett*, 291-92.

101. Roper, *Reviewing Before the "Edinburgh,"* 24 and nn.

102. See also Roper, *Reviewing Before the "Edinburgh,"* 24-25.

103. Roper, *Reviewing Before the "Edinburgh,"* 25-26. See also Paul Kaufman, "English Book Clubs and Their Social Import," in *Libraries and Their Users: Collected Papers in Library History* (London: The Library Association, 1969), 39-43, where he lists more than one hundred provincial book clubs and reading societies.

104. William R. McDonald, "Circulating libraries in the north-east of Scotland in the eighteenth century," *The Bibliotheck* 5 (1968):122. K. A. Manley, "The London and Westminster Libraries, 1785-1823," *The Library*, 6th ser., 7, no. 2 (June 1985):141.

105. *Edinburgh Chronicle*, 26 April 1759.

106. *Edinburgh Evening Courant*, 22 September 1783; McDonald, "Circulating libraries," 135.

107. Kaufman, "Innerpeffray: Reading for all the People," in *Libraries and Their Users*, 154-55.

108. Kaufman, "English Book Clubs and Their Social Import," 57.

109. "A Book of Minutes containing An Account of the Proceedings of the Directors of the Library Company of Philadephia" (Original minutes, on deposit with Library Company), 1:172 and 174. Fabian, "English Books and Their Eighteenth-Century German Readers," 161-65.

110. Roper, *Reviewing Before the "Edinburgh,"* 25. Jan Fergus and Ruth Portner, however, announced research in progress that may qualify or contradict this view, in their paper, "Reviews and Readers: Provincial Subscribers to the *Monthly* and *Critical Reviews* and the Books They Read, 1758-80," Paper delivered at the annual meeting of the Modern Language Association, Chicago, 1985.

111. John Feather, *The Provincial Book Trade in Eighteenth-Century England* (Cambridge: Cambridge University Press, 1985), 51.

112. For this and the following information about the Liverpool and Warrington Libraries, I am indebted to M. Kay Flavell, "The Englightened Reader and the New Industrial Towns: A Study of the Liverpool Library 1758-1790," *British Journal for Eighteenth-Century Studies* 8 (Spring 1985):17-35.

113. Flavell, "Enlightened Reader," 20.

114. Fabian, "An Eighteenth-Century Research Collection: English Books at Göttingen University Library," *Library*, 6th ser., 1 (1979), 223.

115. Fabian, "English Books and Their Eighteenth-Century German Readers," 151-52. See also Fabian, "An Eighteenth-Century Research Collection," 213-18.

116. Moore, "The Life of Tobias Smollett, M.D.," in *The Works of Tobias Smollett, M.D.* (1797), 1:clxiii, n.; quoted in Knapp, *Letters*, 73, n. 3.

117. *Diary of George Ridpath, 1755-61*, ed. Sir James Balfour Paul, *Publications of the Scottish Historical Society*, 3rd ser., 2 (1922).

118. Three examples: the Harvard Library copies of David Fenning, *The Royal English Dic-*

tionary (1768); James Barclay, *A Complete English Dictionary* (1774), and Thomas Sheridan, *A Complete Dictionary of the English Language* (1790).

119. *Boswell's Life of Johnson*, 4:57.

120. *Edinburgh Chronicle*, 26 April 1759.

121. Thomas Underwood, "Liberty," *Poems* (1768), 218.

122. *St. James's Magazine* 3 (1764), 29.

123. Thomas Davies, *Dramatic Miscellanies* (1785), 3:512–13.

124. Goldsmith, "New Fashions in Learning," *Public Ledger*, 22 August 1761; reprinted in *New Essays by Oliver Goldsmith*, ed. Ronald S. Crane (Chicago: University of Chicago Press, 1927), 63.

125. The *Journal étranger* for December 1761 published in translation this review from the *Critical* of September 1761 (Se '61, 203–11).

126. Janssens, *Matthieu Maty and the Journal britannique*, 126.

127. Fabian, "English Books and Their Eighteenth-Century German Readers," 148–52.

128. Fabian, "English Books and Their Eighteenth-Century German Readers," 151–52.

129. Reviewed in the *Critical*, Jl '68, 24–28.

130. I. F. Martynov, "English Literature and Eighteenth-Century Russian Reviewers," *Oxford Slavonic Papers*, n.s., 4 (1971): 30–42.

131. Frank Luther Mott, *A History of American Magazines 1741–1850* (New York: D. Appleton, 1930), 54.

132. For other examples, see Jayne K. Kribbs, ed., *An Annotated Bibliography of American Literary Periodicals, 1741–1850* (Boston: G. K. Hall, 1977), 185–87.

CHAPTER 9. BEFORE ITS TIME

1. Knapp, *Tobias Smollett*, 221–23; see also appendix C. More informative is Wilbur T. Albrecht's recent article on "The British Magazine" in *British Literary Magazines: The Augustan Age and The Age of Johnson*, edited by Alvin Sullivan (Westport, Conn.: Greenwood, 1983), 26–30.

2. *Battle of the Reviews*, 150–51.

3. Albert Smith, *"Sir Launcelot Greaves*: A Bibliographical Survey of Eighteenth-century Editions," *Library*, 5th ser., 32 (1977): 214–37. Many of the details that follow are from Smith's account.

4. *Jackson's Oxford Journal*, 15 December 1759. See also the *London Chronicle*, 20 December 1759 and *Lloyd's Evening Post*, 21 December 1759.

5. *Jackson's Oxford Journal*, 15 December 1759, in Jackson's own file copy, now in the Bodleian Library.

6. Smith, "Sir Launcelot Greaves," 225.

7. *British Magazine* 1 (1760): 216.

8. *British Magazine* 1 (1760): 49, 268, and 382. Such word games and puzzles were used as a kind of advertising well into the nineteenth century, if Mr. Slum the acrostic-writing bard in *The Old Curiosity Shop* (chap. 28) is at all typical.

9. Smollett's license petition, preserved in the Public Record Office (S.P.D., George II, 145, f.25), here quoted from Smith, "Sir Launcelot Greaves," 216.

10. *British Magazine* for February 1760 (Bodleian copy with wrappers: Vet. a5 d.782). See also Smith, "Sir Launcelot Greaves," 216–17.

11. *Public Advertiser*, 2 February 1760 and *Jackson's Oxford Journal*, 9 February 1760.

12. *Grand Magazine of Universal Intelligence* 3 (1760): 90–91; Shenstone to Thomas Percy, 15 February 1760, *Shenstone Letters*, 552; Walpole, *Memoires of the Last Ten Years of the Reign of George II* (London: 1822), 2:421.

13. Wiles, *Serial Publication in England Before 1750* (Cambridge: Cambridge University Press, 1957), 163–69 and passim. See also Smith, "Sir Launcelot Greaves," 217–18.

14. See advertisements in *Jackson's Oxford Journal*, 11 August 1759, 1 December 1759, and 26 January 1760; see also the *Edinburgh Chronicle*, 11 August 1759.

15. "To William Huggins," 24 February 1760, Letter 69, *Letters*, 88.

16. *British Magazine* 1 (April 1760): 212.

17. Advertisement, *Jackson's Oxford Journal*, 15 December 1759.

18. *British Magazine*: 1 (1760): 435; 2 (1761): 102, 159, and 216; 4 (1763): 156.

19. *British Magazine*: 1 (1760): 478 and 536; 3 (1762): 28, 187–88, and 312–13.

20. *British Magazine* 3 (1762): 30–31.

21. Knapp, ed., *Letters*, 74, n. 1. For Carlyle, see above, chap. 7.

22. *British Magazine* 1 (1760): 17–19. For his friendship with Smollett, see Knapp, *Tobias Smollett*, 293–294, and Jones, *Smollett Studies*, 123–26.

23. *British Magazine* 1 (1760): 408–9. For his connection with Smollett, see Knapp, ed., *Letters*, 105 and n.7.

24. Nichols, *Literary Anecdotes* 3: 465.

25. Arnold Whitridge, *Tobias Smollett: A Study of His Miscellaneous Works* (New York: n.p., 1926), 54. *British Magazine* 2 (1761): 178–79; see also Edward W. Pitcher, "Inconsistent Attributions and Arbitrary Signatures in Smollett's *British Magazine* (1760–67)," *Publications of the Bibliographical Society of America* 75 (1981), no. 4: 443–47.

26. "To William Huggins," 24 February 1760, Letter 69, *Letters*, 88.

27. *British Magazine* 1 (1760): 266.

28. Inside front cover, *British Magazine*, issue no. 5.

29. *British Magazine* 2 (1761): 438 and 608; 3 (1762): 103 and 493. See *NCBEL* 2, col. 1304 and Nichols, *Literary Anecdotes* 1: 151.

30. *British Magazine* 2 (1761): 213.

31. "Memoirs of the late Mr. John Cunningham," *London Magazine* 42 (1773): 495–97.

32. Bate, *Samuel Johnson*, 169–71, 189–90, and 202–7.

33. William Wordsworth, "Sonnet, on seeing Miss Helen Maria Williams weep at a Tale of Distress," *European Magazine* 11 (1787): 202.

34. "To Samuel Richardson," 1 May 1760, Letter 70, *Letters*, 90.

35. See Smollett's letters to Richardson on 4 April 1759 and 4 February, 1 May, 31 May, and 12 October 1760 in *Letters*, 78–79 and 87–92.

36. "To the Author of the British Magazine," *British Magazine* 1 (1760): 181.

37. *British Magazine* 1 (1760): 181–84.

38. *British Magazine* 1 (1760): 25.

39. See advertisement, *London Chronicle*, 5 January 1759, warning against such unauthorized reprintings.

40. *British Magazine* 1 (1760): 37–39.

41. See letters written on Johnson's behalf from Smollett to Wilkes in March and April 1759, *Letters*, 75–77.

42. Greene, ed., *Samuel Johnson: Political Writings*, vol. 10 of *The Yale Edition of the Works of Samuel Johnson* (New Haven: Yale University Press, 1977), 279.

43. Greene, "Samuel Johnson, Journalist," in *Newsletters to Newspapers: Eighteenth-Century Journalism*, ed. Donovan H. Bond (n.p.: West Virginia University, 1977), 92 and 100, n. 11.

44. See Smollett's letters to Garrick spanning the years 1757 to 1762 in *Letters*, 52–54, 97–98, and 103–4.

45. *British Magazine* 1 (1760): 709–10.

46. *British Magazine*: 2 (1761): 86–88, 243–45, 313–16, 365–68, 413–15, and 656–58; 3 (1762): 81–84, 132–33, and 653–55; 4 (1763): 7–9, 81–84, and 171–73. The exceptions were: Foote's *Minor* performed at the Haymarket, 1 (1760): 410–11; Foote's *Lyar* at Covent Garden, 3 (1762): 29; Arne's opera *Artaxerxes* at Covent Garden, 3 (1762): 85–86; Foote's *Lecturer on Ora-*

tory at Haymarket, 3 (1762):239; and Bickerstaffe's *Love in a Village* at Convent Garden, 3 (1762):656.

47. *British Magazine* 1 (1760):262–63.

48. Friedman, "Goldsmith's Contributions to the *Critical Review*," 23–52.

49. See J. W. M. Gibbs, ed., *Works of Oliver Goldsmith*, vol. 1 (London: 1884), 406–8; Caroline Tupper, "Essays Erroneously Attributed to Goldsmith," *PMLA* 39 (1924):325–42; R. S. Crane, *New Essays by Oliver Goldsmith* (Chicago: University of Chicago Press, 1927), xi–xx, xxxi, 1–11, and 133–36; *Collected Works of Oliver Goldsmith*, ed. Arthur Friedman (Oxford: Clarendon Press, 1966), 3:87–90.

50. Goldsmith, *Essays and Criticisms*, ed. Isaac Reed, with Thomas Wright (London: J. Johnson, 1798), vol. 2, numbers 1–19 and vol. 3, numbers 1–8. See also *NCBEL* 2, col. 1193.

51. Preface, *Essays and Criticisms* 2:viii–ix.

52. *Works* 3:87–88. See also Crane, *New Essays*, xiii–xv, and Tupper, "Essays Erroneously Attributed to Goldsmith," 325–42.

53. See Friedman, compiler, "Goldsmith," *NCBEL* 2, col. 1196.

54. D. F. McKenzie, *Stationers' Company Apprentices 1701–1800*, 154.

55. Nichols, *Literary Anecdotes* 3:398–99, note.

56. *British Magazine*: 2 (1761):353–55, 434–36, 493–95, 541–44, and 646–49; 3 (1762): 36–37, 89–91, 150–52, 184–87, 262–64, 317–19, 489–91, and 595–97; 4 (1763):17–19.

57. As Crane points out, this essay first appeared in the *Public Ledger* for 9 December 1760. See Crane, *New Essays*, 137. Goldsmith also allowed the *British Magazine* to reprint various of his "Chinese Letters" from the *Public Ledger*; see Albrecht, "British Magazine," 28.

58. A critical edition of these thirty miscellaneous pieces by Goldsmith, together with some other newly discovered Goldsmith writings from the same period, is in preparation by the present writer.

59. *British Magazine* 1 (1760):598–600.

60. See *Works* 3:128–32.

61. This practice was changed between April and May of 1760, when an extra issue marked V was published and the publishing cycle was synchronized with other periodicals, issuing each number on the first day of the following month.

62. Advertisement in the *Oxford Gazette and Reading Mercury*, 7 January 1760.

63. Quoted from the Royal license printed inside the front cover of the *British Magazine* for February 1760.

64. Advertisement in *Jackson's Oxford Journal*, 12 January 1760.

65. *British Magazine* 2 (1761):98.

66. Advertisement leaf bound into *The Orientalist* (Dublin: James Hoey, Jr., 1764).

67. Robert D. Mayo, *The English Novel in the Magazines 1740–1815* (London: Oxford University Press, 1962), 215–16.

68. *British Magazine* 1 (1760):665 and *Critical*, Oc '60, 249–328. Other such examples occur in the *British Magazine* 1 (1760):713–14; 2 (1761):382 and 550; 3 (1762):101–2, and elsewhere.

69. *British Magazine* 1 (1760):155–56 and *Critical*, Fe '60, 133–43, 155–56, and 158. Such simultaneous coverage occurred frequently: see other examples in *British Magazine* 1 (1760):95, 378, 433–34, 489–90, 546–47, and 602.

70. *Man after God's Own Heart* and Bower's *History of the Popes* in the *Critical* for March 1761, and Sterne's *Tristram Shandy*, vol. 3–4, in April 1761.

71. *British Magazine* 1 (1760):89 and *Critical*, My '60, 399–400. The *Critical* article was by Smollett (see appendix A) and he may well have written the earlier one for the *British Magazine* also.

72. *British Magazine* 1 (1760):241–42 and 317 [misnumbered 135]. See Smollett's notice about Frye's designs in the *Critical* (My '60, 400).

73. *British Magazine* 3 (1762):306–10 and 492; and 4 (1763):259–60.

74. *Imperial Magazine* 1 (1760): 2.

75. Martz, *Later Career of Smollett*, 176–80.

76. "History of Canada," *British Magazine* 2 (1761): 83–84.

77. Martz, *Later Career of Smollett*, 176–80.

78. Martz, *Later Career of Smollett*, 1–20 and passim.

79. *British Magazine* 3 (1762): 295–99 and 367–77.

80. See, for example, two essays assigned to him in the *Beauties of the Magazines and other Periodical Works* (1772), discussed in Morris Golden, "Two Essays Erroneously Attributed to Goldsmith," *Modern Language Notes* 74 (1959): 13–16. See also Jones, *Smollett Studies*, 112–16.

81. Buck, *Smollett as Poet*, 52–68.

82. Ph.D. diss., Yale University, 1957.

83. Mayo, *English Novel in the Magazines*, 276–88; Smith, "Sir Launcelot Greaves," 214–37; Boucé, *Novels of Smollett*, 174–90.

84. Mayo, *English Novel in the Magazines*, 276–77. Several of the details that follow are also discussed in Mayo.

85. *British Magazine* 1 (1760), facing 57 and 449. The first of these is reprinted as the frontispiece in Mayo, *English Novel in the Magazines*.

86. Mayo, *English Novel in the Magazines*, 280–81.

87. *Sir Launcelot Greaves*, 41.

88. Boucé, *Novels of Smollett*, 176.

89. *Sir Launcelot Greaves*, 41.

90. Boucé, *Novels of Smollett*, 183.

91. *British Magazine* 1 (1760): 57–64 and 181–84.

92. See for example "Advertisement," *British Magazine* 2 (1761): [i].

93. Knapp, *Tobias Smollett*, 228–29.

94. *British Magazine* 1 (1760): 598–600.

95. Michael Steig, *Dickens and Phiz* (Bloomington: Indiana University Press, 1978), 2.

96. Mayo mentions such examples as the *Novelists' Magazine* (1780–89), among others; see *English Novel in the Magazines*, 366.

97. Mayo, *English Novel in the Magazines*, 284.

98. Martz, *Later Career of Smollett*, 15.

99. For Smollett's review of Battie's *Treatise*, see appendix A (De '57, 509–16). His reviews of works by Shebbeare and of other political pamphlets are discussed above in chapters 6 and 7.

100. *Sir Launcelot Greaves*, ed. Evans, 181 and 231, n.4.

101. Smollett's Dick Distich shares the following details with Charles Churchill: he is "seemingly turned of thirty" (Churchill turned thirty a few months before this chapter was published), he is a chronic and belligerent drunk, his verse attacks "actors, authors, and critics," and Launcelot judges his verse to be "tolerably good," although it attacks many authors of merit—exactly the opinions Smollett expressed in his reviews of Churchill's poetry (e.g., My '61, 409–11). Distich's bosom drinking companion and sworn poetical ally, Ben Bullock, is undoubtedly based on the corresponding figure in Churchill's life, the young poet Robert Lloyd.

102. Steig, *Dickens and Phiz*, 12. Evans notes another possible borrowing by Dickens from chapter 10 of *Sir Launcelot Greaves*: Alfred Jingle's elliptical, staccato speech in *Pickwick Papers* (chap. 7 and following) seems to derive from Captain Crowe's similar "dialect," *Sir Launcelot Greaves*, 82 and note.

103. Alan Dugald McKillop, *The Early Masters of English Fiction* (Lawrence: University of Kansas Press, 1956), 169.

104. It may also be noteworthy that the second, and last, of the historic illustrations Smollett commissioned for *Sir Launcelot Greaves* depicted this scene of a country election for which he was so indebted to Hogarth's engravings. Perhaps the daunting prospect of comparison with Hogarth's works or the realization that the illustrations so far had contributed very little to what were already highly "visual" scenes in prose contributed to the decision to stop the illustrations.

105. Spector, *Tobias George Smollett*, 107; McKillop, *Early Masters*, 169.

106. Knapp, *Tobias Smollett*, 154–59.

107. Knapp, *Tobias Smollett*, 228–29.

108. D. F. McKenzie and J. C. Ross, ed., *A Ledger of Charles Ackers* (Oxford: Oxford University Press for the Oxford Bibliographical Society, 1968), 11–12.

109. Advertisement for the *Royal Magazine* in the *Oxford Gazette and Reading Mercury*, 7 January 1760; the *Library* 2 (1762): 254; Edward W. Pitcher, "The Town and Country Magazine," in *British Literary Magazines: The Augustan Age and the Age of Johnson*, ed. Sullivan, 327.

110. Smith, "The Printing and Publication of Early Editions of the Novels of Tobias George Smollett," 1: 8 and 2: 162.

111. Smith, "Sir Launcelot Greaves," 223 and 225.

112. David Evans, ed., introduction, *Sir Launcelot Greaves*, x.

113. *Library* 2 (1762): 262.

114. Smith, "Sir Launcelot Greaves," 231–32.

115. Smith, "Sir Launcelot Greaves," 232–36.

116. See Miriam Rossiter Small, *Charlotte Ramsay Lennox* (New Haven: Yale University Press, 1934), 30.

117. Mayo, *English Novel in the Magazines*, 286.

118. *Imperial Magazine* 1 (1760): 512–14.

119. Mayo, *English Novel in the Magazines*, 287.

120. Mayo, *English Novel in the Magazines*, 286–87.

121. For example, see *London Chronicle*, 14 July 1763 and *Public Advertiser*, 15 July 1763.

122. *Aberdeen Magazine* 1 (1761): 664–65 and passim.

123. "The Unfortunate Lovers" [i.e., "History of Alcanor and Eudosia"], *Gentleman's and Lady's Museum* 1 (October 1777): 305–8.

124. *Scots Magazine* 21 (1759): 622–23, 636, 666, and 671–72. See also Wilbur T. Albrecht, "The Scots Magazine," in *British Literary Magazines: The Augustan Age and the Age of Johnson*, ed. Sullivan, 299–304.

125. *Journal encyclopédique*, 15 March 1760, vol. 2, pt. 3: 154.

126. *Journal encyclopédique*, June 1761, vol. 4, pt. 3; 101–15 and July 1761, vol. 5, pt. 2: 101–11.

127. These articles were translated by Smollett and appeared in the *Critical* for March 1756 (Mr '56, 181–84).

128. Mayo, *English Novel in the Magazines*, 287.

129. A recent study of borrowings published in the *British Magazine* found more than thirty instances of the *British* reprinting published material from other sources without acknowledgment, *all* of which occurred between 1764 and 1767 (i.e., after Smollett had left); the only known borrowings printed during Smollett's editorship (1760–63) fully acknowledged their sources. See Pitcher, "Inconsistent Attributions," 44–46.

CHAPTER 10. "WHO KILLED JOHN KEATS?"

1. Much of the biographical information that follows is from Knapp, *Tobias Smollett*, 258–301.

2. "To John Moore," 13 November 1765, *Letters*, 125.

3. Knapp, *Tobias Smollett*, 177; Spector, *Tobias George Smollett*, 31.

4. *Continuation* 4 (1761): 120–32.

5. "To David Garrick," 27 January 1762, Letter 83, *Letters*, 103 and n. 2.

6. *Public Advertiser*, 8 October 1761; *Imperial Magazine* 2 (1761): 543–46; *Edinburgh Magazine* 5 (1761): 533; *Aberdeen Magazine* 1 (1761): 567–73; *Scots Magazine* 23 (1761): 673–80.

7. See Knapp, *Letters*, 73 n. 5; Thomas Mortimer, *British Plutarch* (6 vols., 1762).

8. From this one can see how it is no accident that publishers found Smollett's *Continuation* such a valuable account of the mideighteenth century that they routinely appended it, along with the post-1689 years of his *History*, to Hume's *History of England* (which did not come down that far) and published them together as the standard British history well into the nineteenth century.

9. John Gross, *The Rise and Fall of the Man of Letters* (London: Weidenfeld and Nicolson, 1969), 2.

10. Elaine Showalter, *A Literature of Their Own* (Princeton: Princeton University Press, 1977), 74.

11. *Boswell's Life of Johnson* 2: 39–40, and 3: 32 and notes. Johnson's reconciliation with or conversion to the idea of the *Critical* and *Monthly* reviews seems to have been permanent; there were bundles of unbound (recent) copies of both in his library at the time of his death, the only English periodicals in that library according to the auction catalogue of 1785. See Greene, *Samuel Johnson's Library: An Annotated Guide* (Victoria: University of Victoria English Literary Studies, 1975), 22, nos. 633 and 634.

12. Edward A. Bloom and Lillian D. Bloom, eds. Fanny Burney, *Camilla, or A Picture of Youth* (Oxford: Oxford University Press, 1983), xx–xxiii and 915–27. A counterpoint to Fanny Burney's attitude is William Beckford's irreverence in the preface to his novel *Azemia* (2nd, ed., 1798, vol.2): there, posing as the young "authoress" (Miss J. A. M. Jenks) making her debut with *Azemia*, "she" uses twenty pages of (mock-) dedication, "To the Reviewers of All the Reviews," to gush about her lifelong dream of being acclaimed by review critics and then to invent review notices she imagines her book might receive ("Criticisms Anticipated").

13. The self-portrait is developed in an episode that fills most of Jeremy's letter of 10 June, 124–33.

Bibliography

I. WORKS BY SMOLLETT

The Adventures of Ferdinand Count Fathom. Edited by Damian Grant. London: Oxford University Press, 1971.

The Adventures of Peregrine Pickle. Edited by James L. Clifford. London: Oxford University Press, 1969.

The Adventures of Roderick Random. Edited by Paul-Gabriel Boucé. Oxford: Oxford University Press, 1979.

A Complete History of England. 4 vols. London, 1757–58.

Continuation of the Complete History of England. London, 1760–65. Vols. 1–5.

An Essay on the External Use of Water. Edited by Claude E. Jones. Baltimore: Johns Hopkins Press, 1935.

The Expedition of Humphry Clinker. Edited by Lewis M. Knapp. London: Oxford University Press, 1972.

The History and Adventures of an Atom. London: George Routledge and Sons, n.d.

The Letters of Tobias Smollett. Edited by Lewis M. Knapp. Oxford: Clarendon Press, 1970.

The Letters of Tobias Smollett, M.D. Edited by Edward S. Noyes. Cambridge: Harvard University Press, 1926.

The Life and Adventures of Sir Launcelot Greaves. Edited by David Evans. London: Oxford University Press, 1973.

The Present State of All Nations. 8 vols. London, 1768.

Travels Through France and Italy. Edited by Frank Felsenstein. Oxford: Oxford University Press, 1979.

The Works of Tobias Smollett, M.D. Edited by John Moore. 8 vols. London, 1797.

Smollett, Tobias, ed. *A Compendium of Authentic and Entertaining Voyages*. 7 vols. London, 1756.

Smollett, Tobias, trans. and ed. *The Works of M. de Voltaire*. 38 vols. London, 1761–74.

II. EIGHTEENTH CENTURY PERIODICALS

The following list of periodicals consulted is representative rather than exhaustive. Short titles are used except where more information is necessary to distinguish one from another with a similar title. Dates in parentheses indicate only when the periodical was founded and do not imply that all years were consulted.

A. *Periodical Essays*

Adventurer (1752).

Batchelor (1766).

Bee (1759).

Briton (1762).

Busy Body (1759).

Centinel (1757).

Champion, or British Mercury (1739).

Citizen of the World (originally "Chinese Letters" in *Public Advertiser*: 1760).

Connoisseur (1754).

Con-Test (1756).

Covent-Garden Journal (1752).

Crab-Tree (1757).

Entertainer (1754).

Gray's Inn Journal (1753).

Have at You All: or the Drury Lane Journal (1752).

Herald (1757).

Humanist (1757).

Idler (1758).

Man (1755).

Mirror (1757).

Monitor (1755).

North Briton (1762).

Old Maid (1755).

Prater (1756).

Rambler (1750).

Rhapsodist (1757).

Schemer (1760).

Spectator (1711).

Test (1756).

True Patriot: and History of Our Own Times (1745).

World (1753).

Young Lady (1756).

B. Magazines, Miscellanies, and Reviews

Aberdeen Magazine (1761).

Annual Register (1758).

Beauties of All the Magazines Selected (1762).

British Librarian (1737).

British Magazine (1746).

British Magazine: or Monthly Repository for Gentlemen and Ladies (1760).

Cambridge Magazine: or, Universal Register of Arts, Sciences, and the Belles Lettres (1769).

Candid Review, and Literary Repository (1765).

Christian's Magazine (1760).

Compendious Library: or, Literary Journal Revived (Dublin, 1751).

Country Magazine Calculated for the Gentleman, the Farmer and His Wife (1763).

Court Magazine (1761).

Critical Memoirs of the Times (1769).

Critical Review (1756).

Edinburgh Magazine (1757).

European Magazine (1782).

General Magazine of Arts and Sciences (1755).

General Review or Impartial Register (1752).

Gentleman's and Lady's Museum (1777).

Gentleman's Magazine (1731).

Grand Magazine of Magazines, or Universal Register (1758).

Grand Magazine of Universal Intelligence (1758).

History of Learning (1691).

Imperial Magazine (1760).

Journal encyclopédique (Paris, 1756).

Kapélion (1750).

Lady's Magazine: or Entertaining Companion for the Fair Sex (1770).

Lady's Magazine: or Polite Companion for the Fair Sex (1759).

Lady's Museum (1760).

Library (1761).

Literary Journal (Dublin, 1744).

Literary Magazine: or Select British Library (1735).

Literary Magazine, or Universal Review (1756).

Literary Register; or Weekly Miscellany (Newcastle, 1769).

London Magazine (1732).

London Monthly Mercury; or, Foreign Literary Intelligencer (1753).

London Review of English and Foreign Literature (1775).

Magazin de Londres (1749).

Memoirs of Literature (1710).

Midwife (1750).

Monthly Review (1749).

Museum: or the Literary and Historical Register (1746).

New Memoirs of Literature (1725).

Oxford Magazine: or University Museum (1768).

Political Controversy (1762).

Political Register; and Impartial Review of New Books (1767).

Present State of the Republick of Letters (1728).

Repository; or General Review (1756).

Royal Magazine; or Gentleman's Monthly Companion (1759).

St. James's Magazine (1762).

Scots Magazine (1739).

Theatrical Review: or Annals of the Drama (1763).

Town and Country Magazine (1769).

True Briton (1751).

Universal Librarian (1751).

Universal Magazine of Knowledge and Pleasure (1747).

Universal Museum: or Gentleman's and Lady's Polite Magazine of History, Politics, and Literature (1762).

Universal Visiter (1756).

Weekly Amusement: or an Useful and Agreeable Miscellany of Literary Entertainments (1763).

Weekly Magazine and Literary Review (1758).

Weekly Magazine: or Edinburgh Amusement (1768).

Westminster Magazine: or the Pantheon of Taste (1773).

C. Newspapers

Boddeley's Bath Journal (originally *Bath Journal*: 1744).

Bristol Gazette and Public Advertiser (1767).

Bristol Weekly Intelligencer (1749).

Caledonian Mercury (1720).

Edinburgh Chronicle (1759).

Evening Advertiser (1754).

General Evening Post (1733).

Gloucester Journal (1722).

Ipswich Journal (1739).

Jackson's Oxford Journal (1753).

Jopson's Coventry Mercury; or the Weekly Country Journal (1741).

Lloyd's Evening Post and British Chronicle (1757).

London Chronicle (1758).

London Daily Advertiser (originally *London Advertiser and Literary Gazette*: 1751).

London Evening Post (1727).

London General Advertiser (originally *London Daily Post and General Advertiser*: 1734).

Newcastle Chronicle (1764).

Owen's Weekly Chronicle (originally *New Weekly Chronicle*: 1758).

Oxford Gazette and Reading Mercury (originally *Reading Mercury: or Weekly Entertainer*: 1723).

Pope's Bath Chronicle (originally *Bath Chronicle and Weekly Gazette*: 1760).

Portsmouth and Gosport Gazette and Salisbury Journal (1750).

Public Advertiser (originally *London Daily Post and General Advertiser*: 1734).

Public Ledger (1760).

St. James's Chronicle (1761).

Salisbury Journal (1736).

Universal Advertiser (Dublin, 1731).

Whitehall Evening Post (1718).

III. EIGHTEENTH CENTURY BOOKS AND PAMPHLETS

An Abstract from the Monthly Critical Review of the Advertisement Prefixed to the History of Valencia by Don Juan Fernandez, Principal of the Inquisition at Estremadura. London, 1756.

Adventures of a Black Coat. London, 1762.

The Adventures of an Author. 2 vols. London, 1767.

Amory, Thomas. *The Life of John Buncle.* 2 vols. London, 1756–66.

Anderson, Robert. "The Life of Smollett." In *The Miscellaneous Works of Tobias Smollett, M.D.* 6 vols. London: 1796.

[Baker, David Erskine]. "Smollett, Tobias M.D." In *The Companion to the Play-house,* 2 vols. London: 1764.

———. "Smollett, Tobias M.D." In *Biographia Dramatica, or, A Companion to the Playhouse,* edited by Isaac Reed, 4 vols. London: 1782.

The Battle of the Reviews. London, 1760.

Beattie, James. "An Essay on Laughter and Ludicrous Composition." In *Essays,* 321–486. Edinburgh and London: 1776.

Beauties of the Magazines and Other Periodical Works. 2 vols. London, 1772.

[Beckford, William]. *Azemia, A Novel.* 2nd ed. 2 vols. London, 1798.

Churchill, Charles. *The Apology. Addressed to the Critical Reviewers.* London, 1761.

———. *The Author.* London, 1763.

———. *The Ghost.* London, 1762.

Cibber, Theophilus. *Two Dissertations on Theatrical Subjects.* London, 1765.

Comber, Thomas. *A Vindication of the Great Revolution in England in A.D. MDCLXXXVIII.* London, 1758.

Davies, Thomas. *Dramatic Miscellanies.* 2d ed. 3 vols. London, 1785.

A General Index to the Monthly Review. London, 1760.

Goldsmith, Oliver. *Essays and Criticisms.* Edited by Thomas Wright and Isaac Reed. 3 vols. London, 1798.

Grainger, James. *A Letter to Tobias Smollet, M.D. Occasioned by His Criticism upon a Late Translation of Tibullus.* London, 1759.

Griffith, Richard. *The Koran.* London, 1770.

Heathcote, Ralph, ed. "Smollett, Tobias, M.D." In *The New and General Biographical Dictionary,* 15 vols. London, 1784.

The History of Jack Connor, 4th ed. Dublin, 1766.

Hume, David. *Political Discourses.* London, 1752.

Jones, Rowland. *The Philosophy of Words.* London, 1769.

Kenrick, William. *A Scrutiny; or, the Critics Criticis'd.* London, 1759.

"The Life of T. Smollett, M.D." In *Plays and Poems Written by T. Smollett, M.D. with Memoirs of the Life and Writings of the Author,* i–xxix. London, 1777.

Lovett, R. *The Reviewers Reviewed.* London, 1760.

Marriot, Thomas. *The Twentieth Epistle of Horace to His Book, Modernized by* the Author of Female Conduct and Applied to His Own Book . . . An Answer to the . . . Critical Review. London, 1759.

Moore, John. "The Life of T. Smollett, M.D." In *The Works of Tobias Smollett, M.D.* 8 vols. London, 1797.

Murphy, Arthur. *A Poetical Epistle to Mr. Samuel Johnson, A.M.* London, 1760.

—————. *Ode to the Naiads of Fleet-Ditch.* London, 1761.

A New Universal History of Arts and Sciences. London, 1759.

Observations on the Importance and Use of Theatres; Their Present Regulation and Possible Improvements. London, 1759.

Patten, Thomas. *St. Peter's Christian Apology.* Oxford, 1756.

Priestly, Joseph. *The Rudiments of English Grammar, adapted to the Use of Schools.* London, 1768.

Prior, Matthew. *Carmen Seculare for the Year 1700.* London, 1701.

Ralph, James. *The Case of Authors by Profession or Trade Stated, with Regard to Booksellers, the Stage and the Public.* London, 1758.

[Reed, Joseph]. *A Sop in the Pan for a Physical Critick: in a Letter to Dr. Sm*ll*t.* London, 1759.

Reeve, Clara. *The Progress of Romance.* Colchester, 1785.

The Reviewers Reviewed. London, 1779.

[Rider, William]. "Dr. Smollet [sic]." In *An Historical Account of the Lives and Writings of the Living Authors of Great-Britain.* London, 1762.

Rules and Orders of the Edinburgh Society for the Encouragement of Arts, Sciences, Manufactures, and Agriculture. Edinburgh, 1765.

[Shebbeare, John]. Appendix to the Occasional Critic. London, 1757.

[—————]. *Lydia: or Filial Piety.* London, 1755.

[—————]. *The Occasional Critic: or, the Decrees of the Scotch Tribunal in the Critical Review Rejudged.* London, 1757.

Smart, Christopher. *Poems.* London, 1763.

The Theatrical Examiner: An Enquiry into the Merits and Demerits of the Present English Performers in General. London, 1757.

Thompson, Edward. *The Demi-Rep.* London, 1756 [for 1766].

Tickell, Thomas. *On the Prospect of Peace.* London, 1713.

Underwood, Thomas. *Poems.* London, 1768.

Voltaire. François Marie Arouet de. "On the Royal Society and Academies." In *Works of M. de Voltaire*, 38 vols., translated by Tobias Smollett. London, 1762.

IV. OTHER SOURCES

Altick, Richard D. *The English Common Reader*. Chicago: University of Chicago Press, 1957.

Albrecht, Wilbur T. "The British Magazine." In *British Literary Magazines: The Augustan Age and the Age of Johnson 1698–1788*, edited by Alvin Sullivan, 26–30. Westport, Conn.: Greenwood Press, 1983.

———. "The Monthly Review." In *British Literary Magazines: The Augustan Age and the Age of Johnson 1698–1788*, edited by Alvin Sullivan, 231–37. Westport, Conn.: Greenwood Press, 1983.

———. "The Scots Magazine." In *British Literary Magazines: The Augustan Age and the Age of Johnson 1698–1788*, edited by Alvin Sullivan, 299–304. Westport, Conn.: Greenwood Press, 1983.

Anderson, Robert. "The Life of Tobias Smollett, M.D." In *Miscellaneous Works of Tobias Smollett, M.D.* 6th ed., 6 vols. Edinburgh, 1820.

Antal, Frederick. *Hogarth and His Place in European Art*. London: Routledge and Kegan Paul, 1962.

Arnold, Matthew. *Essays in Criticism*. 2nd ed. London: Macmillan, 1869.

Austen-Leigh, R. A. "William Strahan and His Ledgers." *The Library*, 3 (1922–23): 261–87.

Babcock, R. W. "The Idea of Taste in the Eighteenth Century." *PMLA* 50 (1935): 922–26.

Baker, Ernest A. "Smollett." In *The History of the English Novel*, 10 vols. London: H. F. & G. Witherby, 1930.

Barrell, John. *English Literature in History 1730–80: An Equal, Wide Survey*. London: Hutchinson, 1983.

Basker, James G. "Another Smollett Play?" *Notes and Queries*, n.s., 27 (1980): 33–34.

———. "Minim and the Great Cham: Smollett and Johnson on the Prospect of an English Academy." In *Johnson and His Age*, edited by James Engell, 137–61. Cambridge: Harvard University Press, 1984.

———. "Smollett and Literary Journalism, 1756–1763." D. Phil. diss., Oxford University, 1983.

———. "The Wages of Sin: The Later Career of John Cleland." Forthcoming in *Etudes anglaises*, June 1987.

Bate, Walter Jackson. *Samuel Johnson*. New York: Harcourt Brace Jovanovich, 1975.

Benjamin, Lewis S. *The Life and Letters of Tobias Smollett (1721–1771)*. London: Faber and Gwyer, 1926.

Bevis, Richard W. "Smollett and *The Israelites*." *Philological Quarterly* 45 (April 1966): 387–94.

Bindman, David. *Hogarth*. New York: Oxford University Press, 1981.

Birn, Raymond F. *Pierre Rousseau and the philosophes of Bouillon*. Studies on Voltaire and the eighteenth century, edited by Theodore Besterman, no. 29. Geneva: Institut et Musée Voltaire, 1964.

Bisset, Andrew. *Memoirs and Papers of Sir Andrew Mitchell*. London, 1850.

Bloom, Edward A. "'Labors of the Learned': Neoclassic Book Reviewing Aims and Techniques." *Studies in Philology* 54 (1957): 537–63.

———. "Neoclassic 'Paper Wars' for a Free Press." *Modern Language Review* 56 (1961): 481–96.

———. *Samuel Johnson in Grub Street*. Providence: Brown University Press, 1957.

Boege, Fred W. *Smollett's Reputation as a Novelist*. Princeton Studies in English, no. 27. Princeton: Princeton University Press, 1947.

Bond, Richmond P. "Introduction." In *Studies in the Early English Periodical*, edited by Richmond P. Bond, 3–48. Chapel Hill: University of North Carolina Press, 1957.

Boswell, James. *Boswell in Extremes 1776–1778*. Edited by Charles McC. Weis and Frederick A. Pottle. Yale Editions of the Private Papers of James Boswell. N.p. 1931. Reprint. New York: McGraw-Hill, 1970.

———. *Boswell in Search of a Wife 1766–1769*. Edited by Frank Brady and Frederick A. Pottle. Yale Editions of the Private Papers of James Boswell. N.p. 1928. Reprint. New York: McGraw-Hill, 1956.

———. *Boswell's Life of Johnson Together with Boswell's Journal of a Tour to the Hebrides and Johnson's Diary of a Journey in North Wales*. 6 vols. Edited by George Birkbeck Hill; rev. ed. edited by L. F. Powell. Oxford: Clarendon Press, 1934–64.

———. *Boswell's London Journal 1762–1763*. Edited by Frederick A. Pottle. Yale Editions of the Private Papers of James Boswell. London: Heinemann, 1950.

———. *Boswell: The Applause of the Jury 1782–1785*. Edited by Irma S. Lustig and Frederick A. Pottle. Yale Editions of the Private Papers of James Boswell. N.p. 1932. Reprint. New York: McGraw-Hill, 1981.

———. *Boswell: The Ominous Years 1774–1776*. Edited by Charles Ryskamp and Frederick A. Pottle. Yale Editions of the Private Papers of James Boswell. N.p. 1931. Reprint. New York: McGraw-Hill, 1963.

———. *The Correspondence and Other Papers of James Boswell Relating to the Making of the Life of Johnson*. Edited by Marshall Waingrow. Yale Editions of the Private Papers of James Boswell (Research Edition), vol. 2 of *Boswell's Correspondence*. New York: McGraw-Hill, n.d.

———. *The Correspondence of James Boswell and John Johnston of Grange*. Edited by Ralph S. Walker. Yale Editions of the Private Papers of James Boswell (Research Edition), vol. 1 of *Boswell's Correspondence*. New York: McGraw-Hill, n.d.

———. *The Correspondence of James Boswell with Certain Members of The*

Club. Edited by Charles N. Fifer. Yale Editions of the Private Papers of James Boswell (Research Edition), vol. 3 of *Boswell's Correspondence.* New York: McGraw-Hill, 1976.

―――. *Early Papers of James Boswell, 1754–1763.* Vol. 1, *Private Papers of James Boswell from Malahide Castle,* edited by Geoffrey Scott and Frederick A. Pottle. Mount Vernon, N.Y.: privately printed, 1928.

―――. *The Journal of James Boswell 1765–1768.* Vol. 7, *Private Papers of James Boswell from Malahide Castle,* edited by Geoffrey Scott and Frederick A. Pottle. N.p.: privately printed, 1930.

Botting, Roland B. "Johnson, Smart, and the *Universal Visiter.*" *Modern Philology* 36 (1938–39): 293–300.

Boucé, Paul-Gabriel. "Eighteenth- and Nineteenth-Century Biographies of Smollett." In *Tobias Smollett: Bicentennial Essays Presented to Lewis M. Knapp,* 201–30. New York: Oxford University Press, 1971.

―――. *"A Note on Smollett's Continuation of the Complete History of England."* *Review of English Studies,* n.s., 20 (1969): 57–61.

―――. *The Novels of Tobias Smollett.* Translated by P.-G. Boucé and Antonia White. London: Longman, 1976.

―――. "Smollett and the Expedition against Rochefort (1757)." *Modern Philology* 65 (1967): 33–38.

―――. "Smollett Criticism, 1770–1924: Corrections and Additions." *Notes and Queries,* n.s., 14 (1967): 184–87.

―――. "Smollett's Libel." *London Times Literary Supplement,* 30 December 1965, 1218.

Brack, O M, Jr. "The Bicentennial Edition of the Works of Tobias Smollett." *Books at Iowa* 7 (1967): 41–42.

―――. "The Ledgers of William Strahan." In *Editing Eighteenth-Century Texts,* edited by D. I. B. Smith, 59–77. Toronto: University of Toronto Press, 1968.

――― and James B. Davis. "Smollett's Revisions of *Roderick Random.*" *Publications of the Bibliographical Society of America* 64 (1970): 295–311.

Brander, Laurence. *Tobias Smollett.* London: Longmans, Green, for British Council and the National Book League, 1951.

Brewer, John. *Party Ideology and Popular Politics at the Accession of George III.* Cambridge: Cambridge University Press, 1976.

Bronson, Bertrand Harris. "When Was Neoclassicism?" In *Facets of the Enlightenment: Studies in English Literature and Its Contexts.* Berkeley: University of California Press, 1968.

Bruce, Donald. *Radical Doctor Smollett.* London: Gollancz, 1964.

―――. "Smollett and the Sordid Knaves." *Contemporary Review* 220 (1972): 133–38.

Buck, Howard Swazey. *Smollett as Poet.* New Haven: Yale University Press, 1927.

————. *A Study in Smollett: Chiefly "Peregrine Pickle," with a Complete Collation of the First and Second Editions.* New Haven: Yale University Press, 1925.

Burke, Edmund. *The Correspondence of Edmund Burke.* Edited by Thomas W. Copeland. Cambridge: Cambridge University Press, 1958.

Burke, Joseph. *English Art, 1714–1800.* Vol. 9 of *Oxford History of English Art,* edited by T. S. R. Boase. Oxford: Clarendon Press, 1976.

Burney, Fanny. *Camilla.* Edited by Edward A. and Lillian D. Bloom. Oxford: Oxford University Press, 1972.

————. *Evelina.* Edited by Edward A. and Lillian D. Bloom. Oxford: Oxford University Press, 1982.

Byron, George Gordon, Lord. *The Works of Lord Byron.* Edited by Ernest Hartley Coleridge. 7 vols. London: 1898–1904.

Carlson, C. Lennart. "Edward Cave's Club, and Its Project for a Literary Review." *Philological Quarterly* 17 (1938): 115–20.

————. *The First Magazine: A History of the Gentleman's Magazine.* Providence: Brown University Press, 1938.

Carlyle, Alexander. *Anecdotes and Characters of the Times.* Edited by James Kinsley. Oxford English Memoirs and Travels. London: Oxford University Press, 1973.

Chambers, Robert. *Smollett: His Life and a Selection from His Writings.* London, 1867.

Churchill, Charles. *Poems of Charles Churchill.* Edited by James Laver. New York: Barnes & Noble, Inc., 1970.

Clifford, James L. *Dictionary Johnson: Samuel Johnson's Middle Years.* London: Heinemann, 1979.

————. "Johnson and the Society Artists." In *The Augustan Milieu: Essays Presented to Louis A. Landa,* edited by Henry Knight Miller, Eric Rothstein, and G. S. Rousseau, 333–48. Oxford: Clarendon Press, 1970.

Clive, John. *Scotch Reviewers: The Edinburgh Review, 1802–1815.* Cambridge: Harvard University Press, 1957.

Cochrane, J. A. *Dr. Johnson's Printer: The Life of William Strahan.* London: Routledge and Kegan Paul, 1964.

Cole, Richard C. "Community Lending Libraries in Eighteenth-Century Ireland." *Library Quarterly* 44 (1974): 111–23.

————. "Smollett and the Eighteenth-Century Irish Book Trade." *Publications of the Bibliographical Society of America* 69 (1975): 345–63.

Coleridge, Samuel Taylor. *Biographia Literaria.* Edited by James Engell and W. Jackson Bate. 2 vols. Princeton: Princeton University Press, 1983.

Collins, A. S. *Authorship in the Days of Johnson, Being a Study of the Relations between Author, Patron, Publisher and Public 1726–1780.* London: George Routledge and Sons, 1927.

———. "The Growth of the Reading Public during the Eighteenth Century." *Review of English Studies* 2 (1926): 284–94, 428–38.

———. *The Profession of Letters: A Study of the Relation of Author to Patron, Publisher, and Public, 1780–1832.* London: Routledge, 1928.

Copeland, Thomas W. "Burke and Dodsley's *Annual Register*," *PMLA* 54 (1939): 223–45.

———. "Edmund Burke and the Book Reviews in Dodsley's *Annual Register*," *PMLA* 57 (1942): 446–68.

Cordasco, Francesco. *Smollett Criticism, 1770–1924: A Bibliography Enumerative and Annotated.* Brooklyn: Long Island University Press, 1948.

———. *Smollett Criticism, 1925–1945: A Compilation.* Brooklyn: Long Island University Press, 1947.

———. *Tobias George Smollett: A Bibliographical Guide.* New York: AMS Press, 1978.

Couper, W. J. *The Edinburgh Periodical Press.* 2 vols. Edinburgh: Stirling, 1908.

Craig, Mary E. *The Scottish Periodical Press, 1750–1789.* Edinburgh: Oliver and Boyd, 1931.

Crane, R. S., and F. B. Kaye. *A Census of British Newspaper and Periodicals, 1620–1800.* Chapel Hill: University of North Carolina Press, 1927.

———. "A Neglected Mid-Eighteenth-Century Plea for Originality and Its Author." *Philological Quarterly* 13 (1934): 21–29.

Cranfield, G. A. *The Development of the Provincial Newspaper, 1700–1760.* Oxford: Clarendon Press, 1962.

Cross, Wilbur L. *The Life and Times of Laurence Sterne.* 2 vols. London: Humphrey Milford, Oxford University Press, 1925.

Defoe, Daniel. *An Essay Upon Projects.* In *The Earlier Life and the Chief Earlier Works of Daniel Defoe*, edited by Henry Morley, 23–164. New York: Burt Franklin, n.d.

Derrick, Samuel. Papers. Victoria and Albert Museum.

Doherty, Francis. "Letter of Christopher Anstey to Robert Dodsley." *Notes and Queries*, n.s., 32, no. 2 (June 1985): 237.

Dudden, F. Homes. *Henry Fielding: His Life, Works, and Times.* 2 vols. Oxford: Clarendon Press, 1952.

Eddy, Donald D. *Samuel Johnson: Book Reviewer in the Literary Magazine; or, Universal Review 1756–1758.* London: Garland, 1979.

Epstein, William H. *John Cleland: Images of a Life.* New York and London: Columbia University Press, 1974.

Erdman, David V. "Immoral Acts of the Literary Cormorant: The Extent of Coleridge's Contributions to the *Critical Review*." *Bulletin of the New York Public Library* 63 (1959): 433–54, 515–30, 575–87.

Fabel, Robin. "The Patriotic Briton: Tobias Smollett and English Politics,

1756–1771." *Eighteenth Century Studies* 8 (1974): 100–14.

Fabian, Bernhard. "An Eighteenth Century Research Collection: English Books at Göttingen University Library." *Library*, 6th ser., 1 (1979): 209–24.

————. "English Books and Their Eighteenth-Century German Readers." In *The Widening Circle: Essays on the Circulation of Literature in Eighteenth-Century Europe*, edited by Paul J. Korshin, 117–96. Philadelphia: University of Pennsylvania Press, 1976.

Faulkner, George. *Prince of Dublin Printers: The Letters of George Faulkner*. Edited by Robert E. Ward. N.p.: University Press of Kentucky, 1972.

Feather, John. *The Provincial Book Trade in Eighteenth-Century England*. Cambridge: Cambridge University Press, 1985.

Felsenstein, F. "A Note on Smollett's Travels." *Notes and Queries*, n.s., 15 (1968): 452–53.

————. "An Unrecorded Smollett Letter." *Ariel: a Review of International English Literature* 2 (October 1971): 87–89.

Fielding, Henry. *Amelia*. Edited by Martin C. Battestin. Middletown, Conn.: Wesleyan University Press, 1983.

Fielding, Henry. *The Covent-Garden Journal*. Edited by Gerard Edward Jensen. 2 vols. New York: Russell and Russell, 1964.

————. *The Jacobite's Journal and Related Writings*. Edited by W. B. Coley. Wesleyan Edition of the Works of Henry Fielding. N.p.: Wesleyan University Press, 1975.

Flavell, M. Kay. "The Enlightened Reader and the New Industrial Towns: A Study of the Liverpool Library 1758–1790." *British Journal for Eighteenth-Century Studies* 8 (Spring 1985): 17–35.

Forster, John. *The Life and Adventures of Oliver Goldsmith*. London, 1848.

Foster, James R. "A Forgotten Noble Savage, Tsonnonthouan." *Modern Language Quarterly* 14 (1953): 348–59.

————. "Smollett and the *Atom*." *PMLA* 68 (1953): 1032–46.

————. "Smollett's Pamphleteering Foe Shebbeare." *PMLA* 57 (1942): 1053–1100.

Foxon, David. "Letter to the Editor." *Publishing History* 6 (1979): 113–15.

Franklin, Benjamin. *The Writings and Letters of Benjamin Franklin*. Edited by Albert H. Smyth. New York: Macmillan, 1905–7.

Friedman, Arthur. "Goldsmith's Contributions to the *Critical Review*." *Modern Philology* 44 (1946): 23–52.

Frye, Northrop. "Towards Defining an Age of Sensibility." In *Eighteenth Century English Literature: Modern Essays in Criticism*, edited by James L. Clifford, 311–18. New York: Oxford University Press, 1959.

Gallup, Donald C. "Baretti's Reputation in England." In *The Age of Johnson: Essays Presented to Chauncey Brewster Tinker*, edited by Frederick W.

Hilles, 363–75. New Haven: Yale University Press, 1949.

Gassman, Byron. "The *Briton* and *Humphry Clinker*." *Studies in English Literature* 3 (1963): 397–414.

Giddings, Robert. *The Tradition of Smollett*. London: Methuen, 1967.

Ginger, John. *The Notable Man: The Life and Times of Oliver Goldsmith*. London: Hamish Hamilton, 1977.

Goldberg, M.A. *Smollett and the Scottish School. Studies in Eighteenth-Century Thought*. Albuquerque: University of New Mexico Press, 1959.

Golden, Morris. "The British Magazine." In *British Literary Magazines: The Augustan Age and the Age of Johnson 1698–1788*, edited by Alvin Sullivan, 22–26. Westport, Conn.: Greenwood Press, 1983.

———. "A Decade's Bent: Names in the *Monthly Review* and the *Critical Review*, 1760–1769." *Bulletin of the New York Public Library* 79 (1976): 336–61.

———. "Notes on Three Goldsmith Attributions." *Notes and Queries* 203 (1958): 24–26.

———. "Travel Writing in the *Monthly Review* and the *Critical Review*, 1756–1775." *Papers on Language and Literature* 13 (1977): 213–23.

———. "Two Essays Erroneously Attributed to Goldsmith," *Modern Language Notes* 74 (1959): 13–16.

Goldsmith, Oliver. *Collected Works of Oliver Goldsmith*. Edited by Arthur Friedman. 5 vols. Oxford: Clarendon Press, 1966.

———. *New Essays by Oliver Goldsmith*. Edited by Ronald S. Crane. Chicago: University of Chicago Press, 1927.

———. *The Works of Oliver Goldsmith*. Edited by J. W. M. Gibbs. 5 vols. London, 1884–86.

Graham, Walter. *The Beginnings of English Literary Periodicals: A Study of Periodical Literature, 1665–1715*. New York: Oxford University Press, 1926.

———. *English Literary Periodicals*. New York: Thomas Nelson and Sons, 1930.

Grant, Damian. *Tobias Smollett. A Study in Style*. Manchester: Manchester University Press, 1977.

———. "Unpublished Additions to Smollett's *Travels*." *Notes and Queries*, n.s., 14 (1967): 187–89.

Gray, Charles Harold. *Theatrical Criticism in London to 1795*. New York: Columbia University Press, 1931.

Gray, Thomas. *Correspondence of Thomas Gray*. Edited by Paget Toynbee and Leonard Whibley. Oxford: Oxford University Press, 1935.

Greene, Donald J. "Johnson's Contributions to the *Literary Magazine*." *Review of English Studies*, n.s., 7 (1956): 367–92.

————. "Samuel Johnson, Journalist." In *Newsletters to Newspapers: Eighteenth Century Journalism*, edited by D. H. Bond and W. R. McLeod, 87–101. Morgantown, West Virginia: West Virginia University, 1977.

————. "Smollett the Historian." In *Tobias Smollett: Bicentennial Essays Presented to Lewis M. Knapp*, 25–56. New York: Oxford University Press, 1971.

Griffiths, Ralph. Papers. Bodleian Library. MS Add. C.89.

Gross, John. *The Rise and Fall of the Man of Letters: Aspects of English Literary Life Since 1800*. London: Weidenfeld and Nicolson, 1969.

Gunnis, Rupert. *Dictionary of British Sculptors 1660–1851*. Cambridge: Harvard University Press, 1954.

Haig, Robert L. *"The Gazetteer," 1735–97: A Study in the Eighteenth Century English Newspaper*. Carbondale: Southern Illinois University Press, 1960.

Handover, P. M. *A History of the London Gazette 1665–1965*. London: Her Majesty's Stationery Office, 1965.

Haney, John Louis. *Early Reviews of English Poets*. Philadelphia: Egerton Press, 1904.

Hannay, David. *Life of Tobias George Smollett*. London: Walter Scott, 1887.

Hatin, Eugene. *Bibliographie historique et critique de la press périodique Française*. Paris: Librarie de Firmin Didot Freres, Fils et Cie, 1866.

Heidler, Joseph Bunn. "The History from 1700 to 1800 of English Criticism of Prose Fiction." *University of Illinois Studies in Language and Literature* 13 (1928): 9–187.

Henley, W. E. Introduction. In *The Works of Tobias Smollett*, 12 vols., 1899–1901. New York: Charles Scribner's Sons, 1899.

Herbert, David. "Life of Tobias George Smollett." In *The Works of Tobias Smollett*, 7–40. Edinburgh, 1870.

Highfill, P. H., Jr., et al. *A Biographical Dictionary of Actors, Actresses, Musicians, Dancers, Managers and Other Stage Personnel in London 1660–1800*, vol. 3. Carbondale: Southern Illinois University Press, 1975.

Hooker, Edward Niles. "The Discussion of Taste, from 1750–1770, and the New Trends in Literary Criticism." *PMLA* 49 (1934): 577–92.

————. "The Reviewers and the New Criticism, 1754–1770." *Philological Quarterly* 13 (1934): 189–202.

————. "The Reviewers and the New Trends in Poetry, 1754–1770." *Modern Language Notes* 51 (1936): 207–14.

Hume, David. *The Letters of David Hume*. Edited by J. Y. T. Greig. 2 vols. Oxford: Clarendon Press, 1932.

————. *New Letters of David Hume*. Edited by Raymond Klibansky and Ernest C. Mossner. Oxford: Clarendon Press, 1954.

Hunter, Richard A., and Ida Macalpine. "Sir Launcelot Greaves." Letter in

Times Literary Supplement, 16 December 1955, 761.

———. "Smollett's Reading in Psychiatry." *Modern Language Review* 51 (1956): 409–11.

———. "Tobias Smollett, M.D. and William Battie, M.D." *Journal of the History of Medicine and Allied Sciences* 11 (1956): 102–6.

Hunter, Robert. *The History of the Irish Newspaper*. Cambridge: Cambridge University Press, 1967.

Janssens, Uta. *Matthieu Maty and the Journal Britannique 1750–1755*. Amsterdam: Holland University Press, 1975.

Johnson, Samuel. *The Letters of Samuel Johnson*. Edited by R. W. Chapman. 3 vols. Oxford: Clarendon Press, 1952.

———. *Lives of the English Poets*. Edited by George Birkbeck Hill. 3 vols. Oxford: Clarendon Press, 1905.

———. *The Yale Edition of the Works of Samuel Johnson*. Edited by A. T. Hazen, Herman Liebert, John H. Middendorf, et al. 10 vols. New Haven: Yale University Press, 1958–77.

Joliat, Eugène. "Smollett, Editor of Voltaire." *Modern Language Notes* 54 (1939): 429–36.

———. *Smollett et la France*. Bibliotheque de la Revue de Litérature Comparée, 105. Paris: Librarie Ancienne Honoré Champion, 1935.

Jones, Claude E. "Contributors to the *Critical Review* 1756–1785." *Modern Language Notes* 61 (1946): 433–41.

———. "The *Critical Review* and Some Major Poets." *Notes and Queries*, n.s. 3 (1956): 114–15.

———. "The *Critical Review*'s First Thirty Years." *Notes and Queries*, n.s., 3 (1956): 78–80.

———. "Dramatic Criticism in the *Critical Review*, 1756–1785." *Modern Language Quarterly* 20 (1959): 18–26, 133–44.

———. "The English Novel: A *Critical* View." *Modern Language Quarterly* 19 (1958): 147–59, 213–24.

———. "Poetry and the *Critical Review*, 1756–1785." *Modern Language Quarterly* 9 (1948): 17–36.

———. "Smollett Editions in Eighteenth-Century Britain." *Notes and Queries*, n.s., 4 (1957): 252.

———. "A Smollett Note." *Notes and Queries* 174 (1938): 152.

———. *Smollett Studies*. University of California Publications in English, 9, No. 2. Berkeley: University of California Press, 1942.

———. "Tobias Smollett on the 'Separation of the Pubic Joint in Pregnancy.'" *Medical Life* 41 (1934): 302–5.

Kahrl, George M. *Tobias Smollett, Traveler-Novelist*. Chicago: University of Chicago Press, 1945.

Kaufman, Paul. *Libraries and Their Users: Collected Papers in Library History.* London: The Library Assoc., 1969.

Kent, Elizabeth Eaton. *Goldsmith and His Booksellers.* London: Humphrey Milford, Oxford University Press, 1933.

Kerr, Robert. *Memoirs of William Smellie.* 2 vols. Edinburgh, 1811.

Klukoff, Philip J. "New Smollett Attributions in the *Critical Review.*" *Notes and Queries*, n.s., 14 (1967): 418–19.

———. "Smollett and the *Critical Review*: Criticism of the Novel." Ph.D. diss., Michigan State University, 1965.

———. "Smollett and the *Critical Review*: Criticism of the Novel, 1756–1763." *Studies in Scottish Literature* 4 (1966): 89–100.

———. "Smollett and the Sackville Controversy." *Neuphilologische Mitteilungen* 69 (1968): 617–28.

———. "Smollett as the Reviewer of Jeremiah Grant." *Notes and Queries*, n.s., 13 (1966): 466.

———. "A Smollett Attribution in the *Critical Review.*" *Notes and Queries*, n.s., 12 (1965): 221.

———. "Smollett's Defense of Dr. Smellie in the *Critical Review.*" *Medical History* 14 (1970): 31–41.

———. "Two Smollett Attributions in the *Critical Review: The Reverie* and *Tristram Shandy.*" *Notes and Queries*, n.s., 13 (1966): 465–66.

Knapp, Lewis M. "Comments on Smollett by the Rev. Dr. Thomas Birch." *Notes and Queries*, n.s., 12 (1965): 218–21.

———. "Dr. John Armstrong, Littérateur, and Associate of Smollett, Thomson, Wilkes, and Other Celebrities." *PMLA* 59 (1944): 1019–58.

———. "Early Scottish Attitudes toward Tobias Smollett." *Philological Quarterly* 45 (1966): 262–69.

———. "Griffiths's 'Monthly Review' as Printed by Strahan." *Notes and Queries*, n.s., 5 (1958): 216–17.

———. "The 'Prophecy" Attributed to Smollett." *Review of English Studies*, n.s., 16 (1965): 177–82.

———. "The Publication of Smollett's *Complete History* . . . and *Continuation.*" *Library*, 4th ser., 16 (1935): 295–308.

———. "Ralph Griffiths, Author and Publisher 1746–50." *Library*, 4th ser., 20 (1939): 197–213.

———. "Rex versus Smollett: More Data on the Smollett-Knowles Libel Case." *Modern Philology* 41 (1944): 221–27.

———. "Smollett and Garrick." In *Elizabethan Studies and Other Essays in Honor of George F. Reynolds*, 233–43. University of Colorado Studies, 2. Boulder: University of Colorado, 1945.

———. "Smollett and Johnson, Never Cater-Cousins?" *Modern Philology* 66

(1968): 151–54.

——. "Smollett's Admirers in Eighteenth Century America," *Williams Alumni Review* 22 (1929): 114–15.

——. "Smollett's Self-Portrait in *The Expedition of Humphry Clinker.*" In *The Age of Johnson: Essays Presented to Chauncy Brewster Tinker*, edited by Frederick W. Hilles, 149–58. New Haven: Yale University Press, 1949.

——. "Smollett's Translation of Fénelon's *Télémaque.*" *Philological Quarterly* 44 (1965): 405–7.

——. "Smollett's Works as Printed by William Strahan, with an Unpublished Letter of Smollett to Strahan." *Library*, 4th ser., 13 (1932): 282–91.

——. *Tobias Smollett: Doctor of Men and Manners*. Princeton: Princeton University Press, 1949.

Korshin, Paul J., ed. *The Widening Circle: Essays on the Circulation of Literature in Eighteenth-Century Europe*. Philadelphia: University of Pennsylvania Press, 1976.

Korte, Donald M. *An Annotated Bibliography of Smollett Scholarship, 1946–68*. Toronto: University of Toronto Press, 1969.

——. "Smollett's *Advice* and *Reproof*: Apprenticeship in Satire." *Studies in Scottish Literature* 8 (1971): 239–53.

——. "Tobias Smollett's 'Advice' and 'Reproof.'" *Thoth* 8 (1967): 45–65.

Kribbs, Jayne K., ed. *An Annotated Bibliography of American Literary Periodicals, 1741–1850*. Boston: G. K. Hall, 1977.

Kuist, James M. *The Nichols File of "The Gentleman's Magazine"*. Madison: The University of Wisconsin Press, 1982.

Lamb, Charles. *The Letters of Charles Lamb*. Edited by E. V. Lucas. London: J. M. Dent & Sons and Methuen & Co., 1935.

Lettis, Richard Lincoln. "A Study of Smollett's *Sir Launcelot Greaves.*" Ph.D. diss., Yale University, 1957.

Levin, Harry. *Contexts of Criticism*. Cambridge: Harvard University Press, 1957.

Linsalata, Carmine R. *Smollett's Hoax: Don Quixote in English*. Stanford: Stanford University Press, 1956.

Lipking, Lawrence. "A History of the Future." In *New Approaches to Eighteenth-Century Literature*, edited by Phillip Harth, 159–76. New York: Columbia University Press, 1974.

Lonsdale, Roger. "New Attributions to John Cleland." *Review of English Studies*, n.s., 30 (1979): 268–90.

MacClintock, William Darnall. *Joseph Warton's Essay on Pope: A History of the Five Editions*. Chapel Hill: University of North Carolina Press, 1933.

Madden, Richard Robert. *The History of Irish Periodical Literature*. 2 vols. London, 1867.

Manley, K. A. "The London and Westminster Libraries, 1785–1823." *The*

Library, 6th ser., 7, no. 2 (June 1985): 141.

Martynov, I. F. "English Literature and Eighteenth-Century Russian Reviewers." *Oxford Slavonic Papers*, n.s., 4 (1971): 30–42.

Martz, Louis L. *The Later Career of Tobias Smollett*. Yale Studies in English, 97. New Haven: Yale University Press, 1942.

———. "Smollett and the Expedition to Carthagena." *PMLA* 56 (1941): 428–46.

———. "Tobias Smollett and the Universal History." *Modern Language Notes* 56 (1941): 1–14.

Mayo, Robert D. *The English Novel in the Magazines, 1740–1815*. Evanston, Ill.: Northwestern University Press, 1962.

McDonald, William R. "Circulating Libraries in the Northeast of Scotland in the Eighteenth Century." *Bibliotheck* 5 (1968): 119–37.

McKenzie, D. F. *Stationers' Company Apprentices 1701–1800*. Oxford: Oxford Bibliographical Society, 1978.

——— and J. C. Ross, eds. *A Ledger of Charles Ackers*. Oxford: Oxford University Press for the Oxford Bibliographical Society, 1968.

McKillop, Alan Dugald. *The Early Masters of English Fiction*. Lawrence: University of Kansas Press, 1956.

———. *Samuel Richardson: Printer and Novelist*. Chapel Hill: University of North Carolina Press, 1936.

Milford, R. T., and O. M. Sutherland. *A Catalogue of English Newspapers and Periodicals in the Bodleian Library, 1662–1800*. Oxford: Oxford Bibliographical Society, 1936.

Milic, Louis T. "Sterne and Smollett's *Travels*." *Notes and Queries*, n.s., 3 (1956): 80–81.

Moore, Robert Etheridge. *Hogarth's Literary Relationships*. Minneapolis: University of Minnesota Press, 1948.

Mott, Frank Luther. *A History of American Magazines, 1741–1850*. New York: D. Appleton, 1930.

Musher, Daniel M. "The Medical Views of Dr. Tobias Smollett (1721–1771)." *Bulletin of the History of Medicine* 41 (1967): 455–62.

Nangle, Benjamin C. *"The Monthly Review" First Series 1749–1789. Index of Contributors and Articles*. Oxford: Clarendon Press, 1934.

———. *The Monthly Review, Second Series, 1790–1815*. Oxford: Clarendon Press, 1955.

Nichols, John. *Illustrations of the Literary History of the Eighteenth Century*. 8 vols. London, 1817.

———. *Literary Anecdotes of the Eighteenth Century*. 9 vols. London, 1812–16.

———. *Minor Lives: A Collection of Biographies by John Nichols*. Edited by Edward L. Hart. Cambridge: Harvard University Press, 1971.

————. *The Rise and Progress of the Gentleman's Magazine.* London, 1821. Reprint. New York: Garland Publishing, 1974.

Oppenheimer, Jane M. "John and William Hunter and Some Contemporaries in Literature and Art." *Bulletin of the History of Medicine* 23 (1949): 21–47.

————. "A Note on William Hunter and Tobias Smollett." *Journal of the History of Medicine and Allied Sciences* 2 (1947): 481–86.

Park, William. "Change in the Criticism of the Novel after 1760." *Philological Quarterly* 46 (1967): 34–41.

Parker, Alice. "Tobias Smollett and the Law." *Studies in Philology* 39 (1942): 545–58.

Parreaux, André, ed. Introduction and notes. In *The Expedition of Humphry Clinker*, by Tobias Smollett. Boston: Houghton Mifflin, 1968.

Paulson, Ronald. *Hogarth: His Life, Art, and Times.* New Haven: Yale University Press for the Paul Mellon Centre for Studies in British Art, 1971.

————. *Hogarth's Graphic Works*, vol. 2. New Haven and London: Yale University Press, 1965.

————. "Smollett and Hogarth: The Identity of Pallet." *Studies in English Literature* 4 (1964): 351–59.

Percy, Thomas. *The Percy Letters.* Edited by David Nichol Smith and Cleanth Brooks. 7 vols. Vols. 1–5: Baton Rouge, Louisiana: Louisiana State University Press, 1944–57. Vols. 6–7: New Haven: Yale University Press, 1961–77.

Pitcher, Edward W. "Inconsistent Attributions and Arbitrary Signatures in Smollett's *British Magazine* (1760–67)." *Publications of the Bibliographical Society of America* 75 (1981), no. 4: 443–47.

————. "The Town and Country Magazine." In *British Literary Magazines: The Augustan Age and the Age of Johnson 1698–1788*, edited by Alvin Sullivan, 327–30. Westport, Conn.: Greenwood Press, 1983.

Pittock, Joan. *The Ascendancy of Taste: The Achievement of Joseph and Thomas Warton.* London: Routledge and Kegan Paul, 1973.

Pope, Alexander. "An Essay on Criticism." In *The Poems of Alexander Pope*, edited by John Butt, 143–68. London: Methuen, 1963.

Pottle, Frederick A. *James Boswell: The Earlier Years, 1740–1769.* New York: McGraw-Hill, 1966.

————. *The Literary Career of James Boswell, Esq.* 1929. Reprint. Oxford: Clarendon Press, 1967.

Powell, L. F. "Tobias Smollett and William Huggins." In *Eighteenth-Century Studies in Honor of Donald F. Hyde*, edited by W. H. Bond, 311–22. New York: The Grolier Club, 1970.

Preston, Thomas R. "Tobias Smollett—A Rising Misanthrope." In *Not in Timon's Manner: Feeling, Misanthropy, and Satire in Eighteenth-Century*

England, 69–120. Studies in the Humanities, 9, Literature. University, Alabama: University of Alabama Press, 1975.

Price, John Valdimir. *Tobias Smollett: The Expedition of Humphry Clinker*. Studies in English Literature, edited by David Daiches, no. 51. London: Edward Arnold, 1973.

Prickitt, Henry B. "The Political Writings and Opinions of Tobias Smollett." Ph.D. diss., Harvard University, 1952.

Prior, James. *Life of Oliver Goldsmith*. 2 vols. London, 1837.

Rea, Robert R. *The English Press in Politics, 1760–1774*. Lincoln: University of Nebraska Press, 1963.

Read, Allen Walker. "Suggestions for an Academy in England in the Latter Half of the Eighteenth Century." *Modern Philology* 36 (1938): 145–56.

Reid, B. L. "Smollett's Healing Journey." *Virginia Quarterly Review* 41 (1965): 549–70.

Rice, Scott. "The Satiric Persona of Smollett's *Travels*." *Studies in Scottish Literature* 10 (1972): 33–47.

Richardson, Lyon N. *A History of Early American Magazines, 1741–1789*. London: Thomas Nelson and Sons, 1931.

Ridpath, George. *Diary of George Ridpath, 1755–61*. Edited by Sir James Balfour Paul. *Publications of the Scottish Historical Society*, 3rd ser., 2 (1922).

Robberds, John W. *Memoirs of the Life and Writings of William Taylor of Norwich*. 2 vols. London, 1843.

Roberts, Helene E. "British Art Periodicals of the Eighteenth and Nineteenth Centuries." *Victorian Periodicals Newsletter* 9 (1970): 2–56.

Roberts, William. *Memoirs of the Life and Correspondence of Mrs. Hannah More*. London, 1834.

Robinson, F. J. G. *A Preliminary Guide to Book Subscription Lists*. Newcastle: University of Newcastle Upon Tyne, 1972.

Rogers, Pat. "Introduction: The Writer and Society." In *The Eighteenth Century*, edited by Pat Rogers, 1–80. New York: Holmes and Meier, 1978.

Roper, Derek. "Coleridge and the *Critical Review*." *Modern Language Review*, 55 (1960): 11–16.

———. "The Politics of the *Critical Review*, 1756–1817." *Durham University Journal* 53 (1961): 117–22.

———. *Reviewing before the "Edinburgh" 1788–1802*. Newark: University of Delaware Press, 1978.

———. "Smollett's 'Four Gentlemen': The First Contributors to the *Critical Review*." *Review of English Studies*, n.s., 10 (1959): 38–44.

———. "Tobias Smollett and the Founders of His 'Review.'" *Call Number* (Library of the University of Oregon) 19 (1957): 4–9.

Roscoe, Thomas. "Life and Works of Tobias Smollett." In *Miscellaneous*

Works of Tobias Smollett, vii–xl. London, 1841.

Rousseau, George S. "'No Boasted Academy of Christendom': Smollett and the Society of Arts." *Journal of the Royal Society of Arts* 121 (1973): 468–75, 532–35, 623–28.

———. "Pineapples, Pregnancy, Pica and *Peregrine Pickle*." In *Tobias Smollett: Bicentennial Essays Presented to Lewis M. Knapp*, 79–109. New York: Oxford University Press, 1971.

———. *Tobias Smollett: Essays of Two Decades*. Edinburgh: T. & T. Clark, 1982.

——— and Roger Hambridge. "Smollett and Politics: Originals for the Election Scene in *Sir Launcelot Greaves*." *English Language Notes* 14 (1976): 32–37.

Sale, William M., Jr. *Samuel Richardson: Master Printer*. Cornell Studies in English, edited by Robert C. Bald et al., no. 37. Ithaca, New York: Cornell University Press, 1950.

Scott, Temple. *Oliver Goldsmith Bibliographically and Biographically Considered*. New York: Bowling Green Press, 1928.

Scott, Walter. "Prefatory Memoir." In *Ballantyne's Novelist's Library*, vol. 2. London, 1821.

Scott, William. "Smollett, Dr. John Hill, and the Failure of *Peregrine Pickle*." *Notes and Queries*, n.s., 2 (1955): 389–92.

Seccombe, Thomas. Introduction. In *Smollett's Travels through France and Italy*, v–lx. London: Oxford University Press, 1907.

Sekora, John. *Luxury: The Concept in Western Thought, Eden to Smollett*. Baltimore: Johns Hopkins University Press, 1977.

Sena, John F. "Smollett's Persona and the Melancholic Traveler: An Hypothesis." *Eighteenth Century Studies* 1 (1968): 353–69.

Shannon, Edgar Finley, Jr. *Tennyson and the Reviewers*. Cambridge: Harvard University Press, 1952.

Shenstone, William. *The Letters of William Shenstone*. Edited by Marjorie Williams. Oxford: Basil Blackwell, 1939.

Sherbo, Arthur. *Christopher Smart: Scholar of the University*. East Lansing: Michigan State University Press, 1967.

———. *New Essays by Arthur Murphy*. East Lansing: Michigan State University Press, 1963.

Sherwood, Irma Z. "The Novelists as Commentators." In *The Age of Johnson: Essays Presented to Chauncey Brewster Tinker*, edited by Frederick W. Hilles, 113–25. New Haven: Yale University Press, 1949.

Showalter, Elaine. *A Literature of Their Own*. Princeton: Princeton University Press, 1977.

Small, Miriam Rossiter. *Charlotte Ramsay Lennox: An Eighteenth Century Lady of Letters*. New Haven: Yale University Press, 1935.

Smith, Adam. *Lectures on Rhetoric and Belles Lettres.* Edited by John M. Lothian. 1963. Reprint. Carbondale and Edwardsville: Southern Illinois University Press, 1971.

Smith, Albert H. "The Printing and Publication of Early Editions of the Novels of Tobias George Smollett." 2 vols. Ph.D. diss., London University, 1976.

————. "*Sir Launcelot Greaves*: A Bibliographical Survey of Eighteenth-Century Editions." *Library*, 5th ser., 32 (1977): 214–37.

Spector, Robert D. "Additional Attacks on the *Critical Review*." *Notes and Queries*, n.s., 3 (1956): 425.

————. "An Attack on the *Critical Review* in *Political Controversy*." *Notes and Queries*, n.s., 22 (1975): 14.

————. "Attacks on the *Critical Review*." *The Periodical Post Boy*, June 1955, 6–7.

————. "Attacks on the *Critical Review* in the *Court Magazine*." *Notes and Queries*, n.s., 5 (1958): 308.

————. "Attacks on the *Critical Review* in the *Literary Magazine*." *Notes and Queries*, n.s., 7 (1960): 300–301.

————. "The Critical Review." In *British Literary Magazines: The Augustan Age and the Age of Johnson, 1698–1788*, edited by Alvin Sullivan, 72–77. Westport, Conn.: Greenwood Press, 1983.

————. "Eighteenth Century Political Controversy and Linguistics." *Notes and Queries*, n.s., 2 (1955): 387–89.

————. "The End of the *Briton* and *Auditor*." *Notes and Queries*, n.s., 23 (1976): 357–58.

————. *English Literary Periodicals and the Climate of Opinion during the Seven Years' War.* The Hague: Mouton, 1966.

————. "Further Attacks on the *Critical Review*." *Notes and Queries*, n.s., 2 (1955): 535.

————. "Language Control in the Eighteenth Century." *Word Study* 27 (1951): 1–2.

————. "Late Neo-Classical Taste." *Notes and Queries* 196 (1951): 11–12.

————. "The *Monthly* and Its Rival." *Bulletin of the New York Public Library* 64 (1960): 159–61.

————. "Smollett and Admiral Byng." *Notes and Queries*, n.s., 2 (1955): 66–67.

————. "Smollett's Traveler." In *Tobias Smollett: Bicentennial Essays Presented to Lewis M. Knapp*, 231–46. New York: Oxford University Press, 1971.

————. "Smollett's Use of *Tsonnonthouan*." *Notes and Queries*, n.s., 6 (1959): 112–13.

————. *Tobias George Smollett.* Twayne's English Authors Series, edited by

Sylvia E. Bowman, no. 75. New York: Twayne Publishers, 1968.

―――. *Tobias Smollett: A Reference Guide*. Boston: G. K. Hall, 1980.

Sprat, Thomas. *History of the Royal Society*. London, 1667. Reprint, edited by Jackson I. Cope and Harold Whitmore Jones. St. Louis, Missouri: Washington University, 1958.

Stearns, Bertha Monica. "Early English Periodials for Ladies (1700–1760)." *PMLA* 48 (1933): 38–60.

Steig, Michael. *Dickens and Phiz*. Bloomington: Indiana University Press, 1978.

Stephen, Sir Leslie, Sir Sidney Lee, et al., eds. *The Dictionary of National Biography*. 22 vols. Oxford, 1917. Reprint. London: Oxford University Press, 1949–50.

Sterne, Laurence. *The Life and Opinions of Tristram Shandy*. Edited by James A. Work. New York: Odyssey Press, 1940.

―――. *A Sentimental Journey through France and Italy by Mr. Yorick*. Edited by Gardner D. Stout, Jr. Berkeley: University of California Press, 1967.

Stockdale, Percival. *The Memoirs of Percival Stockdale*. 2 vols. London, 1809.

Stone, George Winchester, Jr., and George M. Kahrl. *David Garrick: A Critical Biography*. Carbondale and Edwardsville: Southern Illinois University Press, 1979.

Stout, Gardner D., Jr., ed. Introduction. In *A Sentimental Journey through France and Italy by Mr. Yorick*, by Laurence Sterne. Berkeley: University of California Press, 1967.

Sullivan, Alvin, ed. *British Literary Magazines: The Augustan Age and the Age of Johnson, 1698–1788*. Westport, Conn.: Greenwood Press, 1983.

―――. ed. *British Literary Magazines: The Romantic Age, 1789–1836*. Westport, Conn.: Greenwood Press, 1983.

Sutcliffe, W. Denham. "English Book-Reviewing 1749–1800." D. Phil. diss., Oxford University, 1942.

Sutherland, James R. "The Circulation of Newspapers and Literary Periodicals, 1700–30." *Library*, 4th ser., 15 (1934): 110–24.

―――. "Some Aspects of Eighteenth-Century Prose." In *Essays on the Eighteenth Century Presented to David Nichol Smith*, 94–110. Oxford: Clarendon Press, 1945.

Swift, Jonathan. *A Proposal for Correcting, Improving and Ascertaining the English Tongue*. In vol. 4 of *The Prose Writings of Jonathan Swift*, edited by Herbert Davis, Louis Landa, et al., 3–21. Oxford: Basil Blackwell, 1957.

Thomas, Isaiah. *The History of Printing in America*. Worcester, Mass., 1810: 2nd ed. rev. N.p.: 1874. Reprint. New York: Weathervane Books, 1970.

Tierney, James E. "The Study of the Eighteenth-Century British Periodical: Problems and Progress." *Papers of the Bibliographical Society of America* 69 (1975): 165–86.

Tupper, Caroline F. "Essays Erroneously Attributed to Goldsmith." *PMLA* 39 (1924): 325–42.

Turberville, A. S. *Johnson's England: An Account of the Life and Manners of His Age.* 2 vols. Oxford: Clarendon Press, 1933.

Wain, John, ed. *Contemporary Reviews of Romantic Poetry.* London: George G. Harrap & Co., 1953.

Walpole, Horace. *Memoires of the Last Ten Years of the Reign of George II.* Edited by Lord Holland. 2 vols. London, 1822.

———. *The Walpole Correspondence.* Edited by W. S. Lewis, A. Doyle Wallace, and Robert Smith. Vol. 35. New Haven: Yale University Press, 1973.

Warner, James H. "Eighteenth-Century English Reactions to the 'Nouvelle Heloise.'" *PMLA* 52 (1937): 803–19.

Waterhouse, Ellis. *The Dictionary of 18th Century Painters in Oils and Crayons.* Woodbridge, Suffolk: Baron Publishing for Antique Collectors' Club, 1981.

Watson, George, ed. *The New Cambridge Bibliography of English Literature.* Vol. 2. Cambridge: Cambridge University Press, 1971.

Watt, Ian. *The Rise of the Novel: Studies in Defoe, Richardson and Fielding.* Berkeley: University of California Press, 1957.

Wellek, René. *The Later Eighteenth Century.* Vol. 1 in *A History of Modern Criticism: 1750–1950.* New Haven: Yale University Press, 1955.

Welsh, Charles. *A Bookseller of the Last Century.* London: Griffith et al., 1885.

White, Robert B., Jr. *The English Literary Journal to 1900: A Guide to Information Sources.* Detroit: Gale Research Company, 1977.

Whitefoord, Caleb. *The Whitefoord Papers.* Edited by W. A. S. Hewins. Oxford: Clarendon Press, 1898.

Whitley, William T. *Artists and Their Friends in England 1700–1799.* 2 vols. London: The Medici Society, 1928.

Whitridge, Arnold. *Tobias Smollett: A Study of His Miscellaneous Works.* New York: n.p., 1925.

Wichelns, Herbert A. "Burke's *Essay on the Sublime* and Its Reviewers." *Journal of English and Germanic Philology* 21 (1922): 645–61.

Wiles, R. M. *Freshest Advices: Early Provincial Newspapers in England.* Columbus: Ohio State University Press, 1965.

———. "The Relish for Reading in Provincial England Two Centuries Ago." In *The Widening Circle: Essays on the Circulation of Literature in Eighteenth-Century Europe*, edited by Paul J. Korshin, 85–115. Philadelphia: University of Pennsylvania Press, 1976.

———. *Serial Publication in England Before 1750.* Cambridge: Cambridge University Press, 1957.

Wolf, J. Harry. "Tobias Smollett and *The Orientalist*." *Notes and Queries*, n.s., 15 (1968): 456–63.

Wooll, John. *Biographical Memoir of the Late Reverend Joseph Warton.* London, 1806.

Index

Hill, John, 37, 90, 225, 227, 245, 249, 255, 266
Historical Memoirs of the Irish Rebellion, 227, 263
Historiography, 18, 69, 73, 86, 91, 104–9, 122, 140–43, 158–59, 199–200, 210, 232, 239–40, 242, 245–46, 248–49, 251–53, 256–57, 260–63, 265–67, 271. *See also* Enlightenment; Hume; Smollett; Voltaire
History of Jack Connor, The, 309 n.86, 322
History of Learning, 319
History of the . . . Sumatrans, The, 228, 269, 272
Hoadley, Benjamin, 214–15
Hoey, James, 180, 181, 198, 309 n.86. See also *Magasin des Enfans*
Hogarth, William: in *British Magazine*, 199; in *Continuation*, 116–17, 146, 214; in *Critical*, 110, 113, 146, 221, 225, 251; friend of Smollett's, 114, 116, 225, 251, 257; influence on Smollett, 204–6, 250
Holland, Thomas, 226, 260–61
Home, Francis, 82, 83, 122, 221, 223, 225, 231, 233, 252
Home, John, 45, 57, 93, 151, 214, 306 n.75
Homer, 92, 95, 135, 136, 223, 235–36
Horace, 20, 99, 252, 255, 322–23
Houlton, Robert, 282
Houston, Richard, 143, 144, 226, 257
Hudson, Thomas, 214
Huggins, William: in *British Magazine*, 189; correspondent of Smollett's, 162, 190, 191–92, 294 n.82, 303 nn. 10 and 26; as translator, 51, 135, 137, 191–92, 223, 225, 234, 236, 247–48, 249, 254
Humanist, 318
Hume, David, 175, 306 n.75; contributor to *Critical*, 58, 151, 153, 184; as historian, 69, 91–92, 105–9, 140, 159–60, 215, 221, 222, 225, 230, 240, 245, 251, 316 n.8, 322; and language, 77, 78–79, 82–83, 247
Hunt, James Henry Leigh, 217
Hunter, John, 238, 305 n.71
Hunter, William: contributor to *Critical*, 151, 153, 228, 235, 236, 305 n.71; dispute with Monro, 147, 224, 238, 240,

241, 243, 244–45, 246, 248, 305 n.52; a friend of Smollett's, 19, 213, 237, 250, 252, 267, 268–69, 272–73
Hurd, Richard, 89
Huxham, John, 277
Hydrops, Disputatio Medica, 221
Hylton, John Scott, 175

Idler. See under Johnson, Samuel
Impartial Reflections on the Case of Mr. Byng, 222, 231
Imperial Magazine, 111, 174, 197, 199, 208–9, 216, 281, 319
Important Question Concerning Invasions, The, 221
Ingham, Samuel, 228, 269
Inquiry Concerning the Cause of the Pestilence, An, 225, 253
Institutes of Experimental Chemistry, 225, 226, 255–56, 257–58, 260
Intriguing Coxcomb, The, 225, 251
Ipswich Journal, 321

Jackson's Oxford Journal, 48, 174, 180, 189, 279, 280, 281, 304 n.38, 308 n.49, 309 nn. 83, 85, 88, 90–92; 311 nn. 4, 5, and 11; 312 nn. 14 and 17, 313 n.64, 321
Jago, Richard, 175
Jennens, Charles, 177
Jenty, Charles, 51, 222
Jerningham, Edward, 178
Johnson, Samuel, 17, 88, 123, 127, 186, 226, 323; and *British Magazine*, 193, 194, 285; and his circle, 44, 45, 132, 196; his *Dictionary*, 29, 35, 78, 83, 86, 178; and the *Gentleman's Magazine*, 29, 170–71, 192; *Idler*, 29, 30, 35, 154, 193, 207, 318; lionized by Smollett, 154, 213, 215, 260; and *Literary Magazine*, 20, 33–34, 35, 36, 66, 127, 164, 169, 279; on literature and criticism, 20, 93–95, 158–59, 161, 217–18, 316 n.11; *Lives of the English Poets*, 29, 43, 158, 216, 287 n.2, 309 n.77; and *London Magazine*, 35; *Rambler*, 29, 156, 161, 167, 207, 318; *Rasselas, Prince of Abissinia*, 303 n.8, 304 n.29; as reviewer, 49, 101, 151, 156, 169, 171, 177, 189; *Universal Visiter*, 23, 35, 164, 280. See also *Literary Review*